Earogenous Zones

Genre, Music and Sound

Series editor: Mark Evans, Macquarie University, Sydney

Over the last decade screen soundtrack studies has emerged as a lively area of research and analysis mediating between the fields of cinema studies, musicology and cultural studies. It has deployed a variety of cross-disciplinary approaches to illuminate an area of film's audio-visual operation that was neglected for much of the late twentieth century. This new series extends the field by addressing the development of various popular international film genres in the post-war era (1945–present), analysing the variety and shared patterns of music and sound use that characterize each genre.

Published:

Terror Tracks: Music, Sound and Horror Cinema
Edited by Philip Hayward

Drawn to Sound: Animation Film Music and Sonicity
Edited by Rebecca Coyle

Forthcoming:

Fantasy, Cinema, Sound and Music
Edited by Janet K. Halfyard

Sounding Funny: Sound and Comedy Cinema
Edited by Mark Evans

Earogenous Zones
Sound, Sexuality and Cinema

Edited by
Bruce Johnson

LONDON OAKVILLE

Published by
UK: Equinox Publishing Ltd, 1 Chelsea Manor Studios, Flood Street, London, SW3 5SR
USA: DBBC, 28 Main Street, Oakville, CT 06779

www.equinoxpub.com

First published 2010

© Bruce Johnson and contributors 2010

All rights reserved. No part of this publication may be reproduced or transmitted in any form or by any means, electronic or mechanical, including photocopying, recording or any information storage or retrieval system, without prior permission in writing from the publishers.

British Library Cataloguing-in-Publication Data

A catalogue record for this book is available from the British Library.

ISBN-13   978 1 84553 318 2 (paperback)

Library of Congress Cataloging-in-Publication Data
Earogenous zones: sound, sexuality and cinema / edited by Bruce Johnson.
    p. cm.—(Genre, music and sound)
Includes bibliographical references and index.
ISBN 978-1-84553-318-2 (pb)
1. Motion picture music—History and criticism. 2. Pornographic films—History and criticism. 3. Erotic films—History and criticism. 4. Sex in motion pictures. I. Johnson, Bruce, 1943–
ML2075.E37 2010
781.5'42—dc22
                    2009039112

Typeset by S.J.I. Services, New Delhi
Printed and bound in Great Britain by Latimer Trend & Company Ltd, Plymouth, Devon

Contents

Acknowledgements vii

About the Authors ix

Introduction 1
Bruce Johnson

1 Sound Decisions: Interviews with Ole Ege 12
  Bruce Johnson

2 Beyond the Valley of the Ultra Cliché: Erotic Plenitude in the
  Films of Russ Meyer 38
  Mark Evans (with Matt Burgess)

3 The Push/Pull Game: The Dynamics of Sound in Bertolucci's
  Last Tango in Paris, *The Last Emperor* and *The Sheltering Sky* 54
  Lesley Chow

4 Depraved Desire: Sadomasochism, Sexuality and Sound in mid-1970s
  Cinema 66
  Clarice Butkus

5 The Peculiar 'Love' Music in Oshima's *Ai no korida* 89
  James Wierzbicki

6 Lust in Space: Science Fiction Themes and Sex Cinema (1960–82) .. 102
  Philip Hayward

7 Zero Gravity: Science Fiction Themed Porn Cinema and Its Soundtracks
  1990–2010 125
  Philip Hayward and Emil Stoichkov

8 "It's Gotta Be That New Wave Music": Music in *New Wave Hookers*
  Carries the Joke 140
  Laura Wiebe Taylor

9 Making "a Mall Movie about a Man with a 13-inch Penis": Popular
  Music Representations of Pornographic Intention 158
  Liz Giuffre

10 Musical Loops: *Eyes Wide Shut*... Ears Wide Open 174
   Kevin Clifton

11 Multiple Positions: Sound, Sex and Aural Dominance in *9 Songs* *Andrea Warren*	190
12 Music, Image, Orgasm: Getting off on the *Shortbus* *Marianne Tatom Letts*	203
13 In Extremis: The Roots, Soundscapes and Significations of Twenty-first-century Zombie Porn *Ralph G. Marsh*	217
Index	234

Acknowledgements

I wish to express my thanks to the following, all of whom provided assistance and advice over and above other signed contributions that some of them made to this collection: Clarice Butkus, Kevin Clifton, Karen Collins, Rebecca Coyle, Mark Evans, Liz Giuffre, Philip Hayward, Marianne Tatom Letts, Karen Lury, Fred Maus, David Neumeyer, Jacob Smith, Laura Wiebe Taylor, Andrea Warren.

About the Authors

Clarice Butkus is completing a Masters degree in Gender Politics from the John W. Draper Program in Humanities and Social Thought at New York University, where she is currently writing on gender, sexuality and early silent cinema. She has published articles on media, erotica and the body in film and has taught several courses in Media and Communications Studies at Macquarie University in Sydney.

Lesley Chow is an Australian film writer with a particular interest in dance, music and dialogue in cinema. She writes regularly on film for *Bright Lights* and on art for *Photofile*; her articles have also appeared in *Senses of Cinema, Cineaste* and the *Times Literary Supplement*.

Kevin Clifton is an assistant professor of music theory at Sam Houston State University in Huntsville, Texas. He received his PhD in music theory from the University of Texas at Austin in 2002. He has published analytical essays on the music of Francis Poulenc and Béla Bartók, the Broadway musical *Wicked*, and most recently has written on strategies for effective teaching of music fundamentals.

Mark Evans is the head of Media, Music and Cultural Studies at Macquarie University, Sydney. He is the editor of the forthcoming *Encyclopedia of Film Music and Sound* (Equinox) and series editor for Genre, Music and Sound.

Liz Giuffre has a BA in English and Media from the University of New South Wales, an MA (Research) in Contemporary Music Studies from Macquarie University and is a music journalist and researcher. She is currently a PhD candidate in the department of Media, Music and Cultural Studies at Macquarie University, studying the relationship between the broadcasting and music industries in Australia.

Philip Hayward is Director of Research Training at Southern Cross University and an adjunct professor in the Department of Media, Music and Cultural Studies at Macquarie University in Sydney. He has previously edited volumes on science fiction cinema soundtracks (*Off the Planet*, 2004) and his volume on horror cinema soundtracks (*Terror Tracks*) was published by Equinox in 2009.

Bruce Johnson, formerly a professor of English, is now an adjunct professor in Contemporary Music Studies at Macquarie University, Sydney; Honorary Professor of Music at the University of Glasgow; and Docent and Visiting Professor in Cultural

History at the University of Turku, Finland. He has published prolifically in the field of music and acoustic cultural history. A jazz musician, broadcaster, record producer and arts policy advisor, he was prime mover in the establishment of the Australian Jazz Archives in Canberra, and is co-founder of the International Institute for Popular Culture based in Turku.

Marianne Tatom Letts holds degrees from the University of North Texas and the University of Texas at Austin. Her publications include articles on *Kid A*, the Beatles film *Yellow Submarine*, and indie band Guided By Voices. She is the author of *Radiohead and the Resistant Concept Album: How to Disappear Completely* (Indiana University Press, 2010).

Ralph G. Marsh is a freelance writer and English language teacher with interests in post-war horror fiction and Japanese manga, anime and death metal, who currently resides in Taipei.

Emil Stoichkov is an actor and independent film-maker based in Silver Lake, California.

Laura Wiebe Taylor is a PhD candidate at McMaster University, Canada, in the Department of English and Cultural Studies. She has published articles on the relationship between science fiction, dystopia and metal music, and has also examined the role of popular music in Rob Zombie's first two feature films.

Andrea Warren is a singer and music teacher, as well as a freelance writer, interested in music consumption in everyday life. In articles on *American Idol*, fragrance lines of female pop stars and the relaxation music industry, she has explored sound culture and its commercialism. She recently completed an MA in Ethnomusicology from the University of Toronto, with work on female 'performance practice' in envoicing sexual pleasure.

James Wierzbicki teaches musicology in the Faculty of Arts at the University of Sydney. He is the author of *Louis and Bebe Barron's* Forbidden Planet (Scarecrow Press, 2005) and *Film Music: A History* (Routledge, 2008).

Introduction

Bruce Johnson

While film studies have always been dominated by the visual, film has never been a silent spectacle, even prior to the development of the synchronized optical sound track. All the books in this series explore the power of the sounding/hearing position, the importance of controlling the sonic field. This collection addresses feature-length cinema in which sexuality is central. Setting aside various kinds of ambient noise associated with the cinema, the connection was slow to arrive (Williams, 1989: 121–2; 2008: 88). Because of the relatively late arrival of the soundtrack in sex cinema, the period spanned by this book covers virtually the whole history of the association between the two. With the exception of *Ai no korida* (Nagisa Oshima, 1976), the films featured in the book are all western. This does not necessarily reflect a dearth of sex cinema elsewhere, but that scholarship on, for example, Mexican and South American feature-length sex cinema appears to be as yet relatively underdeveloped. Also, apart from episodic variations, it is heterosexual relations which dominate the collection. This western and heterosexual profile, it must be emphasized, was not a deliberate circumscription of the range covered. Rather, it reflects the repertoire of responses to an internationally promulgated call for papers, and perhaps signals very particular (and regrettable) lacunae in film scholarship.

There are three 'keywords' to this collection: sound, sex, cinema. There seem to be few scholars whose interests in these three fields converge with equal authority. For porn-film scholars themselves, the idea of discussing pornographic film as a sonic phenomenon seemed rather perplexing. In both a 2008 conference on porn that was held by a multi-year funded research project in Helsinki and a 2009 panel on pornography in Stockholm, the most striking feature was the almost unanimous framing of porn as a visual form. Apart from my own contribution, and with only one other exception on rap porn, both events were dominated by visual studies.

This lack of attention to sound exemplifies the more general neglect of aural cultures in favour of the visual. Pornography and erotica are generally regarded as visual phenomena (painting, film, the written word). It is the visuality of porn which is mainly policed, but sounds in popular culture are more difficult to fit into a discourse of censorship. By 'sounds' I do not mean dialogue or song lyrics as bearers of lexical meaning. Warning stickers on recordings address 'lexicality', but never sonicity. While sexuality itself is pervasive in cinema (see, for example, Krzywinska 2006: 1), studies of the topic almost completely neglect sound as such. The example just cited is both recent and representative. In Krzywinska's study there is a passing reference to 'auditory clues' (*ibid.*: 10), but the discussion is conducted broadly without reference to sound. Film is simply 'spectacle' (*ibid.*: 14, 29, 110); there is an index entry for 'spectatorship', but none for sound or music. Thus, there is a prevailing tension between occasional 'lip service' to the auditory and a resolutely scopocentric conceptualization. The cinema audiences are 'spectators', 'viewers', voyeurs enjoying "the pleasure of *watching* a film. This does not mean that *watching* a movie is a form of cold *observation*, however, as there are many ways in which *viewers* can become ... engaged" (*ibid.*: 28, my italics; see similarly deeply entrenched visual tropes at pp. 27, 83, 84, 85). Most of the references to sound concern narrative-driving dialogue; that is, its sonority is not explored at all. Two of the films considered so sonically rich as to be discussed in this collection (by Kevin Clifton and Clarice Butkus) are also dealt with by Krzywinska: *Eyes Wide Shut* (Stanley Kubrick, 1999) and *The Story of O* (Just Jaeckin, 1975). Apart from a virtually unavoidable reference to O's imposed silence, she makes no reference to sound or music (*ibid.*: 59–62, 63–5, 68–9), but there is nothing at all extraordinary in this relentlessly visual focus. This lacuna is even more striking when a scholar addresses a porn genre explicitly framed by music. In a study of 'hip-hop pornography', Mireille Miller-Young's only reference to musical text is to cite four words of a lyric.[1] While acknowledging that she is talking about music, there is no recognition of the role of musicality in the 31-page discussion. Hip-hop porn is seen as exclusively spectacle. In whatever way terms such as 'pornography' and 'erotica' are distinguished as ways of representing sexuality, in the overwhelming majority of such studies they are conceived of in visual terms.

The conceptualization of film as primarily visual has come under challenge with the growing proliferation of studies of sound (most often music) in cinema. Claudia Gorbman, Philip Tagg, Michel Chion, Rick Altman and Kaja Silverman are prominent in a growing body of work in which film music is analysed and theorized.[2] This cross-section exemplifies the varieties of approach to the examination of sound in film: detailed musicological analysis, overviews of affect, narrative functionality and characterization, acoustically based structuralism (internal sonic relationships defined through, for example, tempo, timbre, pitch, and between sound and its absence), the differing functions of diegetic and non-diegetic music in establishing affect, semiotics and narratology. Such studies, both the essays in this collection and the series overall, confirm forcefully the absolutely decisive importance of sound and music in establishing and often inverting the moral, emotional and cultural meanings, and details of place and space, of cinema's visual order.

In studies of cinematic representations of sexuality, one striking exception to the general neglect of sound is the work of Linda Williams.[3] Her analyses demonstrate with great authority the potential explanatory power of music in the discussion of cinema sexuality. Williams attends to sound, recognizing that it is more than the bearer of dialogue; it is also deeply implicated *as sound* in screen affect and gender politics. While her comments on sound are most often *en passant*, in some cases she provides more extensive, and always instructive, analyses of the connections between sound and sexuality in particular case studies, for example, in *Casablanca* (Williams, 2008: 35–9). Apart from discrete case studies, however, she has elaborated more general theorizations of the role of sound in representations of sexuality in film. Her analogy with the cinematic musical interlude (*ibid.*: 82–7) provides a parallel to her discussion of the structural homologies between the musical and porn, arguing that the film musical provides an instructive model for the analysis of porn narrative (Williams, 1989: 130, 133); she explicates and exemplifies the point at some length in an analysis of *The Opening of Misty Beethoven* (*ibid.*: 130, 133, 136–47; see further applications of the model in Williams, 2008: 124, 130, 132–3).

Sound is a distinctive phenomenology with ways of producing meaning that can augment, contest or ambiguate a visual image. Both culturally and physiologically, sound constitutes a distinctive phenomenology which is scarcely tractable to scopocentric analysis. In the contemporary mediatized world it dissolves distinctions which can be sustained through visual modes. It blurs boundaries between public and private, mind and body, objective and subjective, art and nature, aesthetics and sociology. Acoustic orders are characterized by leakages within and between material and intellectual spaces. Throughout the twentieth century these orders became more pervasive and powerful through acoustic technologies.[4] The urge to theorize film visually is to miss one of its distinguishing features, as well as the constitutive essence of sound. In relation to the present discussion, one of the characteristics of the phenomenology of sound is its ability to confound categorizations based on a visual epistemology. In the words of Linda Williams, visual and aural voyeurism are "very different things" (Williams, 1989: 125).

Sound is a medium of very specific and potentially disruptive intensity. The taxonomy of sonic effects published by the Centre de recherche sur l'espace sonore et l'environnement urbain in Grenoble (Cresson) includes the 'ubiquity effect', which entails a conscious searching for the source of a sound, and at least a momentary failure to find it. The uncertainty produced about the origin of a sound establishes a power relationship between an invisible emitter and the worried receptor. The ubiquity effect is an effect of power. It generally produces discomfort, ranging from mild anxiety, a feeling of faintness, to "the most uncontrollable panic, including feelings of flight, aggressiveness, or inhibition, perhaps marked with paranoia".[5] Sound, especially when it is not visibly attached to its source, has a high potential for destabilization. Reviewing various forms of aurally mediated sexuality (including phone sex), John Corbett and Terri Kapsalis asked, "Is it possible that underlying the simple discomfort and embarrassment that naturally accompanies the public airing of such graphic sex sounds is a more profound disturbance: a gentle threat to the stability of sensical representation?"

(1996: 102).⁶ Hearing differs from seeing also in that while the latter clearly establishes a distance from a 'viewer', sound closes that distance. The press kit for the *Cyborgasm* 'virtual reality sex experience' declares: "*Cyborgasm* sounds so real, you're not just hearing sex, you're having it." It advises the user to "Dim the lights and close your eyes ... wear our eco-goggles so you're not distracted by any visual stimuli" (*ibid.*: 107).

Furthermore, as Williams recognizes, 'sound' is not just music and narrative-driving dialogue, but also selective foley enhancement and the voice itself, which is so much more than just the bearer of words that the sonic character of vocalization can radically colour, and even override, the lexical content (Mark Evans, Kevin Clifton).⁷ Silence itself is famously expressive (see Johnson and Poole, 2005: 104–5), and in representations of sexual activity can be a striking way of isolating moments of (literal) climax, as in *The Last Tango in Paris* (Bernardo Bertolucci, 1972) and *Ai no korida* (see Lesley Chow, James Wierzbicki).

Sound is decisive in cinematic representation in general, but in what follows I want to suggest why this is especially so in the politics of sexuality. The word 'politics', by which I mean here relations of power, is central. Williams writes candidly about the problems of writing about explicit sex (1989: x, xi; 2008: 122), which often means having to fall back into a defensive 'should it exist' position (1989: 8). "Sex is rarely ever 'just' sex" (2008: 124). All the essays in this collection address sexuality in cinema; many deal with what may uncontroversially be called pornography. At the beginning of the twenty-first century it was reported that in Los Angeles, for example, more than 10,000 porn films were made each year, compared with the Hollywood feature-film average of 400 (Johnson and Poole, 2005: 120). Its widespread appeal was suggested in an Australian survey, "commissioned by the Office of Film and Literature Classification in 1992 [, which] ... found 70% support for X-rated videos" (Evans and Butkus, 1997: 67). The online communications and information technology website comScore Media Metrix reported that more than one-third of internet users in the USA visited 'adult' websites in April 2007. Famously conflicted, definitions of porn range from attempts to distinguish it through the image on the screen – visual text – to something positioned in a certain way in public discourse – social context (on the latter, see Kendrick, 1987). Scholars of sex in cinema, including those cited here, have addressed the question in a range of ways.⁸

Pornography is represented in this collection, but the coverage also extends to mainstream feature films, covering the grey areas in between. Categorical permeabilities become active leakages in an era of mass mediation and the liberalization of sexual mores,⁹ leaving the boundary between porn and mainstream feature film increasingly uncertain. Changes in social mores, sound and image technology, the distinction between public and private audiences, all disrupted received boundaries between porn and mainstream cinema. Where these boundaries lie is therefore increasingly open to continuing debate, and sound and music themselves contribute significantly and sometimes crucially to the evasiveness of the distinction. The repertoire of films explored in this collection straddles the boundaries between erotica, softcore and hardcore porn.

It is rare for sexual attraction not to be an element in a film; there are simply degrees of explicitness and magnitude. A love story or 'romance' incorporates sexual energy, but so do other genres, including Westerns and thrillers (Hitchcock and the James Bond series, especially, could not survive without this). Less often noted is the way 'fantasy' links, for example, sci-fi and porn – culminating in such films as *Barbarella* (Philip Hayward), *New Wave Hookers* (Laura Wiebe Taylor) and also in the way audiences/viewers often disclaim their interest in both (see Philip Hayward and Emil Stoichkov). Clarice Butkus notes parallels between *The Story of O* and *Alice in Wonderland*, adding to the sense of fantasy a childlike dimension which creates a larger framework within which erotica and porn resonate: a childish pleasure of game-playing.

Sound is decisive in cinema. Can we draw any inferences about the specificity of sonic representations in the representation and foregrounding of sexual activity in particular? In general, whichever style of music attached itself to specific porn categories, it usually existed in an unproblematic relationship with the action – violent sex, violent music; misogynistic sex, misogynistic lyrics; and in the work of Russ Meyer, comic sex, comic music (Mark Evans). Stereotypically, pornographic film is morally flat, psychologically without depth and alienated, with its effects enhanced by featureless loops of funk or metal. Such music actually contributes to the flatness and confirms the seedy formulaic and Fordist mass-produced sexuality that Andy Warhol replicated in his movies. The connections are of mutual reinforcement, or, in its least imaginative deployment, the music is an unchallenging semiotic afterthought, a passive reflection of a moment in lifestyle history, such as spiritless funk clichés that fit with an emotionally drab 1970s/1980s LA milieu.

Williams refers to sex genres becoming associated with particular kinds of music, an evolving codification of the grammar of sound and visuals (Williams, 2008: 98). Hayward and Stoichkov refer to "sex muzak" to describe the rather formulaic approach to porn scores. According to them, relative to improvements in other production values – narrative, special effects – the possibilities of music remain relatively unexplored and non-innovative in the genre as a whole. Sound is linked to spatiality in a literal sense – where something is happening in relation to other events, people and objects. But in virtually all of the cases considered in this collection, it also constructs a moral space and adjusts psychological perspectives. Some musical effects and genres have distinctive affinities with specific forms of erotica and pornography. Well-established 'sonic anaphones'[10] include the saxophone for various moods associated with sex and percussive patterns for climax (Chow, Johnson). Various jazz styles have proved compatible with specific expressions of sexuality, such as 'burlesque jazz' in science-fiction porn (Hayward). Novelty and cartoon sounds and music can turn porn into comedy (Evans), and new wave, metal and indie rock have established links with 'new wave', zombie porn and mainstream explicit sexuality respectively (Taylor, Marsh, Warren). The emergence of electric/electronic media enlarged the possibilities, including in the formation of particular musical genres like rap and metal that rely on electronic mediation for their formal character. This in turn generated changes in the porn aesthetic (Marsh).

As this aesthetic has developed, so has the use of music become more pluralized in its functions in the representation of sexuality. Williams discusses the use of dialogue as a 'screen' or substitute for explicit visual representation (2008: 76–8, 98; see particularly her discussion of *The Graduate,* pp. 79–82), and comments on the scream as a 'screen' (*ibid.*: 96). On the other hand, sound is central in disclosing nuances in sexual relations (Letts). Williams examines at instructive length the narratological and affective role of music in sex scenarios (2008: 75–88). The affective role is perhaps the most prominent function of music in cinema (Tagg and Clarida, 2003), and is crucial in representations of sexuality. It can regulate mood simply through tonal and cadential shifts (Clifton).

Sound (dialogue, music, foley, atmosphere) also plays a central and decisive function in the deepening of perspective. This is by now a truism in film-sound scholarship, but is demonstrated with particular effectiveness in representations of the human being in situations of physical extremity: pain and death, pleasure and copulation, and all the permutations which are covered in these essays. Sound can radically alter the meaning of what are visually the least ambiguous extremities of experience, and in doing so compel a review of how we understand them. Music can literally choreograph these primal moments, can situate sexuality within the category of 'dance' (Chow, Johnson). The point recalls Williams's argument about links with the musical. Hayward and Stoichkov cite an industry director who consciously exploited the connection. Against the 'sex muzak' background of most porn, close attention to the possibilities of sound and music in particular become especially noteworthy. As in any movie, more thoughtful and imaginative deployments of sound and music can defamiliarize and subvert visual representations. If those are explicit representations of sex, then sexual politics themselves are brought under review, as are the meaning of terms like erotica and pornography, and the distinctions implied in the term 'arthouse' (Letts, but also implicitly in most of the essays here).

The most obvious way in which that 'review' works is underpinned by the genre of music that accompanies the visual action.[11] But, as all these essays disclose through their careful analysis of genres and individual case studies, the narratological location of the sound provides even more subtle nuancing – the use of acousmêtre (sound without visible source), diegetic/non-diegetic distinctions which play audience against character and complicate spatial and episodic relationships. The effect is not simply epistemological ('How do we come to know this music?), but ontological ('Which reality are we in?'), and the disorientation disturbs what might otherwise be a formulaic scenario (Warren). Imaginative deployment of sound and music over the visual narratives suddenly produces differentiations and ambiguities which challenge the repetitive homogenization of sexuality associated with pornography. It sets up implied histories and possible futures which disrupt the objectification associated with porn. It introduces humanizing lesions onto the charmless abstract perfection of the pornographied body, suggestions of 'something else' in their lives apart from endlessly repeated penetration, sucking and licking.

Sound and music can introduce into the ahistorical sextopia of porn the cultural specificity of the notion of 'pornography' (Wierzbicki), and indeed the use of music might shift a film in and out of the category of pornography (Johnson). The sight of women undressing, and the naked body more generally, can be sexualized (Hayward) or desexualized (Johnson) wholly by the music. Pornography itself can be critiqued by sound and music that can disturb by a number of means: by a violent disjunction with sexuality, or even with the musical conventions of porn (Hayward). Music can shift the visual representation towards the titillation of pornography, as in Hayward's discussion of music in the 'innocent' representation of semi-nudity. Music can create a subtext to suggest more than may be shown (Giuffre), can function to problematize ideologies playing underneath surface stereotypes, and also to introduce emotional overtones such as playfulness which meliorate the alienation generally associated with porn (Taylor).

Music can also interact with periodization in the representation of sexuality, again giving different inflections in relation to taste, acceptability, and moral status at any given historical moment. In *Ai no korida*, traditional Japanese music may be said to periodize as well as spatially localize sexuality within a frame that ameliorates suggestions of pornography (Wierzbicki); Giuffre and Hayward demonstrate how particular uses of music (and other sound) can both articulate and work around moral conceptions of sexuality in the 1950s. Music can also place pornographic or explicit erotic representations at a safe distance, historically or geographically (Taylor).

I want to conclude this discussion, however, by signalling a far more important role played by sound in pornography or erotica than simply providing an aural affective and narratological supplement to what we are told visually. I have referred to the distinctive phenomenology of sound, and this in turn deeply influences the sexual politics of cinema – and the more central sex becomes, the more arrestingly those politics are played out. Williams has referred to the connections between women and sound in porn (1989: 123) and to the problem of representing female pleasure/orgasm (*ibid.*: x). This is a manifestation of male/female sexuality politicized through the visual/aural binary in cinema. Male sexual pleasure is confirmed visually, female sexuality is represented sonically (Taylor, Letts.)

Both Williams's insights and their development by Corbett and Kapsalis (1996) provide points of departure for the following observations. Williams has noted the importance of the 'money shot' in confirming the climax of male sexual pleasure (1989: 185). By contrast, the evidence of female sexual pleasure is sonic – moans, sighs, shrieks of evident orgasm. That is, the binary of visuality and sound in porn represents also a gendered distinction. Furthermore, while the visible sign of male orgasm is 'single and terminating; female orgasm is heard as multiple and renewable' (Corbett and Kapsalis,

1996: 104). This is intensified through the character of contemporary sound media and the infinite repeatability of sampled sound (*ibid.*: 106).

I want to extrapolate resonances for all forms of such representation, from hardcore porn to erotica, sex comedy, documentary, and in every case study covered in this collection. That is, the sonic/visual divide also marks more profound distinctions in attitudes to sexual appetite and capability and encourages the perception of women as more rampantly sexual, and, as such, both a promise and a threat in the male sexual narrative. There is a further significant and related distinction between the spectacle of male orgasm and the 'oracle' of female sexual pleasure. That is, these aural signals are ambiguous, and are sounds that may express extreme pain or pleasure (Butkus).

A clear political dynamic thus traverses the difference between the specularity of male and the aurality of female sexual pleasure. This suggests that the aesthetics of the representation of sexuality in any category of film are biologically influenced. In addition, it consigns the woman to a sonic information economy, regarded as less reliable than a visual mode in western modernity (see Johnson and Cloonan, 2008: 31–47). Furthermore, the ambiguity in the female articulations of arousal and orgasm is disruptive to male control. Is she pleased, displeased, or even faking? Is she experiencing pain or pleasure, or perhaps disturbingly manifesting the unreliability of the threshold? (Clifton).[12] Ambiguity and lack of explicitness can be both disconcerting and teasingly arousive, as in many sex rituals from flirting to striptease. A further point: the 'renewability' of female sounds of arousal suggests insatiability, as compared with visual evidence of the climaxing male orgasm (Letts). Because of differences between the male and female anatomy in the representation of sexuality, women's sexual pleasure is therefore aestheticized in auditory rather than visual modes, at the same time as it politicizes the relationship: woman as relegated to an unreliable information economy, semiotically evasive and sexually voracious. The signs of her pleasure cannot be securely situated in the model that unequivocally confirms male dominance.

While these dynamics are particularly conspicuous in the explicit domain of pornography, they reverberate in mainstream cinematic depictions of sexual relations. The leakage is demonstrated with notable clarity when a mainstream film scenario incorporates aspects of pornographic explicitness, for example, in Brian de Palma's *Body Double* (1984). The protagonist is an actor, Jake Scully (Craig Wasson), who begins to spy on a woman through her apartment window while she regularly performs a striptease, apparently for her own pleasure. Then one night he sees someone else also spying on her. In the course of attempting to save her from what appears to be the more predatory peeping Tom, Jake finds himself moving in and out of the local porn-film industry. This intensely voyeuristic plot, however, also plays with the sonic dimensions of sexuality in ways that exemplify the points made above. To take one early example, Jake is in good spirits as we see him driving home after work. He arrives home, and it becomes evident that his good humour at least in part derives from his pleasure at the prospect of seeing his partner, since his smile broadens as he enters the house, to hear her voice laughing gently and making sounds of pleasurable assent. In the absence of any other voice, we might assume that she is on the phone to a friend. Jake moves through the house, silently, unable to find her at first, although we can hear her all the time. Finally he enters the bedroom to see her having sex with a silent (male) stranger. The power of this scene is based on the relationship between what we see of Jake and what we hear of his girlfriend. His (ill-founded) pleasure is silent and hers is voluble – but ambiguous to great dramatic effect, an exemplification of the way sexual politics can be played out through the tension between sight and sound.

The foregoing reflections set a context for the essays that follow. It seems pessimistically gratuitous to summarize each essay in this introduction – we would like to assume that the reader will press on. Furthermore, I have already sketchily foreshadowed some of the issues and approaches in parenthetical references. The chapters in this work have been arranged chronologically, and for the most part the analyses of these films are based on 'readings', by which I mean attentive watching and listening as a basis for interpretation. They therefore exhibit the weaknesses as well as the strengths of that general form of critical analysis, and are vulnerable to contestation by different interpretive ingenuities, or sophisticated differences of opinion. One chapter is primarily ethnographic, the interviews with Ole Ege, seeking a film-maker's own account of his work. This is not to imply some master insight into the field – ethnography has its own limitations and mendacities. It simply recognizes that there are other approaches to the study of cultural texts which usefully complement scholarly interpretations. Ege's attentiveness to sound and music tends to confirm the complex ways in which the sonic dimension can transform the meaning of visual representations of sexuality. A film-maker regarded as a major pioneer of unregulated porn thus emerges as deeply troubled by its politics, as someone trying to humanize its subjects through comedy, eroticism and a documentary impulse. Yet the assumption of a documentary model is still, of course, the assumption of a particular kind of power – the cases of *9 Songs* (Warren) and Ole Ege's *A Summerday* (Johnson) make for an instructive parallel, which indeed could have provided a full essay in itself. In both cases, a woman's sexuality is also in a sense wordless; in one case because of a film-maker's narratological decision, and in the other because of a simple equipment malfunction. In both cases the effect is to produce a documentary form, in which the power relations are instructive – sometimes to the female subject's benefit, and at others to her disadvantage. These studies of sound and sexuality in cinema prompt a less-qualified version of Williams's comment. Sex is *never* 'just sex'.

Notes

1. Mireille Miller-Young (2008). My thanks to Philip Hayward for drawing my attention to this article.
2. See, for example, Gorbman (1987), Tagg and Clarida (2003), Chion (1994), Altman (1987) and Silverman (1988).

3. See in particular Williams 1989 and 2008. These represent major benchmarks in the field covered by this collection.
4. See further Johnson and Cloonan, 2008: 13–30.
5. Augoyard and Torgue, 2005: 131. On the implications for music affect, see Johnson and Cloonan, 2008: 43–60.
6. My thanks to Mark Evans for referring me to this source.
7. Undated author citations are references to the essays in this collection.
8. See, for example, Krzywinska, 2006: 63, 65–6, 69, 197; Williams, 1989: 2, 11–12, 15, 29–30, 121, 126; Chapter 1 overall (pp. 1–38) is a discussion of the problems.
9. On connections, see Krzywinska, 2006: 16, 65; Williams, 1989: 12; 2008: 315.
10. The term 'sonic anaphone' was developed by Philip Tagg; expressed simply, it is a musical realization of a non-musical phenomenon, as in "Schubert's babbling brooks, Baroque opera thunder, Byrd's *Bells* or Jimi Hendrix's B52" (Tagg and Clarida, 2003: 99; see further pp. 99–101).
11. As in the incongruities between music and vision in *A Clockwork Orange, Dr. Strangelove* and *2001: A Space Odyssey*, see further Link, 2004; Johnson and Cloonan, 2008: 70.
12. It is worth noting in this connection that aural pleasure can at the same time be aural pain (Johnson and Cloonan, 2008, 13–30).

References

Altman, R. (1987), *The American Film Musical*, Bloomington: Indiana University Press.
Augoyard, J.-F., and Torgue, H. (eds) (2005), *Sonic Experience: A Guide to Everyday Sound*, trans. A. McCartney and D. Paquette, Montreal: McGill-Queen's University Press.
Chion, M. (1994), *Audio Vision: Sound on Screen*, trans. C. Gorbman, New York: Columbia University Press.
Corbett, J., and Kapsalis, T. (1996), 'Aural Sex: The Female Orgasm in Popular Sound', *TDR / The Drama Review*, 40(3), 102–11.
Evans, M., and Butkus, C. M. (1997), 'Regulating the Internet: Cyberporn and the Traditional Media', *Media International Australia*, 85 (November), 62–9.
Gorbman, C. (1987), *Unheard Melodies: Narrative Film Music*, Bloomington: Indiana University Press.
Johnson, B., and Cloonan, M. (2008), *Dark Side of the Tune: Popular Music and Violence*, Aldershot: Ashgate.
Johnson, B., and Poole, G. (2005), 'Sexuality and Australian Film Music, 1990–2003', in R. Coyle (ed.), *Reel Tracks: Australian Feature Film Music and Cultural Identities*, Eastleigh, Hampshire: John Libbey, pp. 97–121.
Kendrick, W. (1987), *The Secret Museum: Pornography in Modern Culture*, New York: Viking.
Krzywinska, T. (2006), *Sex in the Cinema*, London: Wallflower Press.

Link, S. (2004), 'Sympathy with the Devil? Music of the Psycho Post-Psycho', *Screen*, 45(1), 1–20.

Miller-Young, M. (2008), 'Hip-Hop Honeys and Da Hustlaz: Black Sexualities in the New Hip-Hop Pornography', *Meridians: Feminism, Race, Transnationalism*, 8(1), 261–92.

Silverman, K. (1988), *The Acoustic Mirror: The Female Voice in Psychoanalysis and Cinema*, Bloomington: Indiana University Press.

Tagg, P., and Clarida, B. (2003), *Ten Little Title Tunes: Towards a Musicology of the Mass Media*, New York: The Mass Media Music Scholars' Press, Inc.

Williams, L. (1989), *Hard Core: Power, Pleasure and the "Frenzy of the Visible"*, Berkeley: University of California Press.

Williams, L. (2008), *Screening Sex*, Durham, NC: Duke University Press.

1 Sound Decisions
Interviews with Ole Ege[1]

Bruce Johnson

Introduction

Ole Ege was arguably the most important pioneer of pornographic and erotic film during a period of profound change in public and legal attitudes towards the representation of sexuality, and in a country which is still internationally recognized as being at the forefront of those changes. His films won major awards at the first erotic/pornographic film festival in Amsterdam in 1970, but have also enjoyed a very high level of mainstream commercial success in their region. *A Summerday* became one of the most internationally notorious films in the genre of so-called pornography, in spite of the film-makers' own insistence that it was more suitably regarded as documentary.[2] *Pornography* (Ole Ege, 1971) is included in a recent list of 'Danish Erotic Film Classics' (Villadsen, 2005).[3] In the late 1990s Ege was the subject of a documentary, 'Den grimme dreng' (The Naughty Boy) shown on the BBC, accompanied by BBC-conducted interviews.[4] Although he ceased film-making after his feature film *Bordellet* (Ole Ege, 1972; during the interviews, Ege referred to it as *Bordello*, and I have followed suit), he co-founded Copenhagen's Museum Erotica with Kim Riisfeldt-Clausen in 1992. As Chair of its board of directors he remained in a formal position of stewardship until the museum closed in March 2009, owing to unforeseen financial difficulties following the death in May 2008 of Riisfeldt-Clausen, at that time its Managing Director. Ole Ege remains the 'elder statesman' of Danish erotica.[5]

Apart from this, however, he has a special aptness to this volume. As the interviews below demonstrate, Ole Ege has a particular interest in the relationship between music and the cinematic representation of sexuality, and indeed it is the deployment of sound and music in his films that marks him out among his peers and which, in his opinion, helps to identify the contested boundaries between erotica and pornography. For him, it is the way music is used that aestheticizes and humanizes the representation of sexuality on screen. Copenhagen's Museum Erotica was an instructive context in which to encounter his work for the first time. In contrast with the continuous multi-screen presentation of porn films, Ege's productions showed a conspicuous attentiveness to music, for example, in the way Dexter Gordon's band was woven into *Pornography*.

The main topic of the interviews excerpted here was his use of sound in the representation of sexuality, but the two days of discussion touched on a great many related matters which provided context. These included the definition of pornography, its status and history in Danish culture, pornography and alienation, the impact of pornography on his own private and professional life (largely negative), gender and pornography (Ege is sceptical, for example, of the idea that there can be porn for women). It is in these insights into the mind of the practitioner that the distinctive value of these interviews lies. Sophisticated 'readings' of cultural texts often ascribe order and coherence of vision to work which is, as we shall be reminded, in many ways the outcome of creatively opportunistic improvisation and barely articulated ambivalences. What must also be borne in mind is that these interviews are cross-cultural and cross-linguistic. In the way Ege speaks of his work, a turn of phrase will occasionally seem incongruous in English, for example, his use of the word 'naughty'. Some inferences that an anglophone reader might wish to draw regarding, say, gender politics, should also be treated with caution. Words and phrases carry very different cultural baggage across languages. Furthermore, the conversation was conducted with a native Danish speaker who was being interviewed in a second language, translating on the run.

Background

As early as the silent era, Danish film established a reputation internationally for cinema eroticism (Soila *et al.*, 1998: 8–9). "Danish erotic melodramas became infamous in Norway in the early 1910s" (*ibid.*: 103). They inspired early Norwegian films and were exported to Sweden, where they contributed to debates about censorship (*ibid.*: 104, 143). In Finland "the most popular film in the [mid-1960s] was the Danish soft porn movie *The Goat in Paradise* ... ahead of *Zorba the Greek, My Fair Lady, The Sound of Music*" (*ibid.*: 83).[6] In the 1950s, several Danish movies had nude scenes "that would have been unthinkable in American mainstream movies of the same period" (Villadsen, 2005: 1).

Following an initial period of haphazard local regulation, state censorship was introduced in 1913, responding to complaints that film-goers were inspired to criminality by screen crime (Soila *et al.*, 1998: 9). "Danish film censorship has always been somewhat relaxed in relation to sex, worrying more about violence and horror" (Villadsen, 2005: 1). Nonetheless, proscriptions embraced representations of sexuality in text and image until the late 1960s. With a reputation for openness in the public portrayal of sexuality already entrenched, the libertarian atmosphere of the West in the 1960s found special resonance in Denmark. The first stage in the legalization of pornography was under Justice Minister K. Axel Nielsen, with the legalization of written pornography in 1967; the liberalization process was extended to images including film under his successor Knud Thestrup on 1 July 1969.

Career

Ole Ege was born on 23 May 1934, in Hobro, Jutland. After leaving school he saw clerical vacancies being advertised by the Canadian Pacific Railway and went to Canada with a friend who had been trained by Denmark's royal photographer. In Yellowknife, in the Northwest Territories, they worked for a gold mine which had a darkroom, where his friend "taught me what happens after the film has gone through the camera". Ege returned from Canada in 1955, and was living in his mother's flat when his interest in photography led him to start a small business that attracted the attention of the police.

> **OE:** The police were extremely aware of the producers of any of this sort of material. So, in the mid-fifties I had my first case with the police. I was doing a modest mail-order business with photographs of nude girls. No pornography at all, but just the fact that it was nude pictures was sufficient for the authorities to fine me and confiscate all the material I possessed at this time.

In the late 1950s he began shooting 8mm films, circulating them under the name Peter Fleming because it was more recognizable and easier to pronounce for non-Danish speakers. Peter was the name of his son and Fleming was taken from the James Bond author.

> **BJ:** In your first movies, which were black and white, did you add sound, or did you use the sound of the people in the film?
> **OE:** No, they were completely silent. Also, all the colour films that I sold in the 'sixties, when I was at the height of my career, were silent, because there were very few sound projectors circulated amongst the customers.
> **BJ:** Because they were private customers?
> **OE:** Yes.

With the repeal of prohibitions on pornography, Ege's film-making was able to become 'above ground'. At the Wet Dream film festival in Amsterdam in 1970, his short films (under the name Peter Fleming) won the People's Porn Prize and under his own name, the film *A Summerday*, on which he had collaborated with Japanese artist Shinkichi Tajiri, won the Grand Prix.[7]

> **OE:** There were 150 films, I think, screened in several cinemas in Amsterdam at this time. And they were very varied in my opinion as an expression of the pornographic film as such. And I was a little bit surprised that they chose to vote *Summerday* as the Grand Prix, because it's so serious compared [to] all of the films that were shown. Then I was personally pleased that they thought my little films, Peter Fleming films, were worthy of the People's Porn Prize. Because precisely at this time it was very significant that the people, the People's Porn Prize – it's just like the festival itself – it was supporting the hippie movement, the liberty conception.

BJ: Now, I can see why at that time you would, of course, be very pleased at this, at the recognition. But did you have any feeling that "I wish it hadn't been called a pornographic film festival"? Because you've been very strong that the Bodil film's a documentary about a particular way of life. Did you have any worry at all that it won a porn prize?

OE: Tajiri was extremely aware or worried that it should be considered a pornographic feature. I didn't distinguish very much about that, because I felt it was a portrait of a girl who makes pornographic situations appear in front of the camera.

BJ: Yes, of course, but this was simply her preferred way of life.

OE: It was her chosen way... [*A Summerday*] was shot in 16mm, which made it possible to blow it up for the cinema. So when I came back I contacted the Danish expert on eroticism, who wrote the history of eroticism and also a number of books about eroticism. And he also founded the Danish Film [Museum].[8] And then he had a licence to a cinema called Carlton here in Copenhagen. So I thought he would be a good person to contact because the Danish papers wrote about the film. There was quite a lot written about it, that it had won the prize. And I was interviewed. I was known already as one of the main producers in the business. And it was autumn 1970, and I called Mr [Ove] Brusendorff. He was the foremost Danish expert.

At about twenty minutes in length, *A Summerday* was not long enough for a feature, but Brusendorff saw *The Chinese Mask*, at just under three minutes, and offered to show it as a pre-feature short. He suggested that Ege make a main feature called *Pornography*, using ten of his short films. Premiered in 1971, *Pornography* was a great success. It was followed by a feature film, the sex-comedy *Bordello*. Although this was also a very profitable success, nonetheless Ege felt that staging and shooting pornography were having a negative effect on his personal life and artistic ambitions.

OE: It had an effect on my personal life. For one thing, of course, my girlfriend wasn't extremely keen that I was doing this so intensely. After I did the main feature, *Bordello*, I decided, this is enough for me. I don't want to have it cluttering my mind and disturbing my personal feelings to the girl I love. So I left them.

BJ: So you felt that producing and directing and watching pornography was ...

OE: Staging! Imagining!

BJ: So was it the imagining that was interfering with your mind?

OE: Especially that one 'Group Sex'. I constantly played with Santana. And it made me dream about it at night. This banging and the drums of Santana. It's very difficult to explain. But feelings for me are very important. And I felt that I was a dirty old man, doing naughty films. I didn't like that. I was very ambitious about my artistic potential.

Ege took a round-the-world trip, then settled for two and a half years on Aero, a small Danish island, where he opened a nightclub and produced a book of photographs of the island. Returning to Copenhagen in 1975, he became a writer and photographer for Brusendorff's journal on the history of eroticism, and founded his own short-lived erotic magazine *Escort*. He produced a history of Denmark's oldest circus and the book *Erotiske drømme*, a history of erotic photo magazines. He finished the manuscript in 1991 and approached the planner of an erotic fair, Erotica 2000.

> **BJ:** Why was it called 2000 if it was in 1992?
> **OE:** Because it was pointing forward.

Ege asked the planner if he would be interested in some old pictures to add 'atmosphere' to the exhibition:

> **OE:** And he was. And then we made what we called [an] erotic museum, right in the middle of the fair. A major part of the proceeds were donated to the AIDS Foundation. A lot of people really enjoyed watching the old pictures, so we thought it would be a good idea to make a permanent establishment.

Det erotiske museum was set up in 1992 in Vesterbrogade. As a consequence of rising rents, it moved to Købmagergarde 24, in Copenhagen's main tourist area and shopping precinct, opening on 14 May 1994 under the name Museum Erotica. Its last brochure reported that attendances were equally divided between men and women.

Aesthetics and music

From the earliest of Ege's films, such as *The Chinese Mask*, through to *Bordello*, one striking feature is that they are driven not simply and reductively by the explicit depiction of sexual activity. In some of the shorts that make up *Pornography* there is no sexual act at all. Some other aesthetic is at work coterminously, using sexuality as its site, and it is clear that music is implicated. Nonetheless, Ege made no pretence of any form of artistic detachment. In light of his problems with the police, I asked him why, given these legal difficulties, he chose this particular subject instead of photographing, say, birds or cityscapes. He chuckled at these suggestions, and I asked what the attraction was.

> **OE:** Well, the models. Shooting girls in the nude was my prime motive because I thoroughly enjoyed doing it. And also I thought from my own experience [that] the magazines and photographs circulating at this particular time or period could be better quality.
> **BJ:** When you say 'better' do you mean aesthetically, artistically or sensually?
> **OE:** Yes, sensually, artistically and not least technically. Because a lot of the photos were very, very discreet. So I tried to enhance the flavour of the forbidden parts of the female anatomy.

BJ: So the main motive here was not, let's say, political. You were not trying to test censorship. It was an aesthetic pleasure and a sensual pleasure.
OE: Yes.

As the shift to uncensored pornographic film-making developed, however, it brought surprises.

OE: The customers at the time when pornography was liberated were not at all interested in the striptease or the nude art photography; they wanted to see the real thing. And this to me was very peculiar, because I never imagined that I as a producer, photographer, film-maker, for money could tell a female model and a male model to go fornicate when they didn't know each other at all. And it sort of cracked the pedestal on which I had placed the woman, that for mere money you could get her to screw someone she didn't know at all. So then I thought, how can you, within a spectacle of just a few minutes, justify intercourse? So I tried to visualize it with lighting, colours, make-up and everything. And then ultimately [I] set it to music.
BJ: So you felt that producing and directing and watching pornography was …
OE: Staging! Imagining. Just a simple plot, not just man comes in, girl comes in, zips down and phuut [*mimes penetration*]. That to me is straight porn. But [put] a minimum of feeling into it, or at least a pleasant lighting, setting. I have always felt that music accentuates, particularly in films like these short cuts of girls posing in the nude or dancing a little about or whatever they do, much better than the [*simulates the panting of sexual activity*]. Especially in the German films at this time they had these soundtracks that were to my ears abominable.
BJ: In what way?
OE: They were so bad.
BJ: You mean technically or the sound that they were using?
OE: The sound. The blather, the blather these models uttered. I thought, fuck it, it needs music to enhance the mood and the sensuality and the visual stimulant of the girls posing, and then the music to enhance that. That was my aim from the start.
BJ: At the beginning of *Pornography* it said, "The first musical to be presented in Danish cinemas". Do you mean the first musical porn?
OE: Yes.
BJ: Ah, so there's a word missing there.
OE: First erotic musical.
BJ: And the other question that made me think of was this: do you think of *Pornography, Bordello, A Summerday, The Chinese Mask*, as musicals, because the word comes in so often?
OE: Yes. When there's no dialogue. In *Bordello* there's dialogue, but not in *Pornography*, not in *The Chinese Mask*, not in Bodil [*A Summerday*].

> **BJ:** So you think of them very much as musical events. That's interesting. The guide to the Museum Erotica begins with the words 'an erotic musical by Ole Ege'. Now do you mean this DVD is an erotic musical or do you see the museum itself as a musical event?[9]
> **OE:** Both.

These comments provide a useful confirmation of the aptness of Linda Williams's comparisons between two film genres, the Hollywood musical and the hardcore feature film. The musical 'number' in the former performs a role in relation to the narrative that is analogous to a specific sex act – or 'number' – in the latter:

> *To begin with, there is the obvious sense of the musical number, especially the romantic song-dance duet, as a sublimated expression of heterosexual desire and satisfaction. Beyond that there is the fact that the hard-core feature – unlike the silent stag – is quite literally a musical: original music and even songs with lyrics ... frequently accompany numbers, especially the 'big production' numbers.* (Williams, 1989: 132–3)

Ege's use of music is a conscious, and pioneering, application of the analogy. The title of the promotional DVD for the museum is *Museum Erotica: An Erotic Musical* (Ole Ege, 1999). It uses a very broad range of music to complement the voice-over narrative historically, culturally and emotionally, including marching music, jazz, big band swing, operatic and symphonic music, various Eastern musics and light classics.

> **OE:** I made it, edited it and added the music. The music is selected after the recording to the editing.
> **BJ:** And you chose all the music. It must have taken a long time, because there are so many different pieces of music.
> **OE:** Yes, yes, but again it's sort of the third step from the previous films.
> **BJ:** A third step? Explain.
> **OE:** Yeah, well. *Pornography* was the first. *Bordello* was the second. This was the third.
> **BJ:** And when you called it an erotic musical, did you mean the DVD is an erotic musical?
> **OE:** Well, the whole film.
> **BJ:** Yeah, the whole film. So music continues to be very, very central in all your thinking.
> **OE:** Extremely central.
> **BJ:** Did music have any involvement in this work [*points to the book of photographs of Aero*]?
> **OE:** When I looked at the hills of Aero, I felt music. And when I saw the artists in the circus, they had, of course, music. I think everything, if you're not deaf and dumb, is connected to music. Even the way we speak, and our body language, the things we say, is musical. When the birds are singing.

The films and the music

The Chinese Mask (1964)

The Chinese Mask is one of Ege's first short films, shot in colour, and the first of his films to which he added sound of any kind. Just under three minutes long, it shows a woman in a Chinese mask, wearing a black-and-red kimono and underwear of the same colours, slowly stripping and posing. The use of light and colour for abstract effects, the unexplained mask, the apparently artless set, and such editing techniques as double exposures, as well as the stark typography of the opening and closing credits, all have a defamiliarizing effect which challenges the categorization 'pornography'.

> **BJ:** So which film makes you feel best about yourself as a film-maker?
> **OE:** I like *The Chinese Mask* because it's so different from anything that was either then or now.
> **BJ:** It's a very strange film. What were you doing in it?
> **OE:** Well, the model was a model I used for several of the short features. But she had this look that reminded me of Asia.
> **BJ:** You mean under the mask?
> **OE:** Yes. And I used to be a photo editor of a Danish photo magazine. Also, I made my own photo magazine in '63. So I was very interested in the potential of making films. So I had, for instance, sheets of cellophane which I curled together and shot through them.
> **BJ:** For that film?
> **OE:** No, that was for another film. But I liked the abstraction and possibilities of what it would be possible to do on film. And she was a very sensual model.
> **BJ:** And she was Danish?
> **OE:** Yes, she was Danish. And she was married. And every Wednesday she had told her husband that she attended a course in household sewing or something. But then she came to my little studio. And one Wednesday I walked around the city and I passed a Chinese shop. So I bought this mask and the red dressing-gown. Then I thought I will just do an abstract version, just how I think it should be, with her body, the few accessories I had, and make it Chinese.
> **BJ:** And the music. Did you have the music in your mind before the …
> **OE:** I knew it should be Chinese and I had a Chinese record. So I edited the film to the music.
> **BJ:** Edited the *film* to the music?
> **OE:** Yes. That little feature, when I did that I just used my imagination, my desire to show or portray the beauty of a young woman's body.

The fact that Ege edited the visuals to the music and not the reverse is a significant comment on the role of the music in this brief film. "I put sound to that from a Chinese record that I had." The music is in two sections. The first, lasting about two minutes, is dominated by shrill, traditional-sounding stringed instruments in high register, with percussion. The tempo varies, but overall increases to a climax. This is followed by a single lower-register stringed instrument accompanied by a voice in unison, lasting for thirty-three seconds. Someone observed as he watched it with me that, if we imagine a silky sax as the accompaniment instead, it helps us to appreciate the contribution the 'Chinese' music makes to the defamiliarization referred to above. This imagined exercise in film-music commutation underlines the role played by a music not normally associated in the western mind with seduction or pornography. The music is a dominating presence in the piece. Apart from being the only sound, it recalls some of the pieces in Walt Disney's project *Fantasia* (James Algar and Samuel Armstrong, 1940) in its subordination of the visuals to the music and the movement towards rendering the human form as a visual abstraction. The music largely determines the pace, duration and affective arc of the action, and, in addition, the relatively unfamiliar 'Chinese-ness' of the music obscures the sexuality of the visual signals, assisting in their transformation to a form of enigmatic abstraction.

A Summerday (1970)

A collaboration between Ege (camera and musical score) and the Japanese artist Shinkichi Tajiri (director/editor), this is certainly the most confrontational and controversial of his films. Running to about twenty minutes, it is a portrait of Bodil Joensen. Following alleged puritanically driven punitive physical abuse during her childhood, Joensen withdrew to a farm where her main emotional and sexual relationships were with various animals, most notably her dog, the image of which she kept in a locket. The film follows her activities throughout one day, and is interspersed with childhood and family photographs, all of which construct her as having both history and agency. The second half of the film incorporates scenes of bestiality. Further discussion of the controversial issues raised by Bodil's life is to be found at http://alldogs.xtremebeast.com/bodil/bio.html (accessed 11 April 2008). The site includes an assessment of her career and of the film *A Summerday* that achieves a balanced sensitivity extraordinary in relation to such a topic, exemplified in the following summary:

> It is a film of seemingly irreconcilable contradictions: a sympathetic treatment of what most people consider abhorrent and perverted; a non-exploitative take on a subject loaded with exploitative potential. It's a profile of a porno performer that includes explicit sex acts but is not a porno film per se ... *A Summer Day* [sic] ages well, unlike the plenitude of pseudo-scientific sexual documentaries of the period that now seem so dated, artless, transparent and, well, pornographic.

The critique also cites Tajiri:

> Accepting the 'Grand Prix' at the first Wet Dream Film Festival was the worst mistake we made with our film, but we were too flattered by the response at the time to realize it. Today it is referred to as an 'underground

porno classic' and 'porno' was precisely the label [I] was trying to overcome in making a tender documentary about a very special person.

In the film, I wanted to leisurely investigate and give human depth to a person who was being abused as a two-dimensional sex phenomenon, but lack of time, funds and the announcement of the upcoming Wet Dream Film Festival pressed us to complete the film. We didn't think we could ever show it publicly and this seemed the ideal opportunity. Bodil has become, in spite of our efforts, porno's 'superstar', but she remains more than a historical/political/revolutionary personality: she is a fragile and precious human being.

Ege was equally insistent that what became (almost literally) a bête noire of pornography was intended to be a documentary on a chosen way of life, and his distress as he recalled Bodil's later decline (she died of alcohol-related causes at the age of forty) was palpable.

BJ: When did you decide to go back and add sound, and why did you decide? Was it because you were now making movies for people who would have sound projectors, or were you making movies for professional cinemas?

OE: Yes, it was a consequence of the Bodil film *A Summerday*. Tajiri interviewed Bodil, the girl in *A Summerday*, in long sequences, but for some reason it didn't work, the tape recorder. So we ended up with a 16mm colour original, silent. And I had a very comprehensive record collection. So I had hundreds. So we had many sessions at my house, playing very different forms of music, folk music, classic music, jazz, operetta, modern, Beatles and on[wards], contemporary music. And suddenly one day when I put on the Beethoven Pastoral symphony, which, of course, in itself is a portrait of nature. Tajiri was very, very determined that it should not be considered a pornographic movie, but a movie portrait of a true sodomite.[10] And the cardinal question of course: what makes her do it? So this is what she was explaining in the interviews, which unfortunately didn't come out. And so alternatively we portrayed her with the newspaper cuttings and the pictures of her family, the medallion of the dog and these scenes from her private life, to sort of tell, instead of an interview, to portray her feelings. And then of course the Pastoral Symphony was an excellent choice because it both had the pastoral mood of nature and the violence of it in a storm or heavy rain or whatever. And, of course, the film itself is a mixture of her pure innocence as the pastoral idyllic scenery of a landscape, and then the force, the power, the drive of her sexual relations with the animals.

It is notable, then, that the use of Beethoven was as a substitute, not for an array of apparently diegetic sounds which would have largely consisted of coital and animal noises, but for a succession of interviews which sought to humanize, explain and historicize extremely confronting sexual practices. What is also striking is not just that music is used to achieve this, but that it was music that epitomizes the western high art tradition. The cultural distance between the sex scenarios of *Pornography* and its music is not great, given the traditional associations between popular music and the sexualized body. But the aesthetic and moral distance between Bodil's bestiality and Beethoven's music could hardly be greater. It presents an interesting test for the discourses that rhapsodically apply terms like 'elemental' to art music masterpieces. With its suggestions of physical harmonization with the world of nature, Bodil's sexuality is 'elemental pastoral' taken to a logical extreme, and a confronting actualization of a pious tradition of loving all creatures. How would high-art discourse and transcendental pantheism respond to this logic? The use of Beethoven's Pastoral Symphony in this context also constitutes a challenging case study in the potentiality and flexibility of music affect in film.

Pornography (1971)

Pornography is actually a collection of ten short colour films, each of between two and eight minutes' duration, shot between 1964 and 1970.

> BJ: All of these movies in *Pornography* were originally shot as silent films. But even when you were shooting them, did you think, "I wish I could put sound to this"?
> OE: I wished I could put music to this.
> BJ: All the time you wanted that.
> OE: Yes, not sound, not voice.
> BJ: Never sound, always music?
> OE: Always music, because I love music and I think it was a much better way to 'love up' the images with music, to create a mood for the observer, than to have needless utterings of [*makes panting noises*] "Oh fuck me, oh fuck me". And they still do that today, and it's abominable, it's so unartistic. It was a huge success, because it was the first film not to use excuses of morality, aestheticism, subject-wise, but just for the pleasure of viewing nice young people doing naughty things. And I thought, it has to be a musical, also because that's international. Nobody speaks a word in the film. So everybody can understand music and visual enjoyment.
> BJ: Is that one of the reasons you don't use the sounds of the people in the film? So they might be breathing heavily, they might be saying "Fuck me" or something like this.
> OE: No. I avoided that because I detested it personally. I thought it was ridiculous. Because they are not actors. They can't say a line. And to say "Come fuck me" is not to me stimulating in any way. Whereas the music enhances the picture side, brilliantly, and I definitely had this in mind all the time, to combine the two, the silent images and the music to enhance them. No speaking, no "Fuck you", or nothing like that.

In adding music to each sequence, Ege drew on a wide range of genres. The most frequently and interestingly used was the music of Dexter Gordon, discussed below. Ege's comments on other musical choices are also relevant. Danish composer H. C.

Lumbye's 'Champagne Galop' accompanied 'Crazy Strip', which portrays a succession of women in the process of removing and replacing skimpy underwear, exchanging looks with the camera in a way which is more playful than sultry.

> OE: He's [Lumbye] the composer from Tivoli. There's a statue of him in Tivoli. He's a Danish composer who produced the 'Champagne Galop', it's called in Danish.[11] He was greatly inspired by Strauss, the waltz king. And he was the concert-master of the Tivoli when it first opened in [1843]. I used some of his music that is very well known, to at least all Danish people, but also to everybody who loves waltzes and gallops and minuets.

For 'Drømmipigen' ('Dream Girl'), Ege "didn't find Dexter's music appropriate":

> BJ: In 'Drømmipigen' you have a woman who very slowly strips [to] soft-focus romantic music. Do you remember what that music was?
> OE: Yes, it's called [*pauses to recall*] 'The Land, the Sea and the Sky'.
> BJ: And who wrote it?
> OE: The original is French. I think it's 'La Terre, la mer et le ciel', something like that. What fascinated me was that it really is so compelling, sensual, and also extremely nice to listen to. And this particular model was one of the best I had. And I thought the way she smiles and looks into the camera, and her dark hair and the way she moves blended exactly with this music. I still think it's one of the best passages in the whole film.

'Harem' is a pornographic version of the imagery made most famous in the 1921 film with Rudolph Valentino, *The Sheik* (George Melford, 1921). It takes place in a tent, where a man is entertained by a woman dancing, before she strips and joins him on the bed for sexual activity, then the two are joined by a second woman to make a sexual threesome.

> BJ: Now one of the questions I wanted to ask you about 'Harem' is, there are five places in that where it sounds like there's applause.
> OE: Yes, it's from a Mediterranean concert. It's a singer called Fairuz, Lebanese, I think maybe she's Syrian, but the concert was in Beirut.[12] I visited Beirut in '70 [or] '69, and we went to this big casino where she had this concert. Then I went and bought one of her records, vinyl, so the passage in 'Harem' is from that concert.
> BJ: I thought 'Harem' was also very playful and theatrical. The way she danced was almost a bit silly.
> OE: Yes [*laughing*].
> BJ: You meant that?
> OE: Well, it was always a question of the potential of the models, because they were not trained actresses. All they did was, to make money, to strip or even to fornicate, at this point.
> BJ: Because the acting sometimes was not – how shall I put this? – it looked like she was playing a game, and I thought that suited what was happening.

And to me it fitted with the fact of applause. It's like, yes, that's a performance you are doing. Was that part of your intention?
OE: [*with extreme emphasis*] Yes.
BJ: And is that why you chose music that had applause in it?
OE: No, it was because it was the only Arab music I had.
BJ: And it's Lebanese?
OE: Well, I think perhaps she herself is Syrian or Egyptian. But she was the greatest singer at that time in the Middle East. And I must confess to this day I don't know what she is singing about, but there has been no Muslim protest so far. But although you don't understand the words she's singing, you can understand that it's something about love and eroticism. I mean it's not a prayer, prayerly, it's definitely something with the heart and the mind.

'Spanking' is a highly theatricalized sado-masochist sequence involving two women naked apart from minimal leather/leatherette accessories. One, dark-haired, is standing, but with her arms raised by chains attached to the ceiling, while the other whips her. The percussive beat of the music parallels, but not mechanically, the blows of the whip.

BJ: Now, what was the music with 'Spanking'?
OE: Yes. That was a Danish group which was popular at the time.[13] And I thought, as spanking is sort of a more controversial subject than striptease or ordinary straightforward fucking, so I contacted this group and they saw the picture also, and the leader of that group wrote this piece for that particularly. And also there I thought it was not a very known subject at that time.
BJ: Do you mean sadomasochism?
OE: Yes. It wasn't very well-known. I thought exactly that the rhythm of the day would blend very well, which I still think it does today.
BJ: Now, this is one of the sequences that looked a bit camp to me. The make-up looked a bit like a Victorian [melodrama], a silent movie. Now was that deliberate?
OE: Yes, it was also again the models, because the girl getting spanked was a true S/M girl. And this was very significant to me that it shouldn't be just a porn actress, but one who really enjoys it. And when she's strapped, you can see she's edgy, [in] her eyes. And she was a very peculiar girl. But I needed, of course, someone to release that, that tension, that excitement. And I had another model who I thought, "She can do that". Because she was also a lesbian, the S/M girl. And this was the big blonde Ruth and she had exactly the power that excited the other girl, so I just had to get them together to make them perform.
BJ: And when you shot that, did you already think that you knew what music you were going to use?
OE: Yes. Well, I had a good idea. I had a very good idea. Because it was released as a silent film originally.

BJ: But even then you thought, "I would like to put music to this and I know what the music is"?
OE: Not until I heard this group, and I thought, "That's it, the perfect mix."

If any music 'frames' *Pornography*, it is the jazz quartet featuring tenor-player Dexter Gordon, with Kenny Drew's Trio: Drew on piano, an unidentified drummer and Danish bassist Niels-Henning Ørsted Pedersen. Ege thought of Ben Webster as an additional musician, as he was also living in Copenhagen at that time, but the producer's budget did not stretch that far. The film begins with four minutes of the Gordon/Drew quartet. They are in frame to begin with, followed by the film credits over stills from the film, then returning to the visuals of the band playing. The sequence was shot by Ege at the band's performance in Copenhagen's Jazzhus Montmartre. "He was actually performing that evening, so I went with the camera, and I had a sound guy to record it. So it's from an actual concert." Their collaboration with Ege is of particular interest in a review of the latter's 'sound decisions'. Ege had always imagined his short silent films accompanied by music and as they were being assembled as *Pornography*, this represented the most important challenge.

OE: Yes. Well, it's a bigger task than it sounds because when you add music to a film in movement, you have to make them harmonize and blend together. I knew Dexter Gordon through a mutual friend who had an art gallery here, an American living in Copenhagen for many years. And Dexter himself lived here also for some years. So they knew each other. And we all met at my house and explained the idea to Dexter. [We] made an arrangement with Dexter, that composed. We'd run the film in black and white; then he wrote a musical score for the single passages, for the single films.
BJ: Did he express any doubts about playing music for …
OE: No. He loved those little features, considered it a pleasure to write a score and perform it for each of the selected films. Niels-Henning Ørsted Pedersen, he was the most sceptical. He was the only Dane. But he was a brilliant bass player. But he wasn't too keen about it.
BJ: Why not?
OE: Dexter talked him into it, and Kenny Drew also. Dexter loved all the films. He loved girls and pleasure and the sybaritic way of life.
BJ: And what was Niels's problem?
OE: I think he was naturally a shy person.
BJ: When you did this, you got Dexter Gordon, you talked to him about it obviously.
OE: Yes, many hours, many hours.
BJ: Then he sat down, he watched them, and did he actually write?
OE: No, he timed each sequence meticulously and then wrote the score. And a couple of the scores had never been performed before, because he used compositions that he had already put on paper and then he cut them to fit each individual film.

BJ: Did they perform to the film? Did he get the quartet in there and did they watch the film while [they] performed it?
OE: They all saw each individual score.
BJ: They saw each individual score or film?
OE: Each individual film, yes. Then he made the final score, how it should be. They performed it and then it's, of course, edited both on the picture side and on the musical side.
BJ: So first of all he watches and he meticulously times everything. Then did he go back to the band and say, "Here is the song. You will take your solo then, you will take your solo then, and then we finish." Is that how he did it?
OE: Yes, he wrote an individual score for each performer.
BJ: And did the performers see the film while they were performing?
OE: Yes.
BJ: I'm trying to imagine exactly how this took place.
OE: It was in the sound studio.
BJ: Right, and the film is showing while they're doing the performance.
OE: Yes.
BJ: So the bass, for example, he's going, he's watching, dum dum dum, like that [*mimes bass player playing and watching the film*].
OE: Yes. It was sort of tailor-made.
BJ: Do you know if this has ever been done for any other erotic film or pornographic film?
OE: I don't think so. I've never come across any. Also, it took a year, almost a year, to edit the ten pieces and get the music added to it, which I was doing from their recording. I had to make it fit completely. Although they were watching it as they were performing, it still need[ed] final editing.
BJ: What did that consist of? What did you have to do after that?
OE: Well, I had to first of all cut it because the film as it was – there were perhaps some sequences that I took out because they didn't fit the plot or the music score or the overall conception of the final film. So this editing took some time.

Apart from introducing the film, the Dexter Gordon/Kenny Drew quartet accompanied four of the sequences, including playing languidly to the closing visuals. In 'En lystig barbering' (A Jolly Shave), a young woman removes her clothing and shaves her pubic hair, from time to time looking straight at camera in a way which is both self-assured and playful. There is a harmonization, rather than strict synchronization, with the music.

OE: The one where the girl is shaving, for each stroke, there is a bass fiddle plucking. This was very good, of course, because it was as if they were intended for each other, the musical score and the images, the film images.
BJ: While we are talking about that, then, I was interested to notice that it was a blues in fact. And I noticed that there was something playful about it – the girl would look at the camera and smile [*frequent interjections*

of 'yes' from OE in emphatic agreement]. And also I noticed that the performance, the music, was exactly as long as the visual sequence. So did that mean that Dexter Gordon watched it and wrote —
OE: Timed it, and then wrote the score.
BJ: And was it he who looked, for example, at the movement and said, "I will make a bass stroke for each [shaving stroke]"? That was his idea?
[*frequent interjections of 'yes' from OE in emphatic agreement*]

'Ilse' is the name given to one of two women who play good-humouredly with each other, using sex toys they have been given by what appears to be a sex-aid salesman, followed by a threesome with the man joining in. The music begins with an almost martial drum introduction, followed by the entry of the full quartet. A frenzied bass solo accompanies the male ejaculation, and the music finishes with a drum fade. Again, the visual and the musical parallels were the work of the sax-player. "He did it from the viewing of each little film." 'Gruppe Sex' (Group Sex) is a similar scenario. Three women and one man engage in varied permutations of lesbian and heterosexual activity, sometimes simultaneously, as in the sexual climax that concludes the piece, to the accompaniment of another frenzied bass solo complemented by the drums, more or less in tempo with the sexual movements. The music was developed in conjunction with the visual action in the same way as for the other Gordon/Drew collaborations. At the end, the sexual and musical climaxes are perfectly matched. These two are the closest that any of the short sequences comes to conventional understandings of pornography, though they both succeed in avoiding the formulaic porn visual rhetoric of camera-aware simulated ecstasies.

Ege had spoken of the fact that he preferred, if possible, subjects who were in some way personally involved in the filmed scenarios, rather than professional actors completely inventing roles, and who were not acquainted.

> **BJ:** In other sequences, like 'Gruppe Sex' for example, were they models or were they people who knew each other?
> **OE:** [In] 'Gruppe Sex', they were both models and they knew each other. The two of them, the guy and the blonde, they were lovers privately. But she was also a professional hooker. And the other, third, girl was actually a shop assistant who posed just to make a little extra money. But the sequence with the third girl, the dark hair, where she is being really pumped. That is one of the greatest scenes, I think, where I focused on her face. And she really got fucked, and you can see that she is almost crying. Had you said there, "Oh fuck me" [*whistles and gestures signifying a flop*], the whole thing would have been nothing. But with the music and this insisting image of her face, that's I think a very significant thing.
> **BJ:** It's a very abandoned look on her face, as though she's gone beyond pleasure and pain.

OE: Yes, precisely, and that's exactly what I wanted. That she let go of herself and just puffs out the screen with the immense pleasure of being banged.

According to Ege's account, 'Gruppe Sex' had been shown at the Wet Dream festival with music, using Santana's self-titled debut album from 1969.

OE: I put some music to the ones I showed. Santana, for instance. The one called 'Group Sex', I originally put Santana to the [sequence] with the third passage, with the [rapid drums]. Santana, the one with the tiger head. That passage, where he really fucks the girl, I blended with Santana. But for copyright reasons I couldn't do that in the feature movie.
BJ: I see. If you had been able to, would you have kept that music?
OE: [*with great emphasis*] Yes, yes, definitely. It was *perfect*.
BJ: Right, even better than the Dexter Gordon track?
OE: Well. With all respect, it was different.

A much more elegiac piece is 'Forår i Tivoli' (Springtime in Tivoli), which presents a couple meeting in the Tivoli Gardens, then going to an apartment where they dine together, then make love.

BJ: That begins [with] footage, visual footage of Kenny Drew playing solo. And then after four minutes you go into the Tivoli Gardens. And there's a dining sequence, the two are eating on opposite sides of the table. And the music comes into tempo there. Before then it's out of tempo. And the rest of the band joins in. And towards the end of it – it's a very tender section I think – the song drops out of tempo again near the end and you finish with a freeze-frame and the music fades. You actually begin with images of the band.
OE: Yeah.
BJ: Was there a reason for that?
OE: Well, to get in the mood for the sequence, I thought it would be appropriate, as I very much enjoy Kenny Drew's piano. Dexter Gordon sometimes gets a little rough. Kenny Drew is more like Oscar Peterson or Erroll Garner even. I thought to place it in the mood of the piano, the green of the garden and the two persons coming together. And the dining sequence is made at their house, the models' house. Because they were lovers privately. And I thought, it's called 'Spring[time] in Tivoli'. So I thought, this again is not a story to be played by two youngsters who are just models but don't know each other. And I wanted to have a little of the affection, especially from the girl who is so obviously in love with the guy. He didn't care much about it and he was very reluctant to even participate because he was a steward in SAS [Scandinavian Airlines] and he could stand to lose his job if somebody saw this piece. I never heard from them again so I assume they got over it. But to my mind it was important that it was two characters who had real, or shared real, feelings.

BJ: Do you think the music evened up the power relationship? Do you think it produced a more harmonious sense of the relationships?
OE: Definitely.

Bordello (1972)

This was Ege's only full-length feature. The plot draws together several traditions in Danish film: the erotic and the folk comedy. Soila refers to "hyggefilm" ('genial film'), in which "Danish joviality also rates highly and is presented as a national virtue of sorts".[14] It was the first Danish hardcore comedy feature film, and its success inspired a decade of successors in the same vein. It is set in the nineteenth century, and is loosely inspired by John Cleland's 1748 novel *Memoirs of a Woman of Pleasure*, aka *Fanny Hill*. The voice-over narrator is a young country girl, who comes to Copenhagen to seek her fortune, and joins the staff of a very opulent bordello. She participates in a sexual ritual with the other girls in the bordello, the purpose of which is to initiate her into the group. While discussing this scene, Ege revealed an interesting detail about his working method.

> **OE:** But actually there's a funny detail attached to that particular scene. Now I was the director but I had a whole film crew of twenty people doing all the technical things. And that particular scene, where she is initiated into the group of girls in the bordello, they refused to film it.
> **BJ:** Your film crew refused?
> **OE:** To film it.
> **BJ:** Why?
> **OE:** Because they thought it was obscene.
> **BJ:** But we're in a bordello. Why did they think *that* scene was obscene?
> **OE:** I think because of the legs being apart, and the touching. Together with the diamond in her belly button.
> **BJ:** So the film crew had no problem filming [scenes of] people fucking and group sex, but that they thought was obscene.
> **OE:** Well, actually, the fucking scenes I filmed myself. Because you can't have people fucking with a whole film crew around. Today you can, but not in those days.
> **BJ:** You mean for moral reasons or technical reasons?
> **OE:** Moral reasons, I think. Also it makes the models freeze, they don't perform. They perform[ed] when I was alone there with the camera.
> **BJ:** Hand-held?
> **OE:** Yes. I could get them to do anything. So what I did was to let the film crew do all the big scenes with the horse and carriage, all of the outdoor scenes and the cops and all. Then the intimate sessions I filmed myself. I had the film crew put up the lighting, the decorations, everything was arranged. So all I had to do was take the camera and then I shot it myself. And we had loads of theatrical champagne, it's called. It's bubbly water like

champagne, but it has very little alcohol. And then we smoked pot. I always wanted to create the mood to make the models perform optimally. And I very quickly realized that you can't do that with this terrible thing [*mimes*], the slateboard [clapboard]. As soon as that click came [*whistle*], the dick falls. It's a lot easier for women to perform in pornographic movies than men. Because you have to get it up and you have to keep it up. It can take a day to shoot a few minutes.

BJ: So you had to keep a kind of real party atmosphere.

OE: Yes, exactly. I had a very, very large villa of 435 square metres in the most expensive place north of Copenhagen, because I made a lot of money on the smaller films. And so I always wanted to create this atmosphere of intimacy, and pleasant surroundings: colours, lighting, models, make-up, everything.

BJ: What about the sound technician? Because in *Bordello* there are sounds of sighing and groaning.

OE: Yes.

BJ: So did you have a separate sound technician with you?

OE: Yes.

BJ: So there's two people in these scenes. And that wasn't a problem?

OE: No, because most of it was done in the editing process.

BJ: You added the sound later?

OE: Yeah. It was added later as they were speaking into a microphone, again to the images. And the music was also added. For all of the intimate scenes, just me. But that was with the silent camera again. Whereas the major scenes outside with horses, they were done with the sound of the original take.

BJ: So the intimate scenes were basically silent and later you showed them and the actors – the same actors perhaps?

OE: There's a few of them who didn't have the voice which would be feasible in the cinema. We had stand-ins to say their lines. But also that took a year, almost a year.

Ege's attempts to overcome the alienating effect of a large crew with intrusive equipment on set appear to be indirectly related to the way he uses music in his films, and his attempts to address one of the central problems shared by the cinematic presentation of both music and sexuality. I shall return to this in the concluding comments.

In the meantime, as the young girl is indoctrinated into the bordello, a parallel plot is initiated when the male owner suddenly dies (while having intercourse with one of the girls). His will directs that the first of his two sons to arrive will inherit the property. One is a Mormon cleric in the USA, the other is a rogue Count wanted by the police for various offences. Although pursued by two bumbling comic policemen, he arrives first, and enjoys the welcome dinner and its associated entertainments, which include parlour singing and sex games. Part of his objective, however, is the theft of a diamond which he knows to be in the house. The other brother arrives, but for various reasons, including the misguided interference of the policemen, he never gains entry, although one of the policemen does. The plot gradually dissipates in the aftermath of the dinner, when the film's focus shifts to the sexual activities that ensue in various parts of the house. These include comic drunken impotence, the opportunism of the policeman who has gained entry and needs to 'investigate' things very closely, tenderly erotic couplings, and a jovial bacchanalian orgy.

The film is sonically rich, using music that is diegetic, extra-diegetic, and some that is in an indeterminate space between the two. It includes Wagner, Johann Strauss and Borodin, as well as diegetic parlour music and music from a gramophone.

> **BJ:** Gradually, there are many plots coming out and many couples beginning to form. And each of these plots has a different kind of music. For example, there are two people in a bedroom and a woman dances for the man. And the music you've used is a Strauss waltz, I think – it's a waltz anyway. But of course the music is not in the film. This is music added. Now, when we get to the sex scenes near the end, several things happen that I want to talk to you about. First of all, at one point the camera – and you must be shooting at this point – the camera seems to pan in time to a waltz. You know what I mean?
> **OE:** That's me.
> **BJ:** That's you doing that. And any particular reason you did that?
> **OE:** Yes, to make it sway, swing, to make it non-static.
> **BJ:** Here is where it became very interesting. You have a group sex scene and 'The Blue Danube' is played for that.
> **OE:** Yes.
> **BJ:** You have another group sex scene and a sort of old music-hall piano is used.
> **OE:** Yes.
> **BJ:** There's a couple scene with a waltz. And there's a couple scene with one string – it's a violin or a viola – and a piano.
> **OE:** Yes.
> **BJ:** In all of those cases, the music is from outside [extra-diegetic]. But there's one case where the music is inside, and that is where you hear the record player.
> **OE:** Yes.
> **BJ:** And I think this is very interesting. First of all you hear the scratch [*imitates*] noise.
> **OE:** Yes. 'Valentine'. It's a French tune [*whistles*].[15]
> **BJ:** It's a music-hall song. Now that scene is a funny scene.
> **OE:** Yes, with the magnifying glass.[16]
> **BJ:** Now, do you want to talk a bit about why you decided you would have that as recorded music in the film, rather than as music from 'outside'?
> **OE:** I'm a collector, so I had this old record player for '78s, and the sound guy on the film, he had this '78 record. It's called 'Valentine'. It's one of

Maurice Chevalier's old numbers. It's not Maurice performing it. But it's the same tune.

BJ: In fact there's no voice on it. Just a violin.

OE: I think it's from the 'twenties. Well, I thought it was very good to interchange the sound and the modest performance of the two players. The man playing the cop, one of the police officers, he was actually a schoolteacher here in Copenhagen [Gotha Andersen]. He was in a lot of films at that time as a sight ...

BJ: Visual comedian.

OE: So, he was in a lot of Danish films, not a major actor but as a supporting actor. But he was a schoolteacher. But I thought exactly this [whistles 'Valentine'] could blend into her eyes, and when he grabs her. He's a detective, that's what he tells her. "We could make a search, a personal search." Then he says, "I'm trained to wait." And she says, "I can't wait that long."

BJ: I remember the look on her face.

OE: Yes, and she was one of the performers who actually could act a little bit. They were very different, those ten or twelve girls.

BJ: So some of them were – what – models, some of them were actors?

OE: Yes. Semi-actors.

BJ: There were two cases in *Bordello* where the music was in the movie [i.e., diegetic]. One was the record player, the other was the piano, where they had played salon songs. And I wondered how much you had thought about that.

OE: Oh, extremely.

BJ: Tell me the kinds of thing you were thinking about.

OE: Well, I was thinking of, of course, the overall concept of the whole feature, but again to portray the plot and accentuate it with the music. The girl who is singing this song to the piano in the party section, she was a singer, a professional singer [Ingerlise/Inger-Lise Gaarde] in the Bakken Tivoli outside Copenhagen, a funfair. It's called Dyrehausbakken [in English, Deer Park Hill, and located in Dyrehaven/The Deer Park]. In this funfair they have this singing saloon where the girls sing on the stage old familiar Danish tunes and the people throw up money to the stage and they collect it. They sit on chairs, four of them. It's still performed. She was the most well-known of those. As I had a fascination about big women, voluptuous women, I contacted her and asked if she would participate in the film. She was the most known, together with the schoolteacher.

BJ: So most people who saw this would have recognized them as familiar stars?

OE: Yes. The very first to appear in what is later being termed as the first Danish folk comedy erotic in the mixture of Danish folk films set to eroticism.

BJ: You mean *Bordello*?

OE: Yes.

BJ: And you were telling me how much you thought about the music.

OE: Oh, intensely, intensely. I didn't think about anything else, really – well, of course to get the film together. My ultimate aim was to make a feature film, unlike the first one *Pornography*, where it was just a musical score that was new – but to make a comprehensive effort to combine music and sexuality. And I think the most erotic in life, apart from the [*breathes heavily*] moaning and uttering, is music.

BJ: But, of course, sometimes you've used music there as a kind of comedy eroticism.

OE: Yes, yes. Well, it was the producer who wanted it should look a little like the old Danish films in so far as it should not just be portraying nude people or girls or boys or whatever, but also have this humoristic approach to the subject, which at this time *Bordello* was the first film, really feature film who was a light-hearted comedy with specific erotic plot.

Conclusion

It is not my purpose to propose any kind of master key to Ole Ege's psyche on the basis of either his films or his own comments. Indeed, one point to emerge from his descriptions of his working processes is that what a 'textual' critic might interpret as the manifestation of a detailed creative design or the shapely reflection of some critical theory is just as likely to be the outcome of accidents and coincidences. If some believe that massive budgets and commercial appeal compromise artistic vision, it is also the case that working on a low budget with limited technology, and in an initially amateur genre, also deprives the creator of the luxury of an untrammelled 'vision'. Ege did have an articulated aesthetic in his work, but it is also finally shaped by chance and opportunism – a Chinese mask spotted in a shop, a film crew squeamish about shooting certain scenes, equipment breaking down or budgetary constraints. Music is central to Ege's *oeuvre*, but before we ingeniously attribute too much forethought to the detail of any specific musical text, we should remember that sometimes (including one of his most striking uses of music, in *The Chinese Mask*) it simply happened to be a recording he had acquired for reasons that had nothing to do with the movie.

If I draw some extrapolations from his own reflections on his work, it is simply to suggest ways in which they are instructive to the further analysis of the possible roles of sound and music in sexuality in cinema. Ege engages our attention here for the importance he attaches to music in his overall cinematic objective, particularly by contrast with mainstream hardcore porn, in which for the most part music is sonic wallpaper, a secondary budgetary and aesthetic consideration. For him, it is always a high priority and often aesthetically predominant. He often cut the visuals to music rather than the reverse, and even as a cameraman in *Bordello*, he moves – and takes us with him – in a slightly clumsy waltz; it is not an expensive dolly shot, just a man with a hand-held camera doing a sort of waltz. He is thus an instructive case study in relation to Williams's arguments about the musical and the hardcore feature, as noted above.

Williams also echoes Ege's fascination with the paradox of staging spontaneity, of the performance of passion between strangers. Again, this activates analogies with the film musical. Williams paraphrases Jane Feuer's argument in *The Hollywood Musical*:

> the musical as a genre is founded on a contradiction between highly engineered, choreographed, and rehearsed numbers ... and the desire to make these numbers seem unrehearsed, as if they arose naturally and spontaneously out of the rhythms and harmonies of song and dance itself. This contradiction ... animates the musical's extreme valuation of certain myths – of spontaneity, of performers' communion with the audience, of community integration through song and dance – myths that in turn work to overcome the "original sin" of cinema itself: the fact that, as a mass art of canned performance, cinema can never really bring audience and performer together; that it must always be elaborately rehearsed and choreographed for camera and lighting to be right and for lips to synchronize to pre-recorded sound. (Williams, 1989: 146)

She then makes a jump that I feel Ege would perfectly understand, finding similar contradictions in films that seek

> the solution to the problem of sex through the performance of sex. In such films, sex as a spontaneous event enacted for its own sake stands in perpetual opposition to sex as an elaborately engineered and choreographed show enacted by professional performers for a camera. (ibid.: 147)

Ege's switch from nude photography to erotic film brought him up against this paradox. The shift faced him with the alienating effect and affect of filming sex: that strangers would copulate as professional actors, the simulation of coital sound and dialogue, the unadorned close-up of genital images. His production methods seem in many ways to have been a way of addressing this dismay: keeping the camera crew to the least obtrusive minimum, his preference for on-screen participants who knew each other and lived the milieu, actors who were recognizable to the local audience, his use of familiar settings (Tivoli Gardens, the suburbs and canals of Copenhagen), his abhorrence of 'performed' dialogue, and his criss-crossing the borders between feature film and documentary. Alternative solutions were also found in playful engagement with the spectator and in a kind of abstraction that in some way desexualized sexuality, as in *The Chinese Mask*. In that piece the performer goes through the motions of a stripper, but in a disconcerting way that transforms her from a piece of flesh to a play of inscrutable chiaroscuro, the human body going beyond the raw logic of sexuality to a site for the exploration of the aesthetics of the film camera. The music and the visuals do not invite us to desire the subject sexually, but to contemplate her aesthetically. It is significant, I think, that one of Ege's favourite productions is *The Chinese Mask*, while the sequence that disturbed him most was the raw sexual energy of 'Gruppe Sex'. His ambivalent attitude to the process of staging sexual scenarios became an obsession, to an extent that he felt compelled to abandon film-making.

He found the most pervasive solution to these tensions in the use of music as an aesthetic overlay, an attempt to address the central contradiction embodied in such phrases as 'staged intimacy', 'simulated sexual desire'. Music provided a means to create atmosphere and milieu, but above all it was a way of generating emotional depth in a form most often characterized by objectification. He deployed music in two ways: to desexualize the subject, or at least to aestheticize the sexual; and to humanize the representation of sexual activity. Both of these work simultaneously in the case of Bodil, the subject of *A Summerday*. Music is also used to connect with the audience's milieu, in a way scarcely seen in erotic film until *9 Songs*. That is, Ege sought out the sound of the time and place of his audience: Santana at the international Wet Dream Festival; the music and musicians of Denmark's thriving contemporary jazz scene; and its local music-hall and salon traditions. The effect of all of these sounds is to humanize, acculturate and make recognizable the world portrayed visually. Williams's analogy has special significance here. Music seems to have been an attempt to redeem the "original sin" of Ege's chosen film genre.

There are rich possibilities in all this for theorizing about sexuality and music affect. In a collection of essays about sound, sexuality and cinema, however, my primary purpose was simply to listen to what a film producer had to say, and I leave it to others to make speculations or draw conclusions. My intention here is not to impose 'readings' or theoretical grids over the use of music in these films. Rather, these final comments seek to draw out a few threads that emerge from listening to the 'auteur' speak for himself about what kind of sound decisions he made and, as far as possible in such a visceral creative environment, why he made them.

Notes

1. The interviews with Ole Ege (OE) cited in this chapter were conducted by Bruce Johnson (BJ) over two days, 5 and 7 March 2008 in Ege's office in the Museum Erotica, Copenhagen. They resulted in around 35 pages of transcription. Unless otherwise indicated, all quotations are from these transcriptions. For the sake of flow, I have not transcribed all conversational interpolations, hesitancy vocalizations, repeated words, or cross-language clarifications, nor have I indicated ellipses. This editing has tended to obscure the considerable emotional range navigated, from humour to sorrow. I have tried to signal at least some of that continuum through bracketed interpolations. The extracts cited here are the outcome of editing for relevance to the use of sound, and have been reordered for greater cohesion. A number of people have provided invaluable assistance in preparing this paper, and apart from specific acknowledgements throughout, I would like to express my warmest thanks to Nicolas Barbano, Mark Evans, Philip Hayward, Anu Juva and Johannes Juva.

2. The title is given variously as *A Summer's Day*, *A Summer Day*, and *A Summerday*. This last is the version on the opening credits of the film itself, and will be used throughout, unless within quotation. Made in 1970, the credits are Shinkichi Tajiri, director and editor, Ole Ege, camera and musical score. It was basically a closely collaborative production.
3. Apart from more general acknowledgement elsewhere, I wish to thank Danish filmmaker Nicolas Barbano for his assistance in locating and providing this and other sources during the preparation of this chapter.
4. A review by Andrew Billen was published in *New Statesman*, 12 December 1997. My thanks to Mark Evans for drawing my attention to this review.
5. In an unhappy coincidence, Kim Riisfeldt-Clausen died on 17 May 2008, and the funeral service was conducted on Ole Ege's seventy-fourth birthday, 23 May 2008, placing the administrative structure in a fluid state.
6. Soila speaks of the mid-1950s, which must be an error, since the film was made in 1962, and not shown in Finland until December 1963. The other films are all from the 1960s. She also incorrectly gives the Danish title of the film as *Bocken I Paradiset*; it should be *Det tossede paradis*.
7. An account of the Wet Dream Film Festival is provided by Richard Neville, one of the eight judges, who included fellow Australian Germaine Greer (Neville, 1996: 237–43). In the present connection it is notable that the only films he mentions by name are Jean Genet's 'classic' from 1954, *Un Chant d'amour* (*ibid.*: 239), and *A Summer Day* [sic] (*ibid.*: 242), whose subject, Bodil Joensen, he later recalls as 'the darling' of the festival (*ibid.*: 249).
8. Ege mistakenly referred to this as the Danish Film Academy.
9. *Museum Erotica. An Erotic Musical* (Ole Ege, 1999).
10. OE used this term several times; in English the word 'bestialist' would be more accurate.
11. The sheet-music spelling is 'Champagne Galop' by H. C. Lumbye. The colloquial title used by all Danes, however, is 'Champagnegaloppen'.
12. Fairuz is Lebanese. It is, however, instructive to retain the sense of OE's uncertainty. She was a major star in the 1960s and 1970s, blending elements of Lebanese folk, western and Latin American music. She toured the USA with notable success in 1971.
13. The band is listed in the opening credits to *Pornography* as Dr. Dopo Jam. The title of the song is 'Spanking', with composer credit given to Kristian Pommer, the bandleader who played clarinet, guitar and piano. On the website at http://www.alexgitlin.com/npp/drdopojam.htm (accessed 28 May 2008) the band is described as a jazz-rock group specializing in humorous pastiche and reminiscent of Frank Zappa's Mothers of Invention.
14. See Soila *et al.* (1998: 27). The erotic tradition is briefly discussed above. On folk comedy, see *ibid.*: 19.
15. The song was featured in one of the earliest film musicals, the 1929 Paramount production *Innocents of Paris* (Richard Wallace), which starred Maurice Chevalier in his first talkie. Composer credit is shared between Chevalier and Henri Christine. Chevalier recorded the song on Victor 22095 (Kinkle, 1974: 204, 706).

16. The scene involves one of the policemen with a bordello woman. She is cheerfully offering him sex, while he still feels he must dissimulate his desires by conducting an 'official' police examination of her person with the magnifying glass. In the room a gramophone record is seen playing.

References

Billen, A. (1997), 'Goggling at girls', *New Statesman*, 12 December.
Gorfinkel, E. (2006), 'Wet Dreams: Erotic Film Festivals of the Early 1970s and the Utopian Sexual Public Sphere', *Framework: The Journal of Cinema and Media*, 47(2), 59–86.
Kinkle, R. D. (1974), *The Complete Encyclopedia of Popular Music and Jazz 1900–1950*, 4 vols, Westport, CT: Arlington House Publishers.
Levy, W. (ed.) (1973), *Wet Dreams: Films & Adventures*, Amsterdam: Joy Publications.
Neville, R. (1996), *Hippie Hippie Shake: The Dreams, the Trips, the Trials, the Love-ins, the Screw Ups ... The Sixties*, London: Bloomsbury Publishing.
Soila, T., Söderbergh, A., Iversen, G., and Iversen, W. (eds) (1998), *Nordic National Cinemas*, London and New York: Routledge.
Villadsen, E. (2005), 'Danish erotic films', text essay on disc 2 (DVD bonus materials), in *All about Anna* (Jessica Nilsson, 2005), released 24 November 2005 by Team Video Plus, Copenhagen.
Williams, L. (1989), *Hard Core: Power, Pleasure, and the "Frenzy of the Visible"*, Berkeley: University of California Press.

Filmography

The Sheik (George Melford, 1921)
Innocents of Paris (Richard Wallace, 1929)
Fantasia (James Algar and Samuel Armstrong, 1940)
Det tossede paradis (The Goat in Paradise) (Gabriel Axel, 1962)
The Chinese Mask (Ole Ege, 1964; on-screen title in original Danish version *Den kinesiske maske*)
A Summerday (Shinkichi Tajiri and Ole Ege, 1970; on-screen title in original Danish version *Bodil Joensen – en sommerdag juli*)
Pornography (Ole Ege, 1971; on-screen title in original Danish version *Pornografi*)
Bordello (Ole Ege, 1972; on-screen title in original Danish version *Bordellet*)
Museum Erotica: An Erotic Musical (Ole Ege, 1999)

2 Beyond the Valley of the Ultra Cliché
Erotic Plenitude in the Films of Russ Meyer

Mark Evans (with Matt Burgess)

The irreverently warped vision of director Russ Meyer has made him an enduring cult figure among fans and film-makers alike. Meyer, an unabashed breast fetishist and true "public titilla*teur*" (Henderson, 2006), has been referenced in movies by respected Hollywood directors from John Landis to Quentin Tarantino,[1] John Waters to Jay Roach. At the time of his death in 2004,[2] Meyer's films were being taught in tertiary film courses and had been purchased by the Museum of Modern Art in New York. The *Washington Post* decreed him "practically an American institution" (Woods, 2004: 9) and the National Film Theatre in London has afforded him two retrospective film festivals. What makes this acclaim so significant is that Meyer worked for most of his career of 23 feature films in the softcore/erotica genre.

Meyer learnt his film trade as an Army Signal Corps combat cameraman during World War II, and went on later to make 'industrial' films – those used for corporate training and information services. This professional background was one reason why Meyer's films would later stand out from the genre to which they belonged. Meyer's background also meant that he was adept with several areas of film-making, a useful and necessary requisite for those working in early erotic films. Throughout his career Meyer frequently produced, directed, financed, wrote and edited his own films. But it was his skill in direction and editing that would ultimately be celebrated, along with his vivid and engorged subject matter.

Meyer's first film was the landmark *The Immortal Mr. Teas* (henceforth *Mr. Teas*), which he made in 1959 for $24,000. The film went on to return $1 million dollars in profit. *Mr. Teas* is largely acknowledged as the first 'nudie-cutie', a new form of exploitation film that largely operated as comedy (see Schaefer, 2002: 5). While widely considered as the "precursor to the sexploitation genre ... the film lacks the erotic tension, displacements to violence, and general luridness of the sexploitation films of the sixties, including Meyer's own" (Williams, 2008: 89). Nonetheless the film paved the way for a host of similar films that immediately tapped into this substantial, and growing, market.[3] It would be *Vixen* (1968), however, that would catapult Meyer to fame and fortune, and attract the interest of major Hollywood studios. *Vixen* cost $76,000 to make and went on to earn more than $6 million. It was the first film of its type to break into traditional first-run cinemas, where it screened for over a year. Indeed, by the end of the 1960s, Meyer's name had become "so synonymous with his brand of lusty, red-blooded and crudely funny sex fare that he began including his name, à la Fellini, in the titles of his films" (McCarthy, 2004: 100). Meyer's much-anticipated autobiography (credited to the apocryphal Adolph Schwartz), a massive three-volume set, *A Clean Breast: The Life and Loves of Russ Meyer*, was released in 2000.

Despite the critical acclaim that often surrounds Meyer's films today, there have always been, since the release of *Mr. Teas*, those who have derided or dismissed Meyer's work. Apart from predictable tirades against the level of nudity and/or sexual activity in his work, there have been those quick to dismiss his artistic achievements. One newspaper critique, on the occasion of Meyer's catalogue being released on DVD, noted:

> *The thing about Meyer films is that, on the face of it, they are truly dreadful. They have hamfisted acting, ramshackle plots and ludicrous dialogue ... [But] Meyer's films are fantastic to look at. The clothes, the sets and the rapid cutting mean you can put a Meyer film on with the sound off and it won't really matter.* (Armstrong, 1999)

Quotations such as this are readily available. Many are happy to pay homage to Meyer's skill as an editor (by far his most-cited professional attribute), and often the overall look of his films is celebrated. Yet the curse of Meyer's dialogue, with its seeming incoherence and cliché, is often held to be detrimental to any achievements. What is lacking in these accounts is an appreciation of the way the dialogue sounds. That is, how the timbre of the dialogue is utilized by Meyer to further heighten his already enlarged thematic canvas. Furthermore, timbre within the dialogue often works to fulfil Meyer's parodic intentions. As *Los Angeles Times* critic Kevin Thomas noted, Meyer's world is "populated with an abundance of pneumatic women carefully photographed to make them look as cantilevered as possible, dirty old men and blockhead heroes plus dialogue heavy with double-entendre".[4] The final aspect of Armstrong's criticism above pertains to the role of sound generally. And while Meyer is often commended for his filmic sensibilities, little has been considered in relation to his use of sound. This chapter seeks to redress this shortfall. It argues that, while sonicity is not the major drawcard for a Meyer film, it is crucial in the exploration of excess, comedy, violence, sexuality, and other of Meyer's thematic concerns.

Meyer's absurd and artificial sexploitations shaped a soundscape that the adult film industry emulates even today. The main difference is that Meyer used sound to accentuate his satirical assault against prudish, ultra-conservative America and the stigmas it had attached to human sexuality. Meyer was always upfront about his intentions:

> *Stag films were the earliest version of pornographic movies, but then they got hard-core, and I didn't. Mine are put-ons, send-ups, humorous. I think I've got an ability to provoke, be teasing, be provocative. It's all a joke.*[5]

The discussion that follows will detail how the overall soundscape created in Meyer's films is used in similar style to visuals, and in many cases it is sound that achieves Meyer's more mischievous aims.

Meyer's objectives

Meyer's films broadly follow the tradition of burlesque. Burlesque films were popular in the United States from roughly 1945 to 1960, and were situated within the broader context of exploitation films.

> The burlesque film thrived on the fringes of American cinema in the years following the end of World War II, conveying the unvarnished sexual spectacle forbidden in movies governed by the Production Code. (Schaefer, 1997: 41)

Eric Schaefer (2002) has extensively documented the rise of the pornographic feature film, with particular attention to the role of the sexploitation film that preceded it. There is no denying Meyer's crucial role in this history, although he spent most of his career proudly announcing the artistic merit of softcore/nudie flicks over any hardcore sexual depictions (see Meyer, 2000; Woods, 2004). Schaefer has also discussed the purely industrial economics of sexploitation films, an area to which Meyer was all too attuned. Meyer's tactic in exploiting this market was simple: make the most extreme, over-the-top, breast-dominated, daringly fun movies of all time.

Exaggeration and excess

There is no doubt that Russ Meyer set out to make films that were excessive in many senses. His cinematic extremism was demonstrated by cartoonish, larger-than-life pin-ups, shocking colours, playful surrealism and fast-paced editing techniques. Indeed, as his "overactive jump cuts prove, Meyer directs films as though he's perpetually on the cusp of a fantastic orgasm" (Henderson, 2006). Moreover, his films mocked filmic and aural conventions by embracing the stigma of musical melodrama and sexual comedy. Such an approach was not exclusive to Meyer. In many respects he was merely embracing the genre, albeit more so than most film-makers, and the conventions that bounded it. As Schaefer explains:

> On a variety of levels, sexploitation films were always about excess. They were about excessive desire that needed to be fulfilled. They were about excessive display – the skin, the sexual situations. They were often about fetishism that blossomed into obsession ... and they were about excessive bodies. (Schaefer, 2003: 43)

Meyer's depiction of visual and especially feminine excess is well documented; what is less discussed is how he used sound to reinforce and even enlarge the visual tropes present in his films.

The soundtracks of Meyer's movies are consistently used to mimic the action on screen, usually in an exploitative, heavy-handed manner that gives every overtly dramatic or violent activity depicted on screen an unsurprisingly sexual overtone. The gothic, unpredictable allure of Varla, the charismatic, villainous leader of a ferocious gang of go-go dancers in Meyer's *Faster, Pussycat! Kill! Kill!* (1965) (henceforth *Pussycat*) is well accompanied by Igo Kantor, Bert Shefter and Paul Sawtell's bombastic score, which largely consists of furious brass and upright double bass passages reminiscent of Neal Hefti's crime-jazz score in the 1960s adaptation of *Batman*. The film's awareness of audio as a expressive technique is revealed with a startling opening sequence in which the screen is filled with nothing but sonic scratches while the fevered narrator John Furlong welcomes the audience to "violence, the word and the act!" The sound waves twirl to match the changes in the melodramatic narrator's pitch frequency and volume as he foreshadows Varla's downfall into madness: "While violence cloaks itself in a plethora of disguises, its favorite mantle still remains: sex. Violence devours everything it touches, its voracious appetite rarely fulfilled."

It must be said, however, that Meyer's excess is not always as successful musically as it is in terms of dialogue. An example is the lesbian scene in *Vixen*, where Meyer used the uncertainty and timidity of leading actress Erica Gavin, along with some skilful editing, to produce a scene of unusual tenderness. As Gavin herself explained: "Everything else required of me in the script had been really fun and easy, but this was the one scene I was really nervous about" (quoted in Peary, 1976: 63). She attributed much of her nervousness to Meyer's inability to construct the scene and his unrealistic expectations: "The thing that freaked me out in the beginning was all the rough and crude positioning Meyer wanted. I think a woman [director] would have handled it with more sensitivity than Meyer is capable of" (*ibid.*). Listening to the musical track in light of this, we might actually hear in this scene Meyer's misconstruction and insensitivity. As the women begin to make love, a strong march rhythm comes into the mix, the extra rhythmic presence totally at odds with the softness of the vision, especially as the track continues and develops into a quasi-bossa nova rhythm. Over-synchronization of the saxophone, coming in exactly as Vixen's lips touch the skin of the wife, sounds clichéd and harsh. Such overt synchronization is often used by Meyer, for example, later in *Vixen* when the plane is hijacked we hear clichéd brass stabs at entirely predictable moments during the violent struggle. Not all of these extreme moments of image integration (Deutsch, 2008) work against Meyer's intentions, however. During the first bedroom scene in *Supervixens* (1975) we hear Meyer's preferred, smooth lounge music over which the male protagonist continues to talk, despite the overtly sexual advances of the vixen. She uses her generously proportioned body to silence him and then becomes the sonically dominant one. We hear a saxophone come in along with muted trumpet, their entry again timed to coincide, this time comically, with the protagonists' respective orgasms.

Another form of sonic excess employed by Meyer comes through various types of vocalization used throughout his films. From his often dry, corny and at times overly obvious voice-overs, to the threatening vocality of dominant and dangerous females (*Pussycat*), to the ecstatic sexual wailings of many of his (mostly female) lead characters, Meyer exploits the excesses of the human voice. One of the most telling examples occurs in the final scenes of *Beneath the Valley of the Ultravixens* (1979) (henceforth *Ultravixens*). In this vocally charged scene, the homosexual dentist-cum-marriage counsellor (Asa Lavender), unable either to help his patients or capture his male prey, dissolves into hysterical wailings which remain entirely threatening but largely incomprehensible. It is the exaggerated timbre that portrays the narrative most powerfully. There is a sense, however, that this vocality is associated with Lavender because of his homosexuality, a sexuality never treated with sonic or visual sensitivity by Meyer.[6] While Lavender rails hysterically, frustrated in his attempts to gain sexual fulfilment, we see and hear the contrasting lesbians (including his beautiful dental assistant Flovilla) in the next room exhibiting total control over their situation, their dialogue and their general vocality. Meanwhile the radio climaxes with the broadcast of Eufaula Roop's 'sexual baptism' (see below) of Lamar. The loud, rhythmic repetition of "yes" as the baptism, and his sexual emancipation, are completed works in much the same way as Joyce punctuates Molly's cathartic monologue at the end of *Ulysses*. The sonic intensity rises as orgasm is finally achieved, visually represented by a level-meter that is red-lining, indicating extreme distortion and input overload. We are left with vocality and sexuality on the edge, and actually physically hard for the listener to stay focused on. But in a movie of such exaggeration and excess, what other filmic devices remain to represent total sensory overload bar those of extreme sonicity?

Comedy and comment

Stemming from his fundamental cynicism regarding American society, and particularly its disparate public and private views on sexuality, Meyer imbues many of his films with ironic, and often blatantly comedic, commentary. Some of this ironic commentary is aimed squarely at the Hollywood film industry which, for a time at least, Meyer was firmly part of. The use of a pseudo-intellectual narrator was a common technique in Meyer's films to satirize the shallow moral lessons taught in Hollywood films, acting as a knowing wink to the audience. "It's all a joke," Meyer was fond of saying. Occasionally, though, the voice-over,[7] usually working in tandem with a montage, was passing more serious comment, or fulfilling another purpose altogether. Examples include the preacher in *Lorna* (1964) and the narrator in *Mondo Topless* (1966), where, as Fischer notes: "the narrator intones moralistic judgments against the sex and violence of the film in order to provide proof to censors that the film does not appeal to prurient interests" (1992: 24). Indeed it is Meyer himself who is the narrator – although his voice was dubbed by John Furlong for this and several other films – attempting to render a travelogue/documentary tone over his blatant erotic intentions, albeit with tongue in cheek and double entendre aplenty:

> San Francisco, the pearl of the Pacific, has long been recognized as an impressive and significant contributor to the American scene … situated on precipitous peaks … San Francisco thrusts itself into the bosom of the Pacific … San Francisco's arts colony is dominated by the arrogant and imposing Coit Tower, thrusting its bulk majestically to the sky, the Broadway Tunnel offering a yawning orifice through which to enter fabled North Beach … San Francisco! A spumoni-like hodge-podge of wild architecture, harboring wonderful old-world restaurants and emporiums of pleasure, exploding dusk to dawn with the way-out craze of … THE TOPLESS!

While many have noted the comedic qualities of Meyer's films (Woods, 2004; Ross, 1995; Ebert, 1972), as Martin has pointed out, comedy within pornographic texts is hard to achieve. As part of her argument she cites Neale and Krutnick, who noted that "laughter can be inserted in most other genres without disturbing their generic conventions, in most contemporary pornography [however], humor proves far too disturbing" (Martin, 2006: 192), and goes on to state that "comedy and pornography seem to have grown increasingly incompatible" (*ibid.*). Despite this, more-contemporary pornographic films still attempt to prove the congruence of comedy and porn, for instance, the subgenre of 'Clown porn'.[8] Much of the perceived incompatibility between comedy and sex is based on the patriarchal hierarchies present in much pornographic cinema. For Meyer, however, this patriarchal dominance is never sought after. In fact, his male characters are often so dominated, pathetic or twisted that such power is automatically denied them: "My films [contain] … a kind, dumb, industrious male with an IQ of around 38 who, by and large, has some kind of sex problem" (Meyer, quoted in Woods, 2004: 5). And in a genre where "equating the sight/site of the penis with awe" (Martin, 2006: 193) is standard practice, Meyer subverts this by eliminating vision of the penis almost completely, and replacing it with ample female breasts. In concluding her useful investigation of *The Opening of Misty Beethoven* (Henry Paris, 1975), Martin contends that:

> What makes Misty unique, beyond its historical placement in the golden era of porn and its accompanying theatrical screenings and audience attendance, is the film's integrated humor and pervasive libidinousness – the film never takes itself too seriously. (2006: 204)

Unfortunately, to make such a statement ignores Meyer's body of work that preceded *Misty* and, one might assume, had contributed to its construction. Meyer's films are self-aware and intent on poking fun at both the industry and society that have produced them. And it was this element of fun that audiences often responded to, as his longtime friend and collaborator, film critic Roger Ebert, observed in 1972:

> There is a difference, however, in the way a skin-flick audience reacts to a Meyer picture. I noticed it as an undergraduate attending THE IMMORAL MR. TEAS, and I have seen it consistently during my latter days as a film critic. Meyer audiences enjoy themselves more obviously, they laugh. It is such a good thing to hear laughter during a skin-flick. Meyer's films never imply, or inspire, the sense of secretiveness or shame present in so many examples of the genre. (80)

What is important for the present discussion is that, like so many other of Meyer's thematic intentions, this comedic objective is largely delivered sonically.

The movie *Vixen* opens with a patriotic/militaristic theme – composed by Igo Kantor – which continues underneath the documentary-style presentation and associated voice-over. Both soundtrack elements work effectively together to create an authorial comment on US society. Likewise, a brief snatch of the American national anthem is played later in the movie (at 38:40) to enforce Meyer's sarcastic comment. Quirky music cues continue in *Vixen* (at 9:18) to emphasize the punning and sexual interplay vividly depicted on screen. Often the juxtaposition of music and visual achieves the intended lightness. Meyer frequently utilizes a slow 1960s style smooth jazz that borders on innocuous lounge music, most often with saxophone lead. The smooth gentle sound often jars against playful screaming from Vixen and the mandatory vigorous love-making that by default invites predatory readings. Indeed, just when you think Meyer is using music more traditionally, as in the spylike, organ- and trumpet-dominated, band music that underscores the hijacking scenes in *Vixen*, Meyer pushes that to cartoonish lengths (67:00 onwards), easing the tension and revealing more of his directorial intent.

Meyer used music to parody not only society but also cinematic conventions. In *Supervixens* he incorporates trombone-led brass music to parody Western films, further heightening this via the use of a vibra-slap which mocks the genre through its corny, childish timbre, but which also represents the sound of rattlesnakes.[9] Not only are rattlesnakes frequently associated with the American Western, but here the sonic associations tie themselves to Meyer's leading ladies, who have already shown their dangerous, rattlesnake-like ways.

One of Meyer's later films, *Ultravixens*, demonstrates the tight comic sonicity that Meyer developed through careful integration of musical allusions and humorous sound effects. The opening of the film is accompanied by a warlike anthem composed by William Tasker. The track morphs to a piano-only version that we see being played by fugitive Nazi Martin Bormann. However, by the time that Bormann stands to undress, and the music continues, we understand the music is coming from a pianola. Having already played with the sonic assumptions of the audience, Meyer then introduces big, brassy stripping music as Bormann climbs into a coffin. Various sound effects are incorporated for comic value as he begins to achieve erection, including drum rolls and cymbal crashes as the penis grows, followed by a high-pitched electronic wobbling sound as the erection reaches its fullness. As our vixen climbs up to the coffin to mount

Bormann she is accompanied by a militaristic fanfare. As she does, the record player (featured in shot) announces a warning over the improper use of faith and healing, a sonic motif that will become integral to the film.

Following this, the song 'Gimme That Old Time Religion' plays while the couple have sex. A traditional American spiritual – the lyrics were first recorded by Charles Tillman in 1889 – the song offers several levels of interpretation. It was heavily featured in the 1941 war movie *Sergeant York* (Howard Hawks), which if intended intertextually by Meyer would accord with the militaristic sentiments of the opening scene. But one suspects this would be ascribing too much cinematic referentiality to Meyer. It is more likely that he intended only the humorous possibilities of equating Bormann's particular brand of sexual fulfilment with the safe and conservative 'old-time religion'. Given that Bormann's sexual release comes through Fraulein Roop, Meyer is also setting up narrative elements that will reappear throughout the film, namely, those concerning the radio station Rio Dio ("100,000 watts of Faith Healing Power") and the spiritually enlightened sexuality of Sister Eufaula Roop (who is the one and same Fraulein Roop). For not only does Sister Roop possess gigantic breasts and a heady sex drive, she is also a faith-healing evangelist radio DJ, who specializes in emancipating her subjects through sexual baptism. This opening scene shows an interesting adaptation of Williams's notion of the 'musical spectacle' within porn films, and while she initially sets up this paradigm for hardcore films, this episode shows how her conceptualization can also be usefully applied to softcore films. As she notes of musical films: "narrative often permits the staging of song and dance spectacles as events themselves within the larger structure afforded by the story line. Narrative informs number, and number, in turns, informs narrative" (1989: 130).

Meyer shows later in *Ultravixens* that he is not above making topical, intertextual jokes. As our vixen Lavonia strips off to join her naked 'prey' – the virginal student Rhett – in the river (27:40), a very clear homage to *Jaws* (Steven Spielberg, 1975) is heard, played only in the bass register of the piano. Meyer capitalizes on the worldwide success of *Jaws*, which had appeared a few years earlier, and particularly its fear-inducing two-note semitone theme,[10] to create both comment and comedy. Our vixen is clearly positioned as a sexual predator as she enters the water naked, going on to jump on the victim in an unrestrained assault.

Meyer's films also work extensively with foley effects, often amplified and roughly manipulated during post-production for comic and erotic effect. An eager audience hears buttons pop off and zippers pulled apart with lewd abandon as uncontrollable lust overcomes the characters, all heightened by the virtually absurd volume of the events. Meyer's point in all this exaggeration is that sex is inherently ridiculous, a comedy of errors that we might scoff at but can never escape. And what better than cartoon-like sound effects to make this point, over and over again? One of the clearest examples is found on the main menu of the DVD release for *Supervixens*. Here the extended 'boing, boing, boing' sound utilized by Meyer during the movie – indeed, over-used

– is selected as the sonic marker, and heard each time Super Vixen's oversized breasts (that dominate the menu page) move. The quasi-onomatopoeic sound is clearly intended comedically, given its prominence over the smooth middle-of-the-road lounge music that accompanies it. That it has been chosen as such an important sonic signifier reveals how those responsible for the DVD's construction wanted the film to be read by audiences – and since Meyer was still alive for their release, we can assume that in keeping with the rest of his career he was intimately involved in their production.

This cartoonish quality of the sound used in Meyer's films also occurs musically. For example, the Austrian mail-order bride in *Supervixens* is stereotyped not only visually by her costume, but also by the nondescript 'oomp-pa-pa' music that accompanies our first sighting of her. As Meyer shows us more of her domestic situation, the music morphs into Richard Strauss's *Also sprach Zarathustra* (1896) – though seemingly with no reference intended to Stanley Kubrick's 1968 film *2001: A Space Odyssey*, which had used the music extensively. When she attempts to force herself on the newly arrived Clint in the barn, comedic brass stabs enter the soundtrack. Meanwhile her farmer husband is seen striding towards the barn to punish her, accompanied by military motifs that serve only to mock him.

The final sonic element used by Meyer to construct comedic ideas and to provide what is often cynical or sarcastic comment is dialogue. Much has been made of the nonsensical or inane nature of Meyer's (and collaborator Roger Ebert's) scripts: "The scripts are so utterly dire, you'll struggle to sit through them twice. But then, script is the last thing Meyer is famous for" (Armstrong, 1999: 6). Then again, the amateurish quality of his shouted, oddball scripts, which can be heard "like a live action comic book, so convincingly you expect to see word balloons pop up" (Scott, 2005), contribute to the fun of the films. Indeed, the outlandishness of the dialogue, along with the generally colourful chaos of the films, became a major influence on Mike Myers and his *Austin Powers* series of movies (Jay Roach, 1997, 1999 and 2002). Myers is frank, however, in his acknowledgement of Meyer's influence. When Austin and Ms Kensington arrive at the 'swinging '60s' party at his flat, Austin quotes the Z-Man from *Beyond the Valley of the Dolls* (1970) (henceforth *BVD*): "It's my happening and it's freaking me out." Myers even goes so far as to ensure the music playing in the background is straight from *BVD*. The song heard, the psychedelic anthem 'Incense And Peppermints' (1967), was performed by the Strawberry Alarm Clock during a party scene in *BVD*, with one character commenting, "I've been to parties where they've played records by the Strawberry Alarm Clock, but never one where the Strawberry Alarm Clock played!"

Unlike the expensive production techniques and professional comedic delivery found in the *Austin Powers* films, in all of Meyer's films the dialogue is usually badly recorded or dubbed and poorly mixed, with lines getting lost in the soundtrack.[11] While potentially confusing the already complicated plot, this technique works to great effect in capturing the psychedelic haze of rock producer Ronny "Z-Man" Barzell's drugged-out party – where he utters the infamous "This is my happening ..." line. Meyer manages to force the audience to participate in the drama by disorientating them both sonically and visually. Alongside the muddy soundtrack, Meyer manages to cut up the 16-minute scene into 373 shots.

Terror and titillation

The beauty and brutality of Russ Meyer's predatory females are given aural characterization through colorful leitmotifs and recurring noises that bring to life Meyer's "own fantasies of a world of dominant, sexually supercharged women who ruthlessly take out their anxieties on any man who crosses their path or is lured into their web".[12] His energetic, lurid and violent imagery is heightened by a musical fusion of flower pop, smooth jazz, porno groove, lounge, psychedelic, orchestral melodrama and highbrow classical music which complements the often schizophrenic quality of his films and their aggressive eroticism. The tracks chosen for the score are consistently unpredictable and forced together in unusual combinations. What is more predictable is Meyer's concern to render sound appropriate to the violence and extravagance on screen.

Sound is often used, both diegetically and non-diegetically, as a weapon. One of the most pointed scenes in this regard is found in *Supervixens*, when SuperAngel is seducing the policeman Harry Sledge (from 19 minutes onwards). SuperAngel begins by seducing Harry over the standard sax and muted trumpet lounge music, which we soon learn is being used parodically. When the cop can't perform sexually, a blend of musical motifs is heard, with a banjo motif blending with more ominous brass scoring. Meyer also throws in a clarinet trill for suspense (20:20) – and obviously for comedic relief. An uptempo funk groove begins as Harry prepares to leave the house (21:00). However, tension is built as he decides to put banjo-based bluegrass music on the radio, thereby superseding the uptempo groove we now associate with SuperAngel. By doing so Meyer is attempting to equate psycho cop Harry with the worst stereotypes of the southern American male. His impotence in the face of Angel's 'enhanced' sexuality has already positioned him as homosexual, the parodic banjo music now adding a hint of dangerous violence to his character – a violence brought out to hide his nonmasculinity and to regain power over female subjects.[13] Such tendencies are confirmed as he begins to hunt down SuperAngel in her house. Having made his point about the character of Harry, Meyer effectively allows the enraged hunt to occur in silence, save for the threatening foley and effects sounds that accompany his movements around the house. The silence ironically allows music to become a weapon. Safely locked in her bathroom, SuperAngel confidently turns on her own radio, which emits the smooth grooves that have been associated with her throughout. Delighted by this and showing remarkable strength in the face of extreme danger, she begins to dance with herself. She continues even as Harry, now further enraged by the sonic attack, begins stabbing the bathroom door. SuperAngel claims her power back, albeit briefly, through the projection of her music. But as Harry finally breaks down the door, her smooth grooves are replaced with non-diegetic dramatic scoring. After the violent attack, with SuperAngel stabbed and bleeding in the bathtub, Meyer's astute editing allows the soundtrack to again be dominated by the radio, which is now eyed by the assailant as a potential death weapon. As he drops the radio into the bathtub, thereby electrocuting SuperAngel, it is not her music, or Harry's, emanating, but the incessant chat of a radio DJ. Despite her death, Harry has not been able to assert his power and control over her. His music is not left to dominate the soundtrack; it has evaporated as impotently as his own sexuality. In a scene that exemplifies the terror and titillation of Meyer's films, it is the sonic that provides the ultimate indications of character strength or weakness.

Meyer also used standard leitmotif devices for his lead females to endow them with additional sonic ferocity. Unfortunately, these devices often devolved to the lowest common denominator, and worse, a stereotypical/racist construction that is increasingly hard to justify with modern audiences. The imposing, eponymous lead of *Vixen* is given her own theme when she seduces and manipulates the various men around her — a feel-good porn groove with cooing trumpets, bass and free jazz-style drumming that swells dramatically as the sly vixen orgasms and runs her hands down her lover's back. More controversially, each one of the larger-than-life cast members of Meyer's even more cartoonish cinematic fare, *Supervixens*, is given a specific musical styling, revealing Meyer's love of superficial categorization and old-fashioned racist stereotyping. The vicious, bitchy Caucasian SuperAngel is given a rather ordinary ragtime melody, while the mysterious bartender SuperHaji, her nude body bejewelled with sparkling gemstones, has an Eastern-influenced theme with synthesizers and percussion used to mimic more exotic instruments such as the sitar. The exoticism of Rosie, the Mexican lesbian go-go dancer turned gang member in *Pussycat*, is also emphasized for erotic and comic effect, with her heavy accent and preposterous hand gestures constantly jangling her bracelets, most notably during her frisky catfight with her blonde accomplice Billie. While Meyer shies away from portraying his African American characters in this light, this badly dated portrayal of non-Caucasian women can be interpreted as Meyer deliberately ridiculing the sexual objectification of racial minorities within mainstream media culture by rehashing such trite audio cues and 'world music' clichés.

Meyer's use of music to capture the exhilarating thrill of eroticism reached a high with the release of *BVD* – the "camp sexploitation horror musical that opens with gun fellatio and ends in a quadruple murder and a triple wedding".[14] Serving as a classic summary of the cult film-maker's artistic temperament, with "an avalanche of double-D demigoddesses the likes of which the screen had never seen before, or since" (Scott, 2005), *BVD* took Meyer's integration of sonic elements to new, and subsequently unattainable, heights.

Although the soundtrack of Meyer's cult masterpiece *BVD* mainly consists of standard 1960s psychedelic rock numbers and funk grooves intertwined with a schmaltzy Hollywood orchestral score typical of many films of its time, the film features the music of a fictional all-girl rock group the Carrie Nations (an ironic play on the name of the nineteenth-century temperance activist Carrie A. Nation). Meyer collaborated with former Monkees producer Stu Phillips and vocalist Lynn Carey (whose deep, powerful voice was incongruously dubbed over the baby-faced Dolly Read) to create the first fictional girl rock band. In a precursor of many music parody films and 'mockumentaries'[15] that were to follow, the film features a number of original pop songs such as the Partridge Family-esque free-love ballads 'Come With The Gentle People' and 'In The Long Run' (which includes humorous lyrics such as "You spend idle hours talking to flowers who won't even talk back to you") and the swinging rock numbers 'Sweet Talkin' Candy Man' and 'Look On Up At Bottom'. The proto-punk song 'Find It' has a progressive arrangement for its time, connecting it historically to the riot grrl movement of the 1990s. Meyer's promotion of busty, overbearing women allows for the pioneering cinematic appearance of a rock and roll band where all of the vocalists, instrumentalists and songwriters involved are female (as opposed to popular girl groups with multiple vocalists who did not write their own material). The group also includes an African American woman as the band's drummer in a time when such positions were rare within the rock genre. It is doubtful there was any intentional political agenda – merely a plot device used by Meyer to act out his sexual fantasies (especially since each band member is attractive and well-endowed). However, the Carrie Nations still represent an important moment in rock and film history.

This 'moment' in rock history has been picked up by many others over subsequent decades. In relation to the all-girl rock/pop band of the movie, that lineage continues on to such incarnations today as the Spice Girls. As Dribben noted in relation to their 'Say You'll Be There' music video:

> there are a number of similarities to the portrayal of women in the films of director Russ Meyer, particularly the excessiveness of the girls' appearance and predatory behaviour, [even] the notion of an all-girl rock/pop band ... Through the appropriation of traditionally masculine signifiers of power and control the opening sequence [of the music video] constructs a conventionally patriarchal image of femininity as the 'femme fatal'. (Dribben, 1999: 344)

Yet Dribben goes on to note that "the wearing of fetish clothes is both a signifier of sexual liberation and control but may also be a sign that no matter how assertive a woman may be in her world, her private submission to control is what makes her desirable" (*ibid.*: 348). Taken in its totality, however, Meyer's portrayal of his all-girl band remains assured, especially in the broader context of his gendered narrative. As Armstrong (1999) notes: "Meyer's triumph is that he's porn for the new easy-listening generation. His portrayal of women also fits nicely into the Girl Power aesthetic, with most of his men getting their butts kicked by the ladies." As with all texts, and particularly those that find themselves within the softcore/erotica genre, we must be careful not to apportion too much power to the female participants, as Dribben ultimately, and forcefully, concludes in relation to all popular music texts: "Merely to collude in, or be critical of, a cultural representation constitutes a failure to experience the lived tensions of social identities" (1999: 352).

BVD opens with the infamous 'gun fellatio' scene in which an unidentified woman is shot and killed in a sexually suggestive manner – the victim's final scream bleeding into the shrieked opening note of the Carrie Nations' first song, 'Find It', where we cut to the group's frenzied performance at a high school dance, immediately revealing Meyer's obsession with the intermingling of sex and violence. 'Find It' is a proto-punk song that predates punk rock pioneer Patti Smith by five years with snarling vocals, elaborate guitar/bass lines (that work off and against each other in a way reminiscent of modern riot grrl bands) and a fast-paced, repetitive drum beat. The song's bizarre, acid-trip lyrics ("I turn my eyes to lunatic skies of red destruction/sunrise and morning empty out my head") express emotional and sexual frustration, exposing the characters' fragile mental state. Furthermore, the jarring interplay of such deep, powerful female vocals with wide vibrato coming out of *Playboy* playmate Dolly Read's doll-face adds an absurdist quality to the film, typical of Meyer's comic-book surrealism and his large-than-life female creations. It also sets up the unbridled terror that will recur throughout the film, all accompanied, music-video style, by the catchy, sexy tunes of the Carrie Nations.

Conclusion

The films of Russ Meyer will be remembered for many things. Up to now it is fair to say that sound design was probably not near the top of the list. But as this chapter has illustrated, Meyer's films utilized sound elements to heighten, express and develop his broader filmic intentions. Although the terror and titillation of his films might always be generated by his casting of (overly) buxom and sadistic female leads, the effects on the viewer are greatly enhanced through sound effects and vocal manipulation. Likewise, the humour and social comment that are so much a part of his films are stingingly delivered through over-synchronization and musical allusion. Meyer may not have worked with the best technology or influential sound personnel, but he was able to extract optimum effect.

> Sexploitation films ... offer a different tone and feeling compared to Hollywood. Hyperactive musical scores and poor sound recording or dubbing combine with portrayals of perverse, illicit sex to invent a rich repertoire of what Schaefer has called 'strategies of evasion'. These strategies distinguish themselves both from the Hollywood musical interlude and from the direct representation of penetrative sex in hard core. (Williams, 2008: 90)

The sonicity of Meyer's sexploitation films largely accords with Williams's observation. But this is no coincidence. Meyer wanted to express the excesses and sexual exuberances hidden in much of American society. He sought to poke fun at those conservative notions that had produced the dangerous and perverse, and he needed sound to maximize the impact on the audience. Watch a Meyer film with the sound off and it will matter. Not only would you miss much of the sexual comedy Meyer intended, you would also lose the sense of self-referential parody that is woven into his films.

Notes

1. At the time of writing, Quentin Tarantino is thought to be developing a remake of Meyer's classic *Faster, Pussycat! Kill! Kill!* (1965), amid great speculation as to who will play the three female leads (reported in the *New York Post* and *Variety*).
2. Russ Meyer died in his Hollywood home on 18 September 2004 from complications after pneumonia. He was eighty-two years old.
3. One estimate puts the number of imitations of *Mr. Teas* at 150, all within three years of its original release (Turan and Zito, 2004: 19).
4. M. Oliver (2004), 'Skin flick master Russ Meyer dies'; online at http://www.sfgate.com/cgibin/article.cgi?file=/chronicle/archive/2004/09/22/MNGBF8SR181.DTL (accessed 13 October 2008).
5. Meyer, quoted at http://www.madman.com.au/actions/directors.do?-directorId=618&method=view (accessed 16 October 2008).
6. Apart from examples discussed later in this chapter, it is the character of Z-Man in Beyond the Valley of the Dolls that saw many commentators label Meyer homophobic.
7. For a detailed discussion on the role of narrative voice throughout thirteen of Russ Meyer's films, see Sevastakis (2006).
8. Clown porn has been around since the 1990s, emerging first in San Francisco and then later in New York. One of the more popular recent releases is *Clown Porn* (Chris Spoto, 2005). As producers David Quitmeyer and Chris Spoto, owners of San Diego-based Ramco Productions, noted: "Clown Porn is a crazy experiment in stretching the limits of what many people consider pornography nowadays … it's kind of like watching Monty Python with clowns and sex" (http://ainews.com/Archives/Story8477.phtml; accessed 18 May 2009). The films often feature comedy sketch routines and hardcore sex (thanks to Philip Hayward for providing this information).
9. Indeed, during the second act of the film, a vibra-slap is heard as a rattlesnake bites the hitchhiker's assailant, thereby exacting revenge for Angel's violent death.
10. For more on the power of the semitone motif, see Clifton (this volume).
11. Williams (2008) would consider this sonic characteristic part of the sexploitation genre more generally.
12. Gary Morris (1996), 'Faster Pussycat Kill! Kill!'; online at http://www.brightlightsfilm.com/16/pcat.html (accessed 23 March 2009).
13. Meyer enforces this reading through other visual coding during the movie, none more so than his role as officer of the law, a position shown to be about (re)gaining power and control in his life.

14. Ebert quoted in unattributed (1970), 'Populist at the movies', in *Time (USA)*; online at http://aolsvc.timeforkids.kol.aol.com/time/magazine/article/0,9171,942232,00.html (accessed 22 March 2008).
15. Of which *This Is Spinal Tap* (Rob Reiner, 1984) is perhaps the most famous.

References

Armstrong, S. (1999), 'Thanks for the mammaries', *Sunday Times* (London), 23 May, p. 6.

Deutsch, S. (2008), 'Editorial', *The Soundtrack*, 1(1), 3–14.

Dribben, N. (1999), 'Representations of Femininity in Popular Music', *Cinema Journal*, 18(3), 331–55.

Ebert, R. (1972), 'Russ Meyer: King of the Nudies', reprinted in P. Woods (ed.) (2004), *The Very Breast of Russ Meyer*, London: Plexus Publishing, pp. 73–93.

Fischer, C. (1992), 'Beyond the Valley of the Dolls and the Exploitation Genre', *Velvet Light Trap*, Fall, 16–34.

Henderson, E. (2006), 'Film Review: *Beyond the Valley of the Dolls*', *Slant Magazine*; online at http://www.slantmagazine.com/dvd/dvd_review.asp?ID=945 (accessed 23 March 2009).

Martin, N. (2006), 'Never Laugh at a Man with His Pants Down: The Affective Dynamics of Comedy and Porn', in P. Lehman (ed.), *Pornography*, Jersey City, NJ: Rutgers University Press, pp. 189–205.

McCarthy, T. (2004), 'Meyer Stacked Skin-flick Deck', *Variety*, 396(6), p.100.

McDonough, J. (2005), *Big Bosoms & Square Jaws: The Biography of Russ Meyer, King of the Sex Film*, New York: Crown.

Meyer, R. (2000), *A Clean Breast: The Life and Loves of Russ Meyer*, Los Angeles: Hauck.

Peary, D. (1976), 'From Vixen to Vindication', reprinted in P. Woods (ed.) (2004), *The Very Breast of Russ Meyer*, London: Plexus Publishing, pp. 59–66.

Ross, J. (1995), 'Russ Meyer at the National Film Theatre', reprinted in P. Woods (ed.) (2004), *The Very Breast of Russ Meyer*, London: Plexus Publishing, pp. 153–89.

Schaefer, E. (1997), 'The Obscene Seen: Spectacle and Transgression in Postwar Burlesque Films', *Cinema Journal*, 36(2), 41–66.

Schaefer, E. (2002), 'Gauging a Revolution: 16mm Film and the Rise of the Pornographic Feature', *Cinema Journal*, 41(3), 3–26.

Schaefer, E. (2003), 'Showgirls and the Limits of Sexploitation', *Film Quarterly*, 56(3), 42–3.

Scott, C. (2005), 'DVD Drive-in: Beneath the Valley of the Dolls', *DVD Drive In: The Latest in Cult Movie DVD Reviews*; online at: http://www.dvddrive-in.com/reviews/a-d/beyondthevalleydolls70.htm (accessed 22 March 2009).

Sevastakis, M. (2006), *Narrative Voice in Russ Meyer's Films: A Cacophony of Carnality*, New York: Edwin Mellen Press.

Turan, K., and Zito, S. (2004), 'Uncertain Innocence Part One', in P. Woods (ed.), *The Very Breast of Russ Meyer*, London: Plexus Publishing, pp. 15–19.

Williams, L. (1989), *Hard Core: Power, Pleasure and the 'Frenzy of the Visible'*, Los Angeles: University of California Press.
Williams, L. (2008), *Screening Sex*, Durham, NC: Duke University Press.
Woods, P. (ed.) (2004), *The Very Breast of Russ Meyer*, London: Plexus Publishing.

3 The Push/Pull Game
The Dynamics of Sound in Bertolucci's Last Tango in Paris, The Last Emperor *and* The Sheltering Sky

Lesley Chow

The first image in *Last Tango in Paris* (Bernardo Bertolucci, 1972) is a painting by Francis Bacon from 1964, a portrait of Lucien Freud. It shows us a figure of angry modernist posturing: a man with a distorted face and a clear thrust to his sitting position. However, we have only a moment to absorb this before its effect is leavened and lightened by a delicate piano theme. This little phrase – a simple motif with minor melodic embellishments – will come to be associated with the character of Jeanne (Maria Schneider); it suggests an answering, appeasing response to the initial charge of anger. After a few bars, this theme gives way to a wilder progression of drumming, and a saxophone solo by the composer, Argentinian jazz specialist Gato Barbieri. This shows the importance of sound in Bertolucci: the ability of rhythms and individually honed notes to complicate and even override images. In *Last Tango in Paris*, sound frequently softens erotic or violent imagery – yet it also sexualizes scenes which might otherwise be regarded as 'neutral'. At crucial moments, the score implies rifts in the classical style.

While most of Bertolucci's films have prominent soundtracks, *Last Tango in Paris*, his sixth film, is the one which ties its fluctuations of power and desire most intricately to levels of sound. Whereas his earlier, fragmented film *Partner* (1968) used snippets of Ennio Morricone to generate a mood of high parody, the musical themes of *Last Tango* relate intimately to the characters. Paul (Marlon Brando), an American agonizing over the death of his wife, wanders into an empty apartment, where he encounters Jeanne, a young Frenchwoman. Jeanne is willingly drawn into an affair with him, but the relationship is unequal: Paul rages and dominates space, conversation and attention, with his self-lacerating rants. Jeanne is initially intrigued by his strangeness and the conviction with which he pursues her; at one point, she submits to a bout of angry anal sex with him. The scene is now notorious, but within the film it comes across as just another one of the false climaxes in their affair, and the sex has no soundtrack. The major drama of the film is in watching the pair fly between extremes of violence and relaxation, as the score jumps between moods. Jeanne, seemingly the weaker partner, preserves an inner coolness and a lack of desperation. She alternates between excitement at the passion of her lover and fury at his intractable ways, but finally she tires of his overbearing presence and is repelled by him.

Just as the film poses its two characters as a duelling relationship of painted forms – two shapes encountering each other across a canvas or a frame – its sonic structure also refers to duality. The irresistible opening phrase connected with Jeanne is like a promise of renewal, musically as well as emotionally, since it's often used as a segue between sections of instrumentation. Played by Franco D'Andrea, it creates a luxurious feeling of warmth and spaciousness. However, the theme associated with Paul tends to threaten exhaustion, whether played on brass or strings. Its key feature is the repetition of a single phrase on the saxophone, which matches the character's need to perform an act over and over, in order to allay pain; this includes his sex with Jeanne, as well as his sudden howls and screams. Yet this heaviness is occasionally redeemed by the return of the 'Jeanne' theme.

These are two musical cues which cross each other – sometimes fruitfully, sometimes antagonistically. Where the piano is fluid, with long phrases and scalar passages, the saxophone is songlike: narrower in pitch range, with a more considered phrasing (J. Hullick, personal communication with the author, 26 January 2009). On one level, the score might be seen as the tension between two styles, which contest against each other for dominance. However, the themes can also merge or move in counterpoint. Even though certain instruments and rhythms are associated with particular characters, Barbieri and Bertolucci don't create anything as straightforward as a 'his and hers' version of themes. The 'Paul' theme may be wearing and despairing, but it also carries a veneer of romance, especially when played on alto sax. The 'Jeanne' theme is used to accompany the character's gentle, tentative entry into scenes – but it can also be heard from a distance, as a refrain within the heavier, more ponderous, sounds of 'Paul'. The strains of one theme are often coded within the other, and both are heard amidst the relentless noise of trains in the background. Thus the film's emotional tone can shift either rapidly or almost imperceptibly between its two characteristic sounds.

Nevertheless, both themes are usually truncated before they come to a peak. A phrase begins, then tapers off into silence, or moves into a new tempo. Musical cues start off with assurance, but are quickly halted, never to reach catharsis. Is it too obvious to state that this pattern reflects the dynamics of Paul and Jeanne's sexual relationship – the fact that Paul's weight cuts short the natural unwinding of themes? The use of sound defines the pictorial and physical relation of the couple. During their first meeting in the apartment, Paul's hulking form moves into black shadow, while Jeanne correspondingly opens a window to the light. This moment of convergence is accompanied by a swelling of strings, which then stops. The small movement of the characters is matched by a stepwise motion in the music: a major-second ostinato which gives a persistent feeling of advancement, then retreat (J. Hullick, personal communication with the author,

26 January 2009). In the same scene, the camera unconventionally arcs outwards and back, as it films Jeanne's black hat lying on the floor, and the soundtrack re-emerges, as if to etch this circular motion into space. In an outdoor scene, the camera rushes against a lit window, accompanied by a series of chords, as if desperately attempting to press inside. The film encourages us to coast on these moments of soaring orchestration, which are then abruptly dropped. All these sudden stoppages create a sense of tug and flow, protrusion and retraction, and, inevitably, penetration and withdrawal.

This kind of suggestiveness in the soundtrack is necessary, because the actual sex of the film is unscored. To place a layer of sound, with its typical dynamic of plunge and withdrawal, over the sex act would be a doubling of the push-pull effect. Therefore, close attention needs to be given to the rest of the soundtrack. A striking sound never accompanies orgasm, so that the significant moments of climax are to be found in the surrounding score. Post-sex, things are restored to their usual sound and pictorial relation; Jeanne's white form rolls diagonally away from Paul's, as if driven by a form of propulsion. The score returns to its mode of continental dabbling, with a few passages of pleasantly scoping jazz (the phrases are stretched, so as to give a sense of opening out and a smooth trajectory.) However, when Jeanne rushes away from the apartment, the score builds up to a furious vamping on her departure – it's temporarily allowed the impetus of drama.

Any discussion of music in Bertolucci needs to account for the fact that the significant sex in his films is often silent: either soundless, or etched with a few bare scratches and chords. Although music may be heard when supporting or comic characters get together (as in *Stealing Beauty*, 1996, where various unlikely couplings are exaggerated by the score), the use of a soundtrack tends to mark intercourse as 'genre' or 'period' sex – in other words, as sex of a sort. The central, passionate sex in his films is largely limited to the close, quiet sounds of breathing or outdoor noise. Despite the abundance of rich orchestration in *Last Tango in Paris*, a sex scene leaves us to mark the drop in sound levels, especially given the overwhelming musical build-up of previous scenes. In no other director's work are we so aware of the withdrawal of sound, and its relation to sex.

Last Tango in Paris has an intricate aural structure corresponding to values of weight and lightness, sensuality and its removal. The unexpected chords and strokes of orchestration are like little cuts, or deepenings, in the film's texture, provoking attachment and desire. The saxophone theme is marked by a brooding heaviness, while the piano has a lyrical effect, but both are emotional cues which are constantly interrupted. An ascending line is cut off seconds after it starts. When this occurs, we become aware of a sudden deepening of mood, which is then withdrawn. Such a deliberate sense of withholding creates a feeling of absence. In considering how sound influences structural awareness, I was reminded of Bette Davis's famous remark on the set of *Dark Victory* (Edmund Goulding, 1939), about composer Max Steiner: "Either I'm going up the stairs or Max Steiner is ... but we're goddamn well not going together!" (Sikov, 2007:

143). It's an illustration of how music has the ability to 'walk' or carry us through scenes, evoking a pace that replaces or confuses the speed of editing.[1] If sound were to behave as it does in *Last Tango in Paris*, it would take us up half the staircase, and then abandon us midway: it would lift us and then leave us. In Bertolucci, music is something which masterfully takes its momentum: it's a sensual form of involvement which precedes desertion. (In his *Besieged* [1998], the score stops and starts as the camera literally moves up and down a set of spiral stairs, leaving us in a mood of suspension.)

Paul's first scene in *Last Tango in Paris*, with his scream swallowed and obliterated by the noise of a speeding train, already lets us know the degree to which this film is about sound. Like the roaring trains in later scenes, this is an instance of intensity suddenly cut off mid-sound. Sound is used as a device which quickly marks a scene, and is then absent – but which leaves us with the effect of that marking. The structure of the film is built around the precise timing of its cues. Bertolucci often uses a single melodic theme over a succession of scenes. For instance, the scenes in the apartment with Jeanne and Paul are scored with the same theme on the strings, which is varied in length and intensity, and placed in exact relation to the characters' movements. Theme grabs are unusually short, with only one or two phrases used to delineate a point. The fact that one variable is being used to heighten or diminish involvement makes us highly conscious of its manipulation; it's as if all the jumps in the score were controlled by a single finger. We can almost visualize the pattern of sound design in terms of Bertolucci passing a brush over the frame, resulting in an image being subtly touched or deeply underscored. According to Bertolucci, Barbieri "started working by coming to the editing room and taking note of the internal rhythm of the images as they were establishing themselves" (quoted in Ranvaud and Ungari, 1987: 89). The music was then designed to follow the "camera's movements: it announces or underlines them according to whether we were seeking synchronization or conflict" (*ibid.*).

The use of music here is more seductive and less predictable than, say, the lyrical stop-starts in the soundtracks of Godard and Truffaut. Unlike Godard, who often uses jazz to indicate a leap to 'genre' before a return to unshaped real time, Bertolucci's cues are generally free of irony. The only time Bertolucci indulges in a flip usage of music is during the movie's parody of Godard himself, a mini-New Wave film within the film. When Jeanne has a novelettish romance with Tom (Jean-Pierre Léaud), Godard's style is sampled for its over-narration, weightlessly enunciated dialogue, and swirling romantic themes. At one point, Jeanne discusses menstruation, sex and biology, but without heat or impact, and the scene mildly dissolves without implications. While music does not accompany the sex of Jeanne and Paul, the scenes with her and Tom are full of flowing piano phrases and New Wave buoyancy. Theirs is literally a generic relationship – a relationship bound by genre, with all its cinematic inspirations, style and limitations. The soundtrack theoretically encodes the degree and nature of our involvement. The score during Jeanne and Tom's scenes features an appropriation of New Wave composers Georges Delerue – whom Bertolucci used in *The Conformist*, 1970 – and Michel Legrand, with his little diversions on the piano.

In Bertolucci's films, an unexpected use of music is mysteriously effective rather than trifling. Sound marks a space between still moments; when it ruptures silence, it can suggest a specific shape or jutting-out. A shimmer of strings can directly suggest foreboding, as in a conventional thriller, yet the rises in the score come at moments neither obvious nor totally out of place. Whereas most film scores create suspense by using slowly moving chords over rapid percussion, there is a tendency here to use chords which are unresolved, or harmonically unstable (J. Hullick, personal communication with the author, 26 January 2009). We hear sustained dissonant chords, offset by irregular rhythms of percussion. When Paul is seen looking across at jazz musicians in a neighbouring apartment, this is only a partial explanation for the constant riffing on themes and variations; the sound tends to exceed any diegetic source we see. Music is prized for its ability to unleash sensuality onto a sparse or grey landscape. In terms of enlivening bodies, it can be used not just for romantic purposes, but as a way of giving movements an oddly sexualized feel – such as the African-inspired beats which accompany Jeanne's crawling into the room like a cat, almost like a Cubist object entering the frame.

Even the characters use sounds to code one another – most overtly during the scene where Paul and Jeanne develop a system of semi-orgasmic noises by which to recognize each other. In a manner reminiscent of male characters in D. H. Lawrence, Paul insists that "no names" should be exchanged between them: "I'm better off with a grunt or a groan for a name." He asks, "You want to hear my name?" and produces something that sounds like a hoarse baboon, a pained animal choking back cries. With his oval mouth shape, the orgiastic growl is convulsive, inward-turning: a sound made in sex or sorrow. Jeanne responds in turn; Paul's grunt, she decides, is "so masculine". Her signature sound is a sweet little trumpeting, an answering trill. It's playful, high and varied, not shrill – it sounds like something done on woodwind or brass, and she does little runs on it like an instrument. It's appropriate that they identify themselves this way, since the piano associated with Jeanne is melismatic, with each sound flowing over many notes, whereas the saxophone playing is syllabic, broken up into discrete notes; nevertheless, the two parts merge well (J. Hullick, personal communication with the author, 26 January 2009).

It's one of the rare moments of synchronicity between the characters, evoked through sound, although when it ends, the film switches to a farm sequence, with crowing cocks and warbling pigeons. Despite their general lack of communication, Paul and Jeanne's relationship depends on a level of call-and-response. Each throws out a sound element as a signal to the other; for instance, Paul's impromptu playing of the harmonica substitutes for a comment. Even in conversation, both tend to speak in play-voices, especially after sex – she adopting a mock lilt and he an exaggerated version of his customary gruffness. Paul acts as a shock and sound absorber; as Jeanne complains, "You know, it seems to me I'm talking to the wall ... your solitude weighs on me" – a suggestion that silence carries a force and charge, rather than a mere absence. During their tango scene, the two have a clumsy argument, in which Jeanne's cries of "I want to go, I want to leave" are reflected by repeated jabs in the score, until a harmony is once again reached, and both their moods and the music coast smoothly for a while. This kind of musical strategy – where an extreme point is constantly threatened, and then circumvented – mimics the central relationship dynamic. Paul is fond of pushing Jeanne to the brink with exciting inflammatory statements about "going right up into the ass of death" and a discussion of rats' ass-holes, but once that point is reached, energy recedes and peace is a possibility. Paul's famous discussion of pig-fucking is an obscene scrawl which quickly fades out.

A similar pattern of crisis and withdrawal is seen and heard in Bertolucci's *The Sheltering Sky* (1990). Having listened to Ryuichi Sakamoto's soundtrack repeatedly before watching the film, I view the score almost as a kind of overlay: a thin skin laid over the film, so as to deepen it at certain points. The issue is how that deepening relates to sexuality: the characters' rather anguished relationship, and their sex with other partners. When Port (John Malkovich) and Kit (Debra Winger) take their troubled marriage to Morocco, a sense of erotic interest develops between them and their new surroundings. In a hotel suite, they look at each other from different corners of the *mise en scène*; he, reclining in a hotly lit red room, gazes across at her, smoking calmly in bed wearing blue. As he enters her space, he strokes her belly beneath her open shirt, and a cautiously high, shrill violin suggests a mounting moment. Then the sound breaks off – the moment's gone and their contact stops.

Elsewhere, Bertolucci indicates sexuality by introducing a change of rhythm, often by means of fast, irregular drumming. When Port is taken to see a prostitute, he becomes entranced by the rapid beat of the drums, as well as the sound of the *ney* (an obliquely blown flute.) His unfamiliarity with these sounds appears to make him meek; he's submissively led towards a campsite. The seductive music subdues a little when he arrives in the tent and has sex with the prostitute. Afterwards, he grabs his wallet and escapes. Only then do the beats and drums rise to the dramatic force of pursuit. As he leaves, the prostitute gives an ululating cry – another consistent, hypnotic rhythm he does not understand. Richard Horowitz, the movie's specialist in Moroccan instruments, created a sonic language mixing Islamic chants and source noise. Despite his minute control over our rhythmic impressions – with changes in tone and pitch, voices slowed down and speeded up – the score here creates an impression of randomness. In this film, sound serves as a key form of disorientation, which induces an openness to sex. The Moroccan music (partly diegetic, partly of unseen origins) signals a beat which scrambles logic and bypasses the conscious, rational brain. For Port, the drumming, clapping and chanting result in a concentrated pattern of strangeness which make him just susceptible enough.

With Kit, sound is also a route to sexual awareness. Her willing 'abduction' and introduction to a harem of Arab women begins with a scramble of voices, noises and textures she doesn't understand. Eroticism starts with not being able to pinpoint what a sound source is, or where the 'other' is coming from; this opens the door to a form of sexual confusion and blurring. The soundtrack here – source music in addition to Horowitz's work – evokes Kit's dazed consciousness. She's happy to be buoyed by unknown rhythms, with time passing indefinitely, and no sense of beginning or end. As a result, she simply submits to her sexual 'capture'. There's a sense of a continuous present, created by the ubiquitous, 'universal' sounds of rattling insects, animal cries, and excited women.

Contrast this with the all-too-stately manner in which sex proceeds between Port and Kit. The flurry of noise in most of the other scenes makes the silence and strained relations between the couple all the more conspicuous. We're conscious of absence on an aural level, relieved by the occasional light dappling of the soundtrack; for instance, a few strokes of the violin are played whenever Port is curious about what Kit is doing. However, for the most part, the score struggles to penetrate their alienation, as they gaze across the inscrutable desert. The one time when intimacy between them is scored is when they attempt awkward and uncomfortable sex while lying on a bare Moroccan plain. Before long, both are overcome by despair and apathy. The orchestration doesn't contrast with the stiff rhythms of sex – rather, it prevents it from becoming a bad fetish, with the string section extending a warmth which surrounds and shelters alienation. Sakamoto's symphonic strings are gorgeous here, but during this scene, the melody is much slowed. Each stroke of the violin is precisely measured out, in careful steps, perhaps a reference to Paul Bowles's epilogue about the finite nature of passion in a seemingly limitless life.

While the soundtracks of both *Last Tango in Paris* and *The Sheltering Sky* deal with emotion being prematurely silenced and curtailed, silencing is the major theme of *The Last Emperor* (1987). The soundtrack features both a classical orchestra and traditional Chinese instruments: David Byrne scores the Asian instruments, while Ryuichi Sakamoto works with the violins and cellos. Sakamoto's orchestration creates a lush warm bath of romanticism, but Bertolucci makes cuts in that lushness. When, for instance, the emperor runs down a passage in pursuit of a woman, we become lifted by the swell of strings; then the music stops in its tracks and the romantic epiphany is sliced through. The film's theme of hidden emotion and sexuality is suggested in the opening credits, where beautiful distant images of Orientalism come into focus behind a series of shifting black grids.[2] The child emperor's tactile and sexual nature is illustrated through sound. His nanny Ar Mo (Jade Go) tells him stories, with her breast partially exposed, while the camera travels over a lace panel as if it were a storyboard, and an attendant blows on the lace to create a rustling sound. One of the emperor's delights as a boy is to be caught up against a huge bolt of white silk, while the many hands of his servants grasp him, and he dissolves into their murmurs and titters. The boy has a sensual relationship with his milk-breasted nanny; he's suckled by her at a fairly advanced age. When she opens her gown to receive him, he strokes her breast, and we hear a *pipa* (Chinese stringed instrument) in the background. At first, the playing of the *pipa* is impassively controlled, a droll counterpoint to the sensuality, but as the boy becomes more involved, the sound rises and billows with a lurid intensity.

The emperor grows up in a very female, sexualized atmosphere, surrounded by the close giggles and whispers of his attendants. It's the kind of overripe environment Bertolucci loves, yet the characters form serious personal attachments to each other. Sakamoto often quotes his director as shouting during orchestra recordings, "More *emotionale*! More *emotionale*!"[3] When the nanny is torn away from her young charge, the cello creates a luscious injection of mood, but after only a few seconds of plunging orchestration, we switch to silence. It's as if the soundtrack has allowed itself a moment of weakness — just a little wallowing before a return to order. When the empress (Joan Chen) arrives, a drumming greets the unveiling of her face (she is as covered and upholstered as a little side table.) Then we hear her give him a few kisses on the cheek, as if softly daubing its surface, before we pull back to see his face covered in lipstick prints. (Bertolucci's camera often steps back from a scene we believe is sparse, to reveal abundance and fertility.[4])

The film's most explicit sex scene is remarkably similar to one in Joris-Karl Huysmans' classic novel of decadence, *A Rebours* (1959), in which the protagonist caresses prostitutes beneath a flesh-coloured canopy, warmed by pink lights. The film's scene has the emperor cavorting with two women beneath a yellow-peach silk cover, while the camera examines its texture, crossing it again and again. I disagree with Pauline Kael when she says Bertolucci destroys the sensual implications of this image through overemphasis. She finds the scene "much too long", feeling it loses its "voluptuous lyricism" through repetition (Kael, 1989: 398). Rather, I see each of these re-crossings as meaningful; the movements deepen the texture of the silk surface, which flows and courses like water.[5] Little rippling forms appear in the skin, the total flesh that binds the three. There's a loss of boundaries between bodies, which eventually transform into one sexual entity that heaves. Initially, the sex is accompanied by the quiet sounds of nature and chirping crickets. Then the very gentle strains of the *pipa* accompany the flickering of the fabric, finally giving way to the overpowering whirr of a fire which has broken out in the palace. Sensuality then dies down.

As much as Bertolucci may have cried out for it, '*emotionale*' is always quoted sparingly. The constant snatching away of the string theme, just as it approaches its peak, leaves us with the impression of something which is given, then gone. There's a strong feeling of something left unfinished, an arc dangling in space. In addition, the deep pressing of the bow on the cello — each note arrested, rather than trailing off — creates an image of underscore, a scene being forcefully underlined. The carving bow work drives little grooves into the film's surface, almost as if it were being scratched in a very tactile manner, causing the film's texture to shift. Music doesn't crest at the time of sex, but only during the carefully paced closing credits, where we hear an intense vibrato on the strings.[6] At the end, the passages of strident argument on the violin finally relent, giving way to a full orchestration of emotion.

The fact that Bertolucci's scores tend to lilt and change in this way reflects the way that forms shift within his films. In *Last Tango in Paris*, Jeanne's hat appears to change shape, so that it looks flat and opaque at first, before expanding into three-dimensional reality. Paul and Jeanne meet like two vectors on a plane; when they pass each other in the apartment, there's often a quivering of strings, to show the resettling of two elements. This is how Bertolucci constructs the meeting of two forms, in terms both musical and painterly. The director often shows figures spiralling towards each other – encountering each other on architecturally formal terms, across the gulf of a stairway, train track, or corridor. People discover each other in mirrors or frames, as decorative elements – but also as sound features. Sound is a way for Bertolucci to encode the formal play of oppositions: lovers greet each other over a spiral staircase, but they can also meet across the melodic structure of an arpeggio. Both *The Conformist* and *The Last Emperor* show hook-ups between two women: one dominant and the other more relaxed and yielding, like an active theme and its refrain. In *The Conformist*, music and dance refer to the way women stylize and sexualize themselves. There's a note of humour when Delerue's massaging, sympathetic score hits its stride as Giulia (Stefania Sandrelli) recalls her passivity as a teenager submitting to a sixty-year-old. In *The Last Emperor*, when Eastern Jewel (Maggie Han) gets intimate with the empress, the camera fixates on the two women in their slim silver dresses – nearly congruent yet potentially capable of relations in their slightest difference. However, the scene is a little ugly: the room is like an echo chamber, a cold blue-lit space. We hear strange percussive effects, as of heavy metal objects struck, or hollow noises made in a vacuum. Eastern Jewel's malevolent profile is seen in the mirror: reverberations of her image seem to be everywhere, and their sonic equivalent is this chamber of odd, vaguely mechanized human noises. There are little trickles and water-drops, and ominous blowing sounds, while a very distant waltzing orchestration is heard.

This kind of musical echoing is used explicitly in *Besieged*, where a relationship takes the form of a dance between two characters. *Besieged* is a revisiting of *Last Tango in Paris*, this time with the woman as an equal or dominant partner. The English pianist Kinsky (David Thewlis) and his Kenyan housekeeper and medical student Shandurai (Thandie Newton) are fascinating in different ways; they have an equal but opposing weight. Their relationship is the duelling of two musical modes – he fully absorbed in his passages of Bach, versus her exuberant bubbling over Papa Wemba. Curiosity arises when they start investigating each other's space; they are drawn together through sound, hearing refracted noises from each other's rooms. The soundtrack corresponds to Bertolucci's use of curving architectural rhythms: a dramatic spiral staircase is the centrepiece of Kinsky's house, forcing him and Shandurai to perform a pattern of ascents and descents in relation to each other. There's also a dumbwaiter which transmits messages and voices between them. At the same time, Stefano Arnaldi's floating piano work allows phrases to drift across and between the two characters. Bertolucci has a habit of inventing unusual, highly particular structures to link his characters, which are nevertheless naturalized. They exist as both 'devices' and plausible architecture – and also as signifiers of music. As part of her job, Shandurai cleans inside the nooks and details of the spiral structure, getting to know it in detail, at the same time becoming intrigued by Kinsky's music. When she sees Kinsky listening to Coltrane's 'My Favourite Things', she catches a glimpse of his pale skin above the line of his sock, and the sight of him vulnerable and strange leads her to consider him erotically. As he composes a piece of music, trying out a few phrases, her face flushes with a sense of release when he grabs the right note. However, this catharsis is ruptured by the shriek of the telephone, a reference to the shrill bell which later disrupts their bedroom scene, when her husband arrives.

The up/down spiralling leads into the final sex of the characters. Shandurai, who has a very refined face, turns out to have an equally interesting and sensitive body: the camera takes snapshots of her nudity in repose, as she licks her fingers while half-asleep and caresses herself. Alessio Vlad's piano theme registers as an undercurrent while she experiences these sensual tremors; the melody takes notations of her trancelike erotic state, as she touches and uncovers her own body. Later, when Shandurai ravishes Kinsky in bed – delicately unlacing his shoes, undoing each button, unpackaging and revealing the body – the only sound we hear is his heaving breath. After the thundering music of preceding scenes, there is just the quietness of her embrace – and eventually, the piercing sound of the doorbell. At that point, the piano theme reactivates and guides her to the door. From a soundless, nearly amorphous state, to a gradually charged sexual awareness, to consummation, to the shock of an alarm signal, Shandurai's body goes through a number of awakenings in this sequence. All these fluctuating changes are registered in the score.

In *Last Tango in Paris*, the soundtrack is also constantly changeable and surprising, despite being founded on a few key themes. Towards the end, it makes an unexpected move into a new genre, when an implied structure suddenly formalizes itself through music and dance. Although it's initially startling, it seems logical that Jeanne and Paul's sexual relation segues into a tango sequence. As in sex, their bodies are now aligning, now repelling: suddenly in sync, before an abrupt shift and turnaround. Impulsively, Jeanne asks for an encore, and is temporarily lifted into happiness, before wretchedly insisting they leave. The finale occurs when the couple, who have existed in dancelike counterpoint until now, reach a crisis – or in musical terms, a cacophony. At this point, all the spiralling counterpoints come together – the layers of bass, saxophone and strings whirl together chaotically. When Jeanne eventually leaves the dance house, the clamour can only be shut off by Paul's death. The film closes by redirecting itself into genre: it moves into *noir* when Jeanne shoots Paul, and shifts from her normally expressive voice into a toneless repetition of her alibi. Paul's death occurs soundlessly, before the rejuvenation of the jazz line and a final dramatic note on the strings. It's a sudden, striking conclusion: deliberately too quick and unsatisfying. As in *The Last Emperor* and *The Sheltering Sky*, Bertolucci's version of fulfilment involves giving us a climax only at the moment of ending – never one without the other.

Acknowledgement

I would like to thank the musicologist, composer and sound artist James Hullick (http://jameshullick.com) for his perceptive observations on the sonic structures in this film.

Notes

1. Soundtracks need to be careful to avoid this kind of doubling effect, in which the structural imagery suggested by the music veers too close to the events portrayed. For instance, Michael Nyman's score for *The Claim* (Michael Winterbottom, 2000) is extremely effective in suggesting a mountain climb, but when it's laid on top of an actual climbing scene, it forces us to scale every step, arduously.
2. I find this sequence more intriguing than the similar opening of Martin Scorsese's *The Age of Innocence* (1993), which also shows a sensual flowering beneath lacework.
3. See http://www.sitesakamoto.com/update/cinemage.html (accessed 5 September 2008).
4. However, there may be no match for Bertolucci's *Stealing Beauty* in terms of mad, full-blown lushness. When Lucy (Liv Tyler) arrives in Tuscany, she has a habit of discovering everyone asleep or naked, as if succumbing to a sensual enchantment. The film is also musically interesting. Lucy carries her own personal, self-contained soundtrack of Liz Phair and Hole. This Lucy-associated score blends into the source noise; lyrics she reads float across the frame, turning the screen into a tactile medium. Once again, there's the unusual sound source that provokes romantic curiosity, as characters are lured into each other's spaces by music, even something as simple as a jazz standard (Nina Simone, Billie Holiday.) Noemi (Stefania Sandrelli) is serenaded, and then runs off into the woods with a younger man; as in a pastoral comedy, lovers pair off according to theme. Over-abundance is achieved musically, with guitars strummed amid all-night feasting.
5. This criticized scene anticipates one in *Little Buddha* (Bertolucci, 1993), in which the camera and sound could also be accused of being repetitive. At one point, Bertolucci chooses to film the sea for a prolonged sequence. The water shots are unprecedentedly striking – the camera shapes the sea, re-directing it as if spinning skeins of water, almost as if it could mould any form purely through momentum. His camera repeatedly skims the contours of the ocean, like a fine artist remaking the surface with each stroke.
6. Bertolucci is always meticulous with the meaning and pacing of music during his credits. At the end of the closing credits in *The Sheltering Sky*, the orchestration

soars before it heads down into a troubled, 'inward' phase and then stops on that note of irresolution. There's the sense of gaining space and freedom in the upper register, before getting down into the trenches for some psychological work.

References

Huysmans, J.-K. (1959), *A Rebours*, Harmondsworth: Penguin.
Kael, P. (1989), *Hooked*, New York: E. P. Dutton.
Ranvaud, D., and Ungari, E. (eds) (1987), *Bertolucci by Bertolucci*, London: Plexus.
Sikov, E. (2007), *Dark Victory: The Life of Bette Davis*, New York: Macmillan.

4 Depraved Desire
Sadomasochism, Sexuality and Sound in mid-1970s Cinema

Clarice Butkus

Peering back into the complex moment of sexual representation that marked western culture in the late 1960s and early 1970s, cultural archaeologists are presented with a series of vivid, dramatic and problematic texts. The history of sexual representation is in the process of definition, through the writings of authors such as Williams (1989), Andrews (2006) and Penley (2004). Intersecting with these chronicles of ever-more graphic couplings is a more complex history of sexuality's interconnection with violence in a body of texts that range from the marginal mainstream productions of directors such as Just Jaeckin through to more obscure 'hardgore' productions by 'auteurs' such as Joe Davian. Williams (1989) provides a useful point of entry into this field by offering a typology of sadomasochism (S/M) film genre categories. Surveying a range of hardcore porn productions, she identified three principal tendencies:

- *Amateur*, a form which principally comprises prolonged scenes of bondage and domination in which "Everything is focused on the highly ritualized forms of violence and domination enacted upon the body of a woman" and in which conventional sexual activity is absent or minimal (*ibid.*: 197);
- *Sadie-max*, an industry term referring to S/M scenes in porn films that otherwise present more standard sexual interactions;
- *Aesthetic sadomasochism*, whose productions

    self-consciously situate themselves within an elitist sadomasochistic literary tradition where rarefied sexual tastes are explored. Although these films may also focus on prolonged scenes of sadomasochistic torture to the exclusion of all other sexual numbers, they differ from amateur sadomasochism in their comparatively high production values, professional acting, literary sources, and complex psychological narratives plumbing the nature of sexual identities. If the overwhelming effect of the violence in the amateur sadomasochism films is that it seems 'real' in the Bazinian sense – it appears neither acted by the performers, nor faked in the editing – the overwhelming effect of the violence in aesthetic sadomasochism is that it is 'art'. (ibid.: 199)

Jaeckin's work was premised on a cultural pretense of 'literary' erotic film-making and (popularly palatable) softcore aesthetics, and was part of a group of films that saliently 'embodied' the national character of French cinema in the mid-1970s. His controversial softcore erotic feature film, *Story of O* (1975), largely conforms to Williams's third category in portraying a female protagonist who endures elaborate trials of sexual domination, bondage, whipping and branding. Davian, meanwhile, takes up bondage, discipline, sadism and masochism (BDSM) themes across a prolific body of hardcore 1970s 'roughies' (sexploitation films typically depicting acts of sadism or rape). Unlike Jaeckin's releases, Davian's films circulated within the gritty 'underbelly' of New York's Times Square grind-house scene that culturally shadowed the far more visibly burgeoning, and now popularly mythologized, 1970s wave of American 'porno-chic'. His films do not fit so easily within Williams's typology in that the sadie-max elements are prevalent and in that particular scenes also retain elements of what Williams classifies as the "amateur". Expanding Williams's analysis, the comparative exploration of the work of each director in this chapter offers not only an illustrative snapshot of the (sub-)cultural contexts and particular aesthetic moments of their making but, more importantly, identifies two very different examples of the use of sound.

A significant body of theoretical work has explored various facets of cinematic eroticism and violence. Sound analyses dealing with this area have predominantly focused on the prevalent sound effects/affects of classic Hollywood cinema, and of the horror, slasher and sexploitation genres. Often, these have addressed the role and impact of women's voices, screams or vocal utterances. For example, Brophy (1999) analyses the classic female cinematic scream as the complex bearer of darkly violent and misogynistic cultural significations. Chion (1994) takes up the disembodied cinematic voice-over in terms of its sonorous recall to the maternal. Silverman (1988) theorizes the feminine voice in cinema in terms of its fetishization within psychoanalytic relations of the cinematic apparatus. Williams (1989), meanwhile, compares hardcore pornography, in formal terms, to the structure of a musical, wherein sexual sequences become 'numbers' and often (predominantly female) sex sound joins in a free-floating symphony of sonic orgasmic ecstasy, becoming, as Williams notes, the "aural fetishes of the female pleasures we cannot see" (*ibid.*: 123). As part of this analysis, I will look at the role of sound across a range of texts that specifically address violent sexuality, in which cries/screams at the liminalities of pleasure/pain play an explicit role in the sexual 'scene'.

This chapter provides close analyses of Jaeckin's *Story of O* (1975) and Davian's *House of de Sade* (1975) to explore the construction of sound in erotic/pornographic representation. Specifically, I examine how sound and music mediate sexual representation in these texts in relation to the complex themes of violence, sexuality and BDSM that each addresses. For the purposes of this chapter the film texts analysed are those currently available in English-language format on DVD.[1]

Jaeckin's softcore S/M and the sexual odyssey

Just Jaeckin's career as a film-maker followed closely on the heels of his success as a high-fashion photographer. In the late 1960s and early 1970s he worked for magazines such as French *Vogue*, *Nouvel Adam* and *Lui*, producing notable covers of cultural icons including Brigitte Bardot and Jane Fonda. Jaeckin's inaugural film effort, *Emmanuelle* (1974), was one of the first French erotic films to be released on mainstream cinema circuits and one of the most commercially successful films in the history of French cinema.[2] The film was based on an eponymous semi-autobiographical erotic novel written by Marayat Rollet-Andriane (under the pen name Emmanuelle Arsan) and first published in 1959. The film depicts a French diplomat's wife (played by former model and Miss TV Europe 1973 winner, Sylvia Kristel) living in Thailand, who embarks on a journey of sexual awakening, urged on by her worldlier husband. Emmanuelle discovers the pleasures of novel sexual encounters with a variety of male and female partners within the exotic natural settings and privileged spaces of a wealthy expatriate lifestyle. Among Emmanuelle's adventures are a brief lesbian affair and several three-way/voyeuristic sexual encounters guided by her sexual mentor Mario (played by Alain Cuny), who offers accompanying diegetic expositions of 1970s 'free-love' philosophy.

Emmanuelle established several facets of Jaeckin's emerging signature aesthetic, including immersive and dreamy soft-focus cinematography, simulated depictions of sex, and an extended and lingering gaze at the naked female form. In homage to his own photographic background, he also featured self-referential high-fashion/art images and diegetic themes. The film was an unexpected breakthrough success and, as Susan Hayward notes,

> In sixty weeks the film had topped two million viewers in Paris and it was the top film in 1974. Pornography had not just come of age: for that year at least, it was France's leading national cinema product. (Hayward, 1993: 245)

Accompanying the film's box-office *coup* was the notable success of its soundtrack album and single release of its title track, 'Emmanuelle'. Composed and performed by French musician Pierre Bachelet (co-written with Herve Roy), the single sold 4 million copies and the album 1.4 million. The infectious French pop stylings of a lilting piano, guitar and flute lines, and a gently wistful pop refrain are repeated throughout the film. Instrumental renditions of this central leitmotiv also softly infuse various sexual interludes and reflective moments in the narrative. The soundtrack's popular success came as a distinct surprise to its producers, particularly considering that initial requests to score the film addressed to Bachelet's musical contemporaries, most notably Serge Gainsbourg, had been rebuffed.[3] *Emmanuelle*'s popularity motivated Jaeckin to develop other erotic film projects. His second feature was once again based on literary adaptation. This time, the text chosen for adaptation, Pauline Reage's 1954 novella *Histoire d'O*, comprised

Depraved Desire   69

a far more complex and violent sexual narrative that was a less obvious subject for his developing soft-edged erotic aesthetic than its predecessor.

The film version of *Story of O* begins with O, a young Parisian fashion photographer, and Rene, her lover, walking through an abandoned park. O and Rene are picked up by a driver who takes them to the Chateau Roissy. Along the way, Rene asks O to remove her slip and panties and to sit directly on the leather car seat as he cuts the straps of her bra with a penknife. This narrative sequence is depicted twice, and the narrator's voice-over informs us that the second telling is a "simpler, more direct" version of the first. O then enters the chateau, where she is educated in its rules and rituals. These include wearing eighteenth-century clothing, a leather bondage collar and steel bracelets, remaining continuously available to the men of Roissy, and enduring physical torture of bondage, whipping and vaginal and anal penetration. Her entry to Roissy signals her wilful immersion into a ritualized martyrdom of sexual domination, bodily laceration, and psychological debasement. At Roissy, she joins a coterie of ladies-in-waiting who attend to her wounds, feed, bathe and prepare her for sexual encounters and punishments, while themselves also remaining perpetually 'open' to usage by the male inhabitants of the chateau. O successfully endures, as well as (ambiguously) achieves sexual and masochistic pleasure from, her trials. Resuming her life in Paris, she continues her journey by submitting to being sexually possessed by Rene's half-brother, Sir Stephen. Sir Stephen's sadistic machinations intensify into whipping, bondage, the piercing of O's labia and the branding of her flesh as proof of her enslavement to him. O also begins to indoctrinate Jacqueline, the fashion model who appears in O's photographs, by seducing her at the behest of Sir Stephen and Rene, who now desires Jacqueline. O and Sir Stephen fall in love. She continues to submit to his trials and punishments, which culminate in her 'crowning' debasement, the penultimate scene in which she stands naked wearing an owl mask in a highly stylized and surreal display for Sir Stephen's friends.[4] In the final scene of the film (which does not appear in the novel), O asks Sir Stephen if he would submit to similar punishments and upon his answer, "I believe so", she brands him with an O using the tip of her lit cigarette. In the novella version, Reage once again splits the narrative into two, offering one ending in which O returns to Roissy and another in which, when abandoned by Sir Stephen, she asks and receives his permission to die. Reage's fictional depiction of O's wilful submission to her lover's violent sadomasochistic requests, originally published in 1954, received both significant literary accolades (such as the Prix de Deux Magots, awarded in 1955), and public scrutiny and censorship for obscene moral content (remaining unpublished in the United States until 1965 and banned in Britain until 1979). Several literary contemporaries of the author praised the novella as a Sadean feat of erotic existentialism. In his note on the book, for example, André Pieyre de Mandiargues observes:

> Here we are dealing with a genuine novel, one we should not hesitate to categorize as a mystic work ... what we are shown in Story of O is a

> *complete spiritual transformation, what others would call an ascesis.* (de Mandiargues, 1965: xvi–xvii)

O's journey, it was argued, could be read as a kind of sacred asceticism, in which, like the archetypal religious martyr, she reaches a state of apotheosis through trials of (in this case sexualized) constraint and degradation.

With the rapid shifts in the cultural climate of the late 1960s and early 1970s, critical reception of the novella altered dramatically. *Story of O* became the subject of intense feminist critique. Academics such as the anti-pornography feminist Andrea Dworkin (1974) saw the text as the exemplary enactment of a woman's utter self-abnegation within a disturbing matrix of violently oppressive patriarchal sexual, discursive and corporeal regimes.[5] Silverman (1984) advanced a psychoanalytic view of O's condition as synonymous with the constraints of the female subject as a discursively predetermined 'body-to-be-marked'. One notable exception was Susan Sontag's critique in *Styles of Radical Will* (1969), in which she elaborated the basis upon which works such as *Story of O* and *The Image*, Jean de Berg's 1956 novel of sadomasochistic themes, should be seen to function as high literary works within a culturally/artistically significant ethos of "the odyssey of the pornographic imagination" (*ibid.*: 49).

The cultural (and personal) anxiety attending Jaeckin's forays into controversial erotic themes is an important aspect of the making of *Histoire d'O*. In his autobiography, *Tout Just* (2006), Jaeckin characterizes the making of both his inaugural blockbuster erotic film *Emmanuelle* and *Story of O* as significantly influenced by media controversy and critical and feminist reaction to the depiction of erotic themes. Jaeckin has identified his motivation to select Arsan and Reage's works as determined by the sexual politics of the period:

> Don't forget that these films were made in the '70s, and all the feminists were protesting these kinds of films. So I chose books written by women; women are more fantasy-oriented than men. The success of *Emmanuelle* is because the women came to see the film, too. However, many feminists still decried my films, they really gave me hell at the time.[6]

Jaeckin's emphasis on the (stereotyped) fantasy nature of a women's erotica appears to have significantly influenced both aesthetic and narrative representation in the film. As Jaeckin describes, he and the screenwriter Sébastien Japrisot envisaged an Alice-in-Wonderland-like odyssey for O's journey, inscribed through direct visual and narrative references to the popular children's fantasy tale. Though not explicitly mentioned by Jaeckin, the choice of the Alice theme clearly resonates with Jean Paulhan's[7] original introduction to Reage's novel, in which he explains: "I advance through O with a strange feeling, as though I am moving through a fairy tale – we know that fairy tales are erotic novels for children" (Reage, 1965: xxiii). Jaeckin's and Japrisot's self-conscious efforts to couch the story's vivid violent erotic content as childlike fairy tale reflect a curious collision of culturally resonant threads of (purported) female empowerment, sexual liberation and pornographic odyssey.

Score

Accompanied by Bachelet's title composition, the film's initial credit sequence shows the profile of each main actor accompanied by a haunting/ghostly wordless female vocalesque melody. Undulating like a siren song, the ethereal and unreal quality of the sound was created synthetically by a spectrum follower (commonly known as a vocoder), in a score arranged and performed by Matt Camison, which utilized the then-new synthesizer technology to create a cutting-edge modern/futuristic sound. The vocoder analyses recorded vocal (or other) signals, separating them into frequency bands, and then uses this information to provide a signal template that can be realized as note sequences that mimic sung vocal patterns. The score's vocalesque refrains repeat in eerie ascending and descending lines with the slow introduction of lightly crescendoing cymbal percussion underscored by a pulsating bass rhythm. Together, the sounds propel the increasing and intensifying pace of a kaleidoscopic background pattern of stark tree branches shaping and re-shaping to form an engulfing forest. As the moving 'tunnel' and siren sounds draw the viewer into immersion, they signify our entry into the fantasy space of the film and suggest the altered state and symbolic trajectory of Alice's fall down the rabbit hole.

The Alice theme also operates in terms of what Penley argues is the shift in narrative focus towards a "woman and her sexual odyssey" (2004: 320), in this case rather tritely envisioned as a young girl's nonsensical fantasy adventure. As Jaeckin notes:

> The writer, Sébastien Japrisot, added that last scene; we tried to say that Story of O was a fantasy, not a real story. When she brands him at the end, it says to me that the story is like Alice in Wonderland; she goes on a journey and lots of things happen to her, but it has nothing to do with reality.[8]

As Penley argues, 1970s erotic/pornographic film was increasingly bound up in the intersecting moments of sexual revolution and the women's movement, creating commercial interest in establishing products for a larger mainstream audience of heterosexual couples. Penley also notes that the aesthetic consequences of this shift were the introduction of films that were "far more 'tasteful', even pseudoaristocratic, in their demeanour and depicted milieu" (*ibid.*: 320).

Though Penley's remarks are specifically addressed to hardcore examples, *Story of O* certainly evidences a pretension to highbrow literary erotic form, complete with a higher budget, softcore aesthetic and literary themes. As Andrews points out, the "soft core idiom", originally popularized within a sexploitation context by directors such as Jaeckin, Radley Metzger and Joe Sarno, helped to establish a stereotypically feminized mode of sexual representation in which aesthetic features such as soft-focus cinematography and narrative tropes such as the "awakening-sexuality" model "adapted from

European art films" produce an "aspirational" erotic form (2006: 15). Penley's and Andrews's distinctions also apply to the use of sound in the film.

As suggested above, *Story of O*'s soundtrack evidences avant-garde artistic ambitions. In addition to dialogue, it features three major sonic strands: a prominent female voice-over; an original synthesized musical score; and the foley sounds of O's whipping/beating combined with overdubbed screams and cries. In contrast to the abbreviated sound personnel credits of most mainstream sex films, *Story of O* lists eight sound designers, editors and effects editors, including Jean-Pierre Lelong and Laurent Quaglio, who later become pre-eminent in their fields.[9] The soundtrack is also significant for its use of synthesized musical sound. During the late 1960s performers such as Walter Carlos pioneered the use of analogue synthesizers as credible instruments in their own right (rather than simply sources of novelty sound effects).[10] Carlos was closely associated with the popularization of the Moog brand of synthesizer and received considerable public recognition when he wrote and recorded the soundtrack for *A Clockwork Orange* (Stanley Kubrick, 1971), another controversial 'art-roughie' film featuring explicit sex and violence. Bachelet's score for *Story of O* was arranged and performed by Matt Camison, a musician who worked with a rival brand of analogue synthesizer, the ARP, and who had previously recorded an album of synthesizer pop-rock entitled *Pop-arp* (1973), using the pseudonym Mister K. Like Carlos's score for *A Clockwork Orange*, Camison's film soundtrack used the synthesizer as a virtual orchestra and also used a vocoder to produce a vocalesque melody.[11]

Women narrators

One of the most striking elements of sound construction in *Story of O* is the prominent use of a female narrative voice-over, uncredited but performed by Alexandra Stewart in the English-language version (and by Michèle Montel in the French original). The first spoken words of the film, in fact, are those of the (non-diegetic) narrator who begins, "One day O's lover takes her to a place they had never gone before, Park Monceau at Montsouris, somewhere around there", providing a fairy tale-like 'once upon a time' opening. Staying true to the novel, the narrator repeats the two variations of the opening scene, thus explicitly foregrounding the structured artifice, as well as once again reinforcing the notion of a dreamlike non-linearity.

As Chion has argued, use of narrative voice-over in cinema is generally sparing and mostly confined to certain privileged diegetic characters:

> since textual speech does invalidate the notion of an audiovisual scene, the cinema tends to impose a strict quota on its use. This great power is generally reserved for certain privileged characters and is only granted for a limited time. In countless films, therefore, the textual speech of a voiceover narrator engenders images with its own logic (i.e. not that of continuity editing), just long enough to establish the film's narrative framework and

> *setting. Then it disappears, allowing us to enter the diegetic universe.*
> (1994: 172–3)

Jaeckin's narrator, however, does not act as a character in the diegesis. She operates like a voice-of-god interpellator of the action of the film. The narrator of *Story of O* regularly moves in and out of the film, mediating the diegetic scene, rather than being contained within the opening sequence. As McHugh (2001) notes, use of female narration has largely been confined to early usage in film noir (e.g. *Mildred Pierce*, Michael Curtiz, 1945), alternative/avant-garde genres (particularly by women film-makers), and more recently in a televisual context in a contemporary spate of narratives ostensibly directed towards female sexual empowerment (*Sex in the City, Desperate Housewives*). Thus, Jaeckin's choice of this relatively unusual technique is particularly notable in the context of this genre and period.

As Chion's assertion suggests, this narrative construction lends unusual authorial privilege to this female voice-of-god. The role of this voice is particularly important, given the relatively few sequences in which the character of O is able to speak for herself, in large part because of the silence demanded as part of her submission. O's diegetic muteness, which so intensifies the demeaning aspects of her submission, is critically mediated by the voice-over's calm assurances of her pleasure and collusion in the sadomasochistic scene. Upon O's arrival at the chateau, for example, the narrator informs us that she is "surprised at being tied up as she had no intention of not obeying her lover". In another key sequence between the first whipping scene and just prior to a second session in the middle of the night, O lies naked in bed as the voice-over tells us: "O wondered why there was so much sweetness mingled with her terror. Or why she found her terror so delicious." Thus, the narrative voice-over frames and re-positions O's apparent torture with a privileged view into her psyche (an effect that is normally reserved for diegetic voice-overs of inner dialogue), which is split into a third-person disembodied oratory that can project her conscious intellectual investment and pleasure in her masochistic role. This is further supported by several dialogue references in which O is specifically asked by her masters to acknowledge her voluntary participation in what unfolds.

Another key aspect of the film's narration is Stewart's vocal performance. The distinctive low pitch, precise enunciation and texture of her voice strongly convey a marked sense of self-possession. Combined with a detached authoritative delivery, the voice-over offers a cool counterpoint to the sonically jarring scenes of punishment and the sombre and hauntingly dramatic score, further establishing the transcendently detached and empowered impartial observer. On another level, this quality operates as a kind of sonic analogue for the 'voice' of the novella, which Paulhan characterizes in his introduction as "more of a speech than a mere effusion; of a letter rather than a secret diary" (Reage, 1965: xxiv). The relative rarity and particular stylistic choice of a powerfully resonant female narrative voice is perhaps the single most distinctive feature of Jaeckin's film. Voice-over selection also plays an important role in supporting the twin threads of the two types of odyssey discussed earlier – the literary pornographic (as faithful rendition of the literary voice) and the "woman's sexual odyssey" – in the sonic reinscription of a woman's (albeit paradoxical) 'authorship' of her own sexuality.

O's themes

If the overwhelming effect of Stewart's voice-over in the film is to impart a cool, detached intellectual engagement within the sexual scene, the musical sequences in contrast provide heavily laden romantic/emotive cues. Bachelet's original score for *Story of O* is almost entirely instrumental (with the exception of the 'She's A Lady' sequence, discussed below), and features heavily synthesized sounds, processed percussion and acoustic guitar. Described by reviewers as "haunting" and indicative of the "mysterious and foreboding" nature of O's sexual submission, Bachelet's theme variations signify O's psychosexual progression over the course of the film. As Hasan notes, the musical cue "certainly encapsulates the tonal shifts O herself experiences, as the men and women she encounters combine gentle affection with ascending levels of emotional and physical brutality".[12]

O's initial physical immersion into Roissy's masochistic 'Wonderland' is enveloped in an equally immersive discovery theme, which consists of sustained and reverberant synthesized chords with a series of ascending piano changes that create a slow build of tension. Upon O's ascent of the Roissy stairs, a high-pitched electronic melodic thread wistfully ventures, as O does, into the waiting room of the chateau. As she inquisitively pokes around, Alice-like, in the drawing room, the narration reinforces her lost sense of time, intoning that it was undoubtedly her lover's wish that she "wait here pointlessly for half an hour, or an hour, or two. Who could tell? It seemed a century." The music rises up in a romantic swell, with alternating violin and electronic keyboard renditions of the high-pitched theme at times becoming fused in the electronic meld of sustained synthesizer chords. The theme repeats as O's face is shown in a variety of reflection shots, including hall-of-mirrors multiple profile effects. She enters a gilded chamber full of mirrors and glass surfaces where she is depicted in soft-focus shots being prepared by her cohorts, who affectionately dress her in breast-baring clothes and collar, make up her body and brush her hair. Heavy-handed visual markers of O's 'through the looking glass' entry/discovery are accompanied by a violin rendition of her discovery theme.

A key tonal shift occurs with the first Roissy sex sequence. The romantic theme is replaced by a low-pitched piano sequence combined with distorted screeching violin reverberations. As the first master grabs hold of one of O's breasts, a distinctive and dramatic harpsichord line descends to trace the movement across her body. Combined with the violin sequence underlay, the sounds signal the tension and impending danger of her first sexual possession.

The valets and O's lover discuss whether O has been chained or whipped and state their intent to "get tears out of her". The scene then shows highly stylized and simulated intercourse and fellatio with several male valets as the chateau's inmates look on. O is shown in close-up shots, flailing her head and arms as she is multiply possessed against the backdrop of a roaring fire, her anguished face sweating and shivering, as she withstands the sexual tortures. Vocal cries, breathy, high-pitched and sharp, are dubbed over the montage sequence, at times (though not always) synchronous to her mouth movements and intermingled with the repeating downward spiral of the harpsichord, a maelstrom of distorted electronic violin, low rumbling timpani and low-pitched deep flute twitters. The accompaniment dramatizes the visual depiction of O's (slow-motion) physical gestures of being 'taken'. The pseudo-baroque harpsichord passage becomes the signature of O's submission to debasement and, in combination with the historically inspired settings and costumes, provides a proto-postmodern historicity to the scene and broader narrative.

Throughout the Roissy indoctrination sessions, repetition of the sombre harpsichord passage accompanies O's first whipping, her three-way sexual encounter with Rene and a valet and, later, her literal descent into the castle dungeon for an extended period of blindfolded bondage and whipping. Alternately, the entering-Roissy piano and violin sequence and repetition of the initial guitar motif from Monceau Park create intermittent tonal shifts to indicate O's ambiguous, pseudo-romantic bond with the valet Pierre.

The musical and sound motifs that are used during the post-Roissy sequences alternate predominantly to reinforce O's oscillating dominant (though still within a submissive role to Sir Stephen) and purely submissive sexual roles in her sexual encounters, as well as to continue to project, through echoes of original leitmotivs, her ongoing process of sexual discovery. O's initial return to everyday life is distinctively punctuated by the sound of rapid-fire camera clicks and her exhortations to Jacqueline, her fashion model subject, to "Throw your head back" and "Keep moving". Jacqueline moves her face and head for the camera as a fake wind blows her softly lit hair to the sounds of ethereal ambient female vocalization of electronic 'ahhs'. The sounds of camera flashes that cue the physical flicks and poses are distinctly artificial and become more reminiscent of whip cracks than camera noises. The sequence immediately establishes O's returned voice and directly places her in a position of control over Jacqueline through the gaze and sonic 'assault' of the camera.

As O continues her journey into submission, being delivered to Sir Stephen by Rene, the theme 'O Et Sir Stephen' is introduced – a sultry, funky bass and guitar motif that suggests O as sexually assertive (now indoctrinated by the rituals of Roissy) – and she is dressed in the garb of a femme fatale, arriving to meet her new master in fur coat and black widow's dress. Echoes of the Roissy themes return to accompany O's love/punishment by Sir Stephen and a chance encounter with Pierre. A recurring piano motif softly and romantically inflects O's 'ordered/desired' seduction of Jacqueline and is later echoed in a sexual encounter with Sir Stephen as together they recount the story of the two women's encounter. Another encounter with a member of Sir Stephen's cohort,

Ivan, is accompanied by discordant violin, frenzied cymbal percussion and distorted guitar riffs in a scene of 'amped' up (although not sadomasochistic) lovemaking.

One musical sequence stands out from O's recurring thematic progressions. The single 'She's A Lady' is presented (pseudo-)diegetically in a proto-music video sequence. One of O's fashion-shot subjects poses against a backdrop swinging a large light bulb on a cord around herself as she performs various aerobic-style dance moves and semi-splits in hot pink tights, black high heels and a white blouse with Mickey Mouse print. As Hasan notes, the sequence is an "obvious attempt to spin a theme song".[13] The driving electro-rock, shrill and ghoulish male and female shrieks (resonant with a *Rocky Horror Picture Show*-like amalgam of voices), and lyrics of "She's a lady, Drives me crazy" saturate the soundtrack. Despite the film's attempts to emphasize the distinct nature of this song in a spectacle of dance performance, its separation from the main narrative renders 'She's A Lady' less of a key song and more an incidental homage to Jaeckin's fashion oeuvre.

Sound and aesthetic sadomasochism

Jaeckin's approach to representing S/M sequences in the film clearly exemplifies several of the facets of an art-film aesthetic that Williams (1989) identifies as a BDSM film subgenre. As mentioned earlier, the first sex sequence appears as a montage of sexual postures, with slow-motion footage, asynchronous dialogue elements in O's cries, and the classical high-art intoned orchestral motif. Within Roissy, O's punishments most often carry the 'descent' theme, interspersed with her sharp piercing cries. In her first bondage sequence, she is permitted to watch herself being whipped and is shown with her hands tied above her head, as one of the women turns the looking glass so her reflection can be seen. This doubly symbolic gesture reiterates her Alice/psychic journey while lingering over the image in a kind of *tableau vivant* of her nude form cast as beauty in repose of masochistic suffering. Foley cracks of the whip and O's screams figure at times in loose montage with O's facial reactions/protestations, serving to evoke rather than directly depict many of the whip strikes. Foreign-language dubbing in the English-language version further serves to lift the sound asynchronously above the scene. As Williams notes, aesthetic sadomasochism

> is not interested in hard-core evidence of either pleasure or pain. Instead of amateur sadomasochism's fixed stare at the flesh[14] that is slapped, whipped or pierced in order to catch involuntary flinches of pain, in these films we more typically see the whip poised over the vulnerable flesh, hear the noise of its crack, and, in a separate shot, see the reaction on a face. Eisensteinian montage supplants the Bazinian reality of event, and the moment of threat counts more than that of violence. (1989: 199)

Two scenes demonstrate the highbrow sonic aestheticization of sexual violence in the film — one through amplified affective use of musical sound and the other through the distinct absence thereof.

The first takes place at Samois,[15] the garden retreat house presided over by the dominatrix Anne-Marie. O is whipped by one of the former Roissy women after she has accused her of cheating at a chess game. Anne-Marie tells O, "You can cry as loud as you like. No one can hear" and proceeds to play a gramophone record of a waltz. As O's screams rise in volume Anne-Marie turns the volume up, with the music's exacting rhythm quickening the pace of the whipping. The same music is played in a subsequent sequence when O whips Yvonne. O's lashes, reticent at first, become so brutal that Anne-Marie switches off the gramophone and commands her to stop. In contrast to the romantic musical intercession prominent throughout much of the film, this sonic amplification effects a more acute brutality – one, in fact, that requires sonic/narrative intervention. In Pola Rappaport's documentary interview,[16] novelist Reage explains that "Women are as immoral as men. Probably more so." O's awakening to her sadistic drives is met with the heightened affectivity of a highly formalized and disciplinary set of beats per minute. However, this rhythmic excess is quickly remodulated by the next scene in which O heals Yvonne's wounds by making love to her to the tune of soft murmurs and the gentle perambulating guitar echo of the opening credits motif.

By comparison, in a deeply oedipalized spectacle of sexual punishment, Sir Stephen's first possession of O is sonically stark. Musical accompaniment is foregone in favour of O's restrained cries sounded through clenched teeth. He tells her: "You shall learn to obey me without loving me and without my loving you." The unambiguous father figure of Reage's story, Sir Stephen doles out his punishments with paternal exactitude – a kind of high purity of S/M form. Within this regime, a relation of 'purest brutality equals purest love' is established. Sonic choices act to reinforce Williams's notion of aestheticized treatment of "rarefied sexual tastes". One key O/Stephen sequence, in fact, reverts to what might be understood as the 'pure intellect' of the word/voice/text over explicit visual representation of the S/M scene. The voice-over's commentary that "Sir Stephen punished her so cruelly that she lost consciousness" truncates the visual image, showing Sir Stephen holding the whip in what becomes an indicative "moment of threat" (Williams, 1989: 199). Sonically, the voice-over, distinctly feminine, masters and purifies the film's most potently violent thrust across corporeal liminality.

As the above analysis of *Story of O*'s sound suggests, the film essentially dissects O's engagement with sexual violence along three planes – that of 'mind' (voice-over), 'body' (whipping/sex sounds), and 'spirit' (synthesized leitmotivs). Aesthetic S/M sound deconstructs O as singular cohesive subject in the violent sexual scenes. Thus, the film's sonic architecture arguably preserves the novella's perplexing and irreconcilable trajectory of violent, self-abnegating desire. As Paulhan's introduction to the book notes,

> There is no dearth of abominations in Story of O. But it sometimes seems to me that it is an idea, or a complex of ideas, an opinion rather than a young woman we see being subjected to these tortures. (Reage, 1965: xxxiii)

From a narrative perspective, however, Jaeckin departs from the ambiguous and multiple textual ending with a neat 1970s feminist closure. *Story of O* brings the journey to a definitive end when O as femme fatale dominates Sir Stephen by branding him with her cigarette. In this scene, the notion of a woman's liberatory odyssey literally snuffs out the prior narrative trajectory of the unfettered pornographic imagination to become the last governing myth of the film. Consequently, the soundscape alone is left to carry the traces of irreducible tension within this "complex of ideas" (Paulhan in Reage, 1965: xxxiii).

Davian – a hardcore 'auteur'

Joe Davian's film work emerged as part of an underground hardcore pornography 'machine' that would, in contrast to Jaeckin's pedigreed *oeuvre*, serve up a feast of far more vernacular Sadean pleasures. Davian was initially hired by the Avon Theater to direct low-budget pornographic films. In the 1970s the Avon was one of numerous Triple X venues in New York City's Times Square red-light district, with its infamous sleaze cinema houses such as the Venus, the Eros and the Rialto. The Avon came to public notoriety in the Meese Commission's Report of 1986,[17] which charged the theatre chain with producing some of the most violently themed pornography on offer. Avon Theater film productions were typically shot on 16mm and featured budgets of no more than $5,000 to $10,000; they were created primarily for the purpose of quick and profitable turnaround in local and national grind-house cinemas. As Clifford and Landis note, the Avon specialized in

> high frequency adult films that premiered at their string of theaters pocketed throughout Times Square. The Avon schematic serviced the most guttural, shameful and maniacally driven sexualities and play acted them out ... The Avon crew were the bastard children never invited to any adult industry awards ceremonies. Frankly, people were afraid of the directors and cast members. They were too unruly and rough trade.[18]

According to Landis and Clifford, Davian was known as a self-proclaimed Dachau survivor (though speculation existed regarding the veracity of this) and one of a group of Israeli pornography directors working in New York. Despite being perceived as rough trade, Davian was not publicly reported to be violent or abusive. His career and persona were, in fact, shrouded in mystery, and he ultimately disappeared amidst rumours of having either been fatally shot or taken himself to a self-imposed exile in Israel.

In a prolific directorial stint between 1975 and 1981, Davian made a total of fifteen hardcore feature films. A large portion of his body of work explicitly addresses bondage themes, including films such as *House of de Sade* (1975), *Revenge and Punishment* (1976), *Fetishes of Monique* (1976), *Night of Submission* (1976) and *Domination Blue* (1976). Davian's approach was significantly influenced by his miniscule budgets, but nonetheless it features a number of techniques of the classic auteurist. For example, his works regularly include the same rotating stable of actors, including the renowned adult-film stars Vanessa Del Rio and Annie Sprinkle (then a hardcore S/M performer and now a well-known sex guru and performance artist), as well as Jack Teague, Red Baron and Sharon Mitchell. Davian's pictures also focus on concentric 'roughie' themes of kidnapping, prostitution, horror, assault, bondage and revenge, often combining horror-film narratives and settings with explicit hardcore sexual numbers (a genre sometimes referred to as 'hardgore'). As Landis and Clifford note: "Davian created a memorable series of roughies, each one more extreme than the last. His operatic narratives were carried by elaborate narrative twists, snappy dialogue, and unapologetic S&M scenes."[19]

Davian's films depict a multiplicity of classic hardcore sex acts, including a vast array of couplings ranging from orgy sequences to threesomes, masturbation, oral and anal sex, and extensive use of sexual props and toys. As the above quote suggests, S/M themes play a significant role in the diegetic progression of the director's narratives. Davian's signature unapologetic approach constructed S/M sequences that clearly evidence formal features delineated in Williams's sadie-max category. In contrast to aesthetic sadomasochism, sadie-max scenes eschew literary pretension to directly heighten hardcore titillation. As Williams notes, such scenes are designed to add "drama, excitement, danger, and exoticism to otherwise standard fare, functioning perhaps as foreplay to more 'normal' genital acts" (1989: 198). In her analysis, most sadie-max performances depict a female protagonist deriving pain/pleasure from bondage at the hands of a male dominator. Davian's body of films, however, feature a number of female dominatrix performances.

Two such performances are those in *Fetishes of Monique* and *Revenge and Punishment*, both of which offer illustrative examples of Davian's characteristic S/M sound approach. Each film combines conventional hardcore sound with signature Davian music choices to underscore the director's idiosyncratically dark and darkly humorous sexual vision. His films employ inexpensive and rudimentary dialogue recording and sound-editing effects, invariably creating intermittently inaudible speech and relatively raw and uneven soundscapes. Davian's films also rely heavily on the extensive use of uncredited pre-recorded music sequences, typically augmenting sex sound and diegetic dialogue with simultaneous layering and intersection of popular and/or classical music tracks to heighten the affective dimensions of sexual numbers.

Fetishes of Monique opens with a sadie-max scene. Actress Debbie Lee plays 'mad scientist' Dr Angie Verocity, who engages in frenzied intercourse with her male assistant to produce the sperm necessary for a magic sex potion. Interspersed with these opening images is a credit sequence depicting an expressionist-style black-and-white image of electric voltage running up and down two wires, intercut with shots of the couple's intercourse. They perform a scene flanked by a makeshift laboratory with a backdrop of 'science-class' flasks and beakers of bubbling and smoking liquids. Several major sound elements are interwoven throughout this scene. First, three punctuating bars of a halting classical orchestral march commence, which are joined by the sound of a slap and an ominous electrified oscillating buzz. Intercut with these are the female character's moans and groans, which cut across the visual track and credit sequence to form at times a free-floating accompaniment and at others synchronicity with her sexual actions. As the sexual number progresses, shots focus on extremely graphic close-ups of the actors in coitus, creating an almost 'art-film' effect of repetitive patterns of body parts in sexual motion. Throughout the scene, dramatic fortissimo march lines continue to punctuate these movements intermittently. In contrast to the waltz scene in *Story of O*, the classical accompaniment here operates less as aestheticized and ritualistic eroticization than as a darkly humorous inflection to the rough sex skit.

The scene then shifts to the S/M sequence as Dr Verocity drinks the potency serum and dramatically transforms into a dominatrix. The music drops low in the mix as S/M speech takes the fore. She commands her assistant to "kiss my foot", "make your way up" and "do it to me right", as he performs cunnilingus according to her disciplinary demands. She grabs his hair, forces him face down and strikes him with a paddle as she berates him with the words "You bastard, you call yourself an assistant. You're nothing. You're scum." Here the music temporarily gives way to the sounds of slapped flesh. Even when characters' faces do not appear, the aural symphony of oohs, ahhs, and sexual exhortations continues against the slow metronomic backdrop of the lab's repetitive buzz of electrified voltage. Many of the elements of Davian's construction of S/M sex sound in the scene follow the hardcore conventions outlined by Williams:

> In hard core film and video ... the relation of sound to image differs from that in dominant cinema, though without having the function of avant-garde deconstruction. In these films, when characters talk their lips often fail to match the sounds spoken, and in the sexual numbers a dubbed-over 'disembodied' voice (saying "ooh" and "aaah") may stand in as the most prominent signifier of female pleasure in the absence of other, more visual assurances. (1989: 122–3)

Revenge and Punishment depicts the character of an avenging angel, played by Tequila Cheung, who performs in a sadie-max sequence with Gary D. Kid playing Tommy Jordan, the son of a corrupt and abusive senator. The 'angel' commences the scene by commanding her victim to "lick my boots". She then orders Tommy to perform cunnilingus, place himself in a leash, and drink water like a dog from a glass on the floor. S/M acts of whipping and bondage are closely intercut with explicit close-up shots of their feverish sexual intercourse. BDSM sound and dialogue cues play a critical role in signalling the S/M power dynamics of the scene. For example, the female character's imperative sex demands and degradation speech, the crack of her whip, and her partner's doglike panting and slurping of water all circumscribe the role play. Her command of the performance is all-encompassing, complete with final exhortations to her male 'bottom' (in the sense of the submissive role in the S/M relation) to "Come, bitch, come", followed by sharp paddle slaps, and cackling laughter in a mock-drama of revenge domination. This scene unfolds entirely within a confined space of a single armchair placed in the corner of an empty room. This sparse setting repeatedly serves as both the literal platform for extended sequences of sexual calisthenics as well as the film's pseudo-confessional zone, where actors relay critical back story. The single-set staging offers significant narrative economy and enables the diegesis to progress through minimal backdrop changes with the use of often stilted and hyper-performative dialogue to convey overarching plot exigencies (e.g. the senator's abuses that drive the film's revenge motif). Thus, Davian's dialogue arguably works harder by carrying twin weights. Narrative and sex speech awkwardly segue into each other in a collision of impulses that reinforce the amateurish and skitlike lowbrow S/M performance.

In both *Fetishes of Monique* and *Revenge and Punishment*, male S/M 'bottoms' generally respond to their punishments only with low moans of unambiguous arousal, as compared with the hyper-embellished and high-pitched cries of female submissives. This aligns with Williams's analysis of female cries acting as overt markers of female pleasure in counterpart to the externalized "visual assurance" of male ejaculation. Additionally, each of the female sadie-max performances is significantly diegetically cued by special narrative circumstances outside of straightforward heterosexual S/M play. In the case of *Fetishes of Monique*, the trigger is the literal imbibing/embodiment of masculinity through the consumption of the sex potion and in *Revenge and Punishment* the necessity of revenge.

The *Revenge and Punishment* scene also features the single most pervading and signature sonic element of Davian's hardgore signature – use of psychedelic music to establish a dark, ambient, gnawing tension in the sexual performance. In fact, Davian's films are united in their near-universal inclusion of one or more late 1960s/early 1970s experimental Pink Floyd tracks, including 'Careful With That Axe, Eugene,' 'Set The Controls For The Heart Of The Sun', 'A Saucerful Of Secrets', 'Astronomy Domine' and 'Mudmen'. As will be detailed in the reading of *House of de Sade* that follows, Davian's near-obsessive and multiple use of these tracks within each film forms an almost de facto 'sex-song cycle' carried by a psychedelic sonic milieu.

House of de Sade

House of de Sade exemplifies Davian's style of (pseudo-)horror porn. The narrative references familiar devices such as the seance and the haunted house as a premise for unleashing the (sexual) spirit of the Marquis de Sade. With its amateurish settings and skit performance, the film, much like Davian's *Hard Gore*, operates at the border of horror, hardcore and dark comedy. Both *House of de Sade* and *Hard Gore* feature such low-budget horror staples as hunchback sexual deviants, voyeuristic haunting, paintings with eyes that move, and the occasional blood splatter. In fact, *Hard Gore* ups the ante with scenes of necrophilia and murderous sex. These films present a condensed catalogue of taboos, combining multiple forms of sexual fetish and shock hardcore, from graphic orgies to the use of such devices as gynaecological instruments, sex-toy play and sadomasochism.[20]

As noted earlier, the *House of de Sade* soundscape samples various early experimental Pink Floyd songs to create dark psychedelic (and cheap) sound effects. Tracks are drawn from three of the band's early psychedelic rock albums: *The Piper From The Gates Of Dawn* (1967), *A Saucerful Of Secrets* (1968) and *Relics* (1971). *House of de Sade* frequently features the foreboding drum sequence of 'Set The Controls For The Heart Of The Sun', an ominous-sounding track that builds on diatonic progression towards frenzied percussion and then opens out into mimicked 'tweaked-out' space sounds. Additionally, Davian employs the eerie high-pitched notes, oscillators, feedback and guitar distortions from *A Saucerful Of Secrets*. *House of de Sade* uses portions of 'Astronomy Domine's lyrical lines to heighten the impact of sexual interactions. Also featured are the prominent Middle Eastern-style organ melody and creepy, horror-film-like male whispers of the title lyrics of 'Careful With That Axe, Eugene'.

House of de Sade opens with the strange, almost birdlike shrieks of 'Astronomy Domine' and a night-time shot of a haunted house set amidst shadowy tree branches to set the stage for the horror-film adventure. In a cut to an interior house scene, actress Vanessa Del Rio (playing Lucille McLain) receives a phone call inviting her to a seance at the haunted house. She, in turn, calls a friend, who is engaged in an orgy and who agrees to bring her partners along that night. The sequence then cuts back and forth between an extended sexual number featuring Lucille and her partner Brad (played by David Williams) and the increasingly graphic orgy scene.

The sequence between Lucille and Brad depicts rough fellatio/intercourse sonically accompanied by extenuated guitar slides. Intercut with this is a montage of multi-couple orgy and close-up graphic vaginal penetration shots. The orgy participants enact various poses accompanied by low-volume, far-off, 'outer-space' sounds and intermittent shrieks and screams, which mirror the use of 'Astronomy Domine' in the film's opening. Midway towards Brad's climax, his rough sex talk combines with loud female moans in a sharp, aggressive sonic jolt that jarringly overcuts between the Lucille/Brad and the orgy scenes. High-pitched guitar slides segue to the distorted shrieks to create heightened psychedelic intensity, and the two scenes culminate in a double ejaculation montage. The shot immediately cuts back to Lucille and Brad, who begin another round, accompanied by a barely audible repeat of the 'Astronomy Domine' shrieks and twitters. The intense drumming and organ of 'Set The Controls For The Heart Of The Sun' then accompany feverish sequences depicting cunnilingus, slapping of Lucille's flesh and her resulting cries, which intensify in the lead-in to the first sadie-max scene.

House of de Sade's first S/M sequence depicts Brad's domination of Lucille through use of a dog collar and chain leash as she performs fellatio. Actress Del Rio, who gained acclaim as the first Hispanic American porn star, performs the S/M scene with a physical presence and bearing that would seem to contradict her submissive role. As Landis and Clifford note, "With House of DeSade, Domination Blue, and Night of Submission, Vanessa Del Rio perfected her wild style approach toward heavy bondage and discipline scenes"[21] In most of Del Rio's S/M numbers in the film, cries and moans of pleasure dominate in contrast to the seemingly pleasureless punishing screams and asceticism of the *Story of O* sequences. The sounds of flesh being slapped bring louder moans against a backdrop of mild 'outer-space' distortions. Guitar rumble, organ progression and sustained drumming build together to create a continuous underlying tension, but are regularly drowned out by the escalating free-floating groans that aurally mark Lucille's increasing arousal.

The first sadie-max scene includes a sequence of graphic anal penetration. As the intercourse intensifies, the shot is accompanied by Waters's unmistakable primal scream from 'Careful With That Axe, Eugene', a track first performed by Pink Floyd under the title 'Murderistic Women'. The song was later recorded as 'Come In Number 51, Your Time Is Up' for use in Michelangelo Antonioni's high-profile cinematic flop, *Zabriskie Point* (1970). Waters's piercing scream is featured in the *Zabriskie Point* trailer accompanied by a rapid-fire montage of images of late 1960s American capitalist culture, including exploding consumer goods (such as a refrigerator) spreading in extended slow motion against a desert backdrop. The scream creates the sonic effect for a figurative car crash of images, culminating in an abrupt vertiginous pan across a mass free-love orgy in California's Death Valley. Five years after the release of Antonioni's film, *House of de Sade* used the same masculine scream to heighten and primalize the horror-house shocks of orgy coupling and sexual taboo. In this respect, Davian's sound use stands in interesting (and relatively isolated) counterpoint to the typical and typifying female horror-movie scream critiqued by Brophy and the aural centrality of female cries identified in Williams's analysis as sonically figuring (otherwise invisible) pleasures in hardcore. Davian's particular use of these 'masculine' screams invites interpretation as a kind of sonic emanation of Bataille's orgasmic "little deaths."[22] In the case of *House of de Sade* these "deaths" are delivered at the hands of a symbolically murderistic and physically man-eating Del Rio.

The last set of sexual sequences takes place at the haunted house itself. First, Lucille is depicted seductively undressing in her bedroom, where she is harassed in a hallucinatory scene. A hunchbacked butler masturbates as he peeps on her, accompanied by the dramatic dissonance of distorted guitar and crashing cymbal that erupt as part of a surprise ejaculation. Seeking solace from her friends (who are having sex in the next room), Lucille commences a threesome. Prior to leaving for the haunted house, Lucille had been fitted with a chastity belt by Brad, in response to which she gives a conspiratorial wink to the camera and secretes away the key. In the threesome, Lucille effortlessly casts the chastity belt aside so that she may be soothed by her sexual encounter. The gesture provides a striking contrast between O's shackled progression, which demands her rigid psychic and bodily compliance as an objectified pain-aestheticized body, and the powerfully active physicality and apparent pleasure of Lucille's self-empowered sexual encounter.

House of de Sade's final seance scene combines Davian's established sound techniques in a cacophonous denouement of S/M torture sounds, cries, exhortations and lyrical psychedelia. As the group gathers to raise the spirit of de Sade, a bell tolls and Brad exhorts: "Help me bring back the spirit of one of the most notorious sex fiends, the lustful Marquis de Sade!" Lucille, Brad, and the butler then disappear from the table. Once again, the sexual number is structured as a montage between the rough S/M domination of Lucille, in this case with numchucks, leather whip, nipple clamps and feather duster, and increasingly graphic orgy sex. Brad calls out, "Pleasure, pain, sex, lust!" Lucille's moans and screams are interspersed with her words "Oh Master, I'll be your slave for eternity." Increasingly loud repetition of the distorted sound twitters and progressive organ phrases culminate with the lyrics:

> Lime and limpid green ... a second scene ... a fight between ... the blue you once knew. Floating down ... the sound resounds around ... the icy waters underground.

The scene continues to crescendo in a massive orgy sequence accompanied by various screams, slaps, feminine cries, masculine moans, drumming sounds and a second double ejaculation scene. Brad then dramatically removes his S/M mask and casts off his de Sade persona, saying, "So you have found the truth of the Marquis de Sade. His pleasures and pain lie within all of you."

Davian's idiosyncratic S/M staging in *House of de Sade* leaves surprising traces of 1970s female empowerment projected through the dark lens of comedic horror-show. Musical sounds sampled from the Pink Floyd repertoire sonically suture Davian's extended staging of 1970s-style paranoid/ecstatic sexual tripping. The sonic architecture of an enveloping odyssey is once again invoked. However, in contrast to *Story of O*, *House of de Sade*'s sounds trace a parallel undercurrent of dark masculine angst. Across Davian's films, female dominatrix scenes and Del Rio's ultimately 'dominant' submissive performances unfold in tandem with the dramatic refrains of this psychedelic masculinized paranoia. Davian's lowbrow cultural form is consequently rendered more intricate by the selective layering of affective sonic modes from the (sonically complex) countercultural moment of the film's making.

Conclusion

> "I am not a pornographer. I am a dreamer." (Just Jaeckin)

Story of O and *House of de Sade* reflect conflictual moments of 1970s sexual and feminist liberation. In contrast to *Story of O*'s borrowing from high-culture literary erotics (made more popularly palatable through its Alice-in-Wonderland-style narrativization), Davian's work prefers the lowbrow, cheap and dramatically intensified thrills of sadie-max sexual violence. *Story of O* uses the classic art-house cinema strategy of deploying musical/sonic/narrative effects to aestheticize and eroticize its violence and subjugation. The combined sense of the unreality of the sexual pleasure with the psychic reality of torture/pain provides the necessary intellectualization of these erotics to create the high-culture fantasy of the film. Ironically, Jaeckin's signature soft-focus aesthetic would ultimately become the model for what Andrews identifies as the "debased middle brow" form predominant in mass-market commercial video porn (Andrews, 2006: 31–42). Davian's work, meanwhile, offers a shadow discourse to the mainstreaming and "aristocratising" impulse Penley identifies as emergent in 1970s mainstream heterosexual porn films such as *Behind the Green Door* (Mitchell Brothers, 1972) and *The Opening of Misty Beethoven* (Radley Metzger, 1975). Indeed, Davian's work injects a degree of the (albeit dark) lowbrow humour that Penley associates with an earlier generation of stag films. Sound usage in Davian's films propels drama, excitement and psychedelic paranoia and/or acts as a darkly humorous counterpoint to sexual interaction. In contrast to the sound and/or narrative aspirations of emerging mainstream heterosexual S/M porn, such as *The Image* (Radley Metzger, 1974) and *Story of Joanna* (Gerard Damiano, 1975),[23] Davian's sonic architecture 'samples' distinctly vernacular cultural references to construct a darkly humorous, visceral and even primordial titillation, creating what might be argued to be a fourth category of S/M porn cinema premised on a trash-art roughie aesthetic.

Story of O's and *House of de Sade*'s respective use of an 'outspoken' woman narrator and primal masculine screams reflects their own complex registers of the pervading sexual politics of the period. If, as Paulhan opines, "fairy tales are erotic novels for children", both Jaeckin and Davian's works would suggest that, within the context of 1970s sexual liberation, film sound cues may offer unexpectedly productive terrain to explore the dark and complex interior of particular formative moments of western mass culture's collective (hetero-)sexual dreaming and, in particular, the infancy of its modern impulse towards sexual liberalization.

Notes

1. The specific film text versions referred to in this discussion are *Story of O* (Just Jaeckin, 1975; Somerville House Releasing DVD edition, 2000; *Emmanuelle* (Just Jaeckin, 1974; Canal+ Image International widescreen DVD edition, 1998; *House of de Sade* (Joe Davian, 1975), *Fetishes of Monique* (Joe Davian, 1976) and *Revenge and Punishment* (Joe Davian, 1977), all on Alpha Blue Archives Joe Davian Box Set Edition, 2005.
2. The overwhelming success of *Emmanuelle* was followed by over thirty-five screen and home-release sequels (and/or variations) between 1975 and 2006.
3. Gainsbourg later provided the soundtrack for *Goodbye Emmanuelle (1977)* – one of numerous sequels of the original film not directed by Jaeckin.
4. O is dramatically escorted by motorboat to the Commodore's soirée in Brittany. She sits nude, wearing only a mask of owl feathers as the wind blows through the mask to the musical sounds of her original Roissy discovery theme. She arrives at the gathering to be gazed upon by mesmerized onlookers. The voice-over inquires: "Was she made of stone? Of wax?" Reage originally wrote the scene inspired by the purported escapades of surrealist Leonar Fini, who had arrived

similarly adorned to a Surrealist ball thrown by the Dada movement's founder, Tristan Tzara.
5. Dworkin's *Woman Hating* (1974), for example, argues that female characterization in narratives that range from literary pornography, including *Story of O* and *The Image*, to children's fairy tales such as *Cinderella* and *Snow White*, exemplify the feminine cultural position as fundamentally sadomasochistic.
6. From an interview with Just Jaeckin conducted by Nathanial Thompson at http://dvdmaniacs.net/features/interview_just_jaeckin.html; accessed 12 February, 2008.
7. Paulhan was the clandestine lover of Pauline Reage (the pen name of Dominique Aury); he was her colleague at the Gallimard publishing house, and an esteemed member of the Académie française. Aury, who did not reveal her true identity until forty years after the novella's release, originally penned the story as a series of love letters to rekindle Paulhan's waning romantic/sexual affections. His rather cryptic introduction to the book begins with a disturbing parable of freed Barbadian slaves who beg to be taken back into bondage.
8. From the interview with Just Jaeckin conducted by Nathanial Thompson at http://dvdmaniacs.net/features/interview_just_jaeckin.html; accessed 12 February 2008.
9. Lelong went on to work as foley artist and sound effects person in over 200 'respected' mainstream films, including several James Bond movies such as *For Your Eyes Only* (1981) and *Octopussy* (1983), as well as international hits such as *Three Colours: Blue* (1993) and *Three Colours: Red* (1994), *The Tango Lesson* (1997) and *Amelie* (2001). Quaglio later designed sound for *Microcosmos* (1996), *The Triplets of Belleville* (2003) and *March of the Penguins* (2005), among many others.
10. His *Switched-on Bach* (1968), in particular, was considered to be a 'classic' by synthesizer aficionados.
11. Thanks to Philip Hayward for providing information on Camison's use of analogue synthesizers (personal communication, April 2009).
12. M. Hasan (nd), 'Review of Story of O soundtrack CD', at http://musicfromthemovies.com/review.asp?ID=4888; accessed on 4 January 2008.
13. *Ibid*.
14. While Jaeckin does choose to present several of the whipping sequences with a "fixed stare at the flesh", his gaze, however, infuses the scene with an 'arty' aesthetic in which soft-focus lighting and photographic technique frame Clery's body as art/fashion object and the single most 'consumable' aspect of the sadomasochistic scene. One of the most striking examples of this is a later whipping scene in which O instigates her own 'torture' at the hands of Sir Stephen's sadistic maid Nora in order to make a 'fallen suitor' comprehend the depth of her masochistic 'investments'. Appearing face-on to the camera and strapped in cuffs on the whipping dais, O throws back her sweat-soaked hair in a highly stylized posture of 'victorious depravity'. Clery's eroticized head toss and shining nude body mimic current formulaic predatory-eyed fashion poses. The camera's

gaze observes the criss-cross lacerations of the whip marks, but corporeal flinch is displaced in an all-encompassing spectacle of O as 'art'/object/fetish.
15. Samois was later adopted as the name of a high-profile San Francisco-based lesbian-feminist BDSM organization in existence from 1978 to 1983. Key members of the group included Pat Califia and Gayle Rubin.
16. 'Writer of O' (Pola Rapaport, 2004), in Zeitgeist Films DVD edition, 2006.
17. The controversial Meese Commission was appointed in 1986 by then US President Ronald Reagan to investigate the history and social impact of pornography. Its report was heavily criticized at the time for its perceived bias in minimizing evidence which indicated that pornography was not dangerous.
18. B. Landis and M. Clifford, 'The Avon dynasty', online at http://www.alphabluearchives.com/store/index.php?main_page=news_article&article_id=3; accessed 24 January 2008.
19. *Ibid.*
20. Ironically, the films' low-budget aesthetics, amateur performances and (near-'religious') mandates of Sadean fulfilment resonate in a contemporary context as the 'satanic' flipside of a film such as *Hell House*, a 2002 documentary about Christian fundamentalist stagings of 'morality' skits in haunted houses. *Hell House* skits produce similarly bloody and gynaecological (though obviously non-pornographic) numbers such as the "abortion play". (With a strange rhetorical resonance, *Hell House* teen actors clamour to become 'abortion girl' or 'suicide girl', just as the actresses of the hardcore genre occasionally gained reductive monikers according to the acts they were willing to perform. For example, Vanessa Del Rio was known as the 'anal queen' for her regular performances in extended anal sex scenes.)
21. B. Landis and M. Clifford, 'The Avon dynasty', online at http://www.alphabluearchives.com/store/index.php?main_page=news_article&article_id=3; accessed 24 January 2008.
22. See Bataille's discussion of the orgasm as "little death" in *Eroticism: Death and Sensuality*.
23. *Story of Joanna* was reputedly a pseudo-adaptation offering a hardcore American parallel for the *Story of O*. Damiano's film clearly evinces the "aristocratising" impulse outlined by Penley, featuring visual references to 'arty' expressionist horror film and a highly idiosyncratic nude ballet duet, which showcases Terri Hall (Joanna), a former professional ballerina for the Stuttgart Ballet Company.

References

Andrews, D. (2006), *Soft in the Middle: The Contemporary Softcore Feature in Its Contexts*, Columbus: Ohio State University Press.
Arsan, E. (1971), *Emmanuelle*, New York: Grove Press.
Brophy, P. (ed) (1999), *Cinesonic*, Sydney: Australian Film, Radio, and Television School.
Chion, M. (1994), *Audio-Vision: Sound on Screen*, translated and edited by Claudia Gorbman, New York: Columbia University Press.

Chion, M. (1999), *The Voice in Cinema*, translated and edited by Claudia Gorbman, New York: Columbia University Press.

Clifford, M., and Landis, B. (2002), *Sleazoid Express: A Mind-twisting Tour Through the Grindhouse Cinema of Times Square*, New York: Fireside.

Dworkin, A. (1974), 'Review: Woman as Victim: *Story of O*', *Feminist Studies*, 2(1), 107–11.

Hayward, S. (1993), *French National Cinema*, London: Routledge.

Jaeckin, J. (2006), *Tout Just: Souvenirs, Jaeckin, Just*, Monaco: Rocher.

McHugh, K. (2001), ' "Sounds that creep inside you": female narration and voiceover in the films of Jane Campion', *Style*, Summer; online at http://findarticles.com/p/articles/mi_m2342/is_2_35/ai_97074180/; accessed 20 June 2009.

Penley, C. (2004), 'Crackers and Whackers: The White Trashing of Porn', in L. Williams (ed.), *Porn Studies*, Durham: Duke University Press, pp. 309–33.

Reage, P. (1965), *Story of O*, New York: Grove Press.

Silverman, K. (1988), *The Acoustic Mirror*, Bloomington: Indiana University Press.

Silverman, K. (1984), 'Histoire d'O: The Construction of a Female Subject', in C. S. Vance (ed.), *Pleasure and Danger: Exploring Female Sexuality*, Boston: Routledge, pp. 320–49.

Sontag, S. (1969), *Styles of Radical Will*, New York: Farrar, Straus, and Giroux.

Williams, L. (1989), *Hard Core: Power, Pleasure, and the 'Frenzy of the Visible'*, Berkeley: University of California Press.

5 The Peculiar 'Love' Music in Oshima's *Ai no korida*

James Wierzbicki

A notable difference between Asian cinema and its western counterpart has to do with the availability to Asian film-makers, and to Asian audiences, of not one but two distinct bodies of musical 'code'. The soundtrack for a western film can feature music in a wide variety of styles, but almost invariably these styles stem from a single tradition. A western film's underscore might be written in the symphonic idiom of the so-called classical style that has prevailed since the mid-1930s and which to a large extent still holds sway; it might be old-fashioned or modernist, it might borrow directly from the rich treasury of classical music that over the years has somehow come to be 'iconic' for western listeners, it might be cast in a historically specific genre — jazz or rock, hip-hop or country and western — that is contemporaneous either with the film itself or with the setting of its narrative. Similarly diverse can be the western film's source music. But except in those rare cases when a western film-maker is deliberately attempting to violate the norm, or, more often, when he or she momentarily strives to illustrate the obvious 'foreignness' of a certain situation, the mix of music that decorates or accompanies the typical western film — almost by necessity, on the assumption that among the film's goals is connection with the target audience — *always* stems from what may be described as a single musical culture.

By contrast, Asian film-makers have always had the option of selecting their music from a pair of musical cultures. One is that of the West, which had made inroads into such countries as Japan, China and India by the end of the nineteenth century and in most large Asian cities was already well established by the time of the introduction of sound film. The other musical culture, unique to each Asian nation, involves the accompaniments that for centuries had been associated with narrative song and various forms, both popular and courtly, of theatrical entertainments.

Faced with the choice of how to accompany their sound films, Asian film-makers for the most part opted for the musical mode that seemed harmonious with the new medium itself; the sound film was a 'modern' invention, and thus in most cases it was fitted with 'modern', that is, western, music. Writing on Japanese cinema of the 1940s and 1950s, Donald Richie observed that even the samurai films and other historical epics tended to feature western-style scores. The reason for this was that

> no matter how exotic the style and action of the period film appears to foreign audiences, to the Japanese this film style is a part of the realist tradition, adopted from the West and therefore without connection to the classical Japanese drama. Because so much Japanese classical music exists only in relation to the classic drama, the use of this music in [realistic] films must present a severe stylistic clash. (Richie and Anderson, 1958: 9)

This assessment still applies, not just to Japanese film but to Asian film in general. However rich a score might be in 'local colour' (especially in terms of instrumental timbre and performance style), its functionality vis-à-vis the film narrative by and large holds to western models. Exceptions fall into two basic categories. One of them involves particular scenes in which both subject matter and action eschew western realism and instead celebrate, or allude to, a venerable theatrical tradition. (Richie cites the Noh-based ghost segment in Akira Kurosawa's otherwise realistic 1957 *Kumonosu-Jo*, a retelling of Shakespeare's Macbeth story known in the West as *Throne of Blood*.) The other exception, much rarer, involves entire films whose style of acting and presentation might well be international but whose dramatic essence is so much 'of' a particular culture that the only appropriate music is indigenous.

Nagisa Oshima's 1976 *Ai no korida*[1] (愛のコリーダ) seems to be an example of this latter sort, a film whose state-of-the-art production values are thoroughly western yet whose content – quite apart from the obvious *mise-en-scène* – is profoundly, and thus for westerners perhaps inscrutably, 'Japanese'. Indeed, in the West *Ai no korida* probably ranks high among the most misunderstood films of recent decades. With its numerous graphic depictions of sexual activity, *Ai no korida* of course has a reputation for being pornographic.[2] But it is hardly representative of the titillating genre known as *pinku eiga* ('pink film', the Japanese euphemism for softcore porn). Although this might be difficult for first-time viewers to grasp, the film's subject matter is neither sex nor sexual obsession; its focus, rather, is the longing for an aspect of Japanese culture that began to wane with the start of the so-called Meiji restoration (in 1868) and which by the time of the film's setting (1936) had for all intents and purposes disappeared.

Reflecting the film's explicit erotic content but also paying homage to Roland Barthes's essays on Japan, the familiar western title is *In the Realm of the Senses*;[3] significantly, the Japanese title translates as 'Love's Corrida', the latter word suggesting not simply an arena in general but specifically the arena of the bullfight, in which the eponymous protagonist almost by definition is doomed even before the fight begins. Certainly doomed is the film's central male character, a man who manages to sustain his earnest, yet hopeless, struggle only with the help of an arguably psychopathic partner. Taken as a whole – with its detailed enactments of intercourse, fellatio and cunnilingus regarded as incidental elements of a much broader picture – *Ai no korida* emerges as a film not so much about sex as about wistful memories of a still-remembered time when, in Japanese culture, sex for the sake of sheer pleasure was regarded as something quite ordinary. Not surprisingly, the film resonates with music both traditional and newly composed that evokes a distinctly Japanese past.

Ai no korida tells the more-or-less true story of the star-crossed relationship between Kichizo Ishida, the 42-year-old owner of a restaurant in Tokyo's Nakano area, and Sada Abe, a 31-year-old waitress at the restaurant. Kichizo regarded Sada as sexually attractive, albeit no more so than any of the other young females he encountered in the course of his daily activities; Sada, on the other hand, regarded Kichizo's attentions towards her as somehow special, and thus she made herself entirely responsive to what she perceived as her boss's desires and needs. After Kichizo's wife discovered the liaison, Kichizo and Sada ran off to an inn in Tokyo's Ogu district, where for several weeks they engaged in almost non-stop sex. Their affair ended quite gruesomely, with Sada first killing Kichizo (by accident, after ever-escalating efforts to heighten his orgasm by means of strangulation)[4] and then, after he was dead, severing those of his body parts that apparently meant most to her. A few days after Kichizo's death Sada was found wandering the streets of Tokyo, with his blood-drenched penis and testicles clutched tenderly to her bosom.

Sada Abe was tried for murder and sentenced to prison; she was released in 1941. Her official statement – to the effect that all she did was done for the sake of 'love'– obviously struck a chord with the Japanese public. Interviews and articles depicting her not as a sexual deviant but as a sympathetic figure began to appear in the mid-1940s; throughout the 1950s and 1960s she worked as a waitress, a maid and, finally, the proprietress of a small bar. It is not known what became of her after she vanished from the public view in 1969, and perhaps that still on-going mystery helped transform her into something of a folk legend. Before Oshima's film, Sada Abe's story was featured in Teruo Ishii's 1969 *Meiji, Taisho, Showa; Ryoki onna Hanzaishi* ('History of Women's Grotesque Crimes') and Noboru Tanaka's 1975 *Jitsuroku Abe Sada* ('A Woman Called Sada Abe'); decades later, the story figured in Nobuhiko Obayashi's 1998 *SADA* and Sachi Hamano's *Heiseiban Abe Sada: Anta ga Hoshi'i* ('Sada Abe in the Heisei Era: I Want You'), and it was the inspiration for the 1995–96 serialized novel *Shitsurakuen* ('Lost Paradise') (Hori, 2005: 458–9).[5]

Sada Abe had worked as a prostitute earlier in her life, but by 1936 – except for maintaining a professional relationship with a schoolmaster in a distant city – she had basically renounced that line of work. Indeed, as portrayed by Oshima, by the time of her first encounter with Kichizo she had developed an attitude towards sex that was almost prudish. In the film's first scene she is enticed to join a fellow waitress in spying on Kichizo having sex with his wife; while the other waitress plays the part of a snickering voyeur, Sada only stares, as if the observed activity leaves her somehow numbed. Later, once the affair with Kichizo is well under way, and after Kichizo has subtly expressed concern that her interest in sex seems unusually intense, she admits to him that years before she had consulted a doctor to see if, in that regard, there was "something wrong with me". By this time in the film, it is clear that whereas Kichizo is an innocent hedonist Sada is a possessive nymphomaniac.

It is likewise clear, or becomes so soon enough, that Sada and Kichizo regard sex very differently. During their frequent sex acts, Kichizo is depicted as being involved not in 'love-making' but simply in fucking. Sada, on the other hand, is shown plunging ever deeper into states of rapture, with vocalized expressions of pleasure – as well as articulations of what their shared sexual experience means – coming only from her. On two occasions Sada casually suggests that Kichizo rape someone (a passer-by on a rainy street, a maid who has got on her nerves); Kichizo declines, but he does acquiesce to Sada's suggestion that he have intercourse with an elderly geisha while Sada watches. These scenes contrast strangely with Sada's increasingly insistent message to Kichizo, this being the idea that his genitals, so long as they spurt not just sperm but 'love', are for her and her alone. As she straddles him two-thirds of the way through the film, she toys with a pair of scissors and playfully announces that she will "cut it off" if he is ever unfaithful to her; later, after Kichizo visits his home and dutifully has sex with his wife, Sada attacks him with a knife.

The lingering close-ups of sharp blades in close proximity to Kichizo's tumescent penis are enough to make anyone apprehensive; indeed, Kichizo seems bothered by the implications, yet he opts to ignore them in light of the pleasures that Sada so consistently has to offer. Sexually a 'bull', Kichizo of his own volition has entered a dangerous arena from which he likely knows there can be no escape. For the viewer cognizant of the film's Japanese title, the bloody climax of *Ai no korida* is no real surprise.

Ai no korida features a rather large amount of music; its disposition of cues is given in Figure 5.1, with diegetic music shown below and extra-diegetic music shown above a timeline that represents the film's entire duration (of 100 minutes and 42 seconds).[6]

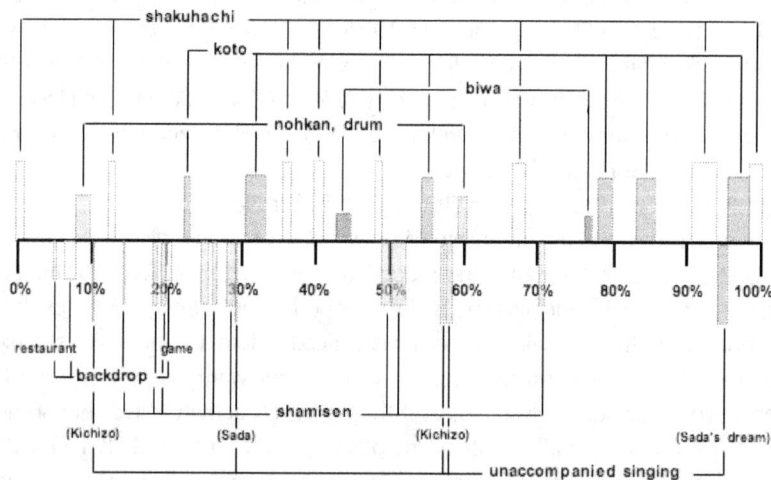

Figure 5.1 The musical cues in *Ai no korida*.

The first two diegetic cues constitute a barely audible 'backdrop' that presumably emanates from live musicians (playing traditional Japanese instruments, but in the popular style of the 1930s) in the off-screen dining room of Kichizo's restaurant. A short while later, similarly inconsequential 'backdrop' music is presented in the form of a song that two of the restaurant employees sing as they leisurely engage, on screen, in a game involving a bouncing rubber ball.

A second group of diegetic cues involves unaccompanied singing by Kichizo or Sada, for the most part merely incidental but towards the end of the film – as Sada 'lovingly' strangles Kichizo to death – part of a dreamlike flashback to, apparently, her early childhood. The subtitles give English translations of the lyrics only for Kichizo's initial 'flirtation' songs and for Sada's 'dream song'.[7] In the flirtation scene, when Kichizo directly approaches Sada the day after their initial encounter in the restaurant's kitchen, he first sings (in translation) "If you fear getting burned, girl, don't play with fire/Little girl, there's a fire", and then, as he reaches under Sada's kimono to fondle her crotch, "This path is filled with hidden treasure/Leading man to eternal pleasure". At the climax of the strangulation scene, when the image shifts from a close-up of Sada's intense face to a distant shot of a little girl playing some sort of chasing game with a slightly older male figure amidst the deserted seats of a stadium, the girl repeatedly sings "Where are you now?" and the male voice repeatedly answers "I'm not there yet"; the song abruptly ends and, still within the dream sequence, an adult female voice cries out: "Kichi-san!!!" The other instances of unaccompanied singing occur as Kichizo waits for Sada to attend him (at 10:38), as she caresses his penis (at 29:55), and later, after he has paid a visit to his home, as he idly shaves (at 57:38) and then just as idly engages in intercourse with his wife (at 58:13).

Significantly, most of the diegetic cues, nine in all, involve traditional Japanese music featuring the sharply twangy plucked sound of the banjolike *shamisen*. Except in three cases, all of this music is performed on screen by geishas who have been hired by Kichizo, doubtless at considerable expense, to entertain him as he indulges in the relaxed pleasures that in the pre-Meiji era were the middle-class norm but which by 1936 were regarded as throwbacks to the past. The third exception occurs 29 minutes into the film, during a scene in which a male *kyogen* dancer performs a comic routine in the aftermath of Kichizo's and Sada's celebration of a mock wedding; it is remarkable only because the source of the accompanying *shamisen* music in this case is not visible, the four geishas who earlier had assisted in the celebration being shown by this time all quite naked, in various poses of post-orgy relaxation, while a fully clothed Sada performs fellatio on Kichizo. The first two exceptions, which form a pair occurring at 18:04 and 19:11 minutes, are more dramatically interesting and, perhaps, amusing. Beginning with tentative music heard from off screen, the scene depicts Sada straddling Kichizo while at the same time attempting, with limited musical success, to perform a standard geisha song; after a brief respite during which Sada complains that she cannot perform musically and sexually at the same time, Kichizo laughs and then helps her with the singing. The purpose of the ruse, of course, is to deflect the suspicions of Kichizo's wife, who allows her old-fashioned husband to enjoy the artistry of geishas but who remains jealous of his extramarital sexual escapades. Listening from the hallway, Kichizo's wife perceives that there is something oddly 'out of tune' in this particular performance.[8]

The six other diegetic cues that feature *shamisen* are both clear in their depiction of 'source' and respectful of the geisha tradition. The first occurs (at 14:02) shortly after Sada and Kichizo have intercourse for the first time; the extra-diegetic music that accompanies the action is abruptly cut off by a knock on the door from the geisha who has been engaged for that evening; Kichizo tells her to wait a moment and then perfunctorily finishes his business with Sada; the geisha enters the room as Sada leaves; after remarking, with a twinkle in her eye, that Sada seems to be a "very attractive" young lady, the geisha begins a song to which Kichizo sings along. The next two *shamisen* songs (at 24:26 and 26:41) occur at the 'love nest' during the lavish dinner that Kichizo hosts in honour of his mock marriage to Sada; the toasts are all very formal, as is the music, but the banter that transpires makes it clear that the four attending geishas know full well what is going on. The second song ends as Kichizo starts to 'deflower' his new 'bride', and there is no music to be heard as the three older geishas – perhaps inspired by what they observe – proceed to rape their younger colleague with an elegantly carved dildo.

As noted above, the next bit of *shamisen* music (starting at 28:44) accompanies the *kyogen* dancer who entertains at what seems to be a post-dinner orgy. The next *shamisen*-accompanied scene in which the source is visible, however, does not occur until 49:49. By this time the relationship between Sada and Kichizo has intensified considerably, and the narrative suggests that Kichizo is perhaps growing physically exhausted. As an on-screen geisha plays lyrically on the *shamisen*, the main characters are shown more or less fully clothed but in a position that suggests Sada has just performed, yet again, oral sex on Kichizo. Using chopsticks, Sada inserts a slice of mushroom into her wet vagina and offers it to an apparently hungry Kichizo; in response to Kichizo's comments as to how much he enjoys the mushroom's flavour, the geisha subtly colours her playing with propulsive rhythmic figures. The *shamisen* music ends at 50:54, for no apparent reason other than that, at this point, Sada and Kichizo have started to engage in kissing and fondling. It resumes two seconds later, after the camera has lingered on the smirking face of the geisha, who obviously takes pleasure in observing the action. The new music is again lyrical, and it remains so as Kichizo, claiming that he is still hungry, takes a peeled hard-boiled egg and forcefully inserts it into Sada's vagina; as he does this he sings, and the geisha modulates her *shamisen* playing to accommodate his song's melody. Clearly in pain, Sada begs Kichizo to remove the egg, but he responds only by advising her to "push" the way a chicken would. Kichizo's singing (presumably a folksong having to do with chickens and eggs) stops abruptly when Sada does manage to expel the egg, but the *shamisen* music continues; it ends only with the change of scene, after an obviously aroused Sada makes Kichizo eat the egg and then declares: "I want you now!"

Shamisen music, again delivered by a geisha, is heard for the last time at the film's 1:10:45 point. Entering an inn room that, according to dialogue in the previous scene, fairly reeks of sex, the geisha professionally goes about her business. Her song grinds to a halt after Sada comments on how attractive Kichizo is and then casually asks the geisha: "Would you like to have him?" There is no music as Kichizo, acquiescing to Sada's bizarre suggestion, dutifully engages in intercourse with the 68-year-old geisha; nor is there music in the scene's aftermath, during which Kichizo says that having sex with the old woman was like embracing the dead body of his mother.

Taken as a whole, the diegetic music in *Ai no korida* reflects the casual attitude towards sex that was pervasive among middle-class Japanese males before the 1868 Meiji restoration. It is the aural representation of what during the Tokugawu shogunate was called *ukiyo*, or 'the floating world', a culture in which it was simply taken for granted that men of a certain status deserved amenities that included, in no particular order of hierarchy, the relaxed sipping of sake and well-brewed tea, the perhaps meditative listening to traditional songs performed by highly trained geishas, and noncommittal sex with both wives and mistresses. Like the antiquated music of which Kichizo remains so fond, sex in the bygone 'floating world' was something for connoisseurs; as represented in the hundreds of *shunga* prints that survive from the Edo period, it was supposed to be always pleasurable but never complicated.[9]

Sex with Sada, unfortunately for Kichizo, involves complications far more difficult than any he might have imagined at the start of their relationship. At first seemingly just another female who suits his physical needs, Sada quickly emerges as a woman who regards sex as the antidote for a psychic poison that courses through her veins. Her jealousy and possessiveness are symptoms not of love but, rather, of the fear of losing the one thing that temporarily eases her inner pain; her torment only increases as she becomes addicted to what Kichizo's penis has to offer, and thus she pushes harder and harder for her own satisfaction. While Kichizo's consistently detached attitude towards sex is coolly enough represented by diegetic *shamisen* music, Sada's volatile attitudes towards the same human activity – always intense, and laden with emotional baggage that neither Sada nor Kichizo can even begin to unpack – are expressed through the film's extra-diegetic music.

The extra-diegetic cues are the work of Minoru Miki, a modernist composer who had been trained in western techniques and then, beginning in the mid-1960s, when he founded the Ensemble Nipponia, became a leader in a Tokyo-based movement to synthesize western and Japanese musical aesthetics as well as sounds (Miki, 1989).[10] Holding to the Oshima-mandated idea that the soundtrack for the film should feature only *hogaku* ('Japanese music'), not *yogaku* ('foreign music'), but by and large steering clear of the *shamisen* which is so closely related to the film's narrative, Miki concocted cues involving four distinct sonorities (shown above the timeline in Figure 5.1).

Derived from the accompaniments to action scenes in the kabuki theatre, the first extra-diegetic cue after the credits highlights the small transverse flute called the *nohkan* in combination with iterations from a *daiko* drum, with occasional punctuations from a *shamisen*. The shrill sound is initially heard during the brightly lit morning scene in which Kichizo playfully 'attacks' Sada as she scrubs a floor at his house; the same sound, and essentially the same music, is heard again late at night after Kichizo has returned home and Sada, having secretly observed him and his wife having sex, determinedly attacks him with a large kitchen knife.

The other sonority heard on only two occasions, and similarly relating to elements of both locale and dramatic situation, is that of the *biwa*, a lute-like instrument whose sharp twang resembles that of the *shamisen* to a certain extent but whose fretted construction and array of strings (four, as opposed to the *shamisen*'s three) lend themselves to a more virtuosic idiom. Whereas the *shamisen* has a long association not just with theatrical music but also with relatively simple ditties of the sort presented diegetically throughout the film, the lofty *biwa* tradition involves bardic songs whose narrative content, accompanied onomatopoetically by harsh tremolos, percussive snaps and fast flourishes, often included descriptions of epic battles. Suiting its sophisticated heritage, the *biwa* is reserved for the two scenes of Sada's visits to her schoolmaster client, an older man she respectfully calls "*sensei*". From a distance, Kichizo derides the schoolmaster as an effete intellectual and likely blames him, and his ilk, for Japan's modernization; appropriately, the *biwa* music in *Ai no korida* is harsh and bitter.

Much gentler music is heard in the half-dozen cues scored for the zither-like *koto* and the eight cues (including those that accompany the opening and closing credit sequences) scored for a pair of end-blown flutes called *shakuhachis*. In gesture as well as timbre this music has a consistently sensuous quality that, for a western listener, perhaps makes it seem apt for a film heavily laden with sex scenes.[11] At the same time, the very softness of this music sometimes puts it strangely at odds with the sex scenes' real content, which increasingly has to do not with love or erotic pleasure but with emotional disturbance.

The first *koto* cue (at 21:59) accompanies the seemingly romantic carriage ride that brings Kichizo and Sada to their 'love nest', but it follows immediately after a fantasy sequence in which Sada, after witnessing Kichizo and his wife having passionate intercourse at their home, imagines herself slashing the wife's throat. The next *koto* cue (at 31:04) is heard the morning after the mock wedding feast; the scene begins with Sada quietly singing to herself as she strokes and licks Kichizo's erect penis; awakening from his sleep, Kichizo bemusedly asks if she has been "holding it" all night; he says that he has to urinate, but Sada demands he "take her" right there and then. The *koto* music lasts almost three minutes as Kichizo, knowing very well that his full bladder will not allow him to orgasm, performs cunnilingus on her. As with the first *koto* cue, the third one (at 54:48) suggests a romantic situation; it follows the 'love nest' scene during which Sada, scissors in hand, warns Kichizo that she will "cut it off" if he ever "makes

The Peculiar 'Love' Music in Oshima's *Ai no korida*   97

love" to another woman, and it serves as accompaniment for their rain-soaked late-night walk back to Kichizo's home (ironically, it is during this romantic stroll that Sada casually suggests that he rape a female passer-by).

The last three *koto* cues come during the extended final scenes at the inn, and they all support moments during which Kichizo and Sada explore the idea – introduced by Kichizo – that controlled strangulation "is said" to increase one's sexual pleasure. The first of these (starting at 1:18:30 and lasting 2 minutes and 10 seconds) accompanies conversation; the initial, largely unsuccessful, attempt at a 'strangle fuck' is conducted without music. The next *koto* cue begins at 1:23:58, after Kichizo suggests they try again, this time with his hands tied and the scarf around his neck pulled tighter; it ends almost two and half minutes later, as Kichizo, after being strangled nearly to death, gasps the words: "Whatever gives you pleasure gives me happiness."

The last bit of *koto* music – possibly the most disturbing cue in the entire film – is heard after Sada emerges from her reverie and realizes that she has, indeed, killed Kichizo; sounding just as tender as in its earlier variations, the music (beginning at 1:36:19 and lasting almost 3 minutes) accompanies Sada's calm sawing off of Kichizo's genitalia and fades only after a voice-over narrator explains that everyone in Japan, after Sada's arrest, was "surprised to find how happy she was".

This last instance of *koto* music segues into the *shakuhachi* duet that plays through the final credit roll and which, with eight iterations throughout the film, serves as *Ai no korida*'s dominant aural motif. Like the *koto* cues, the *shakuhachi* cues, in keeping with traditional compositional practice for both of these 'high-art' instruments (Malm, 1959: 180–1), involve statements of and variations on a single theme. But whereas the *koto* music is for the most part figurational, the *shakuhachi* music is solidly melodic and thus for western ears more easily memorable. Although some of the *shakuhachi* music involves virtuosic spin-offs, the foregrounded cues feature only the basic material as presented during the opening credits and transcribed in Figure 5.2.

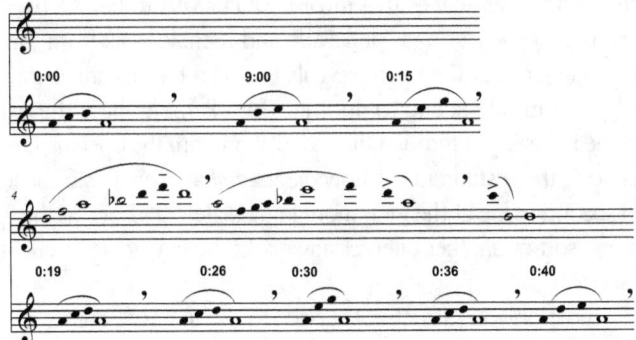

Figure 5.2 The *shakuhachi* duet that underscores the title sequence of *Ai no korida*

As noted, this music occurs no less than eight times during the course of the film. That it is cast in the Japanese *in* scale, with flattened second, third, sixth and seventh steps, identical to the western mode known as Phrygian that since early in the nineteenth century has been stereotypically associated with 'Spanish' music, is perhaps just coincidence. Had the music featured the *shakuhachi*'s other preferred scale – the *yo* scale that corresponds with western music's Dorian mode – it might well have come across as just as touching, just as melancholy.

In any case, this music recurs throughout *Ai no korida*. Its first and last iterations, accompanying the opening and closing credits, in effect 'frame' the film. In between, the music for two *shakuhachis* is heard as Kichizo first fully engages with Sada (at 12:03); as Kichizo expresses his initial concern that Sada is perhaps unusually demanding (at 36:09); as the two of them, upon Sada's financially necessitated departure to rendezvous with her "*sensei*" client, exchange odour-filled kimonos (at 40:16); as Sada tearfully explains how during her session with the schoolmaster she thought only of Kichizo (at 48:47); as Sada tentatively attempts a 'strangle fuck' involving not a scarf but simply her own hands (at 1:07:04); and, finally (at 1:31:32), as Sada launches with all her strength into the strangulation that results in Kichizo's death.

During the final credit roll the audience member, after witnessing close-ups of Kichizo's posthumous dismemberment, hears exactly the same music that introduced Sada's ostensibly prudish character. Vis-à-vis sex, Sada, as Kichizo would soon enough discover, is much more than at first she seems. And thus it is hard to say precisely what, in terms of psychology, is represented by *Ai no korida*'s recurrent *shakuhachi* theme. Depending upon how at any point in the film an audience member relates to the female protagonist, the *shakuhachi* music can be heard either as an articulation of Sada's blissful dreams of fulfilment or an expression of her abject loneliness. Like Sada's character, the nuances of the Japanese *in* scale are infinitely complex.

Most of the music in *Ai no korida* serves a structural purpose. Figure 5.3 shows the film's narrative divided into segments that represent, along with the opening and closing credits, the four scenes at Kichizo's restaurant and house, the eight scenes at the 'love nest' inn, the two scenes that involve Sada's visit to her "*sensei*" client, and the single transition scene during which Sada and Kichizo walk from the inn back to Kichizo's home. A glance at the figure reveals how in a few instances music serves as a 'sound bridge' from one scene to another (for example, how the extra-diegetic *shakuhachi* theme is sustained through the modulation from the opening credit sequence to the first scene at the restaurant, or how diegetic *shamisen* music carries over from the first to the second scene at the inn); more immediately, a glance at the figure reveals how music of one sort or another often clearly marks the beginning or ending of various of the film's scenes.

The music's most obvious structural service to the film, of course, is the 'framing' provided by the *shakuhachi* theme that underscores the opening and closing credits. The subtler – and thus more intriguing – structural service that music offers the film comes

The Peculiar 'Love' Music in Oshima's *Ai no korida* 99

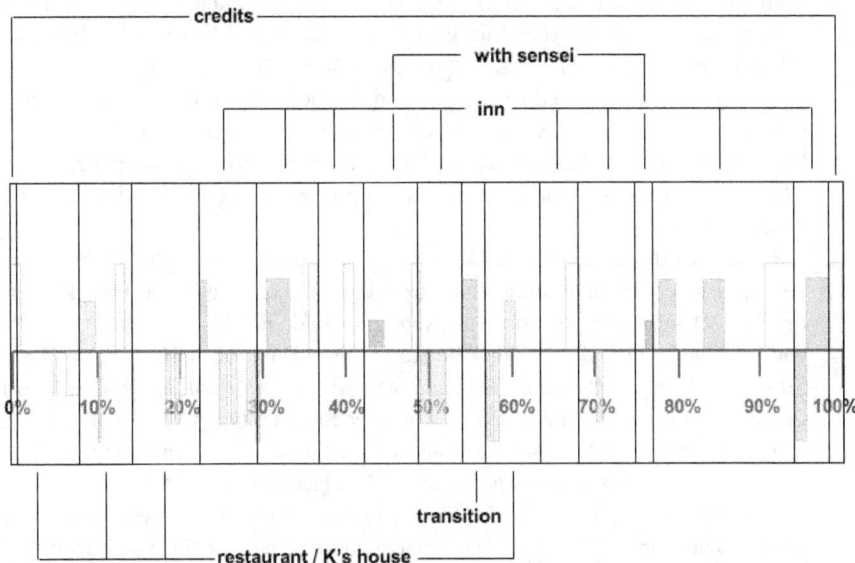

Figure 5.3 The scenes of *Ai no korida*, overlaid with representations of diegetic music (beneath the timeline) and extra-diegetic music (above the timeline).

with the interplay of the ostensibly 'romantic' *koto* music and the ineffable *shakuhachi* music that seems to represent the complexities of Sada's character. As the narrative moves towards its climax, these two types of *hogaku* music come increasingly to the fore; especially in the last two scenes, they seem not so much to contradict one another as to amplify each other's deepest resonances.

Upon her arrest, the real Sada Abe told the police that she did what she did only for the sake of 'love'. On this we can take her at her word. But as the music of *Ai no korida* so poignantly suggests, Sada's idea of love was of a very peculiar sort.

Notes

1. Except in cited titles, throughout this chapter Japanese names are presented in the western style, that is, with given names first and family names second. The title of the film can also be transliterated as *Ai no corrida*.
2. After the sensation-generating premiere of *Ai no korida* in 1976 at the Cannes Film Festival, prints of the film were impounded by customs officials when they entered the United States, Germany and the United Kingdom. When a book containing the film's script and selected stills was published in Japan in 1977, Oshima was officially charged with obscenity; it was not until 1982 that the charges were dropped.

3. Barthes's collection of essays, *L'Empire des signes*, was published in 1970 (Paris: Flammarion); it was translated into English by Richard Howard and published in 1983 under the title *Empire of Signs* (New York: Hill and Wang).

    The French title affixed to the print on the occasion of the Cannes premiere was simply *L'Empire des sens*; however, the opening credits gave the names of the principal actors Tatsuya Fuji and Eiko Mastsuda as appearing 'dans' ('in') *L'Empire des sens*, and subsequently the preposition was considered to be a part of the western title.
4. According to the official report, Sada said that she fatally strangled Kichizo while he was asleep; the final attempt to strengthen Kichizo's erection was made for the sake of increasing her own pleasure, she said, not his.
5. For a detailed study of the Sada Abe story, see William Johnson's *Geisha: Harlot, Strangler, Star: A Woman, Sex, and Morality in Modern Japan* (New York: Columbia University Press, 2004). For anecdotes related to the lore that has sprung up around Sada Abe, see Nicholas Bornoff's *Pink Samurai: An Erotic Exploration of Japanese Society* (London: Trafalgar Square, 2001).
6. This is the running length of the film as presented in the readily available VHS and DVD versions. The original film included a scene in which Sada pulls torturingly at the penis of a young boy who has observed her sexual activity with Kichizo, but this scene was eliminated before the film's showing at the Cannes festival.
7. The spoken or sung words in the dubbed version of the film are for the most part exactly the same as what is offered in the subtitled version.
8. Contrary to impressions that might have been gathered from seeing the film based on Arthur Golden's 1999 novel *Memoirs of a Geisha*, it would have been unlikely for an actual geisha to engage in sex with a client. The word *geisha* means simply 'performing artist'; in essence that is all a geisha was, albeit to an exquisitely refined degree. For more on geisha culture and tradition, see Liza Dalby's *Geisha* (Berkeley: University of California Press, 1983); Jodi Cobb's *Geisha: The Life, the Voices, the Art* (New York: Alfred A. Knopf, 1995); and Kyoko Aihara's *Geisha: A Living Tradition* (London: Carlton Books, 2000).
9. For commentary on the culture in which the *shunga* flourished, and for many examples of representative prints, see Tadashi Kobayashi's *Utamoro: Portraits of the Floating World* (Tokyo and London: Kondansha International, 2001); Bret Norton's *Shunga: The Essence of Japanese Pillow-book Eroticism* (New York: Astrolog Books, 2002); Timon Screech's *Sex and the Floating World: Erotic Images in Japan, 1700–1820* (London: Reaktion Books, 2004); and Margarita Winkel's *Japanese Erotic Fantasies: Sexual Imagery of the Edo Period* (Tokyo: Hotei Publishing, 2005).
10. Participants in the widespread but informally organized movement included Joji Yuasa, who provided music for Oshima's 1964 film *Esturaku* ('Pleasures of the Flesh'), and Toru Takemitsu, who scored Oshima's 1970 *Tokyo senso sengo hiwa: Eiga de isho o nokoshite shinda otoko no monogatari* ('The Battle of Tokyo, or The Story of the Young Man Who Left His Will on Film'), 1971 *Gishiki* ('Ceremonies'), 1971 *Natsu no imoto* ('Dear Summer Sister') and 1978 *Ai no*

borei ('Empire of Passion'). Among the other composers who around this time began to incorporate traditional elements into their modernist music were Ryohei Hirose, Toshio Ichiyanagi, Maki Ishii, Yoritsune Matsudaira, Teizo Matsumura, Shuko Mizuno and Osamu Shimizo (Heifetz 1984; Galliano 2003).
11. For commentary on the still-prevalent, yet controversial, theory that Japanese music can only be truly understood by native speakers of Japanese, see Nuss 2002.

References and further reading

Dresser, D. (1988), *Eros Plus Massacre: An Introduction to the Japanese New Wave Cinema*, Bloomington: Indiana University Press.
Galliano, L. (2003), *Yogaku: Japanese Music in the Twentieth Century*, trans. Martin Mayes, Lanham, MD: Scarecrow Press.
Heifetz, R. (1984), 'East–West Synthesis in Japanese Composition, 1950–1970', *Journal of Musicology*, 3(4), 443–55.
Hori, H. (2005), 'Representing a Woman's Story: Explicit Film and the Efficacy of Censorship in Japan', in J. Bagchi, G. Lovink, M. Narula and S. Sengupta (eds), *Sarai Reader 2005: Bare Acts*, Oakland, CA: AK Press, pp. 457–65.
Malm, W. (1959), *Japanese Music and Musical Instruments*, Rutland, VT, and Tokyo: Tuttle.
Mellen, J. (2004), *In the Realm of the Senses*, London: British Film Institute.
Miki, M. (1989), 'The Role of Traditional Japanese Instruments in Three Recent Operas', *Perspectives of New Music*, 27(2), 164–75.
Nuss, S. (2002), 'Hearing "Japanese", Hearing Takemitsu', *Contemporary Music Review*, 21(4), 35–71.
Richie, D., and Anderson, J. (1958), 'Traditional Theater and the Film in Japan,' *Film Quarterly*, 12(1), 2–9.
Takemitsu, T. (1989), 'Contemporary Music in Japan', *Perspectives of New Music*, 27(2), 198–204.
Turim, M. (1998), *The Films of Oshima Nagisa: Images of a Japanese Iconoclast*, Berkeley: University of California Press.

6 Lust in Space[1]
Science Fiction Themes and Sex Cinema (1960–82)

Philip Hayward

Introduction

Science fiction is predicated on the representation of aspects of futurism, imagined technologies and/or interplanetarism. This set of references allows for a wide range of representations of alternative lives or realities, including, in many instances, contact with alien 'others'. In cinema it exists alongside an aggregate of other, partially overlapping, genres. Within this matrix 'pure' science fiction is an elusive commodity, since even core films of the canon often employ elements of other genres for important structural and thematic elements – such as Ridley Scott's use of film noir in *Blade Runner* (1982) or the 'Haunted House' horror subgenre in *Alien* (1979); the disaster movie, as in *The Day the Earth Caught Fire* (Val Guest, 1961); and those elements of the war film and Western genres that are present in George Lucas's *Star Wars* series (1977–) or various alien-invasion features (such as screen adaptations of H. G. Wells's *War of the Worlds*).

Between the early 1960s and mid-1980s a number of (primarily male) production teams working in the USA and western Europe produced films that combined science-fiction themes and representations of heterosexual desire, fantasy and/or anxiety.[2] This initially occurred in the form of low-budget, so-called 'B-movies' and subsequently established itself in the first experimental, genre-crossing phase of what was later to become the mainstream porn-film industry. As subsequent sections detail, the result of this cross-over was not so much a genre hybrid as a set of texts that activated the connections between science fiction and representations of sexuality in various ways. This chapter provides a critical survey of what might be termed the principal texts of this 'canon'.[3] As subsequent sections discuss, the use of music and/or aspects of sound design is a significant index of the orientation and aspiration of the films involved.

In a more general context I have identified the following schema of musical styles in science fiction (henceforth SF) cinema in its post-war phase (Hayward, 2004: 2):

  1945–60   The prominence of discordant and/or unusual aspects of orchestration/ instrumentation to convey other-worldly/futuristic themes

| 1960–77 | The continuation of other-worldly/futuristic styles alongside a variety of other musical approaches |
| 1977– | The prominence of classic Hollywood-derived orchestral scores in big-budget films together with other-worldly/futuristic styles and, increasingly, rock and, later, disco/techno music + the rise in integrated music/sound scores |

With regard to non-musical sound, the periodization is less marked and can be characterized in terms of intermittent engagements with sound effects and sound design to convey other-worldly/futuristic elements. The relationship to the sonic conventions of the other genres that have supported representations of sexuality is not so easily schematized, given their variety, and is advanced in this chapter through discussions of particular films, series and/or subgenres.[4]

Early engagements

The 1968 feature film *Space Thing* (B. Ron Elliot) opens with a short sequence showing a couple in bed bickering about the male's obsession with pulp SF magazines. Tensions are resolved when he turns his attention to her and they make love. Satisfied by his exertions, she falls asleep, allowing him to pick up a copy of *Fantastic Stories* magazine and resume his reading. The remainder of the film is presented as an extended dream sequence in which he stars as an interplanetary hero. The narrative begins with him boarding a spaceship which is intent on attacking his planet. He disrupts the mission by sexually distracting the (somewhat easily aroused) female crew members, thereby undermining the authority of the lesbian captain. His efforts succeed and the ship diverts and lands on an asteroid, giving him the opportunity to blow it up with a 'mini atom bomb'. As the prelude to the main narrative suggests – and as subsequent interviews with the producer David Friedman have confirmed[5] – the inspiration for the film's scenario, characterization and general imagination were SF magazines and, in particular, their cover designs. In its inspiration and realization *Space Thing* epitomizes the films discussed in this chapter.

SF-themed sexploitation cinema has its roots in the literary (and associated visual) tradition of science fiction writing that emerged in the pages of magazines such as *Amazing Stories* in the 1920s and flourished in the immediate post-war decades. One of the most original contributors to this area was Philip José Farmer, whose representations of sexual encounters between humans and aliens attracted fame and notoriety in the 1950s. Farmer was overt about his project, even presenting a paper to the Worldcon SF convention on the theme of 'Science fiction and the Kinsey Report' in 1953 after receiving an inaugural 'Hugo' science fiction award. The publication of an anthology of his sex-themed stories under the title *Strange Relations* (1960) promoted further awareness of this area of his work.[6]

The preoccupations of authors such as Farmer were visualized in a series of lurid cover designs for American SF magazines loosely inspired by stories featured in their issues.⁷ *Planet Stories*, which commenced in 1939, was an early specialist in such covers and deployed a wide range of sexually charged images, such as the metallic brassièred 'Black Priestess of Varda' seen flogging a reptilian alien on the cover of the Winter 1942 issue. A substantial proportion of these covers featured scantily dressed young human females being menaced by various types of aliens or, alternatively, similarly clad extraterrestrial female humanoids harassing humans. The August 1956 and May 1957 issues of *Amazing Stories*, for instance, provide striking examples of the former, showing (respectively) a woman on a beach being terrorized by a giant hairy creature with barbed feet and a woman being stalked by a robot. Avon publications of the 1950s also specialized in such imagery. *Fantasy Reader* no.14 (1950), for example, featured a diaphanously clad woman under the caption 'Temptress of the Tower of Torture and Sin', while issue 2 of the *Avon Science Fiction Reader* (1958) featured the title 'Sacrifice to the Lust Queen of the Flame Rite' above the image of a bikini-clad redhead sitting inside a barrier of fire.

The imagination evident in 1950s SF magazines spilled over into cinema in various forms. One of the most notable partial precursors of the type of film discussed in this chapter was David MacDonald's *Devil Girl from Mars* (1954), a distinctly British foray into kinky sexuality in the immediate post-war period. The 'Devil Girl' in question is a dominatrix dressed in a fetish outfit who lands her spaceship in a rural area in order to kidnap Earthmen as breeding stock. The film is open to various interpretations; one being that the Martian woman represents an extreme characterization of anxieties about female sexuality in the post-war period (also manifest in the femmes fatales of the film noir series). A second is that the film is as much a depiction of metropolitan post-war decadence and deviance set against stoic rural resistance (with the 'Devil Girl' representing Soho as much as Mars).⁸ Despite this intriguing range of possibilities, the film's score – one of the first by prolific British composer Edwin Astley – eschews the experiments in dissonance and electronics in SF scoring being pursued in Hollywood at this time by composers such as Bernard Herrmann or Dmitri Tiomkin (see Hayward, 2004). Similar themes to MacDonald's feature also surfaced in a group of US SF productions that featured predatory female aliens,⁹ one of which, *Cat-Women of the Moon* (Arthur Hilton, 1953), was graced by an Elmer Bernstein score.¹⁰

The year 1961 saw a convergence of SF themes and sexploitation cinema in the form of *Nude on the Moon* (Doris Wishman and Raymond Phelan¹¹). Following the 1957 judgment of the US Supreme Court in the *Roth v. USA* case that nudity per se was not obscene,¹² a number of US film-makers produced films that were ostensibly documentaries about nudism in order to represent nudity (and, primarily, bare female breasts) on screen.¹³ By carefully avoiding the representation of any sexual activity – or even less-overt lewdness – these films managed to slide round censorship restrictions and provide some coy titillation for their consumers. *Nude on the Moon* provided the genre with a novel twist by framing its nudist sequences within a narrative of two astronaut scientists travelling to the Moon, where they observe and photograph the activities of lunar maidens (and their accompanying men), who go about their activities naked from the waist up. As the dialogue emphasizes (on several occasions), there is some ambiguity whether the verdant landscape they explore is the Moon, or some earthly fantasy projection.[14] The latter aspect is underlined by the actual location of the film's 'lunar' sequences – shot in the grounds of the Coral Castle, an architectural folly completed in the 1930s on the outskirts of Miami. This provides the film with an exotic setting reminiscent of the Polynesian-esque 'Tiki' locations that became fashionable in the late 1950s and early 1960s.[15] The combination of this exotic backdrop and the presentation of semi-clad women for male appraisal also typified the sleeve designs for albums by musical exoticists such as Arthur Lyman and Martin Denny, who were at the peak of their popularity at the time of the film's production[16] and also recalled the SF/erotica cover stylings of releases such as the futuristic instrumental album *Music Out Of The Moon* (1947).[17] Despite these connections, such musical styles are absent from the film.

Nude on the Moon's orientation around earthly male desire is made explicit in the lyrics of its opening song, a big band ballad entitled 'Moon Doll', sung by Ralph Young over a painted graphic of the Earth as seen from the Moon and then reprised at various stages. Along with this contribution, the film score features a variety of other elements. Orchestral sequences, composed by Daniel Hart, are principally used to accompany the opening (pre-launch) sequence, set in a Miami suburb, and to supply the occasional dramatic cue. The remaining music, used primarily in the 'lunar' section, draws on more contemporary idioms. Several sequences are accompanied by (unattributed[18]) 'burlesque jazz' instrumentals. The term 'burlesque jazz' refers to a loose aggregation of bluesy, small ensemble, instrumental jazz styles used in (and commonly associated with) burlesque and striptease performances in the 1950s and 1960s.[19] These tracks feature at various moments, providing sonic accompaniments to 'tasteful' tableaux of topless women sunbathing, posed around pools or gently playing ball games with male companions. The film's use of a music form with such a substantial connotative coding can be understood as an attempt to infuse these 'Edenic' images with the sleazy erotic undertones of the music – attempting to imply more intensely erotic scenarios than its screen images could actually depict. This 'gap' is also manifest in the two dance sequences, which are freestyled by individual women in quasi-modern ballet styles, rather than the sexualized routines more commonly associated with burlesque.

In terms of sound design, effects editor Stuart Hersh contributes two distinct SF elements. The first comprises the bubbling and bleeping laboratory noises of the pre-launch sequences and the rocket noises accompanying the transit scenes. The second is the echoic processing of the alien queen's whispered 'telepathic' vocal parts in the Coral Castle section. This latter aspect is somewhat token and, indeed, the general muteness of the aliens renders them more as animated mannequins than believable humanoids. The denouement of the film concerns the reluctant return of the younger astronaut, Dr Huntley (William Mayer), to Earth after being erotically enraptured by the persona and physique of the queen (played by glamour model Marietta). Shaking off the doggedly asexual, workaholic attitudes he evidences in the film's introduction, he sees his faithful assistant Kathy (also played by Marietta) in a new light, undressing her with his eyes and finally making a move on her that concludes the narrative. In this manner, his voyeuristic encounter with physical beauty in an other-worldly sylvan setting enables him to unlock his repression and enter the overtly sexualized 1960s society that the advent of the 'nudie' films suggested.

Exploiting the growing acceptance of (semi-)nudity on screen, in 1964 sexploitation director Bethel Buckalew (under the pseudonym 'Seymour Touchus') produced a mixed-genre feature entitled *Kiss Me Quick* that drew strongly on stage burlesque performance traditions for its humour and sexual spectacle. The film's narrative involves an agent from a distant unisexual (male) galactic society travelling to Earth. His mission is to find a perfect specimen of a female to bring back for testing and evaluation as a servant class. The alien, named Sterilox, played in bumbling Stan Laurel style by Frank Coe, beams down to the laboratory of a mad scientist, Dr Breedlove (Max Gardens), who keeps a host of nubile females in thrall and under close observation. The laboratories are also populated by a cross-gender monster figure, known as Frankystein, and a Count Dracula character. This narrative framework serves as the pretext for a number of sexual spectacles, such as topless go-go dancing routines, performed by a trio of women in the laboratory to surf-rock instrumental tracks, and scenes of women undressing to various musical accompaniments, such as ensemble and solo piano jazz. Despite the various females paraded past him, Sterilox remains unimpressed until finally he encounters a vending machine, whose functional capacity enraptures him. The film's most novel combination of SF sounds and sexual spectacle occurs in its opening sexual scene. Exploiting the absence of Dr Breedlove from the laboratory, one of his captive females lies on a table and undresses, in increasing erotic heat, as the rays of the scientist's 'sex ray' bombard her body. As she disrobes and writhes in pleasure, her mounting sexual tension is communicated through a collage of crackling electricity and oscillator sounds that both indicate the sex-ray's operation and its effects on its target.

The mid-1960s also saw the production of more mainstream films that combined erotic and science fiction elements. Norman Taurog's *Dr Goldfoot and the Bikini Machine* (1965), a spoof on the James Bond film series (1962–present), was a notable early contribution, with an original score composed by musical exoticist Les Baxter.[20] The SF element of the film involves its villain producing attractive female robots that dress in bikinis in order to exploit vulnerable rich men. Baxter accompanied this narrative with a mixture of quirky pop arrangements. The title song is sung by the Supremes over the film's initial animated credit sequence, with a standard Tamla Motown backing augmented by melody lines performed on tuned bottles and occasional sound effects (electric zap and oscillator noises, explosions, car crashes, etc.) with the bikini-clad robots also providing some spirited dancing. The film was popular enough to spawn a follow-up in 1966, made in English and Italian versions, entitled *Dr Goldfoot and the*

Girl Bombs (*Spie vengono dal semifreddo*), directed by future horror-film specialist Mario Bava. The narrative upped the ante on its predecessor by having its robots literally explode during sexual activity. The US version had a score provided by Baxter with contributions by bands such as the Sloopys and Mad Doctors, while the Italian version featured a score by Lalo Gori. In both cases the light, uptempo music emphasizes the humorous aspects of the narrative and serves to disarm any radical edge that the explosive plot device might have suggested.

The associations of sexual liberation (at least, as understood in terms of male access to female sexuality, sexual representation of [young] women and the SF genre) were present not only in cinema. The iconic 1960s magazine *Playboy* also contributed to the convergence by featuring the work of rising SF authors (it even published a SF-themed book anthology in 1966[21]). The objectification of the female body and its imagination for masculine access was rendered manifest in films such as *How to Make a Doll* (Herschell Gordon Lewis, 1968), in which two socially inept mathematicians attempt to make fully functioning android sex toys. As the subsequent section argues, one of the many charms of the film version of *Barbarella* (produced in the same year) is that it offers a more pluralist representation of female sexuality (albeit within the overarching context of male-orientated erotica).

Barbarella on screen

The style of visual imagery and narrative themes of the 1950s US science fiction magazines discussed above were developed by the French writer Jean-Claude Forest, who in 1962 originated a *bande dessinée* (comic strip) serial about a young earthwoman's interplanetary sexual adventures, entitled *Barbarella*, for the publication *V-Magazine*. The episodes were subsequently published in book form in 1964 by Parisian specialist publisher Eric Losfeld and, despite a ban on the book's public display by the French censor's office, the publication was an immediate success, selling 20,000 copies. Various translations followed and US publications such as *Newsweek* and *Playboy* favourably reviewed its English-language publication, with the former describing its lead character as "a mythic creature of the space age" and the latter praising her as "the very 'apotheosis' of eroticism" (Lofficier, 1985). A key to the strip's appeal was its ability to push the bounds of sexual representation through the 'distancing' context of its SF scenarios. The eponymous heroine is frequently represented in various fetish outfits and regularly loses her garments in interactions with both aliens and astronauts.

Barbarella's appearance and demeanour were modelled on the French actress Brigitte Bardot (*ibid.*), who became an international sex symbol through the *succès de scandale* of Roger Vadim's 1956 film *Et Dieu créa la femme*. Set around St Tropez, in the South of France, the film not only introduced Bardot's impressive physique to the screen but also allowed her character to flaunt her sexuality with complete disdain for traditional social values and mores. As a result, French Catholic bodies condemned the film and the US National Catholic Office for Motion Pictures[22] campaigned against its release in the United States. Despite the latter, an English-language version entitled ... *And God Created Woman* received limited specialist distribution in 1957 and was subsequently re-released more widely in 1958.[23]

The impact of Bardot's appearance and persona in the film was so great that critic Chuck Stevens has described her as "more a force against reason, or a blinding special effect – not unlike Einstein's equations, or Elvis's pelvis – Bardot warped cultural memory as easily as she bent a projector-beam of light."[24] Quoting Vadim's characterization that "She comes ... from another dimension. [Once] people spotted her, they couldn't take their eyes off of her. That's down to her presence, which comes from outer space somewhere" (*ibid.*). Stevens went on to characterize her as "Superabundant and extraterrestrial. Bardot was far too human, yet far beyond 'real' " (*ibid.*).

In Vadim's next major international success, he took these allusions literally, presenting another nubile female in outer space rather than the South of France. Now, some forty years after its release, Vadim's filmic adaptation *Barbarella* (1968) is commonly regarded as an amusing, light-hearted and charming example of 1960s kitsch and has been frequently evoked in subsequent popular culture. The mad scientist featured in the film gave his name to the popular British band Duran Duran[25] (formed in 1978 and currently enjoying a revival). The director of the video clip for Kylie Minogue's 1994 single 'Put Yourself In My Place' created a homage to the film's opening sequence (discussed below) and former Eurhythmics composer/guitarist Dave Stewart wrote the music for a 2004 stage musical version.[26] At the time of writing, a remake of the film, scheduled to be directed by Robert Rodriguez, was also in development. But despite this current interest, the original film release occupied a distinctly different position with regard to respectability and mainstream acceptance. Emerging in 1968, at the height of popular cultural engagement with (and popular social perceptions of) 1960s countercultural permissiveness, the film was decidedly more risqué and boundary-pushing than it now appears.

Vadim's choice of Jane Fonda for the title role of his interpretation of Forest's *bande dessinée* contributed significantly to the film's notoriety in the United States. Born in 1937, Jane was the daughter of actor Henry Fonda and prominent socialite Frances Ford Seymour. Her father appeared in a number of films, most notably John Ford Westerns such as *My Darling Clementine* (1946) and *Fort Apache* (1948), where he embodied classic 'all-American' values of resilience and morality. His daughter initially worked as a fashion model in the 1950s, before moving into cinema after studying with Method acting guru Lee Strasberg. She established a modest profile with drama features such as *Sunday in New York* (Peter Tewksbury, 1963), but her comic skills were recognized with the success of the comedy Western *Cat Ballou* (Eliot Silverstein, 1965). Another event in the same year provided a fresh inflection to her career. Her marriage to French director Vadim, known as something of a roué, was in itself an act of minor rebellion against the US establishment that was amplified by her role as Barbarella in 1968. Word-of-mouth and pre-release publicity ensured the film extensive press coverage that redefined Fonda's image: the March edition of *Playboy* included her in a photo-feature entitled 'The Bizarre Beauties of Barbarella' and *Life* magazine featured her in a PVC fetish outfit on the cover of its March 29 issue.

Barbarella's opening sequence is playfully ambiguous. Initial dramatic 'atmos' sound gives way to an edgy high string motif as the camera zooms into the interior of a small spacecraft where a silver-suited astronaut (of ambiguous gender) floats in zero gravity. A bright, high xylophone melody joins the strings and added arpeggios also warm the sound, but it is not until a manicured hand emerges from one glove and slowly teases off the other (in classic striptease style) that the gender of the astronaut is implied. The opening theme song then commences with a mid-tempo drum rhythm, electric guitar chords and woodwind parts, building to a brass-accentuated climax as the astronaut removes her leggings, revealing smooth, slender thighs. As the astronaut's helmet visor is slowly lowered (again, the tease) a mass of sensual light brown hair appears, then her eyes, as the first verse kicks in (sung by Mike Gale), announcing "It's a wonder – wonder woman/You're so wild – and wonderful", interspersed with a vocal chorus of female 'aah' sounds. During the instrumental break following the first verse, Barbarella removes her helmet and shakes her hair free, scattering animated letters from her tresses that come together to spell her name on screen. As she pulls off her sleeves other letters emerge, first spelling the film's title, then the names of her co-stars. An extended second verse follows, extolling her virtues further. As she undoes her remaining garment and floats naked, the singer renders his desire explicit, announcing that he's "dying to make love". The sequence ends abruptly as Barbarella reaches down and turns the ship's gravity field on, falling to the (thickly carpeted) floor as the music cuts out.

A rich, complex sonic environment immediately asserts itself as the ship's computer asks her – over its burbling electronic processing noises – to prepare to receive a communication from the president of Earth. Before she has time to dress, a brass salvo signals the commencement of the message and the face of the president arrives on screen to brief her. She is ordered on a mission to track down renegade scientist Durand Durand (played by Milo O'Shea), inventor of the 'positronic ray', who is intent on reintroducing weaponry and warfare to a peaceful Galactic order. To this end she sets course for the Tau Ceti system, where she encounters various perils and makes love with a number of colourful male characters (including a blind angel) before confronting the evil rulers of the planet.

In genre terms, the film's most striking sonic elements are the range of synthesized sounds that are used to auralize the futuristic technologies represented in the film (computers, matter-transference devices, ray guns, etc.). The variety and prominence of these are significant in the history of the wider SF film genre. The initial – and still seminal – exposition of such synthesized sound effects was Bebe and Louis Barron's electronic score for Fred Wilcox's *Forbidden Planet* (1956) (see Leydon, 2004). Along with the accomplishment of the duo's "electronic tonalities" (as the film's end-credits have it), the manner in which these operate both diegetically and non-diegetically, moving freely between each mode, was a major innovation. In that *Barbarella* includes synthesized sounds in a more diegetically functional manner and combines these with conventional musical cues, its score is more directly comparable to the East German/Polish co-production *Der schweigende Stern/Milczaca Gwiazda* (Kurt Maetzig, 1959).[27] The bleeping, burbling electronic sounds occurring on board during the spaceship's journey to Venus in Maetzig's film are reminiscent of *Barbarella*'s opening sequence (see Hayward, 2004: 11), and the scenes following the landing of the ship on Venus (which combine conventional orchestration with sonic oscillations) are also comparable with sequences in *Barbarella*'s on-planet narrative.

The style of *Barbarella*'s introductory song sets the template for Charles Fox and Bob Crewe's score, which mixes strong guitar, percussion and brass numbers with quieter, jazzy mood pieces. The musical style, which now appears quaintly retro – evoking an era just before the advent of full-blown psychedelia and progressive rock[28] – reflects the extent to which Barbarella's persona, sexual conduct and dress styles were (similarly to those in *Devil Girl from Mars*) as much an evocation of an (imagined) cultural 'now' as they were that of a far-distant future. Using a plot device that has seen future sex reduced to a tablet-enhanced transfer of energy flows, Barbarella's transport to a barbarian world where male attentions are manifest in more traditional forms allows the film to depict her rapid – and rapturous – sexual awakening: a moment of delirious 'liberation' that accords with dominant stereotypes of 'Swinging Sixties' permissiveness and promiscuity. Despite the film's striptease opening, Barbarella's sexual couplings are not captured on screen. Her post-coital demeanour, such as when she reclines blissfully in Pygar the Angel's feathered nest, crooning softly to herself, attests to the effectiveness of 'traditional' physical interaction.

In a cross-over between its sound design and music score, the film makes effective use of sonic leitmotifs, such as the electronic tonalities that accompany the black-leather-clad guard robots that protect the planet's rulers. Further underlining the sonic emphasis of the film, one of its key scenes involves a musical assault. Captured by the mad scientist, Fonda finds herself (literally) trapped within the body of an 'orgasmatron' (a keyboard instrument shaped like a bed). On the floor behind her – but out of sight – lie the bodies of several young women. Their presence is explained by Durand as he reveals the title of the piece he commences to play on Barbarella's body – 'Sonata for executioner and various young women'. As the sequence begins, Durand plays coolly and fluidly, producing exclamations of surprised delight from his victim. The tempo and urgency then increase, startling her and eliciting further squeals. Revealing the fate of the young women strewn around the floor, Durand explains that "When we reach the crescendo you will die ... the end will be swift but sweet." Playing increasingly manically, with rapid snare-drum patterns and building brass dissonance, Durand makes Barbarella writhe deliriously, wide-eyed and perspiration-soaked, inside the body of the instrument. As the music mounts she continues to ride its waves, crying out orgasmically as an increasingly perplexed Durand attempts to up the intensity even further. Interlocked in mutual escalation, the music unravels first, descending into cacophony, and then the machine itself gives out, as its connections fray, smoke and burst into flames, defeated by Barbarella's prodigious orgasmic abilities. Berating her for wrecking his device, he angrily asks, "What kind of girl are you? Have you no shame?"

Barbarella can be regarded as both the high- and the end-point of a series of mainstream 1960s films that drew on elements of established SF literature and magazine art to present the female form and various sexual scenarios on screen. In this regard, they represent not so much a (sub-)generic aggregate as a loosely linked series of texts. The soundtracks for these features illustrate the slender and superficial pairing of SF and sexual elements within mainstream narrative frameworks. Reflecting their market aspirations, the soundtracks to these features mainly comprise music scores that use contemporary popular idioms. In *Barbarella*'s case, this is combined with an ambitious use of sound effects and general sound design that is accomplished enough to merit favourable consideration within the history of SF film production more generally (see Hayward, 2004: 1–29). However, Vadim's film is a distinct exception to the limited sonic ambition of its cohort.

1970s Sex Cinema

Invasion of the Bee Girls

Made five years after *Barbarella*'s release, *Invasion of the Bee Girls* (1973),[29] directed by Denis Sanders and written by Sylvia Schneble and Nicholas Meyer,[30] presented a very different project. Unlike Vadim's light-hearted feature, *Invasion* represents its hypersexual female protagonists as darkly glamorous figures who exert a deadly allure on the middle-aged men on whom they prey. The film's narrative centres on a scientist, Dr Susan Harris (played by Anitra Ford), working at a facility in a small rural town when she discovers that injections of bee hormones intensify her libido (and give her 'bee-vision'). After killing her first partner through frenzied coupling, she embarks upon a killing spree and recruits new Bee Girls, whom she converts with injections, radiation exposure and bee cocoons. Eventually their secret is discovered and the laboratory and the Bee Girls are destroyed.

In her discussion of the 'sexual thriller', typified by films such as *Fatal Attraction* (Adrian Lyne, 1987), Linda Williams (2005) characterizes the films as exploiting the connection between eroticism and thanatos (the death drive/instinct) and identifies film noir as a partial precursor. *Invasion of the Bee Girls* explores similar ground. Indeed, the text of the film itself explicitly identifies such a connection. As one male character speculates (in what has become something of a cult line), "Just think about it, boys – coming and going at the same time." Similarly to Williams's characterization of the erotic thriller as a melded – rather than hybridized – form (*ibid.*: 21–8), *Invasion of the Bee Girls* combines thriller, softcore and SF genres somewhat unevenly. This is particularly evident in the film's score, provided by Charles Bernstein.

Bernstein's score is varied and includes distinct genre elements.[31] One strand is based on a late 1960s/early 1970s pop-funk style associated with detective/crime TV programmes and films. This strand is closely associated with the investigating government agent, Neil Agar (played by William Smith), and the plot sequences involving him. The opening musical sequence rapidly establishes this genre feel, with its busy funk rhythm and high melody parts. Further associations are manifest in the sequence where Agar saves his young female companion from a rape attempt and beats up her attackers in an alley. The guitar riff accompanying this closely resembles that used in the introduction to Isaac Hayes's theme for *Shaft* (Gordon Parks, 1971). The uptempo, action feel of these (and other) sequences contrasts with the music associated with the Bee Girls. While male corpses litter the narrative, the actual depiction of the fatal sexual congress that produces them is withheld until the later part of the film, but music plays a prominent role in this scene. Seduced by Dr Harris, a middle-aged scientist lies back and enjoys her ministrations (much as the camera invites the viewer to enjoy her naked form) while a reel-to-reel tape-recorder plays her chosen seduction music – two string-based compositions in late-nineteenth-century European art-music idiom. Similar music also marks the Bee Girls' collective activities, in the form of original score passages that comprise a soprano vocal and violin cue and a small choral section performing what might be termed a 'chromatic counterpoint' to an electric organ accompaniment. The connection between the mutant females and western art music colours their role and representation. Rather than one-dimensional monstrosities, they are represented as refined über-femmes fatales, Europeanized in a manner that resembles the aristocratic hauteur of Hammer's contemporaneous vampire films. The use of vocal and choral music in the laboratory scenes is also inter-cut, and occasionally mixed together, with the film's most obvious SF conventions: a set of electronic melodic motifs, oscillations, mechanical clatters and burbles that signify the operation of lab computers, powered activities and laser operations. In the climactic scene when the Bee Girls perish as the laboratory equipment explodes, this mixture is combined with cries and shrieks, a sonic overload that reflects the Bee Girls' agonies. But other elements of the film work against the closure that this scene implies.

The film's score begins with a brief tympani roll, so quickly succeeded by the pop–funk sequence discussed above that it is easily forgotten. Its brevity – and immediate succession by a different musical style – leaves it 'hanging', and thereby ambiguous. Its sonic function is only made manifest at the film's conclusion (signalling it as a subtle foreshadowing of the themes to unfold). The roll is a direct quotation of the opening tympani part from the theme of Richard Strauss's *Also sprach Zarathustra*, best known in cinema through its use in Stanley Kubrick's epic *2001: A Space Odyssey* (1968). This musical reference returns at the end of the film in more extended form, with a further note of ambiguity. While the Bee Girls themselves are killed in the laboratory explosion, the film's final shots show bees buzzing around flowers. This could simply signify a return to the normal order of nature but a more complex meaning is suggested by accompanying these images with the beginning of *Also sprach Zarathustra*. The music is open to various interpretations, cued by both its immanent musicality and its interpretation as reference. Musically, its rousing ascendance represents a point of departure – rather than an end – suggesting a 'to-be-continuedness' to the image of bees, as if the Bee Girls' narrative is not yet over. Cross-associated with Kubrick's usage, the theme also suggests an epic vision that is not easily associated with closure or with the images of the industrious creatures shown on screen being read at face value. For those able to grasp it, there is also an added effect, in that Strauss's music interprets Friedrich Nietzsche's eponymous four-part literary work (1883–85), his famous declaration of the "will to power" and the concept of eternal recurrences – the return of what appears erased.

Half a decade on from the zenith of the 'swinging' (late) Sixties, *Invasion of the Bee Girls* provides an intense image of predatory female sexuality that can be interpreted as an anxious fantasy reaction to the discourses of 'free love' and female sexual emancipation in circulation in the early 1970s. Indeed, Rebecca Coyle has observed that:

> The technology that empowers the Bee Girls has distinct parallels to the 'technology' of the contraceptive pill (introduced in 1960 and widely available from the mid-1960s on). Both transformed women's physiology and changed gender relationships and power. (personal communication, January 2008)

The film's score emphasizes the separate gender sensibilities of its protagonists, enriches these through allusion and – finally – eludes closure. If anything, its SF elements and, specifically, its use of the Bee Girl motif give it an even greater symbolic 'kick'. Any implicit castration anxieties that may be seen to have pervaded film noir are all the more resonant in *Invasion of the Bee Girls*, given (actual) bees' mating arrangements, whereby male bees die after mating when their penises shear off during sex in order to deliver the semen the queen bee requires (dark pleasures indeed).

Flesh Gordon

Films such as *Barbarella* and *Invasion of the Bee Girls* exploited the loosening of film censorship that occurred in the USA following revisions to the (previously highly restrictive) cinema 'Production Code' that replaced strict guidelines with more diffuse advisory measures and the introduction of a classification for "mature audiences".[32] After a period of tentative transgression into hitherto taboo realms, the early 1970s saw the advent of pornographic feature films which generated box-office income (on dedicated exhibition circuits) that compared favourably to many mainstream releases. In this context, whatever *Barbarella*'s risquéness some four years earlier, its representations of the body and sexual acts were tame compared to the material presented in such 'breakout' box-office hits as *Johnny Wadd* (Bob Chinn, 1971), *Behind the Green Door* (the

Mitchell Brothers, 1972), Gerard Damiano's *Deep Throat* (1972) (reputedly the most commercially successful film ever made)[33] and *The Devil in Miss Jones* (1973).

The first SF-themed film to emerge from this nexus was Howard Ziehm's *Flesh Gordon*[34] (1974). With a single vowel substitution for its referent text – Universal Pictures' seminal 1930s/40s Flash Gordon films – the 1974 film signals its sexualized re-visioning of the original series. While this approach is now well established (with 'porno parodies' of referent film texts characterizing a significant strand of both softcore and hardcore porn cinema), it was relatively novel in the 1970s. Such parody films take their narrative themes from well-known mainstream films, usually flagged by their modified titles, and use these as frameworks for the setting and locations used for the representations of bodies and sexual activity. The first feature production of this type was William Allen Castleman and Robert Freeman's revision of the 'Zorro' film formula (initiated by Fred Niblo's 1920 film *The Mark of Zorro*) in the costume (s)extravaganza *The Erotic Adventures of Zorro* (1972). *Flesh Gordon* revolves around the dastardly plan of Emperor Wang from planet Porno to destabilize Earth by beaming sex rays at it. Dashing hero Flesh Gordon responds as Earth's champion and, accompanied by his colleague Flexi Jerkoff and love interest Dale Ardor, flies to Porno. Numerous colourful interactions eventuate as the brave trio attempt to locate and disable the ray.

Prior to working in erotic cinema, producer/co-director Ziehm had a varied career as a drug dealer, nightclub owner and rock band member. He started directing micro-budget ($400) 'beavers' (short films depicting naked women caressing themselves) in 1969 for a company he established named Graffiti. Their success allowed him to graduate to full-length porn features in 1970 with *Mona – the Virgin Nymph*, an unusual porno-with-a-plot feature, and a film entitled *Hollywood Blue* (documenting mainstream film actors who had appeared in underground sex films early in their careers).[35] The success of these two films on the adult cinema circuit led him to develop *Flesh Gordon* as his third feature.[36] Produced at a time of major commercial success for adult cinema productions that would have been unimaginable as little as five years earlier, *Flesh Gordon* was originally conceived as a $25,000 hardcore project in 1970 but, after various stages and inputs, by 1974 it emerged as a significant, independent production with an estimated budget of well over $500,000.[37] The sizeable budget for the film allowed Ziehm to employ talented young production personnel such as the (now fêted) make-up and special effects designers Mike Minor, Jim Danforth, Rick Baker, Greg Jein and Dennis Muren. Drawing on a $25,000 budget that was raised separately,[38] Ziehm hired arranger/composer Ralph Ferraro to write music for the film at the end of the production process.

Responding to the film's inspiration – and the various homages to the RKO series in the film's visuals – Ferraro wrote an accomplished and extra-textually referential score. Substantial passages comprised orchestral pastiches of the style established by Franz Waxman in *Bride of Frankenstein* (1935) (sequences of which were recycled and/or imitated by RKO in the Flash Gordon series). Somewhat remarkably for an early 1970s porn film, Ferraro's score was recorded by a small orchestra in the main Warner Brothers studios in California. Along with orchestral sections, the score also features earlier stylistic pastiches, such as solo piano and organ extemporizations that derive from classic 'silent cinema' accompaniment. While some orchestral passages also incorporate a more contemporary popular music feel and textures, the dominant mood is nostalgic pastiche. The narrative is further punctuated by occasional short musical numbers, such as the quasi 'tribal' chant that occurs when the Amazon underground attempt to initiate Dale into their lesbian sorority; and the sing-a-long chorus of 'Flesh Gordon Is Dead' that Wang strikes up after he tries to flush Flesh and his accomplices down a drain. A sound production team comprising John Brasher, Dan Dillon and Robert Harman also contributed a series of sound effects for the various ray guns, blasts and mechanisms, together with other comic noise effects similar to those used in animation cinema.

Ziehm's combination of sex scenes and themes with 1930s pulp SF elements, retro music, sound effects, deliberately stilted dialogue and one-dimensional acting serves to distance the film from the porno-functionalism of his earlier (non-narrative) 'beavers'. Indeed, the film operates in something of an ambiguous generic zone. The sexual activity depicted on screen occurs either as part of the narrative or else as visual 'background' to scenes in which other narrative elements occur. There are very few scenes in which the narrative 'freezes' to accommodate sexual spectacle.

The film can be read as a dual parody. The first level is overt, addressing its referent 1930s text (and similar film series) and the second is the contemporary socio-industrial context of its production. Although largely overlooked by previous critics (at least as far as I can ascertain from personal research), the film offers an overt parody of the moral panics around pornography and the permissive society which were on the rise during the film's extended production period (leading to investigations of its production, seizure of footage and censorship of content[39]). In this regard, Planet Porno represents the porn industry, whose texts (symbolized by the 'sex rays' beamed at Earth) destabilize the population and lead to mass outbreaks of depravity. The parodically lascivious Wang (presumably) stands for Ziehm and other industry figures much as the bland Flesh Gordon represents the agents of law and order. The film spawned a later, less-successful sequel, *Flesh Gordon Meets the Cosmic Cheerleaders* (1989), but it remains a highly idiosyncratic production, financially enabled by a particular early 1970s market surge that allowed for highly crafted elements of SF film scoring and effects to be created within a film that also featured graphic representations of sexual acts. Like *Barbarella*, it stands out in its decade as an example of the combination of SF and sexuality within a populist aesthetic.

The Farmeresque – *Wham Bam Thank You Spaceman*

Produced with a similar trash/camp aesthetic to *Flesh Gordon*, William Levey's 1975 film *Wham Bam Thank You Spaceman* is notable as the first SF sex film to feature depictions of inter-special sex (sex between individuals from different species) that recall aspects of the work of Philip José Farmer. The film's plot involves two aliens being sent to Earth to inseminate women with alien foetuses (because of the imminent orbital decay and destruction of their home planet and the need to prepare settlement elsewhere). Their preferred approach is to locate naked women involved in sex acts, teleport them (in a trance state) into their spacecraft and then rapidly have sex with them. Despite their quasi-humanoid appearance, the aliens' approach to the latter involves penetrating their victims' vaginas with long tongue-like penises that emerge from their mouths (a process that brings considerable pleasure to both parties). Rapidly teleported back to their lover's clutches – and unaware of what has taken place – the women's post-coital glows testify to the effectiveness of the alien approach. While various electronic bleeps and drones accompany the scenes in the alien spacecraft, there is little cohesion to the film's sex scenes' score, which comprises source music from a range of genres. Indeed, the most sonically accomplished part of the film is its opening. The soundtrack commences with a theremin-like melody, adds a collage of radio voices, then – shifting the mood to the camp-comedic style that typifies the remainder of the film – features a kazoo part as a crudely costumed alien commander appears on screen. The film's title song begins after the commander announces the aliens' mission. Written by Miles Goodman and David White and sung by Kay Denis, the theme song is set to a lively, uptempo funk track with prominent wah-wah guitar riff and additional electronic bleeps. Its lyrics introduce the aliens' orgasmic prowess in the opening couplet: "You're my UFO Romeo/You give my whole body an unearthly glow" and follow this up with the chorus, "Wham bam, thank you, spaceman". Despite the film's imaginative sexual scenario, the SF element primarily comprises the rapid but regular teleportations that punctuate the standard human-on-human sex episodes that become extended and increasingly disjointed from the narrative as the film unfolds. The ending brings a reprise of the SF theme, as the first alien baby is born, and the title song recurs, but the sequence primarily functions as a somewhat token 'book-end' to the narrative rather than any climactic resolution of narrative themes.

The last noteworthy SF-themed sex film of the 1970s was a softcore, comic and futuristic version of the classic Cinderella story, set in 2047. Its most distinctive aspect was its construction around a number of song-and-dance routines, a format it borrowed from *Alice in Wonderland* (1976), Bill Osco's commercially successful softcore reworking of elements of Lewis Carroll's 1865 book. *Cinderella 2000* was directed by Al Adamson in 1977, with music attributed to Sparky Sugarman. The film is set in a time of sexual prohibition and the narrative provides various opportunities to challenge this hegemony. Despite the film's futuristic setting, the musical numbers are resolutely mainstream pop compositions based on show-tune precedents, with the only nod to the contemporary being a disco-dancing robot number. Sound is similarly unimaginative and the flat acting styles, inane script, weak humour and prim softcore sexual interactions contributed to the film's poor critical response and weak box-office performance.

The early 1980s – *Alpha Blue* and *Café Flesh*

Although the eclectic experimentation of late 1960s and early 1970s porn cinema declined by the late 1970s (much as the form itself did under increased censorship and restriction), it still offered space for film-makers to produce occasional experimental works. Two SF-themed features were released in the early 1980s by film-makers at very different points in their careers. Gerard Damiano directed *The Satisfiers of Alpha Blue* (1981) (also released under the abbreviated title *Alpha Blue*) a decade after his pioneering and highly profitable features *Deep Throat* and *The Devil in Miss Jones*. Stephen Sayadian's *Café Flesh* (1982) was, by contrast, the director's debut feature.

Alpha Blue is set in a twenty-first-century context where sexuality has been separated from love and procreation. The film's title refers to its setting, a space brothel where visitors are serviced by highly accomplished female and male 'satisfiers'. While this location provides the pretext for the series of sex scenes that make up the majority of the running time, the film also features a sub-plot involving one client, Algon (Robert Kelman), who experiences an emotional 'throwback' and becomes romantically infatuated with 'Satisfier 805'. Frustrated by her rejection of romantic involvement he resolves to "fuck her to her senses", a ploy that evidently succeeds since the film ends with them kissing romantically in one corner of the room while a frenzied multi-person coupling takes place in the other. While this element of the film could be construed as a critique of loveless sex, the detailed and varied sexual encounters shown on screen and the boundless enthusiasm of the satisfiers ensure that its pornographic appeal and function are not undermined. Indeed, its function is reinforced by the film's (unattributed) keyboard-based score, which combines relatively gentle mood passages with funky instrumental jams that complement the intensity and rhythmic drive of the sex scenes. The score thereby represents an early example of what might be termed 'sex muzak' – a predictable and functional style of instrumental scoring that avoids distraction from or complication of erotic spectacle.

Working under the pseudonym 'Rinse Dream', former porn magazine satirist Stephen Sayadian[40] produced a markedly darker perspective on futuristic sexual entertainment in his *Café Flesh*. Of all the films discussed in this chapter, *Café Flesh* represents the most conscious subversion and critique of the genre within which it was produced. Funded by mainstream porn cinema producers, Sayadian directed the film with scant attention to standard generic formulae.[41] Inspired by alternative theatre and the cinematic revisioning of late 1920s/early1930s Weimar performances in Bob Fosse's *Cabaret*[42] (released in the same year), *Café Flesh* can – in many respects – be seen as a dark remake of the Mitchell Brothers' *Beyond the Green Door*. The Mitchells' film takes place in a private nightclub. Williams describes this venue as an "escapist sexual utopia [where] the normal rules of stagebound space and time are opened out into cinematically abstract but sexually significant patterns of symmetrical and decorative female bodies transformed, multiplied and fetishized" and where the "utopian energy, intensity, and abundance" on display overwhelm the audience with pleasure (Williams, 1999: 159). By contrast,

Sayadian's film is predicated on a futuristic, post-apocalyptic scenario in which 99 percent of the population has been rendered 'sex-negative' (incapable of engaging in sexual activity). Constantly frustrated, the 'negatives' are reduced to observing members of the remaining 1 percent – the 'positives' – perform for them. As screenwriter Jerry Stahl expressed it, the film was conceived as

> a World War Three musical. We had in mind a kind of high-grade Cabaret in which trendy mutants and atomic mobsters held sway over survivors bombed beyond all normal pleasures. Lots of people made movies about the end of the world, but how many showed what the night life would be like? (quoted in Smith, 2007: 22)

The café of the film's title is a small theatre, guarded by a vault-like door and presided over by a caustic MC, who taunts the audience about their inability to participate in the activities they witness. The performances on offer consist of stage cabaret numbers with particular sets and themes that give contexts for the sexual acts that follow. These comprise 1:1 male/female and female/female and 2:1 male/female couplings which begin with jerky, mannered choreographic sequences that imitate sexual motions. Several of these are extraordinary in their stylization, constituting neo-Brechtian *verfremdungseffekte*, alienating/distancing audiences from the erotic content of the numbers.

The first sex scene exemplifies this element. To the left of the stage a soberly dressed actress sits in an armchair knitting, unmoved by baby cries heard offstage. As the music starts, with an accentuated keyboard bass line and distorted treble melody over a rolling mid-tempo drum pattern, spotlights flick on the rear of the stage, revealing three grotesquely made-up men. Dressed in bonnets, bibs and diapers, these 'adult babies' sit in highchairs and provide a rigid choreography of jerky marionette-like movements in time with the musical rhythm. The sexual aspect is introduced in the form of a man in a rat mask and costume who emerges from behind the woman's chair (audibly) sniffing at her. He then marches around the stage before initiating interaction with her (in which the rat's tail is deployed as a phallic substitute) before actual sexual activity commences – with the babies pounding on their tabletops and grimacing as steam jets emanate from behind them. A gentler keyboard motif then enters the mix and introduces close-ups of the male's rat-masked head closing in on the woman's genitals as he licks her vagina and clitoris, before the rhythmic emphasis re-establishes itself as she goes on to fellate him, with female vocal moans inserted into the mix (despite the actress's inability to voice these, given her activity). With a return to shots of cunnilingus, the keyboards drop away to the rear of the mix, and female moans and a second, indeterminate snuffling voice enter over a stark drum pattern. This persists as the shot switches to fellatio, and a cut-away shot shows the babies, surrounded by steam, imitating the action of ironing on their tabletops. This sound mix continues to develop as the couple fuck, with the drum pattern – somewhat unexpectedly – slowing and loosening (as if in anticipation of orgasmic dissolve) as the passion intensifies and as the babies' movements get even more frenzied.

The music and (uncredited) sound design described above play a major part in setting the tone of the overall film and undermining any comfortable immersion in the sexual spectacles on offer. The score was provided by young composer-performer, Mitchell Froom (later known for his work with artists such as Elvis Costello and Crowded House), working with a brief from Sayadian to "make the music real disturbing".[43] Froom responded to this instruction by producing a score (with additional drum parts by Denny Carmassi) that made frequent use of unsettling chromatic passages, avoiding alternations between narrative music cues and soft, atmospheric muzak for the sex scenes (and, indeed, entirely eschewing the latter).[44] In another deviation from standard porn-film scoring, the style of music used in successive sex numbers varies, so as to keep their distanciation 'fresh' in each episode. In addition to these musical devices, the film provides a further, highly original sonic accompaniment to its first female:female number. Colliding references and associations, the scene features one woman, wearing 'Stars and Stripes' panties pulled to one side, who masturbates, then orally and digitally interacts with another woman to an audio collage of civil alert sirens, marching feet, muffled military commands and the MC's cackling laughter – fracturing the visual/interactional intimacy through a series of harsh, impersonal sonic jars. As Smith identifies, Sayadian's "distinctive soundscapes complicate the meaning of on-screen hard-core action and demonstrate the importance of sound in the cinematic representation of sexual fantasy" (2007: 15).

As the above descriptions suggest, the film can be perceived as an acerbic representation of late-twentieth-century porn cinema and/or live sex-shows enabled by the film's post-apocalyptic SF setting. In this regard, the implicit critique of the spectators' inadequacy no doubt contributed to the film's poor performance on the porn circuit. In addition to its operation as a reflexive, implicitly critical exploration of porn cinema, its original approach to sound and music makes it one of the most significant feature films of the period in any commercial genre.[45]

Conclusion

The series of texts discussed in this chapter deploy SF elements to represent contemporary aspects of sexuality in imaginative, displaced scenarios. Representing their production moments, the films show a distinct shift in themes that mirrors the socio-sexual climate in various ways: from representations of nudity in *Nude on the Moon* and free love in *Barbarella* to the sex industry in *Alpha Blue* and *Café Flesh*; from sex comedies (*Kiss Me Quick*, *Barbarella*, *Flesh Gordon* and *Wham Bam*...), through sex thrillers (*Invasion of the Bee Girls*), to mainstream porn (*Alpha Blue*) and ultimately porno critique (*Café Flesh*). The transition from repressed sexual longing in *Nude on the Moon*, through idealized promiscuity in *Barbarella* and anxiety in *Invasion of the Bee Girls*, to the post-apocalyptic world of *Café Flesh* can be interpreted to reflect the shift from the 'swinging Sixties' to an 'anxious Eighties' dominated by media-driven alarm about the proliferation of genital herpes[46] and the subsequent onset of the HIV/AIDS era.[47]

While these trajectories are in themselves unsurprising, given that SF is a medium that speculates on the development of present trends in future and/or alternative contexts, the role of music and sound in the films is significant. The sonic aspects of the films discussed in this chapter provide a variety of interpretations and embellishments to their projects. Given its relative novelty (in the period in question), the representation of sexual activity on screen had no obvious 'default' musical style and offered composers a range of interpretative options. The films' scores reflect this, moving from attempts to erotically infuse imagery (*Nude on the Moon*'s use of burlesque jazz), gleefully celebrate it (*Barbarella*'s pop rock score), stylistically 'defuse' it (*Flesh Gordon*'s use of pastiche/retro orchestrations), present it in terms of inter-gender conflict (*Invasion of the Bee Girls*'s mixed musical modes), ascribe an industrial functionality to it (*Alpha Blue*'s use of sex muzak) and, finally, problematize it (through the auditory discordance central to *Café Flesh*). In this manner, the space of mid to late 1960s SF-themed sex cinema can be regarded as something of a laboratory, exploring the sonic representation of sexuality within various contexts. As such it comprises an active production zone whose considerable stylistic diversity is all the more marked given the standardization of musical grooves that emerged in sex cinema from the 1990s on.

Notes

1. This title, a pun on the 1960s US TV series *Lost in Space*, is too obvious not to have been used before. Indeed, it has been appended to (at least) three audio-visual products. Two of these are softcore porn items: an episode of the 1995 US pay-TV series *The XXX Files* and the fourth instalment of the Erotic Witch Project film series (John Bacchus, 2005). The third was a 1998 British TV programme (directed by Roger Stevens) that staged a mock trial of the BBC's long-running *Dr Who* series on grounds of alleged sexism. The title is not used here in reference to any of these specific productions but rather to tag a broader thematic area.
2. While research for this chapter did not address the issue of target and/or actual audiences for the films discussed, the primarily male orientation of SF comics and early 1960s sexploitation cinema clearly provided a ground for the two forms' initial convergence.
3. I do not attempt to discuss every feature that combines SF content and representations of sexuality produced in the period. Rather, I have selected the best-known and/or widely circulated examples of the generic niche. The body of non-English-language production in this period merits further research. *Spermula* (Charles Matton, 1976, France), for example, is a softcore film with an SF premise; and the two Italian comedies *Il Disco volante* (Tinto Brasso, 1964) and *Conviene far bene l'amore* (Pasquale Festa Campanile, 1975) also have SF/sex elements. Analysis and discussion of the complex field of Japanese *hentai* (sexually

explicit) anime and live-action cinema featuring SF themes in this era is also an area worthy of attention.
4. The films discussed in this chapter have circulated in various film, TV, video and DVD versions. In all cases, references to specific aspects of texts are to those versions that were available on DVD in the mid-2000s (and these are specified in the concluding Filmography).
5. See, for instance, the film commentary on the DVD version.
6. Also see Jaffrey (ed.) (1985) for a collection of early SF erotica stories by other authors.
7. See Harrison (1977) for an historical discussion.
8. See Chibnall (1999) for further interpretation and contextualization.
9. Including *Fire Maidens from Outer Space* (Cy Toth, 1956), which used extracts from Borodin's 1874 opera *Prince Igor* for its score; the Zsa Zsa Gabor vehicle *Queen of Outer Space* (Edward Bernds, 1958); and *Mars Needs Women* (Larry Buchanan, 1967).
10. Bernstein's score was written during the period in which he was *persona non grata* at major Hollywood studios, due to concerns about his alleged leftist political affiliations. The score for Hilton's film features orchestral passages along with quieter sequences featuring harpsichord and celesta.
11. Working under the pseudonyms 'O. O. Miller' and 'Anthony Brooks'.
12. *Roth v. United States*, 354 U.S. 476 (1957) U.S. Supreme Court (June 24, 1957), footnote 20; archived online at http://vlex.com/vid/20013436 (accessed 16 June 2009).
13. See Storey (2003) for a history of the nudist film genre, dating back to the 1930s.
14. An aspect reinforced through both the astronauts' unexplained lapse into sleep before the ship lands itself and by the graphic representation of the spacecraft landing and taking off from a cratered lunar surface entirely unlike that which is represented in the film.
15. See Kirsten (2007) for a history of this vogue.
16. See Hayward (1999: 1–18) for further discussion.
17. The album features compositions by Harry Revel arranged by Les Baxter with Samuel Hoffman's theremin as a lead instrument. Its cover depicts a diaphanously clad 'moon maiden' and the album gained renewed currency when Neil Armstrong took a cassette copy to the Moon on his successful Apollo 11 mission in 1969.
18. While the burlesque jazz numbers used in the film appear to be pre-recorded, their composers and performers (and the featured guitar instrumental, which is strongly reminiscent of Barney Kessel's style) are uncredited, and have not been subsequently identified.
19. See, for example, the Verve Records compilation *Tease!: The Beat Of Burlesque* (2005), featuring tracks by Slim Gaillard, Barney Kessel and Charlie Parker.
20. See Leydon (1999).
21. *The Playboy Book of Science Fiction*, first published in 1966 and republished in 1998 by HarperCollins, New York.

22. Which, in its early incarnation as the Catholic League of Decency in the 1930s, had successfully campaigned against the 'indecency' of films such as those featuring actress Mae West.
23. C. Stevens, 'And God Created Woman', *Criterion Collection*, online at http://www.criterion.com/asp/release.asp?id=77&eid=87&section=essay (accessed 16 June 2009).
24. As an example of (safely sophisticated) European cinema, *...And God Created Woman* gained wider exposure in the USA than domestic sexploitation features. Indeed, as David Andrews has identified: "And God Created Woman showed sexploiters like [Russ] Meyer and [Radley] Metzger the forms that might succeed in arthouses and grindhouses alike" (2005: 264: fn. 14).
25. With the band dropping the silent 'd' at the end of the name.
26. The musical *Barbarella* opened in Vienna in March 2004 and ran for nine months. A cast recording was made but was not commercially released (see Lash, 2004).
27. Released in an abridged English-language version as *211 First Spaceship on Venus* and also distributed (in various versions) as *The Silent Star, Planet of the Dead* and *Spaceship Venus Does Not Reply*.
28. Interestingly, in this regard, Frank Zappa and the Mothers of Invention were initially considered to compose the music for the film (in autumn 1967) before the team of Bob Crewe and Charles Fox was selected (Gray, 1985: 100).
29. Also released under the title *Graveyard Tramps*.
30. Meyer later directed *Star Trek: The Wrath of Khan* (1982) and *Star Trek VI: The Undiscovered Country* (1991).
31. Thanks to Jon Fitzgerald and Michael Hannan for their comments on music cues used in the film.
32. The Production Code was administered by the Production Code Administration, which was established in 1934, as a more powerful version of the previous Motion Picture Producers and Distributors of America office. The original Code was designed to stem the perceived indecency of mainstream Hollywood cinema in the 1930s and it continued to exert a powerful influence on the themes and content of national and imported films until the 1960s.
33. See Fenton Bailey and Randy Barbato's 2005 documentary *Inside Deep Throat* for a discussion of its profitability, estimated as $600 million return on a production budget of $25,000.
34. Credited as co-directed with Michael Benveniste in recognition of his contribution to the early phase of its production.
35. For a cameo autobiography, see H. Ziehm (nd), 'The Ziehm Story (… in Howard's own words)', *PicPal*, online at: http://www.picpal.com/fleshgordon/fleshg.html (accessed 30 July 2008).
36. In this regard his personal career trajectory exactly parallels the stages of evolution of the fully-fledged porn feature as outlined by Williams (1989: 96).
37. Ziehm, in director's commentary on DVD release.
38. Ziehm has stated, "A friend of mine, Peter Tevis, raised money from Canada to do the music. Peter had worked for Capital Records and he hired Ralph Ferraro to do the score" (quoted in Stevens, online; see note 23 above).

39. See Ziehm in note 37 above.
40. See Smith (2007) for a discussion of Sayadian's early career.
41. Composer Mitchell Froom has recalled that Sayadian informed him, "Look, these pussycat theaters are funding this film, so I've got to shoot this porn footage, but my idea is to shoot it with the instructions that everyone act as if their mother just died. I want it to be really dark" (quoted in J. Klein (1998), 'Mitchell Froom interviewed by Joshua Klein', AV Club, online at http://www.avclub.com/content/node/23190; accessed 16 June 2009).
42. The genealogy of Fosse's film is complex. It was based on John Kander and Fred Ebb's Broadway musical *Cabaret* (1966), which was, in turn, based on Christopher Isherwood's 1946 novellas *Goodbye to Berlin* and *Mr Norris Changes Trains*, John Van Druten's dramatic interpretation of these in *I Am a Camera* (1951) and the eponymous screen adaptation of this play (Henry Cornelius, 1955).
43. Quoted in J. Klein (see note 41 above).
44. Froom's music attracted sufficient attention to gain release on Slash Records in 1984 under the title *The King Of Cool*.
45. My use of the term 'commercial' cinema excludes reference to consciously experimental cinema, such as that of Jean-Luc Godard and his collaborators (as exemplified by films like *British Sound* [1970]).
46. The incidence of herpes rose in North America during the 1970s and attracted major media 'panic' coverage in the 1980s (see Mirotznik and Mosellie, 1986).
47. The term Acquired Immune Deficiency Syndrome was coined in 1982 following recognition of a new aggressive STD in the previous year.

References

Chibnall, S. (1999), 'Alien Women: The Politics of Sexual Difference in British SF Pulp Cinema', in I. Q. Hunter (ed.), *British Science Fiction Cinema*, London: Routledge, pp. 57–74.

Cook, J. R. (1999), 'Adapting Telefantasy: The Dr Who and the Daleks Films', in I. Q. Hunter (ed.), *British Science Fiction Cinema*, London: Routledge, pp. 113–27.

Coyle, R., and Hayward, P. (2009), 'Texas Chainsaws: Audio Effect and Iconicity', in P. Hayward (ed.), *Terror Tracks: Music, Sound and Horror Cinema*, London: Equinox, pp. 125–36.

Farmer, P. J. (1960), *Strange Relations*, New York: Ballantine.

Forrest, J.-C. (1964), *Barbarella*, Paris: Éditions Le Terrain Vague.

Gray, M. (1985), *Mother! The Frank Zappa Story*, London: Plexus.

Harrison, H. (1977), *Great Balls of Fire: An Illustrated History of Sex in Science Fiction*, London: Penguin.

Hayward, P. (1999), 'The Cocktail Shift: Aligning Musical Exotica', in P. Hayward (ed.), *Widening the Horizon: Exoticism in Post-war Popular Music*, Sydney: John Libbey/Perfect Beat Publications, pp. 1–18.

Hayward, P. (2004), 'Sci-Fidelity: Music, Sound and Genre History', in P. Hayward (ed.), *Off the Planet: Music, Sound and Science Fiction Cinema*, Sydney: John Libbey/Perfect Beat Publications, pp. 1–29.

Jaffrey, S. (ed.) (1985), *Sensuous Science Fiction from the Weird and Spicy Pulps*, Bowling Green, OH: Bowling Green University Popular Press.

Kirsten, S. (2007), *Tiki Modern*, Los Angeles: Taschen.

Lash, L. (2004), 'Interview with Dave Stewart', *Financial Times*, 4 March: online at http://search.ft.com/ftArticle?queryText=%22Dave+Stewart%22&y=8&aje=true&x=21&id=040315006753&ct=0&nclick_check=1 (accessed 16 June 2009).

Leydon, R. (1999), 'Utopias of the Tropics', in P. Hayward (ed.), *Widening the Horizon: Exoticism in Post-war Popular Music*, Sydney: John Libbey/Perfect Beat Publications, pp. 42–71.

Leydon, R. (2004), 'Forbidden Planet: Effects and Affects in the Electro Avant Garde', in P. Hayward (ed.), *Off the Planet: Music, Sound and Science Fiction Cinema*, Sydney: John Libbey/Perfect Beat Publications, pp. 61–76.

Lofficier, J.-M. (1985), 'Cruising the Galaxy with Barbarella', *Starlog 92*; online at http://www.hollywoodcomics.com/forestint.html (accessed 16 June 2009).

Mirotznik, J., and Mosellie, B. (1986), 'Genital Herpes and the Mass Media', *Journal of Popular Culture*, 20(3), 1–11.

Storey, M. (2003), *Cinema au Naturel: A History of Nudist Film*, Oshkosh, WI: Naturist Education Foundation.

Smith, J. (2007), 'Sound and Performance in Stephen Sayadian's Night Dreams and Café Flesh', *Velvet Light Trap*, 59 (Spring), 15–29.

Williams, L. (1999), *Hard Core: Power, Pleasure, and the "Frenzy of the Visible"* (expanded edition), Berkeley: University of California Press.

Williams, L. (2005), *The Erotic Thriller in Contemporary Cinema*, Bloomington: Indiana University Press.

Principal filmography

Barbarella: Queen of the Galaxy (Roger Vadim, 1968), Paramount widescreen DVD edition, 2001.

Café Flesh (Stephen Sayadian, 1982), VCA DVD edition, 2002.

Flesh Gordon (Howard Ziehm and Michael Benvenist, 1974), Hen's Tooth Video widescreen DVD edition, 2002.

Invasion of the Bee Girls (Denis Sanders, 1973), MGM Midnite Movie DVD (part of double-sided DVD with *Invasion of the Star Creatures*), 2004.

Kiss Me Quick (Bethel Buckalew, 1964), Something Weird DVD edition, 2001.

Nude on the Moon (Doris Wishman and Raymond Phelan, 1960), Something Weird DVD edition (on single DVD with *House on Bare Mountain*), 2001.

Space Thing (B. Ron Elliot, 1968), Something Weird DVD edition, 2001.

The Satisfiers of Alpha Blue (Gerard Damiano, 1981), Alpha France DVD edition (on a single DVD together with *The Devil in Miss Jones* and *Deep Throat*), undated.

Wham Bam Thank You Spaceman (William A. Levey, 1975), Something Weird DVD edition, 2001.

7 Zero Gravity
Science Fiction Themed Porn Cinema and Its Soundtracks 1990–2010

Philip Hayward and Emil Stoichkov

As Chapter 6 outlined, the period between 1960 and the early 1980s saw a number of inventive explorations of science fiction (henceforth SF) themes in a disparate group of (s)exploitation, B-movie and early porn feature films. These films drew their inspiration from the intertwining of SF and sexual fantasy in 1950s magazines and fiction; the trajectory and rhetoric of the 'space race'; and the changes in socio-sexual behaviour, mores and imagination triggered by the sexual liberalization of the 1960s and the associated availability of the contraceptive pill.

By the mid-1980s the experimental, 'freewheeling' porn sector that had facilitated many diverse and often experimental productions[1] had given way to a more standardized industry that aggregated around two axes, softcore and hardcore. In both cases their textual form was premised on the alternation of narrative and sex scenes (both of which were enacted by the same cast members). Williams has identified the differences between the feature-length porn-film format that arose in the 1970s and earlier, short 'stag' films in terms of the organization of sex scenes around a thematic thread:

> Most relevant ... is the greater narrative coherence of both the feature film as a whole and each of the sexual 'numbers.' In feature-length 'pornos', these numbers tend to be complete dramas of arousal, excitement, climax, and (usually) satisfaction that permit both the (male) characters in the film and the (usually male) viewers of the film to withdraw satisfied. (Williams, 1999: 73)

With regard to feature-length porn cinema it is also possible to assert that the form's duration not only allowed but actively *required* an overarching frame to aggregate and orientate sex scenes. As became apparent in the 1960s and 1970s, previously established genre conventions offered instant associations that could provide thematic colour and expectations to (often skeletal) narratives, particularly when accompanied by complementary titles, marketing hooks, cinema posters and video/DVD cover art.

Despite producers' ready embrace of other established genres in the 1980s, the decade that followed the release of *Café Flesh* (1982) was undistinguished in terms of creative aspiration or achievement in SF-themed porn cinema. The small body of SF-themed hardcore productions produced in the late 1980s were either parodies (such as John T. Bone's minuscule-budget *Bimbo Cheerleaders from Outer Space*, 1988); thinly themed ventures (such as Ron Jeremy's *Sex World Girls*, 1987, about a futuristic sex-fantasy service offering material 'projections' for clients); or rare excursions into gay SF-themed porn (such as Jack Major's *Blacklode*, 1985, a 'blaxploitation' porn feature centred on male models providing sperm samples for scientific research into orgasms). The soundtracks for these productions were (at best) unremarkable, particularly in comparison to their thematic predecessors.

Despite this creative downturn, inventive engagements with the genre cross-over revived in the mid-1990s, and this chapter analyses the manner in which music and sound operate with regard to sexual spectacle, narrative and overall textual cohesion in a range of soft- and hardcore films produced in the mid- to late 1990s and 2000s.

1990s SF-themed softcore

Contemporary softcore cinema emerged in the 1990s specifically aimed at pay-TV and domestic video markets that would not accept hardcore material. As Andrews details, the essence of softcore cinema is a product whose

> diegesis is punctuated by periodic moments (typically between eight and twelve, though more is not exceptional) of simulated, non-explicit sexual spectacle ... [It] also leans on standardized forms of pornographic spectacle such as striptease numbers, tub or shower sequences, modelling scenes, voyeur numbers, girl-girl segments, threesomes, orgies, and the like. (2006: 2)

The principal difference between this form and hardcore is the actual (rather than simulated) activity depicted in the latter, and, in particular, hardcore's privileging of the 'money shot', i.e., the representation of male ejaculation, as the peak moment of the spectacle. This 'softer' product also differed from hardcore in another way. Whereas hardcore was exhibited and consumed in public environments largely patronized by men,[2] softcore was circulated and consumed in private, domestic environments. The less-graphic representations on offer and the more discreet viewing environments were regarded as more conducive to couples and female consumers, and producers tailored their product to this market.

As the genre established itself, it became necessary to diversify styles and themes in order to distinguish product and to allow niche marketing strategies to develop (*ibid.*: 151). In the early 1990s Surrender Cinema, a subsidiary of Charles Band's Full Moon production company, developed a distinct brand identity through its use of 'harder' core elements – such as shots of the female pubic area and occasional (non-erect) penis images. Surrender's films were shot on relatively high budgets and featured members of the company's stable of highly photogenic actresses. One of Surrender's regular directors was Sybil Richards,[3] who made over fifteen features in the mid- to late 1990s, which presented a series of 'spectacles' with plot frames and genre attributes derived from mainstream cinema. Her slate included a number of SF-themed productions that commenced with *Femalien* (1996) and concluded with *The Erotic Time Machine II* (2000) – along with forays into other genres, such as horror (*The Erotic House of Wax* [1996]) and costume drama (*Virgins of Sherwood Forest* [2000]). As might be expected, the majority of Richards's SF-themed productions deploy SF elements as devices that 'frame' or otherwise inflect the delivery of the sexual spectacles that constitute their central focus. This is exemplified by the (somewhat misleadingly titled) *Lolida 2000*, in which Jacqueline Lovell plays a future censor employed to destroy sex videos, who becomes aroused by them and presents them to the viewer through direct-to-camera links; and *Virtual Encounters* (1996) and *Virtual Encounters 2* (1998), which use the plot device of individuals entering virtual-reality programs to observe fantasy sex scenes.

As Andrews discusses (2006: 230), Richards's first SF-themed production, *Femalien*, proved a significant commercial success for Surrender and prompted the production of similar SF-themed features. Unlike those of the 1960s and 1970s such as *Barbarella* (Roger Vadim, 1968) or *Flesh Gordon* (Howard Ziehm and Michael Benveniste, 1974), the film is set on Earth and its action includes little in the way of conflict (let alone violence). The film concerns an alien sent to Earth to collect data on human sexual activity. Arriving in a suburb of San Francisco, 'she' assumes the pneumatic physique of actress Vanessa Taylor and the character name Kara. During her visit Kara observes a variety of sexual interactions (female/male, female/female and group), and eventually participates in a 1:1 interaction with a young female (named 'Sun'). She enjoys her encounter so much that she decides to extend her stay (thereby cueing the sequel in which fellow aliens arrive to discover what has happened to her). The film's music (written by a composer using the pseudonym 'Ollie Wood') is used highly functionally, principally during scenes of sexual activity, where diegetic sound drops out. The music for these scenes is based on digital percussion grooves with simple overlaid keyboard motifs, often with prominently ascending and descending melody patterns, which are complemented by distorted rock guitar lead lines as the on-screen passion heightens. In the male/female sequences the music usually climaxes abruptly in (rough) synch with the male's orgasm but subsides more gently in the female-on-female sequences. While noteworthy, this musical approach is congruent with styles used in other Surrender productions and, as such, represents more of a house style than a specific SF inflection. The final climactic sex scene between Kara and Sun is accompanied by the film's only song, a pop-rock number delivered by a female vocalist, which is repeated over the end credits.

The only overt reference to SF musical conventions in *Femalien* occurs during the title sequence, where the high-set vocal part evokes the choral vocables used in the title sequence of the TV series *Star Trek* over similar images of space travel. Despite the minimal SF reference of the music, the sound production team[4] produces a variety of sounds more closely aligned to those used in SF cinema. Kara's alien companion (who remains aloof from the action she participates in, only appearing as a fuzzily rendered mechanical apparatus) talks in a calm, processed electronic voice. Other sound-design features include a 'whoosh' when Kara teleports from location to location and a brief sonic sting when she touches a human. *Femalien 2* (1997), with music written by Wayne Scott Jones, follows a similar sonic model to its predecessor but also includes a brief diegetic performance at an 'alternative' San Francisco coffee house (more suited to the mid-1960s than the mid-1990s), which allows a visiting male alien to freestyle a brief 'beat' poem about outer space over a conga backing. Richards's approach to SF erotica was subsequently imitated in made-for-TV episodic series such as *Star Whores* (2000), which explored interspecial (humanoid) sex, with a particular emphasis on female–female interaction (in a series of punningly titled episodes such as 'Hitch Dykers Guide' and 'Plan 69 from Outer Space') but without the concern for sonic elements that distinguished Richards's work. Similarly, the small corpus of softcore SF films produced in the 2000s, such as *Lust in Space* (John Bacchus, 2004) – the improbable fourth instalment of the *Erotic Witch* series[5] – also exhibit minimal sonic imagination or originality.

1990s SF-themed hardcore

As Williams discusses, hardcore cinema is premised on providing evidence that "not only penetration but *also* satisfaction has taken place" (1999: 73). As she emphasizes, in contradistinction to the silent stag film,

> This satisfaction might be signaled in a variety of ways. For example, the addition of sound permits performers to communicate their pleasure in groans, moans, and sighs, as well as in actual verbal articulations, an ability that immediately enhances the sense of the sex as an event occurring between the performers rather than a show ... put on for the camera. (ibid.)

Yet, even in combination with the genre's other ubiquitous "sounds of pleasure", including "the smack of a kiss or a slap, the slurp of fellatio and cunnilingus, the whoops of penetration-engulfment" (*ibid.*: 123), Williams argues that vocal expression in hardcore's sex scenes departs from dominant cinematic codes of realism in that

> When characters talk their lips often fail to match the sounds spoken, and in the sexual numbers a dubbed-over 'disembodied' female voice ... may stand as the most prominent signifier of female pleasure in the absence of other, more visual assurances. (ibid.: 122–3)

While the former aspect is less remarkable than Williams asserts – being a common characteristic of European film productions aimed at multiple language markets that tolerate dialogue overdubbing without precise lip-synch fidelity – her general characterization is accurate and pertinent. Indeed, the vocal conventions of hardcore sex scenes are so standardized that the hardcore films discussed in this section show very little deviation from this approach (and certainly do not attempt any SF-related experimentalism). In terms of musical style, there is also a clear tendency for both soft- and hardcore to use particular forms of non-intrusive instrumental music to accompany sex scenes. This style, which might best be described as 'sex muzak', also has its generic subsets, such as the use of soft jazz/jazz-rock in more sensual-softcore productions to signal their 'classiness'. Similarly, there is a general avoidance of songs as anything other than title or end credit numbers.

Hardcore films with SF elements produced in the 1990s included Richard Leather's *Renegades* (1995), featuring rampaging post-apocalyptic gangs; two productions by prolific mainstream porn director Stewart Canterbury, *Rocket Girls* (1993) and *Pleasure Dome: The Genesis Chamber* (1994); five low-budget *Star Trek* parodies, the *Sex Trek* series (1990–);[6] and two short hardcore BDSM films directed by Rick Masters which depict the abduction and torture of hapless Earth females by aliens, *Alien Probe* (1993) and *Alien Probe II* (1994).

In terms of music and overall sonic design, *Rocket Girls* was the most notable of this limited cohort. In a manner common to subsequent productions in this niche area, *Rocket Girls*' title sequence establishes its SF theme through both 'star field' graphics and atmospheric instrumental keyboard music, with SF-referentiality emphasized by the electronic zap sounds layered over it. The film is based on the scenario of a mixed-gender space crew setting out on a mission to 're-seed' the Earth's dangerously depleted ozone layer – a mission that nearly comes unstuck after the crew are troubled by a mystery virus that makes them uncontrollably randy. Recovering just in time, after numerous couplings, they finally manage to activate their technology and save the planet. In terms of sound design, the spaceship sequences are sonically distinguished by the use of background electronic bleeps and burbles and occasional low, rumbling tones (suggesting engines). The film also attempts to represent zero-gravity sex through a scene in which images of a couple copulating are superimposed over a number of interior shots, suggesting weightlessness. This is accompanied by fairly standard sex muzak in the form of a slow to mid-tempo keyboard groove, with distorted treble embellishments providing the only hint of unearthliness.

Contemporary hardcore

> Y'know, in some ways there are similarities between how people perceive our industries. Some people watch science fiction movies, enjoy them, but then turn around and make fun of 'Trekkies' or Star Wars fans. In much the same way, people enjoy our products and services, but often don't admit to it in public.[7]

Berth Milton, president of the Private Media Group (PMG), made the above statement in May 2000 upon hearing that his company's film *The Uranus Experiment Part 2* (John

Millerman, 1999) had been nominated for a Nebula Award for best (film/TV) script. The Nebulas, administered by the Science Fiction Writers of America, were established in 1965 and are the SF/fantasy equivalent of the Oscars in terms of prestige and profile. Although the film did not make it past the shortlist, the nomination of a hardcore porn feature for such a prize was seen by the porn-film sector as firm evidence of mainstream recognition for its genre.

Founded in Sweden in the 1960s, PMG has steadily diversified its production and distribution over the past four decades to encompass a range of magazine, film and, more recently, DVD, CD-Rom and web media. In a detailed study of the company's history, Sjoberg (2002)[8] identifies PMG's policy of aiming for 'top-end' production standards and integrated production and distribution networks as key to its establishment as a major player in the global porn industry, a position that was enhanced by its listing on the US stock market system NASDAQ[9] in 1998. Releasing around seventy anthology and feature film titles per year on DVD, the company continues to retain a major presence in the 'high end' of the market.

The Nebula Award nomination reflected PMG's investment in a three-part film series that upped the ante on the production values of previous SF porn productions. The trilogy was made in 1999 and released in DVD instalments (and then as a 4-disc compilation) from 1999 to 2000. While an accompanying 'making of' DVD feature identifies the trilogy as inspired by George Lucas's *Star Wars* film series (1979–) and Isaac Asimov's 'Foundation' trilogy of novels (1951–52), the films lack the epic scope of such models and, instead, explore a simpler scenario. The trilogy's plot concerns two space shuttles docking in orbit, one Russian, one American. While the Americans are simply concerned to interact with their foreign colleagues professionally, mounting a joint mission to Uranus, the Russians have a secret agenda of testing a new libido-enhancing drug in space. Steamy couplings eventuate and the sexual interactions are shown live on television all over the world, much to the chagrin of the US administration. Powerless to resist their impulses due to the drugs, the astronauts continue their sexual activity throughout the mission. Episode 2 ends with the shuttles reaching Uranus. The astronaut delegated to explore the surface of the planet lands, exits his vehicle and is immediately accosted by two naked, blue-skinned female humanoids who – despite not having ingested Russian pharmaceuticals – quickly engage him in oral sex. Buoyed by this convivial encounter with extraterrestrial life, the astronauts' return to Earth is also celebrated with sustained sexual action that takes up the majority of the third episode.

A major aspect of the first film's appeal and media coverage was that, in one scene, at least, the cast didn't simply *simulate* weightless sex, they actually performed it. Millerman facilitated the first (known) act of sexual congress and male ejaculation in zero gravity,[10] with cast members Sylvia Saint and Nick Lang coupling on board a plane used by NASA to simulate weightlessness in space (by going into a steep dive from a high altitude). In addition to this notable 'first', Millerman sought to further elevate the trilogy's reputation in media coverage by claiming an integration of sex scenes and narrative comparable to that of classic Hollywood genre practice:

> ... it is definitely something new in the porno market. The way it was done and the way it is cut. It is done as the old fashion[ed] musical movies, Fred Astaire's type. In those films there was a story and in the story line there was music and dance performances. In this case there is a story and within the story line there is sex. But sex moves the story, is an indispensable element.[11]

This is overstated, as some sex scenes – particularly in Part 2 – are entirely extraneous to narrative progress or cohesion. Nonetheless the general alternation and interrelation of sex scenes and narrative bear comparison along the lines that the director claims, and, indeed, that Williams (1999) claims for the genre as a whole.

In terms of the films' (unattributed) music, there is a relatively straightforward divide between the digital–orchestral score that opens Episode 1, which emphasizes its SF aspect, and the music for sex scenes, which follows a particular (non-SF) format. The opening score is reminiscent of Hans Zimmer's studio style, beginning with a martial drum pattern, succeeded by a deep, unsettling minor-key brass melody (giving a sense of gravity and tension) followed by an intense melodic and rhythmic lift and then a calmer textural passage. The sex scenes are, by contrast, accompanied by a succession of instrumental blues jams, featuring prominent lead guitar lines with supporting (and occasionally lead) electric organ parts. These operate in relative synchrony with the on-screen action, instrumentally climaxing with the male cast members.

Unlike many serial porn films released on the market in rapid succession, the second instalment had a fresh element that succeeded in attracting media attention. Surprisingly for the genre, this concerned its score rather than on-screen activities. Part 2 featured music sequences commissioned from the well-known British dance/rave performers Liam Howlett and Robert ('3D') Del Naja. Howlett rose to prominence in the early 1990s with his band the Prodigy,[12] which mixed techno, industrial and rock styles in a manner that achieved commercial success while maintaining a degree of credibility with a techno/industrial 'underground' fan-base. While the Prodigy's commercial success waned in the late 1990s and early 2000s, the ensemble's use of driving electronic rhythms and digital 'orchestration' of timbral and textural patterns continued to appeal to the producers of video games, TV commercials and film soundtracks.[13] Del Naja's ensemble, Massive Attack, was formed in the late 1980s[14] and achieved popularity with a mix of reggae, soul and techno (often referred to as 'trip-hop') on albums such as *Blue Lines* (1991) and *No Protection* (1994). The lush, highly atmospheric nature of their productions also proved attractive to film producers.[15]

Del Naja and Howlett's collaboration for *The Uranus Experiment 2* involved them producing separate tracks in dialogue with each other. Howlett's track, entitled 'Titan',[16] and Del Naja's 'In Flight Data'[17] are repetitive digital grooves with simple melodic patterns and shifting timbral and percussive textures. *The Uranus Experiment 2* uses these as extended – and constantly repeated – musical motifs that override the separation of narrative and sex-scene elements manifest in the first film. Indeed, they dominate the first half of the film to the almost complete exclusion of all other musical elements. In this, their repetition serves to disassociate them from any particular image/narrative correspondence and they function more as sustained leitmotifs signifying a particular 'modern' aspiration for the film. Showing a lack of coherence, the second half compromises this by featuring both the blues jams of the first film and Del Naja and Howlett's digital grooves (with little apparent logic to their alternation). Both styles of music feature in the third film, again with little coherent clustering.

The most obviously SF-related sonic elements of the trilogy feature in the second film. The first occurs when a brief zero-gravity scene is accompanied by an extract from Johann Strauss II's 'Blue Danube Waltz' (in clear allusion to its use during a weightless exercise scene in Kubrick's *2001*). The second accompanies the shuttle's touchdown on Uranus. This sequence is introduced by a stirring digital orchestral passage that gives way to eerie, unsettling electronic tones that suggest danger and/or the planet's intractably alien difference. The tension is soon dispelled, however, when the Uranians appear and provide one astronaut with a particularly warm welcome.

Operating in a different generic niche, Jonathan Morgan's 2003 feature *Space Nuts* was a well-budgeted hardcore porn parody of Mel Brooks's previous parody of the *Star Wars* films in his 1987 feature *Space Balls*.[18] Morgan's film involves the beautiful Princess Hubba Hubba (Stormy Daniels) being pursued through space by the ugly 'Evil Overlord' (Mike Horner), accompanied by her android butler (named 'Jeeves') and occasionally aided by the film's Hans Solo equivalent, the aptly named Buzz Starfokker (Evan Stone). Unusually for a porn comedy, the latter aspect of the hybrid genre is well developed – in a manner that recalls the humour of Brooks's model – and the film balances and integrates its narrative, sex scenes and comic sequences in a coherent manner, rarely sacrificing flow for spectacle. Produced with a Dolby digital sound mix (prominently announced in its credit sequence), the film (again, like *Space Balls*) opens with a scrolling text receding into the middle distance which introduces the film's theme. The film's score was written and performed by guitarist and keyboard player Brian Rogers (under his professional moniker 'Leaky Brain') and combines several of his distinctive musical approaches to 'production music'.[19] These can be characterized as the use of electronic keyboard ambience/underscore, hard-edged electric guitar passages and what Rogers terms "modern and vintage synth engines reinforced with aggressive beats constructed of industrial electronic textures [to] add a modern edge".[20] The latter aspect is one of the more distinctive musical elements of the film. In addition to unsurprising uses of atmospheric music to evoke space travel, several of the film's sex scenes are accompanied by medium- to fast-paced instrumental tracks in which rough-edged guitar sounds give the scenes a particular (tension-building) sonic intensity more akin to action genres than porn comedy. While this is somewhat at odds with the general Brooksian comic tone of the overall production, it provides distinct sonic impact for the sex scenes – combined with their prominently mixed vocal exhortations – and, indeed, provides a "modern edge" appropriate for futuristic space fantasy.

Sound also plays a prominent role in the film's humour, particularly with regard to the communication skills and sexual adaptability of Jeeves. In one notable scene the android butler becomes attracted to a small computer appliance. Addressed seductively in English, the device responds with increasingly anxious electronic burblings (similar to CP3O's in *Star Wars*) as it begins to suspect what is in store for it as Jeeves carries it off screen. Returning after completion of some unspecified digital interaction, the device's slow, distracted bleeps contrast to Jeeves's more satisfied demeanour. Later in the film Jeeves's own sonic skills are explored when he is pressed into service as a sex droid, pleasuring a female customer. In order to get his client in the mood he runs through a variety of vocal personae before she settles on a French-accented one as most seductive. Further humour is provided in a scene where the Dark Overlord interacts with an electronic door that plays soft easy-listening music to him when he becomes frustrated at its reluctance to open. He responds to its attempts to soothe him by blasting it open with a raygun.

The high-profile *Uranus* trilogy and *Space Nuts* were followed by another ambitious hardcore SF production in the form of *Porn Wars*, a three-part pastiche of (themes from) *Star Wars* that commenced with *Episode 1: Cum Join the Force* (Kovi, 2006). The premise of the trilogy is that the Galaxy is under the thrall of dark powers (the villainous Sith) and that groups of activists (the Jodi Knights) are hidden in secret locations training to combat the evil empire. In addition to learning to use 'the force' to move objects and animate their light-sabre duelling, the (male and female) Knights also practise sexual skills intended to overwhelm potential enemies without recourse to violence. The films' visual special effects (mini robot droids, spacecraft, light sabres, etc.), stark otherworldly locations and a reasonably coherent narrative attest to the ambitiousness of its production, even if the acting – let alone graphic sexual content – problematizes the director's claims for a potential cross-over porn/SF status (made in the accompanying 'making of' video). The films' music comprises a digital keyboard score provided by a composer identified as 'Sugarman'. Aside from its opening sequence, with low brooding brass and string sounds providing a suitably solemn accompaniment to the *Star Wars*-style typographical prelude, there is little other music typical of the SF film genre. In the main the score alternates between slow to medium-tempo variations on keyboard motifs (some of which evoke the opening tempo and melody of Ravel's 'Bolero', providing a vague exoticism suitable for the films' un-Earthly location) and more uptempo digital funk grooves for sex scenes and fight sequences. In addition to the standard repertoire of exaggerated moaning, grunting and squelching sounds and linguistic exhortations, the only distinct SF genre elements are the whooshes and sizzles of the light sabres and occasional other electronic effects. For all its apparent ambitiousness, *Porn Wars*' sonic text is distinctly formulaic and lacks either the musical variety provided by Howlett and Del Naja's contributions to *The Uranus Experiment* or the inventive approaches to non-musical sound in *Space Nuts*.

Other imaginations: sci-fetish porn cinema

In addition to mid- to high-budget mainstream porn productions such as PMG's series, a number of lower-budget fetish niche providers have also recently turned to SF (and particularly its film and TV histories) as sources of inspiration. One of the more surprising forays into SF-themed porn saw specialist female/female spanking company CPE producing its first 'Extravaganza' feature, *SpaceGirls!*[21] (Chelsea Pfeiffer, 2006). The film features the arrival of two humanoid alien females (from the planet Callipygios), interested to experience the 'disciplinary spanking' they have heard is common on Earth. Shortly after arriving, they are captured by a Callipygian bounty hunter, who tests, examines and disciplines them before sending them home. Pfeiffer has explained her inspiration as deriving from:

> *The early impression the* Star Trek *TV series made on me. The crews' encounters with beings from far-flung galaxies allowed for the introduction of 'alien' behaviours and sexual attitudes ... and* Barbarella *was also an inspiration – from the orgasm machine to the costuming.* (personal communication with the authors, November 2006)

Reflecting its 'Extravaganza' status, the production featured special effects (including a flying saucer and laser images and 'zaps') and a music soundtrack supplied by an established composer (identified in the credits by the pseudonym 'Longjohn Williams'). The presence of musical soundtrack is, in itself, unusual for a subgenre that usually features location synch sound only. As Pfeiffer recounted:

> *Since* SpaceGirls! *takes a deliberately camp approach to its subject, our composer appropriated musical styles from low-budget Sci-Fi and other action/adventure movies, especially those made in the fifties, sixties and seventies ... with a SciFi feel here and there. Cue the theremin!* (ibid.)

The film's opening sequence presents the credits emerging from a middle distance over a digital bass and drum rhythm, repeated keyboard motif and whooshing sound. This music drops in level as the bounty hunter introduces herself in a voice-over. A flying saucer then appears over the road she is driving along, announced by a high digital orchestral wash and a sudden zoom as the spaceship veers off to the hills, where it eventually crash-lands. Images of the saucer, and of the two space girls who emerge from it, are accompanied by short, theremin-like motifs. In addition to their short silver dresses, the space girls' alien nature is emphasized by their speaking a variety of English that uses standard grammatical structures but invented words for key activities.[22] Pfeiffer has identified this as a pastiche on the subtitling of foreign-made films:

> Use of foreign language dialogue accompanied by subtitles has become an established way for contemporary films to establish the supposed authenticity of their characters. The chance to parody this conceit by having our spacegirls speak in a patently ridiculous 'alien tongue' was irresistible. (ibid.)

Despite its specialist BDSM emphasis, the film's playful deployment of classic SF conventions within a fetish framework – acknowledging and revisiting classic SF musical and sonic formulae – makes *SpaceGirls!* closer in approach to *Barbarella* and *Flesh Gordon* than the more sober pastiche of *Porn Wars* or the quasi-realist SF orientation of *The Uranus Experiment*.

While *SpaceGirls!* (unsurprisingly) flew under the radar of mainstream media coverage, a second specialist film received more attention. In November 2005 the British media published various colourful items about the appearance of the Daleks, the arch-villains of the long-running British TV SF series *Dr Who*, in an unauthorized British sexploitation film.[23] The film was originally entitled *Abducted by the Daleks* (with the latter quickly altered to 'Daloids' in an attempt to avoid action by the BBC), and the director entered into the spirit of things by adopting the pseudonym 'Nick Skaros' (after the group of quirky, individualistic Daleks who featured prominently in the programme's 2005–2006 TV series).[24]

The film's scenario involves a female slave-trader bringing three skimpily dressed young women into an area of woodland at night. After scaring them with tales of a serial killer who skins his victims, she abandons them. Following an interlude in which they remove their clothes and 'comfort' each other, they are beamed aboard a Dalek spaceship, where they are interrogated and tormented in ways familiar to regular *Dr Who* viewers (and in a few novel ways as well). The Daleks' iconic visual presence (resembling large pepper pots with frontally mounted raygun and plunger arms, for the uninitiated) is matched by the film's retention of the Daleks' trademark staccato, monotonal voices delivering stock phrases (such as "You must obey" and "Exterminate!").[25] After the slave-trader is beamed aboard, the women mount an unsuccessful escape bid, in the course of which they are killed. The final part of the film involves the slave-trader returning to the woods and being menaced by the (alien) serial killer, only to be saved at the last moment when the Daleks beam the killer aboard and exterminate him.

Embracing the media nostalgia manifested in its choice of the Daleks as villains, the majority of the film's music comprises sections of the orchestral score for *The Mole People* (Virgil Vogel, 1956),[26] extracts from Akira Ifukube's score for *Godzilla* (Ishiro Honda, 1956)[27] and Dominic Frontiere's theme music to the mid-1960s TV series *The Outer Limits*. The extracts from these scores allow the film to use rich, atmospheric orchestral passages to add substance to a narrative that is often impeded by the actresses' minimal dramatic skills. Additional material includes a lengthy sequence from Pink Floyd's 1968 track 'Interstellar Overdrive'[28] used – in combination with a collage of confused Dalek voices – to enhance the narrative excitement of the women's escape attempt. The film's utilization of vintage Hollywood and 1960s rock represents an embrace of classic cinema and TV SF themes and associations within a particularly British lens. While its musical appropriations may have been determined by its unauthorized/illegal status and (related) minuscule budget, its assemblage of extracts of 1950s SF film scores and vintage psychedelic rock passages can be seen to represent 'temp tracks' towards an aesthetic of SF sexploitation/porn that engages more directly with the dynamics of the SF genre rather than simply draping its iconography around a series of sex-scene spectacles.

Conclusion

Over the last decade high-budget productions such as *The Uranus Experiment* and *Porn Wars* have upped the ante for visual effects and set design in SF-themed porn. However, with the exception of the comedy feature *Space Nuts*, similar imagination and resources have not been directed to mainstream films' soundtracks. This reflects the extent to which the SF elements of such films are essentially colorations of a form whose principal function is to deliver sex scenes intended to arouse and gratify its audience in an essentially predictable manner. Given this industry context, it is unlikely that more adventurous approaches to sound design will emerge from the established porn media sector (unless the hardcore genre shifts even further into the cinematic mainstream). While a gambler might well put money on the likelihood of porn parodies following close on the heels of Universal Picture's long-awaited *Barbarella* remake, the immediate past of such niche productions suggests that the future of sonic experimentation in mainstream porn will be limited. In this regard, the specialist fringes of the porn industry can be seen to be less constrained in style and content and more experimental — *playful* even – in their uses of sound and music. It is perhaps appropriate that sexual 'specialisms' of the kind represented in Pfeiffer's and Skaros's productions generate greater sonic experimentation. These productions' eschewal of standard coupling dynamics and a predictable series of male ejaculations facilitated less-formulaic approaches to sound.[29] The presence of such experimentation at the margins conforms to a well-established cultural pattern and provides further confirmation of the porn media industry's replication of mainstream cultural phases of development and entropy. In this regard, in direct contrast to the standardized menus of mainstream porn media, science-fetish cinema offers a greater variety of sonic approaches for those prepared to consume its specialized product.

Notes

1. See Williams (1999: 153–83) for further discussion.
2. Following the brief bloom of (so-called) 'porno chic' in the late 1960s and early 1970s, when it became fashionable for mixed-gender couples and women to attend screenings of pornographic material such as *Deep Throat* (Gerard Damiano,

1972; see the 2005 documentary *Inside Deep Throat* [Fenton Bailey and Randy Barbato] for discussion), the pattern of predominantly male patronage resumed.
3. Whose first name is also spelt 'Cybil' in some credits.
4. The team comprised Patrick M. Griffith (supervising sound editor), John R. F. Halaby (sound mixer) and John Kohlbrenner (sound effects editor).
5. Which commenced with *The Erotic Witch Project* (John Bacchus, 1999) a porn parody of *The Blair Witch Project* (Daniel Myrick and Eduardo Sánchez, 1999).
6. Commencing with *Sex Trek: The Next Penetration* (Scotty Fox) in 1990.
7. Berth Milton, quoted in ' "To Boldly Go": Star Trek, Sex and Space', *Space.Com* (2000), online at http://www.space.com/sciencefiction/movies/milton_interview_000516.html (accessed 19 June 2009).
8. A Swedish-language publication summarized and extracted in English on http://www.lukeisback.com/essays/essays/private.htm (accessed October 2007).
9. The National Association of Securities Dealers Automated Quotations system, the USA's major electronic stock index.
10. The film was produced shortly after Kohler (2000) alleged that secret sex experiments had occurred on board NASA craft in orbit.
11. Quoted in interview with John Millerman (1999), private media press release, on http://kotta.abso.net/uranus2.htm (accessed 30 July 2008).
12. Initially a name Howlett coined for self-produced material. Extra performers were added for live performances and aggregated into the ensemble that achieved major chart success in the mid- to late 1990s.
13. Sequences from the band's 1997 single 'Smack My Bitch Up' were, for instance, used in *Charlie's Angels* (McG, 2000). The SF films *The Matrix* (Wachowski Brothers, 1999) and *Event Horizon* (Paul Anderson, 1997) also used previously recorded tracks by the band – the track 'Mindfields' being featured in the former, while the final sequences of *Event Horizon* incorporated passages from the band's 'Funky Shit'.
14. The group was originally formed by Del Naja, Grant Marshall and Andrew Vowles with irregular collaborator (and later successful solo artist) Tricky.
15. The band provided a cover of the Marvelettes' 1967 Tamla Motown hit 'The Hunter Gets Captured By The Game' for *Batman Forever* (Joel Schumacher, 1995) and a new composition, entitled 'Superpredators', for the soundtrack of the 1997 thriller *Jackal* (Michael Caton-Jones) based around samples from Siouxsie and the Banshees' song 'Metal Postcard'.
16. As yet unreleased in any format.
17. Only released on a limited-edition CD *Nocturne Sessions* (Disk 2) in 2002.
18. The film's commercial success, and the boost it gave to the career of lead actress Stormy Daniels, was reflected by a brief sequence in the hit comedy film *The 40-Year-Old Virgin* (Judd Apatow, 2005), when the male lead (played by Andy Carell) watches her on-screen performance in a DVD of *Space Nuts*.
19. They are concisely summarized on his personal website http://leakybrainmusic.com/leakybrain.htm (accessed 19 June 2009).
20. 'LeakyBrain production music', in *ibid*.

21. Despite its title the film has no relationship to the xxxSpaceGirls website operation.
22. Such as 'zingle' for arousal and 'paddapoos paddapoos' for the principal activity depicted in the film.
23. See, for instance, the text of the Sky News TV item 'Daleks Do Not Do Porn', archived online at http://news.sky.com/skynews/article/0,,30000-13471117,00.html (accessed 19 June 2009).
24. Known as 'The Cult of Skaros'.
25. See Cook (1999) for discussion of the origins and appeal of *Dr Who* and the less-successful attempts to adapt it for cinema.
26. Written by Heinz Roemheld with additional contributions from Hans Salter and Herman Stein and orchestrated by David Tamkin.
27. See Hosokawa (2004) for discussion.
28. The score also features brief musical extracts from two other 1968 Pink Floyd tracks, 'Lucifer Sam' and 'Pow R. Toch H'; Black Sabbath's 'War Pigs' (1970); and the 101 Strings' instrumental version of Rodgers and Hammerstein's song 'Climb Every Mountain' (1996).
29. As *Space Nuts* star Stormy Daniels expressed it in an interview broadcast on the Adult Movie Channel in 2007, it's difficult providing anything different in porn cinema since "most of the people watching the movie ... is a guy at home 'doing his business' ".Interview with Stormy Daniels and Joy King, AMC (2007), archived online at http://uk.video.yahoo.com/video/play?ei=UTF-8&b=4&vid=1348336&gid=709607 (accessed 19 June 2009).

References

Andrews, D. (2006), *Soft in the Middle:The Contemporary Softcore Feature and Its Contexts*, Columbus: Ohio State University Press.
Cook, J. R. (1999), 'Adapting Telefantasy: The *Dr Who and the Daleks* Films', in I. Q Hunter (ed.), *British Science Fiction Cinema*, London: Routledge, pp. 113–27.
Hayward, P. (2004), 'Sci-Fidelity: Music, Sound and Genre History', in P. Hayward (ed.), *Off the Planet: Music, Sound and Science Fiction Cinema*, Eastleigh, Hampshire: John Libbey/Perfect Beat Publications, pp. 1–29.
Hosokawa, S. (2004), 'Atomic Overtones and Primitive Undertones: Akira Ifukube's Sound Design for *Godzilla*', in P. Hayward (ed.), *Off the Planet: Music, Sound and Science Fiction Cinema*, Eastleigh, Hampshire: John Libbey/Perfect Beat Publications, pp. 42–60.
Kohler, P. (2000), *La Dernière Mission: Mir, l'aventure humaine*, Paris: Calmann-Levy.
Sjöberg, T. (2002), *Private med Milton och Milton*, Stockholm: self-published.

Principal filmography

Abducted by the Daloids (Nick Skaros, 2005), Star Films DVD, 2005.
Femalien (Sybil Richards, 1996), Surrender Cinema (Director's Unedited Cut) DVD, 1996.

Porn Wars Episodes 1, 2 and 3 (Kovi, 2006), Private Media DVDs, 2006.
SpaceGirls! (Chelsea Pfeiffer, 2006), Chelsea Pfeiffer Entertainment DVD, 2006.
Space Nuts (Jonathan Morgan, 2003),Wicked DVD, 2003.
The Uranus Experiment Parts 1, 2 and 3 (John Millerman, 1999), Private Black Label
    DVD boxed set, 2003.

8 "It's Gotta Be That New Wave Music"
Music in New Wave Hookers Carries the Joke

Laura Wiebe Taylor

Music is central to the plot of *New Wave Hookers* (Gregory Dark, 1985), the Dark Brothers' hardcore feature fantasy about pimps, prostitution and the hypersexualizing effects of new wave music. As a plot device, popular music in the film offers an easy solution to the problem of turning women on, serving to neutralize the threat of difference posed by female sexuality and stereotyped notions of black virility and sexual potency. The music heard in *New Wave Hookers* also supports the film's humorous tone, offering and fuelling puns, irony, satire and mockery that sometimes underscore and often complicate its misogyny and racism for any viewer in on the joke. Highly self-conscious and allusive, *New Wave Hookers* uses music to express a heightened awareness of pop culture trends, moral debates and cinematic stereotypes. Some of *New Wave Hookers*' humour derives from the "bisociative" incongruity of meaning that defines the popular-song pun,[1] and the movie's proliferation of dirty jokes supports Constance Penley's assertion that "lumpen bawdiness" pervades US porn production (2004: 313). Yet the laughs here do not rely only on puns and lewdness. *New Wave Hookers* foregrounds a deliberately inauthentic hipness, satirizes moral panics about popular music and pornography, and plays with gender and racial stereotypes – and it is the film's incorporation of popular music that carries the joke.

The title of *New Wave Hookers* is itself a rudimentary pun, denoting both the new-wave style of the narrative's hookers and the core of the plot – the fantasy that women become and perform as insatiable hookers when they listen to new wave music. The premise is deceptively straightforward, the terminology less so. The *new wave* tag, even when confined to musical discourses (rather than extending to art, literature or cinema), is a slippery term, its meaning changing depending on whom you look to for a definition, and when. In a broad sense, new wave music refers to the popular genre that was born from the short-lived explosion of punk in the late 1970s (Garofalo, 1997: 329). At various times, the 'new wave' label has been used interchangeably with 'punk', as a complementary term capturing the artiness that the more vulgar connotations of punk excluded, as a way to distinguish post-punk bands from first-wave punk artists, or as an umbrella term for either the UK or New York underground music scenes (Gendron, 2002: 227, 270–3). New wave also came to represent the commercialization of punk, a 'co-opted' form of punk rock that was toned down, repackaged and marketed as new wave for mainstream audiences (Leblanc, 1999: 48, 235). In this sense, new wave provided the ideal non-threatening MTV-friendly successor to original punk (Reddington, 2007: 145–6). New wave, as invoked by *New Wave Hookers*, is a similarly slippery signifier, encompassing a wide range of punk and new wave music and fashion, but the film's version of new wave ultimately functions as a satire of subcultural subversiveness, recuperating the imagery and sounds of underground music and style to fuel masculine sexual fantasy.

New Wave Hookers empties punk of its original ironic and parodic potential to make room for the film's own ironic and satirical gestures, including the way it cashes in on new wave's mainstream currency to manufacture an inauthentic sense of hipness years after the explosion of punk and new wave as a subcultural scene. Punk is well known for its oppositional stance, embracing 'outcast status', challenging traditional values and showcasing the forbidden (such as bondage gear) out on the public street (Hebdige, 1979: 107–10). Female punks parodied stereotypes of female sexuality with hypersexual and asexual extremes (Leblanc, 1999: 45), and even a more accessible new wave artist such as Blondie's Deborah Harry maintained a "campily ironic distance" (Lester Bangs, quoted in Gendron, 2002: 289) from the "vulnerable sexuality" and conventional femininity that she performed (*ibid*.: 288). Yet new wave and punk outsiders could (and did) adopt the subculture's styles without understanding the message (Hebdige, 1979: 222). Female punks' play on feminine sexual stereotypes might also be misread – still shots of a fetish-gear-clad Siouxsie Sioux (Siouxsie and the Banshees), for example, might seem like a deliberate attempt at "soft porn" (Laing, 1985: 94). Similarly, the aggressively confident exhibitionism and sexually explicit performances of female new wavers and (post-)punks such as Wendy O Williams or Lydia Lunch could leave a mainstream audience perplexed.[2] The characters in *New Wave Hookers* are like those subcultural outsiders, showing up on screen wearing studded collars and bracelets, handcuffs or bondage belts as signifiers of sexual fetish without any sense of critical irony or subversive critique. One of the male leads, Jimmy (Jamie Gillis), wears a shirt bearing a large anarchy symbol for most of the film, yet his commitment to punk appears to go no deeper than his outfit – his only social deviance is pimping. The women adopt punk and new wave trends, including torn shirts and multi-coloured teased-up hair, as a result of their exposure to new wave music, yet their performance of objectified sexuality only challenges traditional, passive femininity through their heightened (music-induced) sexual desire.

As for new wave sounds, the film's musical soundtrack comprises a mix of popular songs and sections of songlike score that predominantly draws on new wave and punk musical conventions. *New Wave Hookers* eschews the more aggressive and angry punk styles, going instead for more laid-back reggae- and R&B-influenced songs with atypical lyrics alluding to courtship and romance, or more avant-garde new wave tracks that mix or replace traditional rock structures, harmonies and timbres with experiments in atonality or non-melodic patterns, wandering structures or jagged rhythms, and abrasive, often electronic, tones. One new wave song, in particular, serves to transform young women into "new wave hookers" on two separate occasions; it is an up-beat track combining old-school rock and roll and lyrics about romance and desire with a reggae-influenced guitar tone and beat, imbuing the sex scenes it accompanies with a playful vibe. Other musical accompaniments are used to signify settings, such as the sound of a marching band identifying a pennant-decorated space as a college dorm, or the eastern-inflected track that plays during a 'desert' sexual number featuring an 'Arab' man or 'Sheik' (sounding somewhat like a new wave interpretation of Jefferson Airplane's 'White Rabbit'). Like its adoption of new wave visual style, the film's appropriation of new wave music is superficial; it is new wave in the co-opted, commercialized sense – subcultural sounds without the threat of ideological challenge or any indication of gender-role critique. That this sanitization occurs within hardcore porn is part of the film's comic irony: one underground subculture exploiting and recuperating another.

Linda Williams captures the importance of music to the film when she describes *New Wave Hookers* as a "music video-style musical" which culminates in a "big production number" (1989: 163). Classifying the ultimate sexual number as "big production" relies on comparison; this scene runs the longest and features the largest on-screen cast (although the version I viewed showed only three women in the final number rather than the twelve Williams refers to),[3] but the film, or more accurately video, largely maintains a low-budget minimalist aesthetic. Its theatrical, rather than realistic, sets appropriately evoke the "alien/unstable backgrounds" that E. Ann Kaplan associates with new wave/punk videos in the "nihilist" style[4] – another of the film's connections to the commercialized, MTV version of new wave. Director Gregory Dark recalls shooting *New Wave Hookers* "pretty much as a music video ... We had these speakers out while shooting the sex scenes, and I cranked the music up on the girls to get live sound. So they were inundated with this music collectively" (quoted in Petkovich, 2002: 46). Unsurprisingly, Dark's more recent work includes directing music videos as well as feature films. He has directed videos for artists such as the Melvins, Xzibit, Sublime and even Britney Spears, in addition to the second, third and fourth films in the *New Wave Hookers* series (O'Brien, 2002: 483; Petkovich, 2002: 42; http://www.imdb.com/name/nm0201283, accessed 3 February 2008).

"Hip, politically incorrect 'New Wave' straight porn": porn humour and new wave fantasies

Williams classifies *New Wave Hookers* as a "separated utopia," like other Dark Brothers films that "separate the utopian world of sexual performance from the real world" while exaggerating their own "misogyny" and "sleaziness" (1989: 162–3). Drawing upon Richard Dyer's analysis of the Hollywood musical for her classification of pornographic film styles, Williams compares the separated utopia to a Busby Berkeley film, with its "tendency toward non-representational abstract formal patterns" and the "famous Berkeley production numbers associated with surrealist fantasy or dream" (*ibid.*: 160). While "dreariness and [sexual] scarcity" may characterize the non-fantasy narrative sections of these separated utopias, such problems are resolved through the "phallic and commodified intensity and abundance" of the utopian sexual numbers, which offer unrealistic solutions to contemporary sexual problems (*ibid.*: 161–3).

New Wave Hookers frames its narrative in the reality of dreariness and scarcity – opening in a messy and sleazy apartment and closing with a return to the apartment and emergence into the grim night outside. But the film spends most of its time in the completely separate shared dream of the two male protagonists, Jamal (Jack Baker) and Jimmy. In the waking world, porn-watching Jamal and Jimmy want sex but have no "chick" to "bop". As Jimmy says: "You gotta find one or buy one. See, if we was pimps we'd have all the pussy we wanted. That's the good life." Their dream world puts this fantasy into action: they imagine themselves as pimps, running a prostitution agency from a dingy office and having unlimited access to horny women. But while pimp Jimmy describes himself as "rich" and "satisfied," back in the waking world the film leaves him literally running after one of the women he had sex with in his dream. The problem, as this scene demonstrates, is not simply finding or buying a woman. When you find her she still may not want to have sex with you – women's desire is unreliable. The most obvious way the film deals with the problem of female difference and desire is to neutralize it through the instantaneous and automatic aphrodisiac of new wave music, but *New Wave Hookers* also manages gender tensions by making women (as well as men) the butts of multiple jokes.

Separated utopias, like the early cinematic pornography of the stag film, offer identification with the male point of view and reproduce a form of "males only" camaraderie (Williams, 1989: 163). Crude humour is typical of American stag films, suggests Williams (*ibid.*: 62), a point which Constance Penley elaborates in 'Crackers and Whackers: The White Trashing of Porn', noting that stag films are "full of humor" and that the narrative "is itself structured like a joke" (2004: 314). Responding to Peter Lehman's critique that Williams underestimates the "fleeting moments" of humour in pornographic film, Penley suggests that the tone of pornography is generally humorous, "closer to *Hee Haw* than Nazi death camp fantasies," and that women are not the only object of laughter – pornography often situates the man as the "butt of the joke" (2004: 314). Although bawdy humour declines with the social conservatism of "golden-age pornos" in the 1970s, Penley observes a return of "trashy" laughs in the 1980s and 1990s as porn-film producers "threw off the 'quality' trappings of the golden era to start manufacturing [populist] product for the rapidly expanding VCR market" (2004: 321). Such humour features prominently in *New Wave Hookers*, mocking middle-class sexual morality, playing on gender and racial stereotypes, and even making fun of male characters' displays of sexual immaturity. But the too-naïve viewer may also become the target of laughter for taking too much, including the film's musical references, at face value. The self-conscious new wave 'hipness' of *New Wave Hookers* is one of the several characteristics at which the discerning audience member can knowingly wink. Among the uses of popular music in film, as Robb Wright notes, is the potential to represent, at least at face value, the domain of the hip (Wright, 2003: 19–20); thus, a film may seem hip, "contemporary" and "aware" by association. When Williams describes Gregory Dark as a pioneer of "hip, politically incorrect 'New Wave' straight porn" (Williams, 2004: 282), we might make the explicit connection that she only implies – that Dark's use of music is tied up in the sense of 'hipness' which films such as *New Wave Hookers* convey. Yet Wright's caveat – that pop music only represents the hip "at face value" – is crucial to an understanding of one of the ways Dark uses music as joke. Of the actual songs punctuating the score of the film, at least two are several years old: 'Electrify Me,' which plays throughout the opening credits, is the title track from a 1979 album by Latino punk band the Plugz, and 'Blue Sofa,' which appears near the end, is from their 1981 album, *Better Luck*.[5] These not-quite-current songs impart a slightly nostalgic, behind-the-times quality to *New Wave Hookers*, an out-datedness that Dark most likely intended, as one of his later comments on the film indicates:

> *I mean, the whole new wave music thing was at its conclusion in '84. Of course, the porn industry is incredibly backwards – with media, advertising, marketing. And when NWH* [New Wave Hookers] *came out, new wave music had already pretty much been replaced by alternative music.* (Petkovich, 2002: 46)

In part, this joke – the incongruity of the purportedly hip but subculturally passé – mocks the porn industry, but it also mocks the two main characters, the middle-aged new wave punk Jimmy and his non-new wave African American friend Jamal, who want to tap into the hipness of offering "new wave hookers" or "today's chicks", as Jimmy refers to them, to their clientele. The joke additionally makes fun of the viewer who too readily accepts the hipness attributed to the film by what is actually a commercialized and nostalgic appropriation of a musical scene that has passed its subcultural prime.

The twist to Jamal and Jimmy's plan to become pimps, the key to their gimmick, fuels and carries much of the film's humour; it is the pseudo-science fictional fantasy that women can be programmed or conditioned for sex with new wave music. *New Wave Hookers* signals the connection between humour and female arousal in its opening frames with a musical pun: the Plugz' lyrics, "I got this fire burnin' inside me", synchronize with a shot of a woman rotating her pelvis while reaching her hand inside her panties ('Electrify Me'). The reference to desire is straightforward, but the identification of who is "burnin' inside" is ambiguous – the image is female, the voice male, perhaps asserting that the one (a masturbating woman) produces the other (an aroused man). Throughout this title sequence – a montage of shots featuring "lesbian" sex, masturbating women and female genital display – the film's title remains ambiguous as well, potentially referring to the hookers' visual style, their musical preference, or the 'nowness' of their sexual predilections. Some of the women look 'new wave', with studded leather accessories, heavy make-up and multi-coloured hair offering a mass-market version of punk and new wave style, but their arousal already coincides with (and may originate from) the performance of new wave music on the soundtrack, setting up the main premise of the film's plot.[6]

New wave: the ultimate sexual solution

As a narrative device, new wave music represents the ultimate answer to sexual scarcity and female difference and desire: access to new wave music, at least in *New Wave Hookers'* fantasy realm, guarantees access to unlimited sex. "You pick these chicks up and program 'em to fuck by music, man," Jimmy explains to Jamal as they formulate the fantasy that their shared dream will soon enact. Up to this point in the opening narrative sequence, the scene's background music has featured parts of two new wave songs – first distorted guitar and synthesizer with a barely discernible vocal chorus and then an instrumental track with a heavy funk beat, both foreshadowing the new wave music that will accompany sex later. But as the waking fantasy prepares to shift to vivid dream, the new wave sounds abruptly wind down and are replaced by the dream cue of harp glissando. When music is heard next on the soundtrack (in a fantasy scene with a roller-skater named Candy), it is to demonstrate that *New Wave Hookers'* solution to female desire and pleasure is the same answer it poses for scarcity – the programming of women with music. No seduction is necessary; just get young women to listen to new wave music, something they already want to do, and they will automatically, inevitably and amusingly become aroused, desiring and deriving pleasure from sex. The music gives them no other alternative.

Hanging around the dream-world office of New Wave Hookers, Incorporated, Jamal and Jimmy discuss the comical incomprehensibility and benefits of women's response to new wave. They repeatedly refer to their use of music to "condition" and "programme" "bitches," reducing these women to animalized automata – more organic versions of the female robots "programmed for pleasure" in science-fiction films such as *Westworld* (Dery, 1996: 193), or the "pleasure model" replicants in *Blade Runner* (Barr, 1991: 30), whose only purpose is to serve men's sexual needs. Embodying male fantasy, "new wave hookers" are always ready for sex if there is new wave music involved, and they express no desires or gauges of pleasure that differ from the men's own. The women's response to music, as if it were their "sex drug", encourages Jamal to see them as beings "from another planet", but when Jimmy refers to women as "aliens" Jamal quickly denies it. "Hell, they ain't nothin' but bitches," he says, minimizing and containing their gendered difference. He later refers to the new wave hookers as "natural bitches", in effect implying that their prostitution and enthralment through music is "natural" as well.

In Jamal's eyes, women are inherently sex and music junkies, such slaves to desire and unable to control themselves that for the promise of drugs (new wave music) they will give away "that pussy for free". This image of women as lacking in will-power, self-discipline or self-determination operates to legitimize Jamal and Jimmy's roles as pimps and justifies their paternalistic management of the women's sexual lives.

The druglike relationship between women and music that Jamal describes is comically dramatized in two sexual numbers that take place inside the office. In these scenes the women's reaction to new wave music is immediate, and any semblance of free will they initially demonstrate quickly disappears once Jamal places a set of headphones over their ears. As soon as the music starts — it is the same up-beat, reggae-influenced new wave song in each case — the women begin to writhe and masturbate. The first prospective prostitute, Candy (Desiree Lane), rolls into the office on skates in response to a job ad. Jamal and Jimmy sit facing each other at desks placed at opposite ends of the grimy, graffiti-decorated room; a couch sits along the adjoining wall, and a young blond male (identified alternately as a "bum" and as Jamal's pet "dog") is on the floor. Candy initially resists Jimmy's and the dog/man's groping and grasping hands and seems unaware she is applying to work as a hooker. Rather than discussing the job, Jamal asks her, "Do you dig that new wave music?" and begins listing what sound like band names: the Dead Rats, the Bandidos, Band Aids ... At the mention of the Band Aids, Candy excitedly asks, "Have you heard their latest release?" and bends forward to hear it at Jamal's suggestion. She begins to touch herself as soon as the song starts, then soon pulls out a vibrator, and while the lyrics repeat: "She wants my ... what? / She needs my ... what? ... love," she moves from self-pleasure to sex with Jimmy and the dog/man character while Jamal watches and masturbates. The connotative possibilities of the song lyrics, which take on a "pornographic resonance" (Smith, 2001: 427) by association, result in another musical pun.[7] The ensuing sexual number illustrates that "love" is code for "sex", or even more precisely, "cock", as Candy (headset long gone) fellates and manually stimulates the dog/man while Jimmy penetrates her from behind.

The second office number begins similarly but with even less effort on the men's part. The young woman (Kristara Barrington), a sushi delivery girl, kisses Jimmy even before she has heard any music, and Jamal does not even mention "new wave" this time; he merely offers her the chance to listen to some music. She asks, "What kind?" but puts on the headset without waiting for an answer. With the first notes, reprising what sounds like an extended chorus from the track that triggered Candy's sexual excitement earlier, she lifts up her miniskirt and begins to masturbate. In the sexual number that follows, the woman — Jamal calls her "Susie Sushi" at one point but she reveals her name as Kammy — engages in oral and/or vaginal sex with each of the three men, her obedient responses to Jamal's orders emphasizing her lack of self-determination. He removes her headphones and "tastes" her, she fellates him and the dog/man, and the latter penetrates her while she lies on one of the desks, Jimmy and Jamal holding her in place. Meanwhile the new wave music, having performed its role as a catalyst for sexual activity, fades and surges beneath Kammy's moans of sexual pleasure, the song's own vocal track and lyrics subordinated to the sounds of sex. The musical soundtrack then shifts from what is essentially rock music to the more dreamy timbres of the score – a soft, high-pitched, bell-like melody and an electronic pizzicato bleep.[8] When the reggae beat returns Jamal gets his only 'money shot' of the film; Kammy's obedience here ("Lick me clean," he says, "lick my balls" – and she does) and Jamal's assertion, "You're gonna come work for me", suggest that new wave music has transformed Kammy into a sex slave.[9] Thus the popular music soundtrack supports one of the film's most misogynistic representations.

Moral panics and musical satire

The satirical resonance of Kammy's and Candy's susceptibility to the sexual influence of new wave music derives from the way in which this scenario echoes moral panics about the effects of rock and roll. Crusades against rock's sexuality would have been familiar demonstrations of middle-class anxiety by the 1980s, with young women often identified as the listeners most at risk (Frith and McRobbie, 1990: 388), and *New Wave Hookers*' depiction of music as a drug and/or programming input functions in part as a satire on such conservative fears. In the 1970s, for example, the Reverend Jesse Jackson spearheaded a campaign which blamed sexuality in rock lyrics for increases in illegitimate births and abortions (Chastagner, 1999: 184), and by the early 1980s the American National Parent/Teacher Association began to express concerns about 'obscene' or 'pornographic' lyrics in rock music (*ibid.*: 181). This latter panic led to the formation of the Parents' Music Resource Center (PMRC) in 1985 and the group's efforts to establish a causal link between rock music and problems such as rape or teenage pregnancy (*ibid.*: 181). The masculinity of rock music's sexuality is one of the reasons it was deemed a threat to young women, who were meant to conform to ideals of feminine passivity and yearn for romance,[10] but rock also provided the soundtrack for sexual liberation – accessible to some women, even if it was presented as a masculine prerogative (Frith and McRobbie, 1990). In effect, rock music "operates both as a form of sexual expression and as a form of sexual control" through its ideological constructions of masculine and feminine sexuality (*ibid.*: 373). *New Wave Hookers*' narrative use of new wave music draws upon both these associations, enabling the expression of sexual arousal and, for men, fulfilment of sexual desire while providing a means of controlling women's sexuality.

In keeping with the film's humour, this plot device is employed haphazardly, its use never very thorough, precise or serious. The young women barely put on the headsets before they begin to respond with hypersexual behaviour, and in the office scenes the headphones, which have large plastic breasts for earpieces, are not even connected to any sound source.[11] Each earpiece sports a dangling cord that leads nowhere, and the music that starts up as the women put on the headsets comes from no identifiable diegetic source. The use of headphones in other sexual numbers is even more perfunctory. Music plays throughout each of the film's sexual numbers but acts as a trigger for sex only in the office scenes. The three women who go out on calls wear a small earpiece in one ear at the beginning of their numbers but soon remove it; the cords dangling from the earpieces lead to no sound source. In the final 'big' number the film makes even less effort to establish a direct connection between the music and the women's sexual excitement; these three women are supposedly "hooked up", undergoing "conditioning", but they wear no headsets at all and again music with no visible diegetic source plays throughout the scene. This comic carelessness sabotages any attempt to take the idea of "programming chicks to fuck by music" seriously while mocking any moralist who believes in a direct causal relationship between the sexuality of rock music – or porn – and actual sexual behaviour.

Moral panics about the link between rock music and sex are much like the arguments of anti-pornography activists who try to establish a causal relationship between pornography and sexual violence (see Williams, 1989: 16–23). *New Wave Hookers* satirizes both and demonstrates that the difference between the two arguments unfolds along gender lines. While it is the music's effect on the women that the film emphasizes, the men are equally quick to respond to any sexual stimulus; the women may be vulnerable to the sexual influence of music, but for the men the 'sex drug' is pornography. When Jamal and Jimmy are first introduced we find them watching pornographic videos, and Jamal notices that the "flicks" have a "weird" effect on him: "Makes me wanna go out and bop some chick." The characters' exposure to pornography goes beyond the videos on Jamal's television; pornographic posters adorn his living-room walls, pornographic magazines are piled up on his couch and table, and the dream office maintains a similar porn-themed decorating style. Conditioned by all this pornography, the men in the film are unable to control themselves in the presence of women, and faced with a woman who has been aroused by music they do not even try; they immediately engage in sex with her or masturbate while watching her have sex with someone else. Even the vice cops who show up during the final number are unable to resist the temptation and agree not to arrest Jamal or Jimmy in exchange for free sex: access to "any of these fuckin' bitches [that they] want any fuckin' day of the week" and the chance to "pile on" then and there. Although such behaviour is conventional for a pornographic film, after Jamal's initial comment on the effects of viewing porn the men's lack of self-control might also be read as a satire on moral outrage about pornography, paralleling the satire on moral panics about the sexual influence of rock. The characters' programmability, including the implied programming of men through porn, satirizes fears of pornography's "power to override or short-circuit our sense of propriety" and snidely mocks resulting debates about the relationship between pornography and how viewers will act (see Clover, 1993: 3). In the filmic world of *New Wave Hookers*, both music and pornography lead to unrestrained sexual behaviour, turning moralists' nightmares into jokes.

The irony of gender and race

Comic satire turns to irony when it comes to the particular type of music that releases women's sexual proclivities. In *New Wave Hookers* it seems like any old porn will inspire men to act out on their sexual desires, but for the women, as Jamal tells a prospective customer,

> "If you wanna screw these bitches, you gotta be playin' that new wave music. You know, that silly ass rock 'n' roll shit? No man, no nigger music, no nigger music. It's gotta be strictly the new wave."

A short time later he wonders, "What the hell does that new wave music got that black music doesn't?" and is perplexed that the women do not respond to "soul". While the choice of new wave is tied to the film's construction of hipness, it also serves as an ironic comment on punk and new wave's complicated relationship with sexual pleasure and with African American and Afro-Caribbean musical influences, and the emphasis on black music's sexual ineffectiveness is a play on and ironic reversal of racialized sexual stereotypes.

Traditionally, it has been African American genres of music that have inspired the most white middle-class sexual anxiety (Chastagner, 1999: 183), and moral panics about rock and roll were inspired in part by the music's African American origins in rhythm and blues (Garofalo, 1997: 152). Rhythm, a defining element in rock and one of R&B's key contributions to the genre, has been understood as "naturally sexual" (Frith and McRobbie, 1990: 386), the beat seeming to command a physical response (Frith, 1978: 240). As Frith and McRobbie point out, "Rock's rhythmic insistence can be heard as a sexual insistence" (1990: 388). Pornographic film has taken advantage of the relationship between beat and movement in its sexual numbers, capitalizing on the similarity between the rhythmic and melodic features in the sounds of music and of pleasure (Williams, 1989: 124). However, *New Wave Hookers*, in its insistence on the whiteness of new wave music, distances itself from the sexuality of rhythm and blues, 1950s rock and roll or 1960s rock.

The punk and new wave music cultures the movie alludes to and borrows from have a much more antagonistic relationship with conventional ideas of sexuality than does traditional rock. Punk music and style have been read as a disruption of rock's equation between sex and pleasure[12] and a rejection of the "sexual language" of rock's musical roots (Frith and McRobbie, 1990: 384), even as an "asexual" expression of "castration-paranoia" (Reynolds and Press, 1995: 23) or as a marker of sexual deviance (Hebdige, 1979: 121). Punk and new wave was also the site of female sexual resistance. UK bands like the Slits confounded gender performance, while the Raincoats attempted a musical "revolution" (Reddington, 2007: 109–10). Meanwhile, the New York punk/new wave scene served as the setting for violent and aggressive expressions of female sexuality from Lydia Lunch's performances in and out of Teenage Jesus and the Jerks (O'Brien, 2002: 158–9) to "ex-porn-star" Wendy O Williams's bondage garb and blowing up of cars while fronting the Plasmatics (Leblanc, 1999: 50). *New Wave Hookers* captures none of this subversiveness or female aggression. In another ironic and potentially satirical twist, the film strips new wave of its sexual deviance, explicitly associating the style and music of punk and new wave with relatively conventional (at least in pornographic terms) images of sex and arousal.

New Wave Hookers' ironic and comic denial of the sexual potency of "black music" and its rhythm is also a reversal of the stereotype that portrays blackness as innately sexual. The discursive construction of the hypersexualized black man, as Richard Fung has observed, is a familiar stereotype in western popular culture (cited in Hoang, 2004: 224). *New Wave Hookers* is conscious of this stereotype – Kammy once refers to Jamal as "big bad black man", and at one point Jamal (telling Jimmy he is not allowed to sample the merchandise) says, "You ain't black – I'm the only one that can taste the bitches until I say different." While Kammy's comment foregrounds the stereotype to heighten the pleasurable and threatening eroticization of Jamal's black body (see Williams, 2004: 281), the film attempts to neutralize the threat which black male virility and sexual potency pose to white masculinity. Classical cinema enacted a prohibition against sex between black men and white women; in porn this prohibition is a source of sexual excitement (*ibid*.: 271). *New Wave Hookers* takes advantage of this excitement while keeping the African American male's sexuality carefully contained.

In the opening, waking-world narrative sequence Jamal and Jimmy watch an interracial porno, but the spectre of the hypersexed black man immediately rears its head (literally, when a black penis comes into view on the television screen). The film promptly undoes any progressive potential in this portrayal of interracial sex with Jimmy's exclamation, "That fucking guy looks exactly like you! Is that you?" Jamal responds, "That nigger don't look nothin' like me, man", but of course the joke here is that it could be Jack Baker, who plays Jamal, acting in another pornographic video – the image on Jamal's television is not clear enough to tell for certain, but Baker's other porno credits include the 1984 Dark Brothers' film *Let Me Tell Ya 'Bout White Chicks* and a role as "Jamal the pimp" in *Black Throat* (1985) (http://www.imdb.com/name/nm0047323; accessed 11 February 2008). Just before this, the new wave soundtrack features the repeated phrase "white chicks", and though the lyrics are barely discernible, the song encourages the informed viewer to assume it is Baker on the television. Jamal's challenge to Jimmy's racism (thinking that all black men are interchangeable or look the same) is delivered in the same tone of low-brow humour as Jimmy's original joke; however, the racism and the humour both serve to defuse the threat of the black man penetrating the white woman on the screen within the screen. This pattern of containment and neutralization continues throughout the film. Although Jamal appears to run New Wave Hookers, Incorporated, he gets very little contact time with the girls and none at all with any girl coded as unequivocally white. In the first and in the last number he mostly watches the action, masturbating on the sidelines, and the only woman he comes in direct contact with – through cunnilingus and fellatio, not penetration – appears racially ambiguous:

Kammy, the submissive sushi delivery girl played by Asian American Kristara Barrington, is verbally lumped in with the "white girls" but enacts another sexual stereotype, that of the passive and sexually accommodating Asian woman.[13] The containment of Jamal's sexuality culminates in the final number when his masturbation is interrupted by the ringing telephone, denying him a second orgasm while provoking unsympathetic laughter at his frustration.

Yet, as if to add another layer to the musical joke and undermine the film's own neutralization of black sexuality, the music in *New Wave Hookers* is not strictly or purely 'white' music, despite all Jamal's protestations to the contrary. While the straight rhythms of much punk rock tend to "submerge" rock's rhythm and blues origins – specifically its reliance on the African American element of syncopation (Laing, 1985: 61–2) – punk's evolution towards new wave entailed a rebuilding of connections to "black music" through the incorporation of influences from reggae, R&B, and even elements of disco (Garofalo, 1997: 333). Punk and new wave may have been "the first significant rock music movement" to avoid explicit displays of a "blues or soul foundation" (Gendron, 2002: 284), but it was new wave's turn to soul, reggae and disco that produced its first real popular successes (*ibid.*: 286).[14] In *New Wave Hookers*, both the title sequence track ('Electrify Me') and the song playing during the office numbers ("She wants my ... love") rely on a strong reggae beat, exposing punk's and new wave's debt to black musical traditions. This exposure occurs in all of the popular songs on the soundtrack. The penultimate, return-to-reality song ('Blue Sofa') owes a comparable debt to rhythm and blues, particularly in its use of the saxophone as a lead melodic voice. The last song featured on the soundtrack – a reiteration of the instrumental rock-based new wave music playing during part of the final sexual number – draws upon a more contemporary African American genre, incorporating rap vocals. The choice of Latino punk band the Plugz to provide music for the film further complicates simple racialized musical dichotomies; although they were not black men playing soul and nothing in the film points to their Latino background, they pose a challenge to the identification of punk and new wave with Anglo-Saxon 'whiteness'.[15] However, contextualized within the film's frequent recourse to laughter, the disjunctions in *New Wave Hookers*' representations of racialized sexuality and music feature as just another joke, mocking anyone who understands too literally the stereotype of the hypersexualized black man, or Jamal's separation of new wave and black music.

Back to reality: superficial appropriation and (not so) fleeting pleasures

But in the narrative of *New Wave Hookers* the ultimate joke is on Jamal and Jimmy, who awaken to find their elaborate fantasy was only a dream. They wake up surrounded by porn rather than women, and their interaction with each other provides additional humour. In their final scene together the two men act more like a romantic couple than pals, and the song that plays during the transition from dream to reality (the

R&B-influenced 'Blue Sofa') underlines both the implied romance and their removal from the fantasy world, capitalizing on the ambiguity of the pronoun 'you'. The men are still hanging on to their dream-world sex fantasies, as the lyrics imply, but ambiguous pronouns in the line "I'm still an idiot, still in love ... love with you" help shift attention to the two men's seemingly intimate relationship with each other. When Jimmy wakes he tenderly rouses Jamal, saying, "Hey, babe, I'm gonna take off, okay?" As he finally gets up, Jamal asks, with a concerned (yearning?) expression on his face, "Hey, Jimmy, hey, Jimmy, will you call me later?" (Of course, the audience 'knows' one-night stands never call you back.) On his drive home Jimmy speculates that he needs a "straight job," or to get married, but his confusion is ambiguous enough for a viewer to wonder whether it is the dream that has disturbed him or his interaction with Jamal.

Jimmy's comments indicate that his uneasiness arises at least in part from the fact that he and Jamal experienced the same dream, and he is haunted by aural and visual flashbacks while he drives. Fantasy intrudes into his reality and sabotages his half-hearted impulse to settle down. A montage of images from the dream's sexual numbers takes over the screen, and the musical soundtrack reprises the song heard in the final sexual number, now with lyrics such as "new wave hookers" and "new wave makes 'em hot" to identify this as the movie's implicit theme song. When the film cuts back to reality, Jimmy stops to offer a young woman a ride; she turns out to be a real-world version of Kammy, a further intrusion of the dream into his waking consciousness. But when he touches her face and says, "You're real", she responds with disdain – "Cut the shit, Jimmy" – and walks away. Jimmy runs after her, and the following high-angle shot shows the top of his abandoned car, closing the movie with one more, literally empty, phallic symbol. Even as these intrusions of fantasy tantalizingly imply that Jamal and Jimmy's dream may have some basis in reality, Kammy's ability and choice to walk away affirms the impossibility of their fantasy. In the end, Jimmy and Jamal are still just two comical working-class guys who are not getting any sex.

The *New Wave Hookers* videos, the original and six sequels,[16] were successful enough to earn the title of "*Hustler*'s highest rated series" (according to the DVD packaging), a success that could derive in part from the film's ability to generate laughter – *Hustler* is, after all, the print manifestation of mass commercial porn's "deliberately stupid humour" and white trash "raunchiness and sluttiness", as Constance Penley notes (2004: 313). But gags, like musical puns, may function as humorous "throwaways", engaging a "brief affective response" that is immediately forgotten (Smith, 2001: 414–15). Porn humour generated by video titles may have nothing to do with the movie at all (Lehman, 1995/96: 7), and musical puns, while serving a narrative function, often do little or nothing to actually advance a film's narrative (Smith, 2001: 423). As Peter Lehman observes, narrative in porn occupies a contradictory role, perhaps even more so since the transition of porn production from film to home video (and now DVD) and the resulting potential for discontinuous viewing that wreaks "havoc with narrative structure" (1995/96: 5). Feature-length porn films may boast "meaningful" narrative patterns, but there is also truth to the cliché that porn narrative "is indeed a pretext": people watch porn for the sex (Lehman, 1995/96: 13–14) and listen for the sounds of pleasure (*ibid.*: 6–7). If narrative can be subordinated to porn's more erotic pleasures, then an understanding of *New Wave Hookers'* musical humour – which occupies a subordinate "perceptual register" (Smith, 2001: 414–15) – seems even less crucial to enjoyment of the film. New wave music is central to *New Wave Hookers'* aesthetic, plot, narrative development and humour, but the musical soundtrack (and its jokes) may turn out to be just another source of what Lehman identifies as porn's "heterogeneous, fleeting, and fragmentary pleasures" (1995/96: 6–7).

Thus *New Wave Hookers* offers one final joke when the movie is over: that all this semi-sophisticated self-conscious irony and satire may be as superficial as its hipness. Attentive viewing and listening to *New Wave Hookers* reveals the film's relative ironic and satirical complexity – sources of perhaps unexpected pleasure – but the last laugh could come at the expense of the audience that 'gets it', the viewer (or critic) who takes all this embedded complexity too seriously. While the self-conscious reflexivity of *New Wave Hookers* suggests that the Dark Brothers were well aware of the conventions of misogyny and racism their film reproduces, awareness does not serve as disruption or challenge, and, really, the film's sex is only new wave in a very trivial sense. The accommodatingly programmed 'new wave hookers' would be more at home in a music video than at a punk or new wave concert, and Jamal and Jimmy latch onto new wave not for its ideological associations but as a potential business gimmick and a fantasy solution for their sexual problems. At the same time, while *New Wave Hookers* enacts no real subversion, the film's new wave music is inseparable from its vocalizations of sex, the musical soundtrack dipping and surging in a cinematic duet with the actors' moans and cries in a recurring series of sonic climaxes, competing for attention at the aural, if not the visual, register. At that level, and in the realm of sexual fantasy, new wave music remains integral to the *New Wave Hookers'* basic claim that new wave music guarantees good sex – perhaps a not-so-fleeting pleasure after all.

Acknowledgements

I would like to thank the anonymous referees of this volume for their helpful and thought-provoking comments and questions.

Notes

1. In 'Popular Songs and Comic Allusion in Contemporary Cinema' Jeff Smith draws upon Arthur Koestler's Freud- and Bergson-influenced explanation of "bisocation" in humour – the juxtaposition of two distinct "associative chains of logic" that produces "incongruous ways of seeing something, such as a person, sentence, or situation" – to define the popular-song pun (2001: 416). *Boogie Nights* (Paul Thomas Anderson, 1997), for example, is rife with musical puns, such as the ELO song 'Livin' Thing', which in the context of the film becomes a reference to

fictional porn star Dirk Diggler's very large penis (*ibid.*: 426–7). Smith classifies the use of popular songs for ironic commentary as typical of the self-conscious intertextuality of postmodern cinematic style (*ibid.*: 407–8).
2. Williams, for example, appeared in the porn comedy *Candy Goes to Hollywood* (Gail Palmer, 1979) and was arrested on a public obscenity charge (but acquitted) in 1981 (http://www.imdb.com/title/tt0123627/, http://plasmatics.com/BioPage4.html; accessed 14 June 2008). Lunch's confrontational work includes several collaborations with underground director Richard Kern: "Together they realized Lunch's shocking personal vision of sexual violence and desire in [films such as] *The Right Side of My Brain* and *Fingered*" (http://www.lydia-lunch.org/biography.html; accessed 14 June 2008).
3. This discrepancy could be due to the fact that the film has been recut and reissued since its original release. The original print featured an underage Traci Lords and subsequent North American versions have had her scenes removed (Carnal Cinema review of *New Wave Hookers*, http://www.carnal-cinema.net/new%20wave.htm; accessed 19 February 2008). The recut version is the one analysed here: *New Wave Hookers* (Gregory Dark, 1985; DVD (1999), Chatsworth, CA: VCA Labs, Inc.
4. Such videos feature re-creations of performance, "aggressive use of camera and editing", Expressionist or film noir lighting, and "disorienting and disturbing music", among other characteristics (Kaplan, 1987: 60–1).
5. Los Angeles punk band the Plugz may be better known for their musical contribution to *Repo Man* (Alex Cox, 1984); Plugz member Tito Larriva, who later performed in the Cruzados, has appeared in and/or contributed music to numerous Hollywood films, including *From Dusk Till Dawn* (Robert Rodriguez, 1996) (see Inoue, 1998). A 1998 interview with Larriva suggests that the Plugz composed the score for *New Wave Hookers* in addition to contributing two prerecorded songs (*ibid.*). The film also credits musical contributions by a band (probably fictional) called the Sockets.
6. The association of new wave style with hypersexuality might also be read as a satirical comment on the "androgynous New Wave fashion models" of the independent science-fiction film *Liquid Sky* (1982), whose drug use (heroin rather than music) is associated with gender confusion or withdrawal from/uninterest in sex – basically loss of sexual identity (Bergstrom, 1991: 44–5). *Liquid Sky* also features a sex drug of sorts – not music, but "a chemical substance produced in the human brain during orgasm," which is sought by aliens (*ibid.*: 46). However, even aside from the film, several popular new wave artists played with androgyny as well as sexuality – compare, for example, the androgyny of Annie Lennox in early Eurythmics' videos versus the softcore porn of Duran Duran's *Girls On Film* video.
7. Smith discusses the way in which a popular soundtrack can take on "pornographic resonance" during his discussion of *Boogie Nights* (1997), in which lyrical ambiguities enable most of the popular songs on the soundtrack to be interpreted as references to the size of Dirk Diggler's penis (Smith, 2001: 427, see also Giuffre, this volume).

8. While the "dog" character penetrates Kammy, the soundtrack switches to a hunting bugle and the barking of a pack of hunting dogs before returning to the same new wave song and then the dreamy bells and pizzicato for the number's conclusion.
9. Kammy also wears handcuffs for a short segment of this sexual number; although there are no explicitly S/M scenarios, the film frequently plays with the notion and image of bondage, particularly in terms of tying or hooking women up for musical programming.
10. See also Barbara Bradby, 'Sampling Sexuality, Technology and the Body in Dance Music', in *Popular Music* (1993), 12(2), 156 (quoted in Reddington, 2007: 111).
11. We see an additional headset when Jamal discusses women's reactions to new wave with Jimmy; its earpieces are decorated with erect penises instead of breasts.
12. The "fantasized version of eighties punk subculture in New York City" in *Liquid Sky* draws upon this reading, portraying the subculture's attitude toward sex as disinterested, hostile or aggressive (Bergstrom, 1991: 44).
13. In Hollywood cinema, Asian women are often restricted to roles where they appear as "Lotus Blossoms passively catering to the sexual appetites of white men" (Fung cited in Hoang, 2004: 224). This is the only representation in the film of any woman who might be read as a woman of colour; the perspective of black women is conspicuously absent. *New Wave Hookers* refers to other racialized identities but treats them with even more irreverence. Jimmy puts on an 'Asian' accent and alternately claims a Japanese or Chinese identity during the fantasy sequences, and the film's 'Arab' client is given no comprehensible dialogue and is played by non-Arab actor Peter North. Furthermore, the parallel othering of 'nerds' in the video undermines the realities of race-based discrimination and injustice.
14. Bernard Gendron cites the Talking Heads' cover of Al Green's 'Take Me To The River', as well as Blondie's "discolike" 'Heart Of Glass' and cover of reggae track 'The Tide Is High', as both groups' first real commercial successes (2002: 286). Interestingly, in the UK context, it was the female punk bands such as the Slits and the Raincoats who incorporated strong reggae influences, with even less reliance on rock conventions than male punks such as the Clash (Reddington, 2007: 16, 100).
15. A similar blindness can be observed in 1970s punk discourse, which was unaware of or ignored the number of Hispanic musicians in the garage bands identified as punk's antecedents (Gendron, 2002: 284). However, within the late 1970s and early 1980s Los Angeles punk/new wave scene, the Plugz' ethnic identity was no secret; one of their first recordings was a "nod to their Spanish heritage," a "super charged version" of the Mexican folk song 'La Bamba' (Lee, 1983: 36).
16. The original *New Wave Hookers* has also inspired a 2006 'alt-porn' re-envisioning and update by Eon McKai in which viewing the 1985 film inspires prostitutes to become *Neu Wave Hookers* to a contemporary electro/punk soundtrack. The plots of all the sequels seem to centre on strange narrative twists more than new wave music and reprise the fantasy element of the original in various weird ways.

References

Barr, M. (1991), 'Metahuman 'Kipple' Or, Do Male Movie Makers Dream of Electric Women? Speciesism and Sexism in *Blade Runner*', in J. B. Kerman (ed.), *Retrofitting Blade Runner: Issues in Ridley Scott's* Blade Runner *and Philip K. Dick's* Do Androids Dream of Electric Sheep? Madison: University of Wisconsin Press, pp. 25–31.

Bergstrom, J. (1991), 'Androids and Androgyny', in C. Penley, E. Lyon, L. Spigel and J. Bergstrom (eds), *Close Encounters: Film, Feminism, and Science Fiction*, Minneapolis and Oxford: University of Minnesota Press, pp. 33–60.

Chastagner, C. (1999), 'The Parents' Music Resource Center: From Information to Censorship', *Popular Music*, 18(2), 179–92.

Clover, C. (1993), 'Introduction', in P. C. Gibson and R. Gibson (eds), *Dirty Looks: Women, Pornography, Power*, London: BFI Publishing, pp. 1–4.

Dery, M. (1996), *Escape Velocity: Cyberculture at the End of the Century*, New York: Grove Press.

Frith, S. (1978), *Sound Effects: Youth, Leisure, and the Politics of Rock'n'Roll*, London: Constable.

Frith, S., and McRobbie, A. (1990), 'Rock and Sexuality', in S. Frith and A. Goodwin (eds), *On Record: Rock, Pop, and the Written Word*, New York: Routledge, pp. 371–89.

Garofalo, R. (1997), *Rockin' Out: Popular Music in the U.S.A.*, Boston: Allyn and Bacon.

Gendron, B. (2002), *Between Montmartre and the Mudd Club: Popular Music and the Avant-Garde*, Chicago: University of Chicago Press.

Hebdige, D. (1979), *Subculture: The Meaning of Style*. London: Routledge (available in Taylor & Francis e-library, 2002).

Hoang, N. T. (2004), 'The Resurrection of Brandon Lee: The Making of a Gay Asian American Porn Star', in L. Williams (ed.), *Porn Studies*, Durham, NC, and London: Duke University Press, pp. 223–70.

Inoue, T. S. (1998), 'Tito on Movies: Film Scores Are Just a Side Project for Tito Larriva', *Metroactive*, February 19–25; http://www.metroactive.com/papers/metro/02.19.98/beat-9807.html (accessed 16 February 2008).

Kaplan, E. A. (1987), *Rocking Around the Clock*, New York and London: Methuen.

Laing, D. (1985), *One Chord Wonders: Power and Meaning in Punk Rock*, Milton Keynes: Open University Press.

Leblanc, L. (1999), *Pretty in Punk: Girls' Gender Resistance in a Boys' Subculture*, New Brunswick, NJ: Rutgers University Press.

Lee, C. (1983), 'Los Angeles', in P. Belsito and B. Davis (eds), *Hardcore California: A History of Punk and New Wave*, Berkeley: Last Gasp of San Francisco, pp. 9–40.

Lehman, P. (1995/96), 'Revelations about Pornography', *Film Criticism*, 20(1/2), 3–16.

O'Brien, L. (2002), *She Bop II: The Definitive History of Women in Rock, Pop and Soul*, London: Continuum.

Penley, C. (2004), 'Crackers and Whackers: The White Trashing of Porn', in L. Williams (ed.), *Porn Studies*, Durham, NC, and London: Duke University Press, pp. 309–31.

Petkovich, A. (2002), *The X Factory: Inside the American Hardcore Film Industry*, Manchester: Critical Vision.

Reddington, H. (2007), *The Lost Women of Rock Music: Female Musicians of the Punk Era*, Aldershot: Ashgate.

Reynolds, S., and Press, J. (1995), *The Sex Revolts: Gender, Rebellion and Rock'n'Roll*, Cambridge, MA: Harvard University Press.

Smith, J. (2001), 'Popular Songs and Comic Allusion', in P. R. Wojcik and A. Knight (eds), *Soundtrack Available: Essays on Film and Popular Music*, Durham, NC, and London: Duke University Press, pp. 407–30.

Williams, L. (1989), *Hard Core: Power, Pleasure, and the "Frenzy of the Visible"*, Berkeley and Los Angeles: University of California Press.

Williams, L. (2004), 'Skin Flicks on the Racial Border: Pornography, Exploitation, and Interracial Lust', in L. Williams (ed.), *Porn Studies*, Durham, NC, and London: Duke University Press, pp. 271–308.

Wright, R. (2003), 'Score vs. Song: Art, Commerce, and the H Factor in Film and Television Music', in I. Inglis (ed.), *Popular Music and Film*, London: Wallflower, pp. 8–21.

9 Making "a Mall Movie about a Man with a 13-inch Penis"
Popular Music Representations of Pornographic Intention

Liz Giuffre

Pornography, as it refers to the explicit depiction of sexual acts on film,[1] has been traditionally excluded from the mainstream film industry. Therefore, a "mall movie about a man with a 13-inch penis"[2] sounds ambitious — certain to attract attention due to the titillating nature of the subject, but also a likely target for film regulators keen to ensure that the general public browsing around shopping-mall theatres is properly warned about what it may be exposed to. This chapter will explore two films about pornography that have been distributed generally as commercial feature films, *The Notorious Bettie Page* (Mary Harron, 2005, henceforth *NBP*) and *Boogie Nights* (Paul Thomas Anderson, 1997, henceforth *BN*). *BN* is the mall movie about a man with a large penis, while *NBP* is the mall movie about a female bondage star. What the films have in common is the use of pornography as their main subject matter, but without showing it visually. The core of the following argument is that both deploy sound, including popular music, to express what cannot be seen.

Sound and pornography

Using sound to represent porn and its effects is difficult for a fundamental reason. The effects (and affect) of pornography are at the centre of arguments about its value, and how it is defined in legal terms.[3] Notwithstanding these debates, however, the character and impact of porn are invariably determined in terms of the visual, of what certain images may and might arouse in audiences. This is because images in pornography are considered much less ambiguous than sound. A moan or a sigh may indicate any number of emotions and expressions which are relatively easy to simulate sonically, whereas the sight of ejaculation is almost impossible to mistake for anything else nor is it easily simulated. In terms of the central point of pornography, then, its desired and imparted effect and affect, sound is generally regarded as secondary to what is seen. Linda Williams's inclusion of sound in her 1989 benchmark study of pornography remains one of the few to focus closely on sound's function in this genre.[4] She suggests a number of similarities between sound in pornography and sound in the movie musical genre, whereby sound is often added pre or post recording in order to "seek an effect of closeness and intimacy, rather than a sense of spatial clarity" (Williams, 1989: 123–4), and argues that "there is no such thing as a close-up of sound, as there is of image" (*ibid.*: 124). That is, although the close-up image of sexual activity confirms its occurrence, sound, no matter how it is recorded, generally only suggests rather than explicitly represents in the way an image can. Although *NBP* and *BN* use the porn industry as the setting for their narrative, their agendas deviate from the material produced by the porn industries. As such, both are able to exploit the potential ambiguity of sound in ways that traditional pornography does not.

NBP and *BN* both use the porn industry as their main focus, although they are set at different stages of its development. Neither film, however, actually shows pornography despite this being its subject matter, a symptom of what Catherine Zuromskis calls "The Crisis of Pornographic Representation" (Zuromskis, 2007). Drawing on a suite of non-pornographic films that have been made about the porn industry in the last ten years, Zuromskis suggests that film-makers wanting to appeal to mainstream audiences have chosen to discuss, but not to show, pornography. She argues that in such films "a complicated set of formal and narrative techniques" are employed in order to minimize visual pornography's "inherent threat to the viewer and to the film as a whole" (*ibid.*: 4). Although these descriptions suggest an ideological battle over pornography's value (Zuromskis discusses such battles in depth in her study), first I want to engage with a simpler problem: the threat pornography may pose to commercial success. The visual depiction of explicit sexual material[5] is usually heavily regulated and often restricted by government or other censorship bodies,[6] with the result that some audience members (such as those under 18 years) may be unable to access it, whether they want to or not.

However, there remain obvious advantages to the depiction of sexuality on screen despite the possible loss of audience through censorship classifications. As Tanya Krzywinska (2006) argues, the mainstream film industry has relied on sex on screen to help attract and maintain audiences during times of intense competition from other entertainment forms. Using the example of the 1950s film industry, Krzywinska describes a group of films that depicted sex as part of their marketing, particularly to attract adult audiences back to the cinema and away from their new television screens. Discussing the poster for *Cat on a Hot Tin Roof* (Richard Brooks, 1958), which featured a semi-clad Elizabeth Taylor beckoning the viewer into her bedroom, Krzywinska notes how sex was employed in strong enough terms to attract attention, while remaining acceptable for the mainstream: "the strategic placement of sexual material within the context of more traditional melodramatic forms [gained] acceptance of such films by the mainstream audience" (*ibid.*: 14). Although sex was instrumental in the appeal of such films, the way it was depicted was critical to their mainstream success. Specifically, a sense of sex had to be offered, but any visual depiction avoided. As Johnson and Poole observed, techniques of "indirect representation" of sex, like "the waves washing over Burt Lancaster and Deborah Kerr in *From Here to Eternity* [Fred Zinnemann, 1953] or the exploding fireworks in *To Catch a Thief* [Alfred Hitchcock, 1955]" were essential to this, with sound and music also used to suggest what could not be shown (2005: 99). While mainstream acceptance of what can be shown has changed since the 1950s, sex is still generally portrayed visually with some circumspection.

The Notorious Bettie Page and *Boogie Nights*

Although *NBP* and *BN* are non-pornographic films, Williams's observations about how sound functions in pornography remain relevant. Both films use sound, and particularly music, in ways that engage the audience, but in what is often a process of defamiliarization. Unlike traditional, scopocentric porn, which 'flattens' the sexual scenario and maintains a uniform emotional distance between that scenario and the viewer, in *BN* and *NBP* sound functions to constantly modify that distance and give each film's characters depth and ambivalence in their relations to the industry in which they are participating. This use of sound to adjust perspective is fundamental to how these films represent the porn industry, and is also somewhat atypical in terms of how sound in traditional pornography is generally considered. As Williams argues, "sound [in pornography] functions the same way it functions in mainstream narrative cinema: to situate and give realistic effect to the more important image" (1989: 122). In *NBP* and *BN* more complex and ambiguous narratives and characters are developed, with the allusiveness of sound harnessed in the storytelling. Unlike traditional pornography, which relies on clichéd characterization and the most rudimentary plotlines, *NBP* and *BN* work with complex characters and narratives that seek to engage the audience on a number of levels. Through the use of popular music *NBP* and *BN* are able to deliver detailed portraits of the porn industry to audiences that might not otherwise have engaged with such a subject. In each film, music (both as a presence and at times a strategic absence) works to present pornography in more comprehensive and complex terms than is generally the case in mainstream cinema. Popular music in these films helps the film-makers to challenge traditional views of pornography by moving away from models of objectification and simplistic narration, replacing these with more thoughtful characterization and layered semiotics.

NBP and *BN* sought to capture the widest possible contemporary mainstream film audiences.[7] In each case popular music has been paramount in achieving this objective, working as a substitute for the visual depiction of pornography (thus resolving Zuromskis' "crisis"), but also creating a level of character and narrative detail not normally evident in traditional pornography.[8] *BN* and *NBP* have achieved this through the use of some key film-music techniques. Apart from the terms 'diegetic' and 'non-diegetic', I will conduct the following analysis as far as possible in non-technical terms. At the same time, however, it will be clear that some of the sonic effects I will be discussing have close affinities with, for example, Shumway's formulation of "tie-ins", where pre-existing music is used to create a sense of transferable familiarity between the existing music and the new film text (Shumway, 1999: 37),[9] and Kassabian's definition of "commentary music", whereby popular music is used as a primary source of signification rather than as mere support of the visual action of the film (Kassabian, 2001: 59).[10]

Sounding the porn scene

NBP and *BN* both depict distinct eras in the American porn industry. *NBP* is set in the late 1940s and early 1950s, focusing on an industry driven by the illegal creation and distribution of porn magazines and short films, while *BN* is set in the late 1970s and early 1980s, when feature-length porn films (and later videos) were legal, but clearly segregated from the mainstream film industry. Both films use visual cues to indicate their historical setting, with costumes being obvious markers (*NBP* features 1950s high-waisted bikinis, for example, while *BN* shows men and women in flared trousers). These markers, however, are superficial and help primarily to locate the film's setting rather than to assist with the narrative or character development. By contrast, the aural indicators used, specifically the popular music, provide each film's subject with a depth and texture that are not delivered through the visual indicators.

NBP and *BN* both use popular music to identify their historical settings. At the beginning of *BN*, the Emotions' 'Best Of My Love' begins almost immediately, with its brass-driven staccato introduction sounding just as the graphic "Boogie Nights" appears on the screen in neon (indicating the name of a nightclub as well as the film's title). 'Best Of My Love' creates an immediate sense of familiarity for the audience – the song's upbeat disco production clearly evokes the 1970s. The shot and song follow unbroken as Jack Horner (Burt Reyolds) enters the club and comes into contact with its young occupants, the circle from which he will one day recruit his porn stars. The song becomes meaningful as part of the diegetic setting (some of the characters are seen dancing to it on the dance floor) and as a non-diegetic signifier. 'Best Of My Love' also implicitly foreshadows to the audience that these characters will literally become what the song's lyric describes, "the best love" available. In addition to the lyric, the song's style also implies a type of 'love' that these characters will engage in, one that is carefree and upbeat. While the visual clues hint at such playfulness (the skimpy 1970s costumes, as well as the appearance of Roller Girl on roller skates), for a 1990s audience watching the film at the time of its release the music and the dancing could also evoke a situation of irresponsible exploitation and naivety, particularly as the women are clearly objectified by the men present. The use of popular music and this venue is thus a double signifier, signalling to the audience the socio-historical setting, but also activating value judgements generated in retrospect.

NBP also relies on a synergy of music and visuals to establish the film's historical setting in chronological terms, as well as giving a cultural resonance. The caption "New York 1955" appears as a graphic over black-and-white images of New York streets and the sound of traffic, as the 1950s big band-inspired 'Intro' plays. Although this song was written specifically for the film, its period style functions in the same way as pre-existing music does, inviting the audience into the 1950s with, initially, a comfortable sense of recognition. While the visuals create this effect in themselves (the use of black and white is an obvious technique which establishes historical distance), the music provides something additional. The use of big band music evokes not simply a particular period, but also a form of consciousness as yet untroubled by the distinctive tensions and discontents later projected by rock music and its derivatives.

This introduction is not to posit a pervasive and untroubled innocence, however. Following the first graphic of New York, 'Intro' continues to play over a long shot into a shop specializing in men's magazines. This may be a rather banal setting for a contemporary audience, but the fade and resurgence of music as the shop's owner talks to a customer and makes a sale to him emphasize the perils of the transaction at that time. 'Intro' continues as the shot cuts away from the shop, to introduce Bettie Page (Gretchen Mol) waiting outside a courtroom. The music accentuates the tension between then and now, and also connects Bettie to the episode in the shop, a link of which she is scarcely aware. The style of the song, which to contemporary audiences may appear harmlessly dated, helps to characterize the film's main protagonist, Bettie Page, and to relativize her description as 'notorious'. Just as the music sounds somewhat innocent to a contemporary listener, Page's appearance is also non-threatening, as she sits well-dressed and well-postured. With this small sonic gesture, the film-maker situates the film's subject in a particular way, introducing a puzzling disparity between the way Page is talked about and the way we ourselves perceive her.

Sounding the porn industry

Popular music is also used to illustrate the evolution of the porn industry in both *BN* and *NBP*. In *BN* popular music is used to articulate the developing engagement of Eddie Adams/Dirk Diggler (Mark Wahlberg) with the porn industry. When Adams first 'auditions' for Horner by having sex with Horner's employee, Roller Girl (Heather Graham), Melanie's 'Brand New Key' is played both in the scene (she puts it on the stereo before beginning to have sex with him) and over the scene for the audience as the shot cuts away from the couple on the lounge to Horner watching them. It is used as a substitute for the visual – we hear the song rather than actually seeing Diggler and Roller Girl having sex. However, as such the song suggests multiple layers of meaning in the scene. The song's key lyric, "I've got a brand new pair of roller states" works as a simple, but sardonic, commentary on the scene as we see Roller Girl keep her roller skates on despite taking off all her other clothes. But the particular instrumentation and style of the song also function beyond the level of descriptive commentary. It is sung in a high register by the female vocalist, supported by male backing singers, a gendered figure/ground dynamic that parallels the voyeuristic setting of Diggler and Roller Girl's copulation, and also their future jobs as porn actors. The singer's high-pitched, almost childlike voice also confers a kind of innocence upon the action. In this way the song is fundamental to the effectiveness of this scene as it functions in relation to the rest of the film, infantilizing the spectacle of two strangers having sex in front of Horner as being little more than youthful high jinks rather than anything more sinister.

In *BN* the establishment of a new porn-film era is musically heralded by 'Magnet And Steel' by Walter Egan, which plays non-diegetically over a conversation in the back of a van between Dirk Diggler, Jack Horner and his co-star Reed Rothchild (John C. Reilley). As they talk about wanting to make films that are "sexy" rather than just featuring sex (Diggler defines the former as something that doesn't just "slap some girl around" but instead creates "a whole story"), the relatively unmanipulated sound of the song parallels the new direction the men want their porn movies to take. The more 'organic' acoustic style of 'Magnet And Steel', featuring voices in close harmony, provides a telling contrast to the slick synthesized and fast-paced disco played elsewhere in the film. The contrast provides aural cues for the less alienating and formulaic porn films Diggler and Rothchild are describing. These aural clues play explicitly during the dialogue, as the smooth and prolonged "oohs" of the female backing singers work in tandem with key descriptions by the men as they discuss the ambition to make films that are "sexy", "classy". The organic sounds proclaim a warmth that the visuals to date haven't provided. The sound of the song in conjunction with the dialogue about the proposed films gives the audience some sense of what these porn films will be like, even though we don't actually see them.

Walter Egan's vocals in 'Magnet And Steel' also italicize Diggler and Rothchild's appeal to Horner. Although the visuals suggest a casual and inconsequential conversation, the song gives some force to their conversation as a genuine desire to engage with porn in a more thoughtful way. 'Magnet And Steel' continues over a sequence that sees Diggler win an award at the second Annual Adult Film Awards, suggesting a continuous trajectory between the conversational birth of this new approach to porn film-making and its triumph. 'Magnet And Steel' pauses while Diggler accepts his award (replaced momentarily by a synthesizer-driven instrumental grab recognizable to a contemporary audience as typical porn music), but the song returns again as Diggler triumphantly kicks the air before leaving the stage. Here the music serves as a direct substitute for a visual narrative, both the narrative of Horner's unfolding project and the pornographic content of the new films themselves, of which we see nothing. The music stands in for the visual narrative.

The continuing sound of 'Magnet And Steel' from the van conversation to the awards sequence also prepares the audience for Diggler's individual progression. Just as the porn industry begins to evolve to become something more narratologically sophisticated and closer to the standards of the mainstream film industry, the contemplative pace of 'Magnet And Steel' provides an aural characterization of Diggler that we don't apprehend in his visual image. The musical texture of 'Magnet And Steel' confers upon Diggler some aura, however tentative, of human agency; he is not merely a mechanical instrument for Jack Horner, but a self-reflective industry participant with his own aesthetic. His acceptance speech gives some explicitness to the point: "I promise to keep making better films ... these movies that we make can be better, they can help, they really can."

In *NBP* music also defines changes in the porn industry in much more forceful terms than are shown or described visually. The doo-wop style of 'Sexy Ways' by Hank Ballard and the Midnighters plays over a montage of magazine covers featuring Bettie Page, a sequence that traces her growing success as a model for the porn industry. As the various magazine covers are shown underneath the song (images which show Bettie in more and more suggestive poses, with fewer and fewer clothes on), the music invites the audience to believe, as Bettie does, that her involvement in the porn industry is also unproblematically light-hearted. The song creates a mood that is buoyant rather than threatening, reinforcing the storyline and the character's belief that this incarnation of the porn industry is non-menacing.[11] This technique is used again later when Bettie is first shot by Irving (Chris Bauer) and Paula Klaw (Lili Taylor) at their illegal studio. As she emerges for the camera in extremely high heels and "strange costumes for special clients" (costumes which are actually bondage wear), Paula Klaw puts 'Mucha Muchacha' by Esquivel on the record-player and encourages Bettie to dance as she is being photographed. Here the music functions diegetically to distract Bettie from any ominous undertones of perversion in the industry into which she is drawn, reinforced by the fact that we don't actually see the finished photographs. Music functions as a distraction diegetically and non-diegetically as the photo shoot proceeds. 'Mucha Muchacha' is essential to this scene in normalizing the process of the creation of pornography, presenting it as apparently harmless, creating this impression for both Bettie and the audience. The sense of exploitative objectification implicit in the total visual *mise-en-scène* is musically contested for the film audience, and completely dissipated for Bettie.

Sounding character

Popular music is fundamental to the narrative of the development of the main protagonists in *NBP* and *BN*. Both films use music with and in the dialogue as each of the protagonists enters the porn industry, and both use music non-diegetically to comment on these initial characterizations (Eddie Adams/Dirk Diggler is asked by Jack Horner if he likes music as he is first introduced to the porn industry at a party, while Bettie Page discusses the 'Grand Old Opry' during her first professional photo shoot). These comments remind us of the importance of music in the definition and development of character in *BN*.

When Eddie Adams is first introduced to the other porn actors at director Jack Horner's house in *BN*, he appears as the opening phrases of Three Dog Night's version of Randy Newman's 'Mama Told Me Not To Come' begin to play. This song works on a number of levels. It provides a choric commentary on what has happened so far (Adams has just had a huge fight with his mother about the path his life is taking and he threatens to leave), and it also sonically indicates the atmosphere of the party about to take place.[12] The keyboard introduction that provides the basis of the song underscores the dialogue as Adams is introduced to each character, and, although dating from 1969, its synthesized and heavily produced sound also perfectly matches the milieu and period the dialogue alludes to, as Adams and his prospective colleagues discuss "that new film, Star Wars".

Later in the scene Hot Chocolate's 'You Sexy Thing' becomes the aural signifier of Eddie Adams. The choice of this song underlines Adams's (and as he will become, Dirk Diggler's) qualifications as the ultimate pornstar and encourages the audience to engage with the character in terms of the song – as smooth, sexy, engaging. The song begins as one of the film crew, Scotty J (Philip Seymour Hoffman), meets Eddie for the first time, and serves to reflect Scotty's initial impression. As 'You Sexy Thing' sounds, we see Eddie from Scotty J's perspective, and while the visual indicates the focusing of Scotty J's attention (the shot of Eddie from his perspective appears momentarily through a tunnel lens) its playful nature occludes any sinister undertones in Scotty's reactions. However, 'You Sexy Thing' continues as Eddie is presented to The Colonel (the man who funds all of Jack Horner's films, played by Robert Ridgely), and here it serves a different commentary function. The Colonel gives Eddie advice as someone who is "interested in film" before asking blatantly to see his "great big cock". We see The Colonel's reaction to Adams's penis (he is silent and expressionless, leaving us to assume he is impressed, perhaps shocked) but we don't see the penis itself. This leaves the song as the only descriptor for the audience. Played over these visuals, 'You Sexy Thing' now becomes a signifier of objectification, as it becomes clear that The Colonel sees Eddie only as a commodity, an extremely bankable porn actor, a sexy 'thing'.

Similarly in *NBP* popular music is used to represent pornography and the character of Bettie Page in ways that supplement and comment on the visuals. 'I Surrender, Dear' performed by Artie Shaw is used to situate a flashback to Page's earlier life, and the song serves not only to signify an era, but also to provide the audience with an emotional platform on which to build a sense of the significance of this episode in the context of Page's life. The sequence, set in Nashville in 1942 (as indicated by an on-screen caption), shows Bettie meeting her serviceman husband, and continues to play as we see the happy marriage sour as he turns violent. However, 'I Surrender, Dear' functions as an ambivalent comment on the visuals. Notwithstanding the song's title (perhaps a literal description of Bettie's position as a wife), the sounds of slow-paced clarinet-driven jazz provide a sonic sedative against the hardship of life as a serviceman's wife. As the sequence continues and we see Bettie make a home, then suffer the onset of physical abuse, the continuing saccharine sound of 'I Surrender, Dear' becomes an implicit signifier of the determined ingenuousness and sacrificial self-effacement expected of women at this time, and manifested in Bettie in particular. Functioning in a way similar to 'Mama Told Me Not To Come' and 'You Sexy Thing' in BN, as the sequence unfolds, a gap opens between the visuals and the period music, signalling a false consciousness and the impending loss of innocence.

A similar effect is achieved when Peggy Lee's version of 'It's A Good Day' is played over a sequence showing the lead up to and making of a bondage film. The disparity between the sound and the images underlines an unfolding motif – Bettie's enduring naivety. The sassy vocal and upbeat tempo of Peggy Lee's singing suggest Bettie's attitude to her work as something that is playful, and perhaps even empowering. However, a contemporary audience soon becomes aware of the dangers threatening Bettie, when the holiday she takes with the Klaws and some other models turns out to be a set-up to shoot a bondage film. The danger is emphasized visually, as this sequence moves from colour (with the appearance of a good-time home movie) to black and white with 'noir' overtones (when the girls stop playing games like tennis and begin to simulate a kidnapping). The unremitting refrain of 'It's A Good Day' opens a space between Bettie's understanding of the situation – bondage as a harmless extension of play – and the more ominous ideology underwriting these forms of sexual relations. The song refers forward, to an era in which that ideology is more fully recognized, but also back, to the similar incongruities between 'I Surrender, Dear' and the plight of a serviceman's wife during wartime.

Music's strategic absence

In the sonic effervescence of the early sections of these two films, it is often the sudden silence that first disturbs the apparently innocent idyll. The strategic absence of music is particularly striking when Dirk Diggler makes his first porn film in *BN*.[13] Although traditional pornography also occasionally uses silence (or very sparse sound), it is unusual for this to be a deliberate artistic choice as opposed to economic pragmatism.[14] After the setting up of the scene and Diggler's insistence that he wants to "try and make it sexy", the absence of music when he and co-star Amber Waves begin to apparently have sex is disconcerting in the wake of the upbeat, loud disco sounds earlier (and later) in the film. It is, literally, a sonic 'unmasking' of the reality of porn production. The shot moves away from the couple beginning to undress and kiss, and although the unmasked sounds of sexual activity (kissing, moaning) continue, all we see of them having sex is out-of-focus and inverted writhing images through the camera lens as the porn film is being made. When the shoot is interrupted because the camera runs out of film, Diggler and Waves talk, and when 'action' is called again she begins to moan before we see them begin moving, underlining the artificiality of this sound and the actions it accompanies. We hear them both apparently orgasm, and dialogue between Horner and the other film-makers expressing disappointment that they didn't get the shot they wanted because Diggler "came inside of her". Their disappointment is a confirmation of the scopocentricity of porn: in spite of the orgasmic sounds, the absence of visual evidence of ejaculation deprives the camera (and therefore the film's paying customers) of what they want from the sequence: it is not called the 'money shot' for nothing.

When Diggler offers to "do it again", the shot moves away from the couple to a popping champagne cork (an obvious visual metaphor for a successful shot, this time) and the song 'Boogie Shoes' by KC and the Sunshine Band begins. Like 'Brand New Key', music is used here to mark a new stage in Diggler's career, this time success (confirmed by images of Diggler and the other porn workers going shopping and dancing). After this first film shoot, in the next porn shoot we see Diggler rehearsing positions with Roller Girl, and music is played ('Machine Gun', by the Commodores) as Diggler talks to the film crew about his plans. Instead of the awkward silence, the presence of music suggests a new aura of confidence that is reinforced as the song continues over a montage that shows the film's release, reception and finally all the actors dancing to it in the disco. Like 'Magnet And Steel' earlier, 'Machine Gun' is used as a narrative device to verify Diggler's success as a porn actor, to remove any possible ambiguity in the visuals and confirm that Diggler here definitely considers his progress to date as successful and fulfilling.

NBP also uses the contrast between music and its conspicuous absence, and to the same 'unmasking' effect. In an early scene Bettie is tricked into getting into a car with a group of strange men. As the car stops outside the city there is no sound other than the men talking about their intention to rape her. Silence disturbingly functions to focus our attention on the rape. It has already thus been ominously coded when, following an initial, somewhat informal amateur photo shoot on the beach, Bettie decides to pursue 'modelling'. She goes to a larger agency with a group of photographers, and a sequence begins with 'Goody Goody', sung by Peggy Lee. The song continues as we see Bettie working in a call centre as a secretary, and looking at herself on the cover of *Photo and Model Weekly*, then as she walks up the driveway to the house where a new shoot is being set up. The music has faded to silence by the time Bettie is asked by the owner if she thinks she can handle the shoot, and when she comes out to pose only the sound of the cameras can be heard along with the oohs and ahhs of the photographers. The contrast from the sassy, untroubled atmosphere created by the non-diegetic 'Goody Goody', to the diegetic sounds of the cameras and the active voyeurism of the photographers, changes the way the audience perceives Bettie. As usual, she is not aware of the transition, but the sonic shift focuses the audience's attention on her objectification. This is made even more explicit as she complies with the request to show her 'keister' (her backside). With the return of the non-diegetic music shortly after this point – 'Jordu' by the Clifford Brown/ Max Roach jazz group – it is as though the interval of silence marked, for the film and audience, a transition from the facile insouciance of 'Goody Goody' to a phase that is more darkly textured and more sophisticated, with that word's roots in the idea of falseness.

This studied alternation between musical presence and absence is used throughout the film as Page poses more and more suggestively. During her first naked shoot music is notably absent, focusing our attention on the visuality of the porn industry and the seriousness of Bettie's engagement with it at this point (confirmed in the dialogue as the photographer says, "If you show too much I could get arrested"). Without music, this scene featuring Bettie posing naked in a forest underscores her objectification, again in telling contrast with her own comments about her bikini, "What difference does a little piece of cloth make?"

Thus far, neither Diggler nor Bettie has picked up the signals transmitted non-diegetically to the film's audience. As they begin to suspect the negative ramifications of their growing involvement in porn, they too fall into a form of silence, becoming, as it were, 'spectators' of themselves, with musical commentary. For Diggler, the hazards are represented physically in his addiction to drugs, and then, in a pivotal scene, with his involvement in an attempted robbery. The latter sequence features 'Sister Christian' by Night Ranger and 'Jesse's Girl' by Rick Springfield presented diegetically as music coming from the prospective victim's hi-fi. The effect on Diggler is demonstrated through the affective disjuncture of sound and image. As the easy-listening, soft-pop sounds of these songs play while drugs are delivered, one of the characters begins to play Russian roulette, and Diggler is left to literally run for his life. The disparity between the saccharine music and the violent images, as the drug dealer sings along to 'Jesse's Girl' while playing alarmingly with his gun, increases the disparity between Diggler's perceptions and the actualities of his situation. In this scene Diggler becomes analogous to the audience and, indeed, physically assumes the position of a seated spectator, watching his theatrically framed intended victim take control. Diggler's stunned silence betokens an awareness of the ebbing of his power.

The diegetic use of these songs now dismayingly proclaims the incongruity of his position in a way that he, as well as the audience, cannot ignore. The everyday pop music, in the context of the actions taking place around him, tells him how outrageous his 'everyday' has become.[15] Diggler's 'epiphany' reaches its climax following the attempted robbery, as he returns to Horner's house in tears, begging him for help and apologizing. When Horner hugs him and also apologizes, this is accompanied by a focusing silence, emptied of any music that might distract from the situation. Prior to this point we have seen little sign of regret or acknowledgement by Horner that he has exploited Diggler, and with this silent conclusion this realization is clear.

In *NBP* Bettie's discomforting suspicions regarding the impact of porn are reflected through her increasing insistence on her morality. Ultimately, it is her religious faith that is under threat as she works in the porn industry, to be restored only later when she stops this work. During a bondage shoot that features mainly the strategic absence of either diegetic or non-diegetic music, Bettie is offended when the silence is broken, by a dirty song that the photographer Mr Willie begins to sing. She asks him to stop, telling him she "believes in Jesus" and the two have a discussion about "what Jesus might think" of Bettie's engagement in the porn industry. Her inarticulate dismay at the question heralds her own imminent 'epiphany' about the growing chasm between her situation in the porn industry and the naive way she has perceived it. Like Diggler, she is finally forced to assume the position of spectator of her own environment, silenced in the sense that she can no longer articulate her own justification. Art Pepper's 'Blues In' plays at a party that she and her boyfriend attend soon after this discussion with Mr Willie, and as the music plays we see Bettie transformed from the glamorous guest of honour to someone her boyfriend finds "disgusting" as he looks at a series of bondage pictures in which she has been involved. It is not until Bettie looks at the pictures through his eyes, so to speak, a spectator of herself, that it appears to occur to her how others see her work and the industry. Like Diggler's silence at the failed robbery, her inarticulate confusion is eloquent testimony to a sudden sense of disempowerment. At the same time, the affective neutrality, the abstraction and 'innocence' of the instrumental 'Blues In' become, like Bettie, a blank canvas on which meanings are inscribed by specific contexts and listeners/spectators. Bettie is what Barthes called a 'writerly text', awaiting completion by any reader, working in a 'key' that, like Pepper's music, is unspecified. Both she and the diegetic music take on a 'meaningfulness' in the context of her boyfriend's indignation.

Conclusion

The Notorious Bettie Page and *Boogie Nights* are both films about the porn industry that choose not to depict pornography visually, but through sonic commentary. Each film uses popular music to depict, comment on and explore the realities of the porn industry, particularly through constant adjustments of sonic perspective. They do so by playing off diegetic against non-diegetic signals, opening up seams in the consciousness of both audiences and, more belatedly, the protagonists. Music nuances the narrative, and indeed sometimes bears the main burden of the continuity and detail of defining the narrative arc. By these means, despite their subject matter (pornography) the films are able to remain securely located within what, at the time of their production, was the category of the mainstream feature film and its audience profile. Furthermore, the use of music to sound what is not shown in these films about pornography also nuances the narrative and characterization in ways that are difficult to imagine through visuals alone. Similarly, the pervasiveness of music and a predominantly sonically cluttered soundtrack make the intervals of complete silence both conspicuous and meaningful, isolating critical moments in the films. By the use of sonic commentary audiences are invited to engage with the characters of each porn industry in ways that are beyond the participants' horizons. The use of sound rather than imagery also allows the films to exist within the mainstream without isolating potential audience members.

Notes

1. The definition of pornography is notoriously contested. For the purposes of this chapter I will use the definition which Zuromskis has articulated in relation to contemporary popular film: "'film pornography' defines any film that offers graphic sexual content as its primary focus ... [in which] the function of the film is

to bring the viewer as close as possible to the sexual act itself" (Zuromiskis, 2007: 4).
2. The quotation is from a review of *Boogie Nights* shortly after its release (Stephens, 1997: 11).
3. In 1868 the Hicklin standard was established in the USA and UK to assist in the identification of and legislation about pornography: to provide "a definition for criminally publishable obscenity" (Heins, 2006: 169). Curiously, the definition did not help provide a standard to define the obscene in terms of content (that is, what could be depicted), but rather related the threat back to what effect such material might have on an audience, "those whose minds are open to such immoral influences, and into whose hands a publication of this sort may fall" (Hicklin standard, as quoted in Heins, 2006: 169). Heins discusses the Hicklin standard in more depth (*ibid.*: 169–70), as does Brigman, who refers to the same case but calls it the "Hicklin Test" (Brigman, 1997: 150–1).
4. Williams (1989) was one of the first film or pornography commentators to argue strongly the importance of considering pornography as a genre of film, that is, a particular type of film bound by particular stylistic conventions (Williams, 1989). Since then Krzywinska has also discussed pornographic films in similar terms, and although she resists using the term 'genre', she argues the importance of considering it a distinctive type of film created with particular conventions and audience expectations: "Like mainstream cinema even the most pared-down hard-core film is dependent on the use of established formal cinematic devices to facilitate the viewer's entry into the onscreen space" (Krzywinska, 2006: 28).
5. I emphasize the "visual" depiction of pornography because explicitness in film is generally conceived in terms of visuality – the seeing of genitalia and/or penetration.
6. In Australia, all "film (including videos and DVDs) and computer games, whether produced locally or overseas, have to be classified before they can be made legally available to the public", a process that is overseen by the Australian Classification Board (ACB: www.classification.gov.au, accessed 20 January 2008) and run by the Federal Office of Film and Literature Classification (OFLC). The OFLC is an Australian federal government body that must adhere to Australian federal law when classifying material; it can impose classification ratings ranging from "G" (General) to "RC" (Refused Classification). As explained on the ACB's website, RC means "in other words, banned. ... This occasionally results in material being refused a classification, which means that it cannot legally be shown, sold or hired in Australia" (*ibid.*). In contrast, the USA does not have a centralized classification system but rather a group of dominant, voluntary (and largely industry-based) organizations. The Motion Picture Association of America is the dominant body responsible for classifying films in the USA. However, as it is voluntary, the effects of its classifications are not as binding as they are, for example, in Australia.
7. In various interviews the directors of both films have indicated they wanted to appeal to audiences other than those already interested in porn (Harron in Durbin, 2006: 15; Anderson in Sickels, 2002: 52, 54).

8. Together with emotive and complex concepts like "artistic value" and "substance", narrative is often figured as something superfluous in pornography, as something that doesn't quite hinder its appeal, but is certainly not essential to its success (Krzywinska, 2006: 28). Although narrative is generally very rudimentary in pornography, it is by no means absent or unimportant. The genre of pornography, however, as Williams demonstrated, has very well-established narrative conventions; pornography "consists of sexual action in, and as, narrative" (1989: 121). Williams's definition of hardcore porn includes the delivery of a classic narrative component, the "sense of ending" demonstrated by the showing of external ejaculation (*ibid.*: 93).
9. In particular, Shumway discusses the way tie-ins worked to attract audiences with films such as *The Big Chill* (Lawrence Kasdan, 1983), where the sense of nostalgia which the sounds featured in the movie evoked for baby-boomer audiences also attracted them to the film. Importantly, for Shumway, tie-ins work not only with specific knowledge (that is, when an audience knows the songs and their details), but also just with general details. As he argues, "the assumption that the audience will recognize the artist, the song, or, at the minimum, a familiar style" is enough to create a successful tie-in (Shumway, 1999: 37).
10. This technique has been used in many different types of films and described in different terms. For example, Van Leeuwen (1998) explores music that functions in a similar way in his study of *The Piano* (Jane Campion, 1993), where he is careful to articulate the importance of music as a storytelling device in its own right, as something that can at once relate to, but at times also differ from, the larger story told in the film.
11. Williams (1989) and Andrews (2006) both review the stages of the American porn industry since World War II.
12. Sickels calls this "The Last Golden Age of Irresponsibility" (2002: 49), both in general popular cultural terms and regarding the heedlessness of the 1970s porn industry.
13. Evans (2005) describes a similar use of ambience and musical absence in his chapter about the depiction of violence in *Chopper* (Andrew Dominik, 2000).
14. Instead, as Williams has noted, silence or badly reproduced sound is something that sometimes features in pornography, but as a budgetary decision that hinders the narrative (1989: 124). Although Williams's observations are now almost two decades old, this argument remains valid for pornography today as it is distributed through the internet. Sound tends to produce larger file sizes than images, and so is often omitted or condensed at poor reproduction quality.
15. Here, music works in the same way as Powrie describes, with reference to a similar use of popular song in Quentin Tarantino's *Reservoir Dogs* (Quentin Tarantino, 1992), where "the song, by virtue of its anodyne lyrics, suggests comic incongruity, and that this somehow lulls audiences into a sense of false security, thereby increasing the shock value" of what is depicted later (Powrie, 2005: 102).

References

Andrews, D. (2006), *Soft in the Middle: The Contemporary Softcore Feature in Its Contexts*, Columbus: Ohio State University Press.

Brigman, W. E. (1997), 'Politics and the Pornography Wars', *Wide Angle*, 19(3), 149–70.

Durbin, K. (2006), 'As Costume Dramas Go, Bettie Page's Rather Brief', *New York Times*, 2 April; online at http://www.nytimes.com/2006/04/02/movies/02durb.html?_r=1&pagewanted=print&oref=slogin (accessed 20 June 2009).

Evans, M. (2005), 'The Sound of Redemption in *Chopper*: Rediscovering Ambience as Affect', in R. Coyle (ed.), *Reel Tracks: Australian Feature Film Music and Cultural Identities*, Sydney: John Libbey, pp. 137–46.

Heins, M. (2006), 'Sex and the Law: A Tale of Shifting Boundaries', in P. Lehman (ed.), *Pornography: Film and Culture*, New Brunswick, NJ: Rutgers University Press, pp. 168–88.

Johnson, B., and Poole, G. (2005), 'Scoring: Sexuality and Australian Film Music, 1990–2003', in R. Coyle (ed.), *Reel Tracks: Australian Feature Film Music and Cultural Identities*, Sydney: John Libbey, pp. 97–121.

Kassabian, A. (2001), *Hearing Film: Tracking Identifications in Contemporary Hollywood Film Music*, New York: Routledge.

Krzywinska, T. (2006), *Sex and the Cinema*, London: Wallflower Press.

Powrie, P. (2005), 'Blonde Abjection: Spectatorship and the Abject Anal Space in-Between', in S. Lannin and M. Caley (eds), *Pop Fiction: The Song in Cinema*, Bristol: Intellect Press, pp.100–19.

Shumway, D. (1999), 'Rock 'n' Roll Sound Tracks and the Production of Nostalgia', *Cinema Journal*, 38(2), 36–51.

Sickels, R. C. (2002), '1970s Disco Daze: Paul Thomas Anderson's Boogie Nights and the Last Golden Age of Irresponsibility', *Journal of Popular Culture*, 35(4), 49–60.

Stephens, C. (1997), 'The Swollen Boy: Paul Thomas Anderson's Boogie Nights and Diggler Days', *Film Comment*, 33(5), 10–14.

Van Leeuwen, T. (1998), 'Emotional Times: The Music of *The Piano*' in R. Coyle (ed.), *Screen Scores: Studies in Contemporary Australian Film Music*, Sydney: AFTRS, pp. 39–48.

Williams, L. (1989), *Hard Core: Power, Pleasure and the 'Frenzy of the Visible'*, Berkeley: University of California Press.

Zuromskis, C. (2007), 'Prurient Pictures and Popular Film: The Crisis of Pornographic Representation', *The Velvet Light Trap*, 59, 4–14.

Filmography

From Here to Eternity (Fred Zinnemann, 1953)
To Catch a Thief (Alfred Hitchcock, 1955)
Cat on a Hot Tin Roof (Richard Brooks, 1958)
The Big Chill (Lawrence Kasdan, 1983)

"A Mall Movie about a Man with a 13-inch Penis" **173**

Reservoir Dogs (Quentin Tarantino, 1992)
The Piano (Jane Campion, 1993)
Boogie Nights (Paul Thomas Anderson, 1997)
Chopper (Andrew Dominik, 2000)
The Notorious Bettie Page (Mary Harron, 2005)

10 Musical Loops
Eyes Wide Shut ... Ears Wide Open

Kevin Clifton

Introduction

The marketing campaign for Stanley Kubrick's *Eyes Wide Shut* (1999) mirrored the subject matter of sexual teasing in the film. Before its release, audiences were tantalized with provocative pictures of the film's stars, then-married Tom Cruise and Nicole Kidman, in a marketing blitz that intentionally held back pertinent information about the film. Critics were allowed to see the film two days before its release, adding to the veil of secrecy surrounding it. Kubrick, at the helm of the marketing campaign, was thus able to control the flow of information about his last project, one that effectively drove the media and audiences alike into a frenzy of extended foreplay.

The initial reaction to the film, however, was one of anticlimax (Sperb, 2006: 125–7). Critics and audiences alike found the film "confusing", "overblown" and "unresolved", and, as Mario Falsetto put it, "The audiences that came to see what many thought would be the most sexually explicit film of the summer, were instead confronted with a magisterial, feverish dream movie" (quoted in *ibid.*: 127). Jonathan Romney, in his generalization of the aesthetic of *Eyes Wide Shut*, observed that "the mood is akin to erotic disappointment, which is quite fitting, for that is essentially the film's subject" (quoted in *ibid.*: 126). Romney rightfully points to the significance of erotic disappointment at work in the film, which was certainly at odds with the first viewers' false expectations of seeing overt sexual relations between Cruise and Kidman [as Bill and Alice Harford] on the big screen. Early viewers/voyeurs felt cheated by the 'un-sexy movie', in part because it lacked a cathartic 'money shot', and therefore viewed the film as unresolved. Many recent writers, however, have read the open-endedness of the film not as a flaw in its construction, but rather as strength in its design (Abrams, 2007: 59–83; Sperb, 2006: 125–34; Grodal, 2004; Chion, 2001: 164–73; Nelson, 2000: 260–97; Walker, 1999: 344–59). Writers have also commented on the dialectic between dream and reality, such as film-maker Alex Cox, who interprets the film as a modern-day morality tale; he pointed out that:

> Eyes Wide Shut *seems to be a rake's progress story.* He [Bill Harford] *goes on an adventure that could really turn out any way, so it is an irresponsible adventure for him to embark on. But it's a fantasy, isn't it? It's a dream film. I don't think we're supposed to believe anything that we see, and I think that one thing that people do have a hard time with in the cinema is ambiguity.*[1]

Parallel to Cox's interpretation, my reading of the film considers the broad implications of an 'ambiguous' fantasy/dream world. Of particular interest is the expression and ultimate *repression* of Bill Harford's erotic impulses in this self-constructed world, one that he inhabits for more than half of the film.

My reading foregrounds how the use of pre-existing music — music not composed for the film, but rather *chosen* by Kubrick himself — counterpoints the filmic narrative of erotic repression.[2] What follows is an account of the 'opening' of my analytical ears on three different levels, as identified by Claudia Gorbman in her groundbreaking text, Unheard Melodies (Gorbman, 1987: 12–13). The *first level* of analysis considers the music on its own terms as *pure musical codes*, completely removed from any association with the image track. In a chapter on film-music criticism, Neumeyer and Buhler, drawing from standard music analytic practices in American universities, identify various musical codes appropriate for Gorbman's first level of analysis, such as timbre, musical form, pitch relations, consonance and dissonance, and tonality (2001: 16–38). The *second level* of analysis takes into account the *cultural associations* of various types of music, such as the waltz, the nineteenth-century character piano piece, and twentieth-century modern music, all representative musical styles used in *Eyes Wide Shut*. These musical styles, which other scholars have referred to as *style topics*, provide a rich backdrop of cultural associations for the filmic style and narrative (*ibid*.: 23–6). The *third level* of music analysis, which Gorbman refers to as *cinematic musical codes*, finally associates the film music with the image track itself. Formal structural relationships, informed by the use of diegetic, non-diegetic and metadiegetic music, coexist between image and filmic narrative (*ibid*.: 39–61).

My reading also considers Gorbman's own insightful analysis (2006) of the use of music in *Eyes Wide Shut*. While we both focus on the use of pre-existing music in the film, our analytical thrust, though at times similar (we both identify the interval of the half-step as a powerful unifying force in the filmic soundscape), differs in significant ways. In sum, my reading conceptualizes the half-step motif, first heard in Shostakovich's 'Waltz no. 2' in the opening visual sequence, as a metonymic sound capable of signifying tonal *desire* as well as an ultimate *denial* of that desire. In other words, my reading regards musical structure itself as *representational*, emblematic and, in this particular case, as a type of *warning*. I will uncover the symbolic half-step motif in two additional pre-existing works, both of which occur later in the film in the dream world. I hope to show that by tracing the half-step motif throughout its various musical guises, the audience is able to follow with 'ears wide open' the musical thoughts of Bill Harford as he journeys in (and out of) the quixotic dream world.

Locating *desire* and *denial* in the opening visual sequence

The film opens with Shostakovich's 'Waltz no. 2' (from his *Jazz Suite no. 2 for Jazz Orchestra*) as background music (Figure 10.1). The first four bars of music, a typical

Figure 10.1 Shostakovich, 'Waltz no. 2' (bars 1–59)

vamp pattern in triple metre, accompany a black screen with '*Warner Bros. presents*' in bold white lettering. As the first phrase of the waltz begins, the screen fades and shows the name *Tom Cruise* in the same visual style as the opening credit; exactly midway through the first phrase, the name *Nicole Kidman* is similarly displayed. As the second phrase begins, the visuals cut to '*A film by Stanley Kubrick*'. Precisely midway through the second phrase, the black screen is abandoned and we see the backside of Alice in the bedroom of the Harfords' upper-middle-class apartment. She wears a sexy black dress and high heels. As the third phrase begins, the last in the opening section of the waltz, Alice literally slips out of her dress, revealing that she is not wearing anything underneath, and stands naked in the room with her back towards the viewer, forcing him or her into a voyeuristic position. Then, as in the previous musical phrases, something new happens midway through the third phrase. The stark black screen returns and ironically shows the title of the film, '*Eyes Wide Shut*'. This return of the black screen foregrounds a major theme of the film, namely, that of *desire* and *denial*. While Kubrick initially allows the audience to gaze at Alice's nude body, the abrupt return of the black screen, similar to the closing of a window in a peep show or the shutting of an eyelid, blocks her image, thus denying the audience the virtual pleasure of eroticizing her body.

Up until this point, the visual cues have aligned precisely with either the beginning or the midway point of each musical phrase. The first and second phrases are both eight bars long, with their midway points coming in their respective fifth bar. The third phrase, however, is quite a bit longer than the previous two phrases. In its ninth bar, the black screen is once again abandoned and we see the bustling street outside the Harfords' apartment building. It is night-time and the nocturnal sounds of New York City can be heard, complete with the indexical police car's siren signalling danger. Towards the end of the third phrase, the visuals cut back to inside the Harfords' apartment and we see, for the first time in the film, the handsome doctor, Bill, fully dressed in an expensive-looking tuxedo. At first he is shown standing by the window, providing a visual link with our previous outside perspective, and as the extended musical phrase pushes to its close, he walks directly towards the camera, towards the viewer, with purpose and conviction. Checking his tuxedo pockets, he looks for something as the four-bar vamp returns, setting up a repeat of the first section of the waltz.

Like the visuals, the subsequent dialogue between Bill and Alice is cut precisely to the beginnings, middle, and endings of the musical phrases of the waltz (Table 10.1). The opening scene tells us much about Bill and Alice, as well as the dynamic of their marital relationship. On the surface, Alice can't decide what she wants to wear to the upcoming party of Victor Ziegler (Sydney Pollack). In our first encounter with her, she removes the sexy black dress, to reveal later in the bathroom that she has opted for another outfit entirely, one not so revealing. This time around, too, Alice decides to wear panties, which can be seen as she sits on the toilet. Contrary to Alice, Bill presents himself as a self-confident man, in control, even when he is unable to find his

Table 10.1 Synchronization of Shostakovich's 'Waltz no. 2' and spoken dialogue

Phrase		Character	Dialogue
1	Beginning	Bill	"Honey, have you seen my wallet?"
	Middle	Alice	"Isn't it on the bedside table?"
2	Beginning	Bill	*Finds wallet on bedside table.*
	Middle		"Now listen, we're running a little late."
		Alice	"I know."
3	Beginning	Alice	"How do I look?"
		Bill	"Perfect."
	Middle	Alice	"Is my hair okay?"
		Bill	"It's great."
	Ending	Alice	"You're *not* even looking at it."
		Bill	"It's beautiful. You always look beautiful."

wallet. His self-assurance, however, comes at a cost. When Alice asks for reassurance concerning her appearance ("Is my hair okay?"), Bill answers with his "eyes wide shut", a gesture that is not lost on his wife ("You're *not* even looking at it."). From this brief, but important, interaction, it is clear that Bill is somewhat smug and non-communicative and that he basically ignores Alice and takes her for granted.

Gorbman reads the close interaction between music and spoken dialogue in the opening visual sequence as "quasi-operatic", even going so far as to provide a possible musical setting for Cruise's first line of dialogue (2006: 9). This mickey-mousing of dialogue to music could conceivably continue throughout the first section of the waltz, as is evident from the above chart. But rather than interpreting the scene as quasi-operatic, might the all-too-perfect mapping actually resist such a unified *musical* interpretation? To my ears, Kubrick's carefully controlled synchronization between spoken dialogue and music actually reinforces their sonic differences. In other words, I can easily follow the dialogue as dialogue, and, at the same time, focus my attention on the music itself, appropriate for Gorbman's *first level* of analysis. While Gorbman places the music in a somewhat subordinate position to Cruise's words ("Honey, have you seen my wallet?"), my reading puts the purely musical codes on par with the spoken dialogue as an object of critical study. To be sure, there are many ways in which a listener can approach the waltz. My analysis, informed by an understanding of tonal harmony and voice leading, presents one such way to regard the passage.

Like the visceral images of the opening visual sequence, Shostakovich's waltz depicts moments of desire and denial. If we listen carefully, we can detect cracks underneath a polished musical surface, much like the cracks lurking underneath the veneer of the Harfords' complacent marriage. The home key of the waltz is D minor, a mode commonly associated with sadness and melancholy, in part because of the interval of the minor third above tonic. In the first phrase, the melody follows the shape of an inverted arch, first moving downwards from A, then back up again to its starting referential pitch. The melody, however, peaks a half-step higher on the dissonant pitch B-flat, a non-harmonic tone that creates a sense of dramatic urgency. The pitch B-flat can be interpreted as an ornamental upper neighbour to the more structural pitch, A. The half-step relationship between B-flat and A situates the pitch B-flat as an upper leading tone, encoded with dramatic *tonal desire*; the gravitational pull of B-flat down to A in the passage is palpable. As expected because of this strong directional pull, the B-flat falls downwards to A in the passage, but rather than resolving to A as a true chord tone, it is reconfigured as a non-harmonic tone within the new harmonic context of a pre-dominant, a supertonic seventh chord.[3]

At the corresponding passage in the second phrase, the melody once again reaches B-flat as its highest note. This time around there is new harmonic support for the B-flat by that of the dominant harmony. Now, the B-flat has been upgraded as a possible chord tone, the ninth of the chord. And once again the encoded tonal desire of the B-flat yearns to find melodic resolution downwards by step. But instead of following the expected tonal path of B-flat down to A, as we have just encountered in the first phrase, the melody now leaps down to G-sharp, an appoggiatura, as the harmonic motion comes full circle and cadences on the tonic triad. As a result, melodic claustrophobia ensues at this moment of harmonic repose since the pitch A is surrounded by both its upper and lower leading tones, both a *half-step* away.

In the third phrase, B-flat makes another appearance in the melody, now supported by the subdominant harmony (bars 23–24). Its previous linkage with the A is conspicuously missing as the melody makes a leap from B-flat down to G, thus jumping over (and avoiding altogether) the pitch A and the previous chromatic G-sharp. In the next bar, B-flat moves into an inner voice and is supported by another new harmony. In bar 25, what earlier was labelled as the middle of the third phrase, a temporary tonicization of F major reconfigures B-flat as the chordal seventh of the dominant harmony, yearning, once again, for melodic resolution down by step to the pitch A. For the first time in the waltz, the B-flat does, in fact, find both melodic and tonal solace. However, the next chord in the passage, a B-flat major triad, undermines any sort of extended closure. Within the larger scope of the passage, the harmonic motion to III in bars 25 to 27 moves via a conventional circle-of-fifths harmonic progression to VI in bar 28. Strikingly, the polarity between the two pitches of B-flat and A is reversed since A, the leading tone in B-flat major, *desires* to find melodic resolution up a half-step to its tonic. The B-flat pitch, which up to this point has depended on A for its identity as an upper leading tone, has upgraded its status to a stable temporary tonic, while the pitch A, now encoded with the tonal desire of a leading tone, has been relegated as a pitch dependent on B-flat for its melodic resolution.

In the last section of the third phrase, what was earlier labelled as the ending of the phrase (bar 29), the pitch B-flat is now heard in the lowest voice, thus making a textural journey from the exposed melody, to an inner voice, and finally to the exposed bass line. The polarity between the pitches B-flat and A returns to its original state in that the cadential dominant harmony, supported by A in the bass line, is ornamented by a neighbouring supertonic seventh chord, with B-flat serving once again as an upper leading tone to the pitch A. The tension created by the melodic motion from the A to B-flat, and the resolution of that tension down by half-step to the A, is obsessively repeated four times in the passage. This oscillation of half-step motion, coupled with the extra-musical siren of the police car, gives the music an ominous tone, a musically depicted crack underneath the surface of the lilting waltz.[4]

Kubrick's choice of music for the opening visual sequence is simply brilliant. The genre of waltz music is associated with a particular type of twirling dance in which partners hold each other closely, a perfect choice for the metaphorical dance about to take place between Bill, Alice and other key players in the filmic narrative. The genre of waltz music is also associated with the Old World sophistication of nineteenth-century Viennese culture, appropriate for Kubrick's updated adaptation of Arthur Schnitzler's *Traumnovelle* (1926). Shostakovich's waltz, within the context of the Harfords' chic New York City lifestyle, can be imagined as music heard in a smoke-filled jazz club as the 'sexy' saxophone, instead of the more traditional violin, takes centre stage as the soloist. Shostakovich's waltz, as we have seen, also contains musical seeds of tonal desire and denial; and, as the reading above has shown, the half-step motif hints that this psychological journey may come at a cost.

The employment of the waltz sheds additional light on the character of Bill Harford. From the very beginning of the film, the audience probably assumes that the waltz is non-diegetic music since it does not take part in the narrative on the screen; the music is not attributable to a source in the film, so it is safe to say that the characters are unaware of it. This assumption, however, proves unexpectedly incorrect. Before Bill and Alice leave their bedroom, Bill turns off the stereo system, which has been playing the Shostakovich waltz all along! His decision to stop the music in bar 54 creates an additional moment of tonal desire and denial; the underlying harmony at that moment is a highly charged secondary dominant. Instead of waiting a second or two more to hear the resolution to the very next chord in the passage, Bill cuts off the music midstream, seemingly unconcerned about hearing harmonic resolution in bar 55, let alone the cadence at the end of the phrase in bar 59 – this is the first time that the listener has been denied musical closure. His action, arguably, has a jarring effect on the listener, comparable to the earlier effect on the viewer/voyeur of the black screen that replaced the visual of Alice's nude body. In both instances, our eyes and our ears have been literally shut at critical moments of desire.

Nocturnal journeys and the symbolic return of the half-step motif

Desire and sex intoxicate the saturnalian atmosphere at Ziegler's Christmas party. In one scene, as the live orchestra plays jazz standards like 'When I Fall In Love' and 'I Only Have Eyes For You', an older Hungarian Lothario (Sky Dumont) attempts to seduce a tipsy Alice on the dance floor. But remaining true to Bill, she rebuffs his old-world come-on by holding strong to her vow of fidelity ("because I'm *married*"). Meanwhile, another erotic chase takes place, with Bill this time being the object of desire of two sexy models; they coyly ask him, "Don't you want to go where the rainbow ends?" While we know that this nocturnal journey would inevitably end up in a threesome with the pair, Bill plays dumb in response to their sexually charged innuendo ("It depends on where that is"). For the moment, both Alice and Bill have survived their respective extramarital temptations. The same, however, cannot be said of the party's married host. Bill finds this out when he is called away, or 'summoned' as it were, to attend to a matter upstairs in Ziegler's private bathroom. When Bill enters the room, he finds a naked Mandy (Julienne Davis), a probable hooker, passed out from an injection of cocaine and heroin, with Ziegler in the process of getting dressed.

In the opening visual sequence, the motif of female nudity was first presented, however briefly, with the backside of a nude Alice. Now, in contrast, Mandy faces the viewer head on, with her breasts and pubic hair fully exposed for an extended amount of time. The difference between these two moments has to do with Mandy's complete lack of agency. With no power and no literal voice, she has been reduced to a prop, a decorative mannequin whose sole purpose is to be looked at, to be gazed upon by men in the bathroom. Instead of getting outside help for Mandy, because of the threat of being caught with his proverbial pants down, Ziegler counts on his friend Dr Bill to help him out and to keep quiet about what he has seen ("this is just between us"). Knowing his place within the privileged world of Victor Ziegler, Bill obediently obliges on both accounts.

In the following scene, back in the privacy of the Harfords' apartment, we see a naked Alice from the back once again. Her exposed breasts, an image that signals a progression in the filmic narrative, are reflected in a mirror, in front of which she stands with an undressed Bill. This intimate moment between the couple provides a resolution to both of their earlier extramarital temptations. They are shown together after spending so much time apart at the party. The look on Alice's face, however, tells a slightly different story from that of complete resolution. Instead of being totally in the moment as they kiss and fondle each other, she often reflectively gazes at herself in the mirror, her mind drifting away from Bill to another place and time, perhaps to the earlier cat-and-mouse episode with the Hungarian. The use of diegetic music in the scene underscores this reading as Alice moves her body to the primal beats of Chris Isaak's 'Baby Did A Bad Bad Thing'. Isaak signifies that 'baby' proves to be a destructive force by singing the titular hook from the bottom of his vocal register in a singing style reminiscent of a musical growl. And when Isaak later asks in earnest, in his trademark high vocal register, "You ever love someone so much you thought your little heart was gonna break in two?" he answers his own question ("I didn't think so") at the precise moment that Alice gazes questioningly at herself in the mirror. This moment of self-awareness for Alice is interrupted, once again, with the structural return of the peep-show-like black screen. Shostakovich's waltz returns, too, now undeniably used as wholly non-diegetic music accompanying a filmic montage of Bill's and Alice's daily routine the next day. Dr Bill is shown examining various patients in his office, the first of which is a beautiful woman with directly exposed breasts, while Alice is shown performing various domestic duties in their apartment. During the montage, there is no dialogue to interfere with hearing a recapitulation of the waltz's pure musical codes.

The pivotal scene of the film occurs the next night in the privacy of the Harfords' bedroom. Because of its significance in the filmic narrative, close attention to the dialogue is provided. In the scene, Bill and Alice disagree about sexual desire outside of their committed relationship, fuelled by the events that took place the previous night at Ziegler's Christmas party.

Alice, smoking marijuana, begins the conversation by asking Bill in a seductive, dreamlike way, "Those two girls ... at the party last night. Did you ... by any chance ... happen to ... *fuck* them?" Her musical enunciation of the word "fuck", especially with its hard '-ck' ending, underscores its visceral and highly charged erotic meaning. As their dialogue unfolds, Bill lies to Alice and says that he was not with the two girls, but was rather upstairs with Ziegler, which is, of course, partly true – he fails to mention Mandy, the passed-out hooker, as well as the models' flirtations. Hiding behind his professional credentials, Bill tells Alice that Ziegler wasn't feeling well and he needed his help: end of story, new topic. But undeterred by his will, Alice next recounts the advances of the horny Hungarian. Bill's strategic response turns Alice's own word against her: "He just wanted to *fuck* my wife." Their conversation gains momentum when Bill says that it is understandable for men to desire her because she is such a "very, very beautiful woman". Using her intellect, and not her beauty, Alice turns Bill's logic against him, accusing him of wanting to have sex with the beautiful models from the party, as well as beautiful patients in his doctor's office – this image is fresh in our memory from the montage showing Dr Bill examining a topless patient. For Alice, their conversation takes a turn for the worse, however, when Bill counters by taking an elitist, moral high ground. He claims that he is an exception because he is in love with her; he is married to her; and he would never want to hurt her. Alice is not convinced by his words. She fires back that he is only faithful to her "out of consideration". Her larger point that desire outside of a marriage is completely natural is lost on her husband.

Using another tactic, Alice asks Bill if he ever thinks that his patients might fantasize about *him*, thus placing him in an uncomfortable feminized space as the object of female desire. Obviously annoyed with this scenario, Bill argues that "sex is the *last* thing on this *fucking*-hypothetical-woman-patient's mind" as he hides, once again, behind his professional credentials. And if that were not enough, taking his argument one step further, Bill argues that "*women* basically don't think like that," like men, that is; he says that women want commitment and safety in a relationship instead of desire and sex: end of story, new topic. But Alice's reply, "If you men *only* knew," challenges his self-assurance, not to mention his already fragile ego. This dramatic moment serves as the catalyst for Bill's rejection of reality and escape into the dream world. Alice recounts an incident that happened the previous summer during their vacation at Cape Cod. She confesses that she was so attracted to a young naval officer that she was willing to give up her life, her "whole *fucking* future" with him, even if it was only for one night of sex with the officer. The diegetic ring of the telephone interrupts Alice's confession to a visually shell-shocked Bill. And for the first time in the scene, his overplayed professional credentials get him off the hook, so to speak, as he is called away to a deceased patient's home.

The remainder of the film, which happens over a two-night time span, is all in consequence of Alice's bedroom confession. It is here, in his self-constructed dream world, that Bill embarks on an erotic sexual odyssey, far removed from his mechanical day-to-day routine of work and home. It is not entirely clear whether or not Bill is on a mission to get revenge sex in the dream world; after all, *to him*, Alice has cheated, as is evident from the black-and-white visual loop in his imagination showing her having sex with the naval officer. If he wanted to have sex, he certainly has ample opportunity in the dream world. Almost everywhere he ends up he is the object of someone's desire, such as Marion (Marie Richardson), the daughter of his deceased patient; Domino (Vinessa Shaw), an HIV-infected prostitute; a male hotel clerk (Alan Cumming); and a teenager (Leelee Sobieski), to name a few. And thanks to his musician friend Nick Nightingale (Todd Field), who told him the secret password ('*Fidelio*') at Ziegler's Christmas party, Bill ends up at an orgy for the ultra-wealthy and powerful, like Ziegler, who is also an attendee. At the orgy at Somerton, Bill first encounters a bizarre sex ritual that later turns into a fully fledged orgy, where everyone around him is engaged in some type of sexual act, but not Bill. In every sense of the word, he is an outsider, even in his self-constructed dream world.

At the orgy, Bill is a voyeur. He roams freely as an uninvited guest because he, like the other participants, wears a mask to conceal his identity. His outsider status, however, is eventually noticed by an unidentified woman. She warns him that he is in "great danger" and that he should leave "while there is still a chance". Bill chooses to ignore her warning, resulting in a confrontation with the masked assembly that is the most chilling scene in the film. In it, Bill is forced to remove his mask and reveal his identity to the group. The red-robed master also demands that Bill fully disrobe, targeting him once again as a feminized sexual object, this time for the collected gaze of the rather creepy masked assembly. But we actually never see Bill's "punishment" because the mysterious woman, the same one who warned him earlier that he was in danger, takes his place and "redeems" him, a coded term that is never really explained in the filmic narrative. The master gives one final threat to Bill that he must keep quiet about what he has seen, reminiscent of Ziegler's bathroom request to keep it "just between us", or Bill and his family will suffer dire consequences.

The background music during the interrogation scene is the second movement from György Ligeti's piano suite, *Musica Ricercata* (1953). The minimalist music, which consists entirely of three notes (E-sharp, F-sharp and G), makes a strong impact on the scene because of its total sparseness of musical elements. The texture is incredibly thin, with each sound made painfully audible by the percussive playing style. The main theme alternates between E-sharp and F-sharp, two pitches that are a half-step apart. Thus, the melodic half-step is highly symbolic within the filmic soundscape of the real world and the dream world. We heard a similar motif earlier in Shostakovich's waltz between the A and the B-flat. In the waltz, we traced the emergence of the half-step motif through various tonal and registral contexts, culminating in the ominous half-step alternations in the bass signalling danger. Ligeti's piano music, in contrast, is nothing but an exploration of the half-step motif; all superfluous musical elements have been stripped away.

Obsessive tonal desire, and the subsequent denial of that desire, can be heard throughout the interrogation scene. The ascending melodic gesture from E-sharp to a longer sustained F-sharp encodes the top note as the goal of the half-step motion. The lower note, the E-sharp, can be heard as the leading tone resolving to a more stable F-sharp tonic. This polarity, however, is not sustained. The melody shifts directions and swivels back downwards and comes to rest on the E-sharp. This new descending gesture shifts the polarity between the two pitches, as the F-sharp can now be heard as an upper leading tone, a flattened-second scale degree, to the more stable E-sharp tonic. This dialectic illustrates, in musical terms, as it were, the various impulses pushing and pulling within Bill's psyche. While the upward half-step motion signals an internal expression of desire, the downward half-step motion represents a repression of that desire.

In suggesting that we can actually hear Bill's musical thoughts during the scene, I draw from Gorbman's theoretical work with metadiegetic music, which she first presents in the form of a hypothetical filmic narrative:

> ... early in a film we witness the great romance of protagonist X, which ends tragically during the war. Years later, while X and his best friend Y sit in a bleak café discussing their irretrievable joys, Y brings up the name of X's lost love. This strikes a chord: a change comes over X's face, and music swells onto the soundtrack, the melody that had played early in the film on the night X had met her. On which narrative level do we read this music? It is certainly not diegetic, for the forty-piece orchestra that plays is nowhere to be seen, or inferred, in the filmic space of the café. In a certain sense, we may hear it as both nondiegetic – for its lack of a narrative source – and metadiegetic – since the scene's conversation seems to trigger X's memory of the romance and the song that went with it; wordlessly, he "takes over" part of

> the film's narration and we are privileged to read his musical thoughts.
> (Gorbman, 1987: 22–3)

In the dream world, everything relates to Bill in a cogent way, and that includes the choice and the use of music. Further, it makes sense that Bill's musical thoughts stem from a sonic source from his waking life, especially since many characters and the theme of erotic repression were first introduced in the real world. In the case of the Ligeti theme, the music serves a dual purpose as a double-bind within Bill in that it not only conveys the immanent *danger* that he is in, but it also harkens back to the cracks in his marriage, first signified by the half-step motif in Shostakovich's waltz. In the dream world's orgy, however, we should remember that Bill ultimately remains faithful to Alice, therefore taking an important step in abating his complacency on one level, and perhaps opening his eyes on another.

Making connections in the morgue

In the dream world, the filmic action speeds up the next day as the scope of the story shifts to one of a murder mystery in which Bill, now as self-imagined private investigator, tries to figure out a classic "who done it" narrative. The menacing Ligeti theme, now a constant presence in Bill's musical thoughts, is used effectively to connote danger and to build suspense as Bill learns that his friend, Nick Nightingale, has gone missing under questionable circumstances; he also receives a second ominous warning from Somerton to give up his inquiries about what he has seen; he is stalked on the streets of New York; and the body of an ex-beauty queen, Amanda Curran, has turned up dead from a drug overdose. The Ligeti theme, first heard during the interrogation scene, points to Somerton as the probable source from which all of these disparate events connect in Bill's mind. Did Nick ultimately pay with his own life for giving Bill privileged information to attend the orgy as an uninvited guest? Is Bill being stalked by someone affiliated with the Somerton elite to frighten him, or worse? And is Amanda Curran, the dead ex-beauty queen, really Mandy, the passed-out hooker in Ziegler's bathroom, as well as the unidentified woman who "redeemed" Bill by giving her own life for his? These questions are never fully answered in the dream world.

Bill's subsequent trip to the morgue for further investigation leads one to believe that Amanda could possibly be his redeemer. As Bill stares in disbelief at her nude body, we hear a voice-over from the unidentified woman ("because it could cost me my life ... and possibly yours"). The camera angle shot from above shows Amanda's lifeless corpse, with breasts and pubic hair in full frontal view once again. Throughout the film Amanda/Mandy has been portrayed as a mannequin-like prop, first in Ziegler's bathroom, then as an objectified sex object at the orgy. This scene pushes her sexual objectification to the final threshold, her physical death. The visual of her lifeless body conveys an eerie detached coldness as blood no longer runs through her veins to keep her warm. Her skin, no longer pinkish, has an unnatural blue-coloured hue. Her eyes, however, tell a very different story. No longer closed because of her drug-induced stupor, or hidden behind an actual mask at the orgy, now, in death, they remain physically *open* as she lies lifeless on the sterile slab. In the dream world, her death gaze seems to reach out to Bill's psyche in one of the most real moments in the film. For an extended period of time, he simply looks into her eyes. This moment, while arguably sentimental, is significant in that it recalls Alice's earlier words that he was unable to look at her while she was getting ready for the party. In the dream world, Bill is finally able to look at another.

The use of metadiegetic music in the morgue scene provides an additional case study of Bill's musical thoughts. In the scene, the background music is Franz Liszt's '*Nuages gris*' (Grey Clouds) (1881), a gloomy nineteenth-century character piano piece (Figure 10.2). The home key of the work is G minor, a mode form commonly associated with sadness, as we heard previously in the waltz. In addition, other musical elements, such as a muted dynamic scheme and the prominent use of a low register on the keyboard, contribute to its melancholic affect. The opening right-hand gesture, which is repeated *four* times in the passage, follows the trajectory of an arch, with the D serving as the lowest and highest points in the initial ascent. The structural upper D is ornamented by a C-sharp, a chromatic lower neighbour significant because of its half-step resolution as a leading tone to D. The resolution of the C-sharp to D is effectively drawn out in the passage, thus building tonal desire, since the C-sharp is given special emphasis as the longest-held note. With the third statement of the gesture, the left hand makes its entrance and plays a B-flat tremolo in a submerged register, fading away at the end of bar 7. Later, in bar 9, the ominous B-flat returns in the left hand, this time

Figure 10.2 Liszt, '*Nuages gris*' (bars 1–20)

moving down a familiar half-step to the A in bar 10. This tonal motion inverts the previous C-sharp to D resolution in the right hand since B-flat can be heard as an upper-leading tone resolving down by half-step to A.

As we heard previously in the waltz and the second movement of the *Musica Ricercata*, tonal desire, and the subsequent reversal of that desire, permeates the filmic soundscape during the morgue scene. The left hand alternates between the B-flat and the A, making it possible to hear both as temporary tonics as well as goal-directed leading tones, just as we encountered previously with the same two notes in the waltz. There is an additional transformation of the half-step motif beginning in the right hand in bar 9. All sonorities in the passage are accounted for by *descending* half-step motion, therefore expressing in purely musical codes the climactic point of Bill's repressed desire. Taking another point of view, these highly charged chromatic chords in the right hand, coupled with the ominous half-step motion in the left hand, additionally convey an overwhelming sense of grief and loss appropriate for Mandy's death. Are these two interpretations, one which foregrounds Bill's erotic repressions, and the other Mandy's literal death, somehow connected? Further, might these chords ultimately symbolize a glimmer of hope for Bill outside of the dream world? I intentionally hold back a definite interpretation, holding true, to my eyes and ears at least, the wonderful ambivalence that exists in the dream world. In any case, it is for certain that for the first time in the film, Bill looks outside of himself towards another with his eyes literally wide open.

Conclusion: musical loops and the imagined space of sexual climax

Once back at home, after a heated confrontation with Ziegler in which he tells Bill that they tried to scare the "living shit out of you to keep you quiet", Bill finds Alice asleep in bed. Lying on her pillow next to her is his mask from the orgy. The background music returns to Ligeti's two-note ominous theme, suggesting an aural link with Somerton in Bill's musical imagination. Bill's reaction to seeing his mask next to Alice is a complete emotional and physical breakdown; he sobs uncontrollably as Alice holds him and comforts him. He then decides to tell Alice everything. It is at this critical moment that Bill leaves his self-constructed dream world behind. In other words, he decides to wake up.

In the last scene of the film, shopping in a toy store with their daughter, Bill and Alice discuss their future as a couple ("What do you think we should do?"). While Alice thinks that they should be grateful because they have survived their marital adventures, real or imagined, Bill, still stinging from his dream odyssey, seems a bit more cautious ("Are you ... are you ... sure of that?"). For better or worse, they both agree that they are now awake to each other; their eyes are finally open, "forever" according to Bill. Alice's honesty during this moment is both tender and sad ("Let's not use that word, it frightens me. But I do... *love* you."). Alice is given the last line in the film, one that appropriately recapitulates her highly charged four-letter word: "And you know, there *is* something very important that we need to do as soon as possible… *fuck.*"

The peepshow-like black screen makes one last appearance at the end of the film, effectively creating a visual space of nothingness into which we, the audience, can project our own fantasy of Bill and Alice making love, or *fucking*, as Alice puts it. The open-ended filmic narrative can be imagined, therefore, in as many different ways as there are viewers. The background music of Shostakovich's waltz returns at the end of the film, too, curiously looping back to the beginning of the filmic soundscape. By ending in the same way as it began, enmeshed in a musical loop, the film resists a conventional Hollywood ending. While the waltz is certainly used as non-diegetic music for the end-credits, we might also think of it as metadiegetic: it offers a structural use of music that, up until now, has been reserved solely for the dream world. This reading, arguably, gives one final glimpse into Bill's musical thoughts in the aftermath of his 'eye-opening' experience. We would do well to remember, however, that the waltz is intended as a social activity for a couple, not as a solo dance. And a relationship, or a marriage, takes two to make it work. Might the return of the waltz provide a shared insight into the musical thoughts of both Bill and Alice as they embark together on their next marital adventure? To be sure, there is no visual or musical 'money shot' in *Eyes Wide Shut*. The film ends, as it began, in a state of arousal.

Notes

1. Interviewed by J. Harlan (2001), *Stanley Kubrick: A Life in Pictures* (DVD).
2. I emphasize and clarify 'pre-existing'. This means that Jocelyn Pook's music, which was composed for the film, is outside the scope of this discussion. Even 'The Masked Ball', which is a revision of one of her early works, is considered by Pook herself to be a new composition for the film because the bass voice is turned backwards. I find her music highly effective in the film, but it is very different from the other pre-existing music that was 'chosen' by Kubrick. She worked with him closely to score the scenes. The other pieces, like the Shostakovich, the Ligeti and the Liszt, were not manipulated to fit the scene.
3. One reader of this chapter suggested a different musicological reading of this tonality is possible, one that places the opening B♭ as the beginning of an arpeggiation down to the G, with the A in between a passing note rather than a suspension. While this interpretation makes sense, my reading puts more emphasis on the half-step resolution back to the A, which later, as we see, is extremely important. My main focus is the relationship between A/B-flat. The other interpretation, which does mention the A, gives the final pitch, G, the greater emphasis.
4. Two pitches a half-step apart, like the A and B-flat, are reminiscent of John Williams's two-note motif for Steven Spielberg's *Jaws* (1975).

References

Abrams, J. (ed.) (2007), *The Philosophy of Stanley Kubrick*, Lexington: The University Press of Kentucky.

Chion, M. (2001), *Kubrick's Cinema Odyssey*, London: British Film Institute.

Neumeyer, D., and Buhler, J. (2001), 'Analytical and Interpretive Approaches to Film Music (I): Analyzing the Music', in K. Donnelly (ed.), *Film Music: Critical Approaches*, Edinburgh: Edinburgh University Press, pp. 16–38.

Gorbman, C. (1987), *Unheard Melodies: Narrative Film Music*, Bloomington: Indiana University Press.

Gorbman, C. (2006), 'Ears Wide Open: Kubrick's Music', in P. Powrie and R. Stilwell (eds), *Changing Tunes: The Use of Pre-existing Music in Film*, Burlington, VT: Ashgate, pp. 3–18.

Grodal, T. (2004), 'Love and Desire in the Cinema', *Cinema Journal*, 43(2), 26–46.

Nelson, T. (2000), *Kubrick: Inside a Film Artist's Maze*, Bloomington: Indiana University Press.

Sperb, J. (2006), *The Kubrick Façade: Faces and Voices in the Films of Stanley Kubrick*, Lanham, MD: The Scarecrow Press, Inc.

Walker, A. (1999), *Stanley Kubrick, Director*, New York: W. W. Norton & Company.

11 Multiple Positions
Sound, Sex and Aural Dominance in 9 Songs

Andrea Warren

> *When I remember Lisa, I don't think about her clothes, or her work, where she was from, or even what she said. I think about her smell, her taste, her skin touching mine.*

We do not learn much more about Lisa after this opening voice-over in Michael Winterbottom's 2004 film, *9 Songs*. The young character, Matt, who speaks the line, has a selective memory of the other protagonist, immortalizing her as a fleshy, fragrant female. A more detailed examination of the vocal material in this passage, however, suggests that there is more to their relationship and the ways in which it is conveyed in the film than meets the eye:

> Matt: *(voice-over throughout)* When I remember Lisa, I don't think about her clothes, or her work, where she was from, or even what she said.
> Lisa: *(in bed, having sex with Matt)* Huh, huh.
> Matt: I think about her...
> Lisa: UHH
> Matt: smell...
> Lisa: UNG
> Matt: her taste...
> Lisa: ge...
> Matt: her skin...
> Lisa: huh huh hmm.
> Matt: touching mine.
> Matt and Lisa: hmm huh hum huh.
> Lisa: UHHhaaa! huh huh.
> ...

Lisa's aural presence in this scene is typical of women in heterosexual pornography: her sounds of pleasure and sexual exertion dominate the soundscape in both volume and sonic interest. This, however, is no ordinary porn scene. By contrast, Matt's articulate and factual contribution is emotionally removed, spoken with such retrospective clarity that the two characters sound like they could be in different films. In a sense, they are.

This 68-minute film comprises a string of sex scenes, factual vignettes of Matt at work as a glaciologist in Antarctica, and the nine titular concert performances which the couple attends together at London's Brixton Academy. As these are taken together, the film's audience is made privy to Matt's nostalgia for his summer fling with Lisa. As part-pornographer, part-ethnographer and part-music video director, Matt calls the shots in this film with aural privilege and voice-over. His control over the non-diegetic space sonically navigates the spectator through a convoluted blend of reality and fiction, evoked by the film's combination of pornographic, documentary and musical realities. In many ways, sound causes the fantasy of the narrative to intermingle with the materiality of the action in the film: actors Kieran O'Brien and Margot Stilley engage in a simulated relationship as characters Matt and Lisa, and this fiction is presented alongside concert performances with real, paying audiences, as well as the characters' own unsimulated sex. As spectators, we are visually positioned as concert-goers, yet aurally reminded that we are but film spectators. We are visually privy to sexual pleasure, yet aurally forced to question its authenticity. These conflicting presentations alternately position viewers as participants in a fantasy and as voyeurs of a so-called reality, an ambiguity which creates a pleasurable, if conflicted, visceral engagement with the film. As I will explore, sound mediates this pleasure.

In *Knowing the Score*, film-music composer Irwin Bazelon describes the irony that, although music may be the least natural element in a film, it is often the very element "that gives the film its semblance of reality" (1975: 140). Sound, more broadly than music, can do much more than help the viewer suspend disbelief. As ethnomusicologist Jeff Packman asserts with regard to a 1997 videogame, sound can "obscure the boundary between the real and the virtual" (Packman, 2001). Drawing on what Carol Laderman calls "aesthetic distance" (1991), Packman argues that sound positions players just far enough inside the action to engage them emotionally, but not so far that they lose grounding in their own realities. This description of sound's ability to influence specific viewing positions can help frame the following discussion of the ways that sound manipulates viewers' involvement in *9 Songs*. By encouraging a hyperconsciousness of the viewers' bodies during the nine live performances, by flogging Matt's authorial perspective through voice-over and non-diegetic music, by masking and revealing the sounds of real bodies interacting during sex, and finally by manipulating all of these sonic details in post-production, sound functions to control viewers' stimulation in various ways, but only on *its* terms. This chapter will explore just what those terms entail, including how sound encourages a visceral involvement with the film, privileges a male viewing subjectivity and ultimately problematizes autonomous female sexuality – a troubling progression in light of the film's appeal to reality.

Diegetic dancing to nine songs

The ways in which viewers engage with the titular eight rock songs and single piano composition are convoluted, largely influenced by viewers' initial attraction to the film: for fans of the film's line-up of bands (Black Rebel Motorcycle Club, the Von Bondies, Elbow, Primal Scream, the Dandy Warhols, Super Furry Animals, and Franz Ferdinand), the songs provide the main draw of the film.[1] A 'concert-performance-only' option on the DVD, which omits the intervening sex scenes, is offered as a special feature for these viewers.[2] I did not fall into this viewer category; I had previously heard only a handful of the songs, so for me those opening moments of documentary voice-over set in train an imaginary narrative between Matt and Lisa — a plot I tried to impose on the first few concert performances in the film. Anecdotally, this seems to be a common attempt. Exposure to 'Hollywood scoring' (the association of mood-enhancing musical elements with particular events in the story, such as lush strings to evoke romanticism and undulating minor seconds to foreshadow horror) has instilled in many film-viewers an infectious expectation that most film music will reflect, if not propel, the plot. In this film, however, such an expectation falls flat after several viewings: the lyrics of the songs only vaguely correspond with the narrative of the deteriorating on-screen relationship, and Matt and Lisa are only rarely pictured during these scenes (when they are, their lips move in conversation, but their voices are not included in the mix). Because the songs do not develop the plot, I feel prodded to focus my attention on the bands.

The film goes to great lengths to foster audience involvement in the 'concert-going experience'. In addition to watching the bands on stage, viewers watch the audience on screen, which, in turn, watches and listens to the bands. The camera shifts omnisciently, enabling multiple vantage points, but continually returning to a position submerged within the crowd. The hair of dancing women flies past the camera and the heads of tall spectators obscure its field of view. Despite these visually involving cues, however, the sounds of these concerts — those which are included and those which are masked — remind me of my distance from the fantasy and remind me that despite my toe-tapping, I am watching a film. In the Von Bondies' performance of 'C'mon C'mon', for example, occasional bursts of crowd sounds enter and exit the mix, the back-up singer walks away from the microphone but is still heard singing, and the audience changes its dance patterns every few seconds without any audible cue from the music. Whether these incongruities were intentional or simply examples of sloppy editing, their combination with the reality of the live venue, the live bands and the live surroundings remind me of my own reality. They encourage a level of self-consciousness in viewing and listening that keeps me from completely giving myself over to the experience and thereby heightens my awareness of my own body.

When time after time these scenes cut to sex, that heightened bodily awareness leaves me exposed, stripped of the critical distance of film viewership. Physically involved while watching the concert performances, I suddenly become a spectator to the sex or acted dialogue preceding it. What happens to that bodily awareness from the concerts when viewers watch the sex? Popular-music scholar Simon Frith argues that the effects of music and sex are not greatly different: "Music is 'sexy' not because it makes us move, but because (through that movement) it makes us feel; makes us feel (like sex itself) intensely present" (Frith, 1998: 144). The same can be said of being a spectator to music-making and sex: the materiality of these acts involves us in real time. If sexual interest is not aroused, it seems inevitable that we will be moved in some corporeal way, be it out of revulsion, sympathetic fascination or anything in between. What happens, though, when the film elicits this very real kind of involvement and then immediately juxtaposes it with depictions of fantasy – sex which is packed with sexual assumptions and presented from one character's perspective? When the music ends, does bodily involvement convert into sexual arousal, alignment with the dominant perspective in the fantasy, or something else? How does sound affect how viewers receive the fantasy and how much of its baggage stays with them after the film is over?

Questions of perspective

I have suggested that the dual experiences of concerts and sex in *9 Songs* appeal to viewers beyond their usual involvement in a film narrative. The alternating concerts and sex scenes elicit physical involvement with relatively little narrative distraction. Where the treatment of the concert scenes departs from the sex, however, is in the matter of perspective: the concert scenes are characterized by the multiple viewing positions they provide, but the sex scenes favour Matt's subject position. The presence of the camera in any dramatic or documentary work produces such questions about the perspective it privileges as: who is behind the camera, whom does it favour, how do its choices manipulate our understanding, etc.? These questions are compounded in *9 Song*'s sex scenes because *Matt controls both the visual and aural perspectives.*

Aural representations of Lisa are abundant in this film. They come in the form of narrated descriptions and are often positive, even nostalgic.[3] Nevertheless, in almost every case Lisa is aurally dominated by Matt. In Matt's voice-over, for example, he comments on many aspects of his relationship with Lisa, including his memory of her, details of how they met, how she celebrated his birthday and how her demeanour improved after she had booked a flight home to America. Although he never specifically comments on their sex, his frequently present non-diegetic voice reminds us that the entire depiction of their relationship, indeed the entire film, is from his perspective. Matt's voice-over also functions to establish the only other subplot in the film – a vaguely metaphorical depiction of his job as a glaciologist (ancient work on a vast and unchanging Antarctic landscape, lonely "like two people in a bed", he says). This somewhat gratuitous plot detail seems to be an effort to open up the scope and expectations of the documentary form, a genre that encourages the presence of an authoritative perspective. Matt is more than simply the storyteller, therefore; his scientific career earns him credibility as a truth-teller, someone who will objectively unfold this relationship before the audience. Factual vignettes about glaciers in Antarctica, the couple's unsimulated sex, live music and other truths in the film further contribute to the sway of Matt's truth-telling, 'objective' perspective.

The idea that 'having a voice' represents social presence and political freedom is as compelling in film as it is in other media representations in popular culture. As film scholar Rick Altman says, "In the narrative world, the right to speech invariably conveys narrational power, for by convention it carries with it a secondary right, the right to appear in the image" (1980: 68). The documentary voice-over changes this model somewhat, because the speaker may never actually appear in the image. Mary Ann Doane cogently theorizes this to be the very power of the voice-over: it is, "in effect, a *disembodied* voice ... It is its radical otherness with respect to the diegesis which endows this voice with a certain authority" (Doane, 1980: 42). As she describes, it is almost an ethereal voice, gaining its power through its facelessness. Its truths cannot be questioned. Matt's voice, though separated from his image during his voice-over, is recognizable as the voice of the on-screen character, but its power derives from its ability to dodge the diegesis. Instead of 'eavesdropping on dialogue', we are overtly connected to Matt's voice as an authoritative source of information about Lisa and his relationship. Matt's voice-over reaches beyond the plot and positions him as a 'real' person, similar to the way in which the music scenes reposition film-viewers as participants in the events. Hearing the voice-over, the viewer is, as Doane puts it, "an empty space to be 'filled' with knowledge about events, character psychology, etc." (*ibid.*: 43). The sound of Matt's voice, in effect, herds the viewer into this position.

Since the 1970s, film scholars have debated the role of film in shaping viewers' subjectivity. When Laura Mulvey (1975) sparked discussion about how models of spectatorship might be gendered constructs and questioned how women identify with characters on screen, she challenged the idea that film dictates spectators' viewing position. Teresa de Lauretis (1984) theorized a complex system that argued for viewers' ability to identify with various subject positions in a film – both male and female – regardless of their own gender. Janet Staiger (2000), in turn, stressed that modes of reception are not predetermined, but influenced by instance-specific factors at play in the theatre (such as distraction, stress and interest). In these theories, film spectators are given the ultimate agency in choosing their viewing positions, yet I am not convinced that such generosity is applicable in the case of this film. The production choices which align this film with the documentary privilege Matt's voice as an authorial one. The use of sound further asserts his authority and seems to heavily inform spectators' reception of the film.

This film suffers from many of the same problems of representation and power inherent in documentary genres, and these problems do not simply disappear when the voice-over does. The disappearance of Matt's dominating voice from the audience's aural radar, for example, does not mark the disappearance of the documentarian's authority, nor the perception that he is feeding viewers aural and visual 'truths'. Doane argues that when the voice-over steps aside to allow the event being documented to "speak for itself", this actually disguises the reality that every aspect of the film is shaped and chosen (manipulated) by the documenter, a reality that can be dangerous – indeed, manipulative – when masked (Doane, 1980: 46). Beyond the obviously influential sound of Matt's voice, the sound of his non-diegetic musical choices and his choices to mask or feature the sounds of sex thinly veil his sexual predispositions and, furthermore, subject viewers to his antiquated sexual discomforts.

Composer Irwin Bazelon raises an important issue about the specific effects of musical gestures in films: he muses, do "cool-jazz drum-rhythm patterns" cause the audience to eat "their popcorn a little faster?" (Bazelon, 1975: 96). In *9 Songs*, music has a distinctive impact on how I receive and retain the stimulus of the film, especially within the heightened trust that documentary conventions such as the voice-over seem to elicit. As Frith cogently elucidates:

> *The issue is not how a particular piece of music or a performance reflects a people, but how it produces them, how it creates and constructs an experience – a musical experience, an aesthetic experience – that we can only make sense of by taking on both a subjective and collective identity.*
> (Frith, 1996: 109)

In *9 Songs*, how does the non-diegetic music of the sex scenes and the manipulation of the sounds of sex during post-production affect the aesthetic spectating experience and, ultimately, viewers' comfort with the sex on screen?

Acoustic accolades and sexual idealism on the ivories

Matt's voice, as virtually the only occupant of the non-diegetic space of the film, seems to assume territory there. Because his voice-over asserts that the story is from his perspective, within the fantasy of the plot, the entire non-diegetic realm seems to be his – his locus for analysing memories of the relationship and his venue for coupling these memories with the music which shares the space with his voice. The consistency of Matt's vocal presence in the non-diegetic space gives the listener no reason to doubt that he chose the music that often accompanies the sex scenes. I would like to suggest, then, that the music in this space is at the whim of Matt's nostalgia, sometimes emphasizing the sounds of sex (a soundscape dominated by Lisa's voice) in an otherwise 'naked' aural space, while at other times completely masking these corporeal sounds. The non-diegetic music used throughout the film fleshes out how Matt remembers Lisa and how he represents her womanhood through sound.

If Matt controls the non-diegetic music, then solo piano is his instrument of choice – a choice which provides an easily edited and unprogrammatic aural background, one which can continue uninterrupted amid the film cuts. In an early scene in the film, Michael Nyman's composition 'Debbie' continues uninterrupted while shots of Matt and Lisa's sex reveal a hanging wall clock in the frame which jumps incrementally with every cut. Nyman's music here is so harmonically stagnant (structured on three repeated triads) and rhythmically repetitive (plodding bass with either a running eighth note or predictable appoggiatura pattern in the treble) that the music functions just as an original score would: it fades out unobtrusively when the sex ends. This role of music to smooth out the "temporal–spatial gaps created by editing" aligns the use of this piano music with music in pornography (whose traits Linda Williams [1999: 122] has outlined).

Melissa Paramenter's two piano pieces in this film, the only music originally composed for it, function somewhat differently, creating more than enabling continuity. In some of the more explicit sex scenes of the film, with close filming of the couple's genitals and slightly more adventuresome play, her music connects different locations (from a walk outside to sex in the bath) and power dynamics (from laughing passion to light slaps across the face). This music choreographs strings of sexual scenarios into cohesive groups and representations of the couple's relationship, almost distracting from the action of these scenes in favour of a series of musical vignettes with the now normative sound of the piano and the sex it has come to accompany.

Loaded sex and the threatening buzz of electric organs

When, for the first time, this non-diegetic space is breached by a singer (and a female singer at that), the music begins to comment upon the on-screen action and new musical and sexual meaning is created. This meaning is relative to the ways the singer's song departs from the previous uses of non-diegetic music as outlined above and, importantly, is related to the declining state of Matt and Lisa's relationship. Lisa makes this relationship failure explicit when she exclaims, "Sometimes when you kiss me I want to bite you. Not in a nice way; I want to make you bleed." Shortly thereafter, 'Horse Tears' by the UK duo Goldfrapp fades in, while the scene cuts to a dark and seedy bar, foggy with smoke and dull green light. Sitting on a couch at Venus, the "Really Nude Table Dancers" bar, Matt becomes increasingly uncomfortable with the attention Lisa attracts and enjoys from a female lap dancer. As Alison Goldfrapp's voice croons slowly and sorrowfully, the camera cuts between the bar, Lisa masturbating in bed, Matt leaving the bar alone, Lisa interacting with the dancer and, finally, Lisa bringing herself to orgasm with her vibrator.

Matt's discomfort with Lisa's autoeroticism, her interest in this woman at the bar and the fact that the combination of these might signal trouble in their relationship is encapsulated in his choice of accompanying song. When Matt allows another voice into his narrative space during Lisa's masturbation, he distances himself acoustically from the scene. Beyond the theoretical significance of a woman's voice invading this otherwise male territory, every musical detail of this song coddles Matt's discomfort: the minor key, the strings playing tension-building appoggiaturas, Alison Goldfrapp's voice sighing with descending gestures ... the composition uses dozens of musical tropes of sadness and regret. Although plodding piano chords run the length of the song, as in the other music Matt has matched with his sexual memories, a synthesized electric organ aurally dominates the track. The organ's electric whirring – its timbral contrast with the acoustic piano – seems to signal Matt's discomfort with Lisa's autoerotic pleasure which technology (her vibrator/'electric organ') now affords her. The singer's voice, too, is dramatically enhanced by technology: in the chorus, her voice becomes breathy and is matched with an electric guitar for a result that sounds distinctively buzzing and inhuman. At this point in the song, Lisa's otherwise obscured sound of masturbation fades into the mix. Now, the sound of her vibrator is nestled into Alison's buzzing voice track while Alison's breathing and vocal inflections colour Lisa's own. Goldfrapp's technologically mediated music (with its pointedly contrasting instrumentation) is paralleled with Lisa's technologically mediated pleasure. This is the perfect break-up song for Matt to include on his soundtrack: one which combines nostalgia with masochistic reminders of his own shortcomings and the likely comforting representation of Lisa's 'self-indulgence'.

The remainder of this subplot (appropriately encapsulated on the DVD within a chapter titled "She's All She Needs") confirms that Lisa's autoeroticism is a source of guilt for her and disappointment for Matt. The scene directly following Lisa's masturbation reveals the couple lying in bed while Matt tries to stop Lisa from crying. Sounds of a car alarm and a yelping child leak in through the window, and the camera trails Matt's hand as he rubs Lisa's naked body. His gesture looks understanding and concerned, while the camera eroticizes Lisa's guilt; her masturbation begins to appear as a gimmick or even a marketing ploy for the film.[4] After Matt has prepared dinner, he walks into the bedroom to find Lisa using her vibrator once more. He stands spectating, silent but with obvious disappointment, while another Nyman piano piece fades in. The composition is not much different from Nyman's others in the film, yet it takes on a defeatist quality in spite of itself, through the combination of Matt's look of utter vulnerability and the unobscured sound of Lisa's vibrator, now loaded with the memory of the previous scene. To add insult to injury for the watching and listening Matt, Lisa's vocal expressions are louder and more varied here than during any other sex in the film.[5] Despite the fact that throughout the film, the vast majority of vocal sounds during sex are Lisa's, she ups the ante of aural representations of her pleasure in these masturbation scenes, using her voice in a much more guttural, occasionally even multiphonic, way.

The fact that Lisa sounds like she's enjoying herself during these two scenes of masturbation may suggest that this film proactively creates a space for Lisa's autoerotic pleasure, but it is not that simple. Although she is granted the aural space to express her pleasure within the diegesis, especially during her masturbation scenes, this space is curtailed by Matt's dominating soundtrack, which is laced with doom-filled musical tropes, as discussed above. Liz Kotz argues that the act of labelling porn 'progressive' or 'feminist' because, say, the woman is on top or dominating encourages the dated notion that women viewers identify with women characters on screen (Kotz, 1993: 104). In Lisa's masturbation, the rich sounds of her orgasm do not diminish the fact that viewers of all genders are simultaneously enveloped by the most plodding, depressing sounds of musical anxiety heard at any point in the film. Musical anxiety becomes sexual anxiety, and although, as Kaja Silverman notes, our viewing position is "assignable", we are nonetheless entranced "by the authorial system of a given text" (1988: 233), in this case, by the authority of our visceral involvement with the film. In a film which straddles both sides of materiality and fantasy, encouraging our bodies to engage with the former, there could be contagious effects of the narrative fiction within the film. When considered in tandem with the repertoire of documentary tropes within the film, Matt's antiquated perspective of female sexuality (connecting female autoeroticism with the demise of a relationship) begins to sound all the more convincing.

Post-production and the 'man-handling' of aural pleasure

The post-production 'sweetening' of sounds, common to all cinematic genres but especially prevalent in pornography, causes Lisa's voice to lose even more of its agency in envoicing sexual pleasure. Pornographic film is characterized by close-miking, close genital shots and the fostering of both fantasy and reality: actors must try to create attractive representations of pleasure while everyone working behind the camera has to capture these representations and supplement them where necessary to create a product which will arouse spectators. The technical similarities between pornographic films and *9 Songs*, therefore, extends further than explicit sexual content. In *9 Songs*, the actors negotiate the reality of sexual pleasure with its fictional expression. With an eye and ear to the final product, a team of professionals tidy and tighten, boosting the actors' performances of pleasure with their editing technology. The difference between such mediation within pornographic genres and the hybrid of *9 Songs*, however, is in the narrative result. Peter Lehman argues that sex in porn is not about the diegesis:

> Attraction ... is both extended and patterned, but within a pattern of curiosity, arousal, display, and satisfaction rather than one within a diegetic framework. The hard-core feature's diegesis has little or nothing to do with its display of sexual attractions. (Lehman, 2006: 89)

Lehman's is a progressive view of pornography, which argues that narratives are only subtexts. But in *9 Songs*, Matt's documentation of his failing relationship and his perceived reasons for its failure often infiltrates the sex through sound, as explored above. Thus, the post-production sonic manipulation of aural pleasure, which is expected in pornography, becomes narratologically and ideologically problematic here, clashing with previous attempts to depict reality and stripping Lisa of control over her erotic voice.

While the sounds of orgasm are often supplemented with 'banked' sounds in pornography, this same disjunction in *9 Songs* confuses an already convoluted web of materiality and fantasy. The sound of Lisa's orgasm, the sonic highlight throughout the film, is actually recycled in the final sex scene, dubbed non-synchronously from her orgasm 13:35 minutes into the film. This duplication is not likely to be something the average film spectator would notice without comparing Lisa's orgasm sounds one by one, especially in light of what Michel Chion has termed "synchresis", or "the forging of an immediate and necessary relationship between something one sees and something one hears at the same time" (Chion, 1994: 224). Nonetheless, it is more than theoretically significant. First, it suggests that the authenticity of "unsimulated sex" which the film boasts in its advertising (particularly on the DVD's 'special features') is purely a visual matter; in other words, that authentically produced sound is not a factor in the description "unsimulated sex". Second, it seems as if the post-production team usurps Lisa's control over demonstrating her pleasure when it manipulates the sounds of her orgasm. These editors act as a collective ventriloquist, who, as Altman describes in another context, "lures [his] audience into believing the (strong but mistaken) visual evidence rather than the (weak but correct) testimony of the ears" (Altman, 1980: 77). This false testimony is common in pornography's representations of female sexuality, as Linda Williams suggests: "the aural 'ejaculation' of pleasure, especially in post-synchronized sound, gives none of the same guarantee of truth that the visual ejaculation does" (Williams, 1999: 125). Nevertheless, this duplication and non-synchronization of Lisa's body and voice disempower her erotic voice as a tool of arousal; it does not act to deconstruct image hegemony (as in Silverman, 1988), but disenfranchises Lisa's agency in her expression of pleasure.

(In)discrete events and merging genres

On the topic of pornography Lehman notes, "since porn does not invest much in the believability of its fictional world, it acknowledges that spectators are really watching actors perform sexually, not characters" (Lehman, 2006: 89). For similar reasons, it is becoming increasingly difficult to discuss sounds associated with Lisa's sexual pleasure within the supposedly unsimulated reality of the film. In the conflicting 'suspension of belief' and 'suspension of unbelief' that *9 Songs* fosters, Lisa's sounds could be a result of post-production mixing, a product of actor Margot Stilley's own sexual personality or a creative invention she developed for her character. Other realities of the film complicate this discussion, such as the possibility of directorial coaching and even miking choices. These kinds of possibilities certainly challenge the romanticism of director Michael Winterbottom's methodology, which he describes in the DVD's 'special features' as an attempt to capture "the atmosphere of being in love" by filming sex "closely enough and honestly enough in enough detail". In an e-mail correspondence with the author, *9 Songs* sound recordist Stuart Wilson mused about the difficulty of upholding this kind of 'honesty' amid the realities of sound recording:

> I take responsibility for the sound either working around director and camera, or sometimes, getting the results I want by stealth, without letting [the director] be distracted by what I am doing. (Michael often has ideas about

> how he wants the sound which wouldn't work practically, so I sometimes have to plant mics without telling him [in order] *to get the results I want without him feeling his aesthetic approach is being compromised!*) (personal communication with the author, February 2008)[6]

It seems that although the sex in this film is made more graphic and 'real' by isolating its sounds (for example, Matt's condom slipping up and down the shaft of his penis, Lisa's mound moving beneath Matt's hand, and Lisa's vocalizations of orgasm), the reality within the diegesis is diffused by the knowledge of the realities and limitations that sound technology imposes on filming. Beyond technology, the nine songs themselves are rarely heard in conjunction with the sex. Instead, the alternation of sex-song-sex-song in the final cut mirrors the experience of film-making: the concert scenes were filmed as a break from a week's worth of filming the sex scenes, as if the change of pace and medium provided some relief to the actors from the intimacy of the film. For the viewer, the alternation between concert performances and sex minimizes any risk of becoming desensitized to either experience. The separation between these two themes continually rearticulates their individual impact.

Marketers for this film certainly emphasized its separation of music and sex. The film's promotional website features two frames on its homepage: one, a music frame featuring a photo of a drummer behind his kit with the words "Where do you find love?" and the other, a sex frame featuring a half-naked photo of Lisa with the words "How do you see love?" (http://www.tiscali.co.uk/events/2005/9songs/main.html). Surrounding each frame is an unplugged ¼-inch audio cable. When you scroll your cursor over either of these frames, the male end of the cable penetrates the female, connecting it and closing the border around the frame. Browsing the site, you can only scroll over either the music or sex frame at one time, so the two are never connected simultaneously. Although music is eroticized by this penetrative gesture, the two cable frames visually separate those images representing music and sex in the film. Music and sex appear at odds. The advantages to separating music and sex are not difficult to isolate: by featuring internationally renowned bands on one of Europe's most famous stages,[7] *9 Songs* averted classification as a pornographic film, despite its explicit imagery, and gained much of the 'artistic merit' needed for air-time in theatres and film festivals. While we do not know if these outcomes marked the original intention behind the songs' inclusion in the film, it is notable that the director's aims seem to have shifted during the filming process. When Winterbottom first asked Kieran O'Brien (Matt) if he would be interested in making this film, O'Brien admitted "he didn't mention bands or anything, there was none involved at that stage" (interview with Kieran O'Brien, *9 Songs* DVD). Furthermore, as Winterbottom himself describes, "the heart of the film, the way the film was going to be told was through the sex" (interview with Michael Winterbottom, *ibid.*). The DVD packaging bears testimony to this change in emphasis: highlighting the music, with the sex as a kind of fringe benefit, the DVD back cover boasts "9 Live Performances Not Available Anywhere Else!" but makes no mention of the film's

"Abundance of Real Sex Scenes!" In practical terms, the music provides the film with an easily marketable, autonomous feature.

So could this film have just as effectively alternated between unsimulated sex and a gallery crawl or hockey season, for example? I doubt it. If, as Mary Ann Doane suggests, different cinematic genres manipulate the viewer's perception of spatial realities differently (1980: 39), *9 Songs*'s thematic and methodological flirtation with pornography, documentary and music video is a finely balanced one. It herds the viewer into specific viewing positions, controlling a significant proportion of the viewer's belief in fictional realities on screen. The live rock performances intersect with live sexual performances in convoluted representations of reality, encouraging viewers to question their own positioning as participants in the concerts, question the materiality of the sex, and in doing so, question their own propensity to be sonically aroused, duped or, more generously, moved.

Notes

1. A quick look on Internet Movie Database (www.imdb.com), under the *9 Songs* message-board, gives a sense of what attracted many viewers to the film. Notable is the thread posted by 'alexito' titled, "If only they'd screened it without these stupid music scenes!", a post which encouraged a host of replies in both support and rebuttal.
2. There are parallels between this 'concert-performance-only' version of the film and pornographic 'compilation videos' in which, as Peter Lehman describes (2006: 92), sexual acts from different scenes or films are sewn together with the foreplay and narrative edited out.
3. One example of this nostalgia is in Matt's sighing emphasis in one line of his voice-over: "she was twenty-one – beautiful, egotistical ..."
4. Indeed, because Lisa's only instances of masturbation are held within this single chapter, the chapter functions as a kind of 'compilation video' (see note 2). Her masturbation begins to look and sound suspiciously deliberate on the film's promotional website, where these images are prominently featured (http://www.tiscali.co.uk/events/2005/9songs/main.html). Her masturbation is clearly fetishized.
5. Speculating about the reasons for Lisa's changed vocalizations raises issues concerning the film's appeal to reality. Is Lisa using more of her voice to provoke Matt, or perhaps the film viewer? Her increased vocality might suggest a kind of performance rather than an earnest expression of pleasure.
6. In this quotation, Wilson is discussing his frequent collaboration with Winterbottom in general terms.
7. Most of these bands have international fame: a prerequisite for them to tread in the footprints of the likes of Madonna, the Rolling Stones and other stars who have performed at the Brixton Academy, where *9 Songs*' concert scenes were filmed.

References

Altman, R. (1980), 'Moving Lips: Cinema as Ventriloquism', special issue on Cinema/Sound, *Yale French Studies*, 60, 67–79.

Bazelon, I. (1975), *Knowing the Score: Notes on Film Music*, New York: Van Nostrand.

Chion, M. (1994), *Audio-Vision: Sound on Screen*, edited and translated by Claudia Gorbman, New York: Columbia University Press.

de Lauretis, T. (1984), *Alice Doesn't: Feminism, Semiotics, Cinema*, Bloomington: Indiana University Press.

Doane, M. A. (1980), 'The Voice in the Cinema: The Articulation of Body and Space', special issue on Cinema/Sound, *Yale French Studies*, 60, 33–50.

Frith, S. (1996), 'Music and Identity', in S. Hall and P. du Gay (eds), *Questions of Cultural Identity*, London: Sage, pp. 108–27.

Frith, S. (1998), *Performing Rites: On the Value of Popular Music*, Cambridge, MA: Harvard University Press.

Kotz, L. (1993), 'Complicity: Women Artists Investigating Masculinity', in P. C. Gibson and R. Gibson (eds), *Dirty Looks: Women, Pornography, Power*, London: British Film Institute, pp. 101–23.

Laderman, C. (1991), *Taming the Winds of Desire: Psychology, Medicine, and Aesthetics in Malay Shamanistic Performance*, Los Angeles: University of California Press.

Lehman, P. (2006), 'Revelations about Pornography', in P. Lehman (ed.), *Pornography: Film and Culture*, New Brunswick, NJ: Rutgers University Press, pp. 87–98.

Mulvey, L. (1975), 'Visual Pleasure and Narrative Cinema', *Screen*, 16(3), 6–18.

Packman, J. (2001), '*Quake* Sounds: The Video Game as Multimedia Work of Art', paper presented at the Society for Ethnomusicology National Conference, Detroit, 28 October.

Silverman, K. (1988), *The Acoustic Mirror: The Female Voice in Psychoanalysis and Cinema*, Bloomington: Indiana University Press.

Staiger, J. (2000), *Perverse Spectators: The Practices of Film Reception*, New York: New York University Press.

Williams, L. (1999), 'Generic Pleasures: Number and Narrative', in *Hard Core: Power, Pleasure, and the "Frenzy of the Visible"*, 2nd edn, Los Angeles: University of California Press (first published 1989).

12 Music, Image, Orgasm
Getting off on the Shortbus

Marianne Tatom Letts

"Voyeurism is participation." So says a minor character in director John Cameron Mitchell's *Shortbus* (2006), notable for its many sexually graphic scenes. *Shortbus* is not pornographic cinema, but it was released as 'unrated' in the United States because it surely would have received an NC-17 (formerly X) rating otherwise; NC-17 was originally meant to release adult-oriented 'art' films from the stigma attached to X-rated hardcore pornography (Gerosa and Thompson, 1990). *Shortbus* grew out of Mitchell's desire to make a film that would present images that were sexually positive, in order to counteract the unfortunate trend of "increasing prudishness in American cinema", coupled with the "increasingly joyless and formulaic porn that floods the Internet".[1] Mitchell has said that

> We have to keep reminding people it's not pornographic – it's not a film that's meant to arouse ... We try to de-eroticize the sex to see what kind of emotions and ideas are left over when the haze of eroticism is waved away.[2]

The sole intent of most explicit films seems to be to titillate or arouse the viewer, rather than to explore characters' motivations or further the plot. In *Shortbus*, by contrast, sex functions as a device to connect characters emotionally, even in the scenes in which partners seem to copulate almost casually; by depicting sex in this way, the film allows viewers to connect emotionally with the characters in a way they probably would not in conventional porn. The central story in the film is a woman's quest for orgasm, something not normally talked about in polite society, but each character has his or her own sexual problems to confront. Sofia's mission both fascinates and drives the other characters, most of whom make an attempt at satisfying her, if not personally, then by pointing her in the direction of someone who can. Normally, when women have problems reaching orgasm, they resort to self-pleasure, buying a vibrator and using it in the privacy of their own room. Unable to achieve orgasm this way, Sofia moves into a public space, the salon, which is where she ultimately climaxes. Her experience functions as a microcosm for Mitchell's stated goal of bringing sex into the public eye, where it can be celebrated communally as a positive event rather than as a hidden, often shameful, act.

Mitchell and the other film-makers put out a call in 2003 for people willing to participate in a film project involving on-screen sex; after an initial group was selected from home-made audition tapes, people were brought together in person and paired up on the basis of chemistry and attraction. Various characters and storylines were then improvised in workshops over the scriptwriting period, so that the actors were also co-creators of the final product. Mitchell has stated that he "wanted an in-depth audition process where the actors were creative partners and trust could be built".[3] This trust and the relationships formed through the lengthy film-making process come through to the viewer, making the sex seem less erotic or sensational than revealing of the characters' fears and desires. After an initial scene that may be shocking to the viewer in its graphic depiction of various sexual acts, the sex becomes simply part of the narrative. As critic Manohla Dargis (2006) writes,

> This integration goes a long way to normalizing the sex, making it seem matter-of-fact, natural, and it also normalizes watching this kind of material in the kind of public space where you don't need a roll of quarters to keep the images flowing.

Actress Sook-Yin Lee, who plays the protagonist Sofia, has commented that Mitchell "wanted to see what [sex] would look like if it were funny, because sometimes sex is really funny. Sometimes it's full of pathos. Sometimes it's joyous" (Verge, 2006). Other critics have described *Shortbus* as "explicit sex treated as a facet of shared existence rather than taboo raincoat material" (Ridley, 2006) and have observed that "the sex becomes so integral to *Shortbus* that eventually you barely notice or think about it" (Zacharek, 2006) and "its net effect is almost the opposite of pornography" (O'Hehir, 2006).

The movie's title refers to the small yellow schoolbus that carries special-needs children to school; Justin Bond, cabaret singer and self-described "mistress of Shortbus", describes the New York City salon where much of the movie's action takes place as a "salon for the gifted and challenged", whose participants include hetero-, homo- and bisexual as well as transgendered characters. Mitchell has stated that "society views people on the shortbus as people who couldn't keep up with the mainstream". In the film, though, it is "a much more interesting place to be" (Tamaki, 2006). Each of the characters in *Shortbus* uses his or her sexuality to search for meaning: Sofia, a sex therapist (though she prefers the term 'couples counsellor'), is trying to reach the elusive orgasm; her husband, Rob (Raphael Barker), has insecurities about their relationship and his inability to satisfy her sexually; James (Paul Dawson) and Jamie (PJ DeBoy), collectively known as "the Jamies", are redefining their relationship by opening it up to other sex partners; and Severin (Lindsay Beamish), a dominatrix, is becoming demoralized by her profession and simply wants to make an emotional connection with

Table 12.1 DVD tracks and songs in *Shortbus* (track titles from DVD listing)

Track	Song
1. Opening sequence	'Is You Is Or Is You Ain't My Baby?'
2. I'm Home	
3. Jamie & James	'If You Fall'
4. The Mistress of the Shortbus	'Wizard's Sleeve'; 'Winter Love'
5. Yenta 650	end of 'Winter Love'; 'Surgery'; 'It's Not Safe'
6. Bitch	'Beautiful'
7. About New York	'Language'
8. Star-spangled Banner	'Soda Shop'; 'The Star-spangled Banner'; 'I Can't Give You Anything But Love'
9. A Place of Love	
10. Non-smoking Environment	Jazz song
11. The Egg	'Upside Down'; 'Boys Of Melody'
12. Three-way	'This House'; 'Little Bird'
13. Truth or Dare	Jazz-styled piano piece
14. You Gave It Away?	'This Piece Of Poetry Is Meant To Do Harm'; 'Kolla Kolla'
15. For Jamie	
16. This One's for Her	
17. My Film	'Winter Love'
18. Calm	'In The End'
19. In the End	'In The End'; 'Winter Love'
20. End-credits	'Winter Love' (continued); 'Surgery (Remix)'

someone. These characters (and others) converge at the Shortbus, where art, music and sex occur almost interchangeably and copulation is accompanied by a DJ and various live performers (notably Justin Bond, of the famed cabaret duo Kiki and Herb, and singer-songwriter Scott Matthew). The Shortbus provides a safe place within which characters can experiment and interact sexually, which they may not be able to do in the outside world. Likewise, a variety of musical styles and performances (classical, techno, folk) can co-exist and intermingle in ways not normally experienced by audiences.

Rather than simply describing the songs as they appear chronologically throughout the narrative, I have provided a table that lists the tracks on the DVD and which songs appear in each one. In Table 12.1 I have left out songs that are either too short or too faint in the sound mix to play a significant role in the on-screen action; a complete list of songs is provided in the closing credits to the movie, but not all of them are important to my argument here. After a discussion of three pivotal scenes in *Shortbus* and the pronounced use of diegetic music in the movie, I will focus on the two final scenes, and specifically on the songs 'Winter Love' (Animal Collective), excerpts from which occur three times over the course of the film, and 'In the End' (Justin Bond and the Hungry March Band; written by Scott Matthew), which is performed 'live' in the salon at the movie's (and Sofia's) climax.[4] There are many other themes present in *Shortbus*, such as the use of light, animation (including the cityscape model featured in the linking scenes), water, colour, power/domination, gender/sexual variability, and particularly the gaze; while I will touch upon several of these themes, I will in large part confine my analysis simply to the music as it relates to both the on-screen sexual action and the fluidity between viewer/voyeur and performer/participant. Specifically, I will draw out some ideas on the music's relation to female and male sexuality.

Fred Maus has written that music

> *doesn't just convey information or maintain sociability; with its pulsating rhythms, hypersensitive surfaces, and elaborate patterning of climaxes, it can give a particularly intense, concentrated, sensuous pleasure. The music ... has the active role of initiating and controlling the interaction that gives the listener pleasure.* (1993: 272–3)

Film music typically functions to produce an effect on the audience rather than on the characters, who are often unaware of its existence. The music in *Shortbus*, however, plays a more crucial role than just an accompaniment to the sexual acts occurring on screen; it underscores the characters' search for meaning and emphasizes the fluid movement between their various roles: observer/participant, man/woman, straight/gay, monogamous/polyamorous, dominant/submissive. Since *Shortbus* is the follow-up to Mitchell's successful movie musical *Hedwig and the Angry Inch* (2001), it is not surprising that music is given great significance. Much of the music in *Shortbus* is diegetic, which can be divided into two categories: pre-recorded songs that are played within a scene, and songs that are performed 'live' by a character in the scene. Both inside and outside the salon, musical performance is equated with sexual involvement. Often at the salon, a band or DJ is playing in front of people engaged in sexual acts; at the Shortbus, everyone is a participant, and everyone is an observer. The lines between participant and observer are further blurred by the appearance of real-life couples in the movie: DeBoy and Dawson, Bitch (a New York City 'musical poet'[5] playing herself) and Little Prince (Daniela Sea), and Shanti Carson and Jan Hilmer (Leah and Nick), as well as the sea of 'sextras' in the Sex Not Bombs room. Going a step further, Mitchell has stated that all but one of the on-screen orgasms are real.[6] The preponderance of diegetic music seems to make the point that the music, as well as the sex, is 'live' (even in the scenes in which the music is obviously mimed, since it matches the soundtrack CD exactly).

Three pivotal scenes in *Shortbus* illustrate the importance of the music to the initial establishment and subsequent development of the characters. These scenes are the opening sequence of sexual acts ('Is You Is Or Is You Ain't My Baby?'); the sequence with Sofia on the park bench, James with Caleb (Peter Stickles), and Severin with Rob (the second 'Winter Love' scene); and the final scene at the Shortbus when Sofia finally climaxes ('In The End', followed by 'Winter Love'). All three scenes involve a multitude of characters having a variety of sexual experiences. All the characters change partners from one scene to another: Sofia moves from Rob to just herself and then to Leah and Nick; James moves from himself to Caleb to Jamie; and Severin moves from Jesse to Rob to herself (non-sexually). The final scene adds the couples of Rob and an unnamed woman at the salon, and Ceth (pronounced 'Seth' and played by Jay Brannan) and Caleb, along with various others. The characters have also changed locations: from their own apartments to foreign spaces (the park, a stranger's apartment, a hotel room) to a communal sexual and musical space (the salon). The accompanying music illustrates this move: in the first scene, the music is non-diegetic, but the characters produce physical sounds that accompany the song (see below); the listeners have become the participants. In the second scene, the music is non-diegetic, yet there is the air of familiarity, as it recalls a scene from earlier in the movie when the same music was played. In the third scene, the music is represented as wholly diegetic, emanating from the participants as well as from the onstage performers. The musical style is different for each scene: the lyrics of the first song seem to be commenting on the mutability of the characters' relationships; the second is a pulsating blend of drums, guitars and chants (evoking the tribal associations of the band's name, Animal Collective); the third starts as a schmaltzy cabaret number but is enlivened by the appearance of the oompah band and the group chorus of "We all get it in the end", as Justin Bond grabs a megaphone to be heard over the cacophony. The song 'Winter Love' had ended without resolution in the second scene, mirroring the characters' sexual frustration; at the end of the movie, the 'climax' (both orgasmic and plot-wise) ends before the song returns, so that the music no longer has to furnish the resolution. The tables have been turned, and the visual now provides the resolution for the musical.

The director suggests from the opening scene that music will play a larger-than-usual role in the narrative. The film opens with Anita O'Day, a jazz singer active from the Big Band era until the 1960s, singing 'Is You Is Or Is You Ain't My Baby?' as various characters are introduced.[7] The camera first wends its way around the body parts of a model of the Statue of Liberty, noting the sensuous curves of its eyes, hands, feet and lips; the view then opens up to show New York City in vibrant colours, as an animated cityscape. The camera flies over the city and in through windows, showing us various individuals and couples engaged in sexual acts. The light streaming through the windows emphasizes for the viewer that sex is going to be treated openly in the film, and that there will be a variety of sexual experiences shown; we are watching the characters in their most intimate actions, which are occurring simultaneously in many different rooms. The animation emphasizes the interconnectedness of all the characters; all are living in the same city, and all are struggling with aspects of their sexual relationships. The song's lyrics seem to be casting doubt on the stability of each relationship ("Is you is or is you ain't my baby? The way you treat me lately makes me doubt"). As each character performs a different sexual act (James takes a bath, then performs auto-fellatio; Severin flogs her client, Jesse [Adam Hardman]; and Sofia and

Rob frantically change sexual positions to try to bring her to orgasm), the scenes are cut to appear as though the characters are also engaged in performing to the music, which itself is clearly non-diegetic. In James's bathtub, a bubble escapes to the surface, making a 'plink' that fits into the piano arpeggio; Severin bangs down her flogger on the windowsill and later on the bed in time with a crashing sound in the music; and Rob performs oral sex on Sofia on top of a piano keyboard, the resulting chords almost fitting into the underlying song. The camera cuts away from the piano to show a few sheets of music fluttering to the ground, drawing our attention to the music's importance. All the dialogue in these interlocking opening scenes occurs during instrumental vamping in the song, and the music stops altogether as all of the male characters virtually simultaneously reach climax. When Severin begins to walk around the room, signalling the end of her session with Jesse, the song's walking bass line begins again. The pause in the music recalls Severin's earlier comment to Jesse that, in the moment of orgasm, it felt like "Time had stopped and I was completely alone". The music's resumption signifies her almost-immediate realization that "Time hadn't stopped and I wasn't alone". In other words, orgasm offers her only a brief moment of respite from everyday life. Given that James is shown crying immediately afterwards and Rob and Sofia launch into a discussion of a 'client's' inability to reach orgasm, the moment has been equally brief for the men.

In addition to showing graphic sexual scenes to which non-participants would not normally be privy, the film-makers allow the viewer to have analogous auditory experiences to the characters by distorting or muffling the diegetic music. James compulsively records scenes from his life with a small camera; he is compiling a film that we later learn will function as a suicide note to show Jamie that, as James tells Caleb, "it wasn't his fault". As James edits his film, the song 'I Can't Give You Anything But Love' (words and music by Dorothy Fields and Jimmy McHugh; performed by Fats Waller and Una Mae Carlisle) plays over scenes of his and Jamie's childhoods, intercut with scenes of him and Jamie sleeping and shots of James's prescription medications. We learn later that James's choice of a soundtrack is ironic; he tells Caleb late in the movie that he feels he cannot love Jamie enough, and that that is at the root of their relationship problems. Despite the song's lyrics ("I can't give you anything but love, baby/That's the only thing I've plenty of, baby"), love is the one thing James cannot give. When he rewinds the tape to insert another scene, we hear the sound of the tape rewinding and then the song starting up again; 'I Can't Give' continues to play over the following scene of James taking his antidepressants. The music is also muted for the viewer when James jumps into the pool at the 'gym-jacuzzi' where he works, to retrieve a dead body; and when Sofia shoves toilet paper in her ears to muffle the sound of Rob's music from the next room so she can concentrate on masturbating. In the scene in which Sofia and Severin are floating in an immersion chamber, a jazzy saxophone plays; we may assume it is emanating from an external source, but the film-makers show us a boom-box in a plastic bag floating by, indicating that the characters have brought their own music to set the mood. Even here, we are assured that we are experiencing the music as the characters do.

The music at the Shortbus salon alternates between DJ'd and live performance, depending on which room the characters are in, but it is always diegetic. The experience for the viewer is marked by the fact that we can hear the changes from one DJ'd track to the next, or can see that a live band is playing a different song in another room. We feel as though we are close to the musical action as well as the sexual. Scott Matthew is often shown performing in front of a live audience, along with other spectator-participants from the salon, most notably Bitch, who figures prominently in the scene in which Sofia discusses the orgasmic experience with a group of women. At times the characters make comments about the songs playing in the background without seeming to be aware of them, casting ambiguity on whether the music is commenting on the characters' actions or vice versa. When Sofia first visits the Shortbus, the instrumental 'Wizard's Sleeve' by Yo La Tengo is playing in the background. As the host, Justin Bond, shows Sofia around the salon, he points out a woman named Alice and comments that part of her anatomy is "like a wizard's sleeve", perhaps an odd detail for a transvestite to know, but one that shows immediately that sex is a communal matter within this space. Likewise, everyone seems to already know about Sofia's 'problem' by the time she visits the Shortbus for the first time.

Scott Matthew's 'Surgery' plays as Ceth talks to Sofia while playing with his Yenta 650, an electronic matchmaker that is meant to find him a husband. The song begins with the lyrics "Transplant my heart into yours" and the chorus states that "It's life-saving surgery". The song foreshadows the next scene, in which Ceth meets Tobias, a former mayor of New York City (played by Alan Mandell and purportedly loosely patterned on Ed Koch), and Ceth's Yenta interferes with Tobias's pacemaker. Again, the lyrics of the song are commenting, though a bit obliquely, on the action in the movie. These characters have a 'heart connection' of a more literal kind. Sofia has an unusual reaction when she meets Shabbas Goy (played by Ray Rivas), a transgendered performer who tells Sofia that "if you're Jewish", she can "help you turn on your lights".[8] The song playing over this scene is 'It's Not Safe', by Gentleman Reg (Reg Vermue, pictured in a cameo immediately prior to this as an albino who speaks to the Jamies), which has the line "It's not safe to be naked, young or creative anymore". The song begins as Shabbas starts to describe her performance-art piece 'Ode to the Female Secretion', which includes five movements covering lubrication, lactation, ejaculation, urination and menstruation. The lyrics underscore the discomfort and incredulity Sofia feels at Shabbas's suggestion that she donate her menstrual blood for the latter to use in her performance art. Sofia is being asked to enter a space that doesn't feel safe to her, which could also apply to her inability to reach orgasm; likewise, the viewer is probably experiencing on-screen sex in ways that are at least initially uncomfortable. At times the non-diegetic music in one scene becomes diegetic in the next: Scott Matthew's 'Upside Down' plays over scenes from James's film and then cuts back and forth between Matthew's live performance at the Shortbus (with two women singing while hanging upside down on a swing) and James throwing away his antidepressants. While the women are literally upside down, James is turning his life upside down by drastically altering his mood, and perhaps viewers are also turning their expectations upside down as they watch the acts being depicted on screen.

The song 'Beautiful' by Lee and Leblanc plays in the background as Sofia quizzes a roomful of women about their own experiences with orgasm.[9] Although most other songs in the movie are sung by men, 'Beautiful' features a woman's voice – while Sofia listens to a roomful of women's voices. One character (Jid, played by JD Samson) compares the experience of orgasm to "shooting out creative energy into the world, and it was merging with other people's energy, and then there was no war", echoing the theme of the salon's orgiastic Sex Not Bombs room; another, Bitch, simply comments that it was "really slow and still, and I felt like I was finally not alone" (the opposite of Severin's experience). The women's descriptions are as varied as their physical appearances and personalities, but all are still accepted. The song's repeated line "I was lost, and I'm still lost" underscores Sofia's frustration in her quest to reach orgasm, and it attains an extra layer of meaning when we know that Lee is the real singer. Despite acknowledging all the women's descriptions as legitimate, Sofia is no closer to reaching orgasm herself than before; her own description of sex as "kind of like somebody's gonna kill me and I just have to ... smile and pretend to enjoy it, that way I can survive", immediately after extolling its aerobic virtues, is especially poignant after the other women's glowing descriptions. Scott Matthew's song 'Language' furnishes the soundtrack to Ceth's discussion with Tobias about New Yorkers' search for redemption, as well as the Jamies' initial acknowledgement of Ceth from across the room. The song continues to play as Sofia watches the people copulating in the Sex Not Bombs room; as Matthew sings the line "Oh, we wished for, ever",[10] and hits a loud, high note on the final word, one of the participants (Leah) reaches orgasm with her partner, then turns to see Sofia watching her. The lyrics and pitch have underscored Leah's climax and have also made us notice Leah as she notices Sofia noticing her; we may guess (correctly) that Leah will play a pivotal role for Sofia later in the movie.

Participating in both musical and sexual performance brings the characters of James, Jamie and Ceth closer. After the Jamies pick up Ceth at the Shortbus, the three men sit on the couch at the Jamies' apartment, awkwardly making small talk. Eventually Ceth is coaxed into performing an original song ('Soda Shop', written by Brannan), and the Jamies exchange looks while Ceth is performing, confirming to each other that they are comfortable with introducing him into their relationship as a new sexual partner. Although a version of 'Soda Shop' is included on the *Shortbus* soundtrack CD, the filmed rendition is truly diegetic, emphasized when Ceth messes up one line and has to start it again. The song continues to play, non-diegetically, as Ceth and Jamie discuss modelling tips and techniques. The song then cuts out abruptly, before the final few chords (although after the final lyrics), as the scene shifts to a three-way sexual act, in which each man is both giving and receiving oral and/or manual sex. In response to a request from Ceth to make more noise to heighten the experience, Jamie begins to sing 'The Star-spangled Banner' into Ceth's anal cavity, accompanied by percussive slapping. By the end of the scene, all three men are singing along, with Ceth holding James's penis as a microphone. Again, the characters have shifted between musical and sexual performance, and between audience and participant. The film shot cuts back at one point to show James's stalker, Caleb, watching from his window across the street. By showing us this on-screen voyeurism, the film-makers extend the participatory nature of the action to the cinema audience as well. Just as Caleb is watching, so are we. Voyeurism is participation.

Animal Collective's 'Winter Love', the first of two noteworthy songs in *Shortbus*, furthers the participatory feel because of its structure and sound. 'Winter Love' is divided into two parts: a subdued, shorter, wordless section; and a longer section with louder strumming and actual lyrics. As it exists on the *Shortbus* soundtrack, the song's first section fades in as though we are coming in on the middle of it; it sounds like a demo recording for the more fleshed-out second section. Both sections contain wordless, primal chants that furnish a suitable accompaniment to the scenes of live sex. The first section of the song features wordless 'da-da-da's' in harmony with the main instrumental melody; in the background are drums or handclapping and strummed guitar, with the squeaking of strings. Although the song is non-diegetic in each scene in which it occurs, the sounds of the music-making are clearly audible. This first section gradually fades out, and after a beat's pause, the second section begins more strongly; we now seem to be hearing a slightly more polished, 'studio' version, which adds louder instruments and more vocals, along with lyrics. This second section begins with a loudly strummed guitar, then a chanted section of nonsense syllables. This wordless melody is sung a few times before the lyrics come in. These are difficult to understand and fairly nonsensical ("I love this light in wintertime/The frost cakes in the carpet") rather than anything explicitly sexual. The song concludes with more wordless 'da-da-da's' and finally resolves to a sustained chord with three-part harmony; this resolution is not heard in the film until the very end, however.

'Winter Love' is first heard in the film when Justin Bond leads Sofia to the Sex Not Bombs room, where a DJ presides over a roomful of couples engaged in sexual acts, the pulsating acoustic groove marking a contrast from the mostly electronic/techno songs heard thus far. In this scene, only the second section of the song plays, and the effect is that of a circle of people participating wholeheartedly in a communal ritual, which seems entirely appropriate for the Sex Not Bombs room. The undulating of the copulating bodies matches the tribal atmosphere of the song. Similarly to the interaction of characters and music in the first scene, a man in the Sex Not Bombs room gives his partner a percussive slap in time with the music. The song fades out before the end, hinting that the couples will also continue their actions indefinitely without resolution. Likewise, because Sofia has begun watching the couples in the Sex Not Bombs room in the middle of her evening at the Shortbus, she experiences the action in the room as having no beginning or end. Sofia seems appalled yet intrigued by what she sees and hears, but the music and the room both have an encouraging participative feel. She does not overtly join in the action, but she feels compelled to keep watching (voyeurism is participation). When the song reoccurs later in the film, it reminds the listener (and perhaps the masturbating Sofia) of this very primal Sex Not Bombs room and signifies the sensation of raw sexual energy.

The second time 'Winter Love' is heard, all the characters are on the verge of epiphany: Sofia has escaped into a fantasy during her therapy session with Brad and Cheryl, in which she claws her way through a forest and emerges onto a beach to see a beckoning street light next to a bench. Rob has booked a dominatrix session with Severin, in order to "be dominated but not totally lose control", things his wife "wouldn't understand". Ceth is talking to the hospital admissions desk on the phone while Jamie looks through James's computer files, trying to understand why he checked himself out of the hospital after his suicide attempt. James has decided to allow Caleb, his stalker, to penetrate him, something he has never allowed anyone else, even Jamie, to do. This scene, cutting back and forth between many characters engaged in sexual acts, recalls the opening scene, in which all the characters try desperately to reach climax. Here, 'Winter Love' begins at the first section, fading in as though it has already begun (as it does on the soundtrack CD). We see Sofia lie down on the bench and begin to masturbate, James and Caleb take their clothes off, and Jamie find James's film stored in his computer. As the first section of the song fades out, Jamie clicks 'play' on the film and Caleb asks James, "Are you sure?" James nods, believing that the penetration will allow him to finally feel something. James is penetrated during the break between sections of the song; he gives a sharp intake of breath, and the second section begins. Images from James's film are then intercut with the scene of him and Caleb, as though his life is flashing before his eyes, and with the scene of Jamie and Ceth watching the same images on the computer. (The 'real' soundtrack to James's film, 'I Can't Give You Anything But Love', is not heard here.) This trio of scenes (James's film, Caleb penetrating James, Jamie and Ceth watching James's film) is matched by the pairing of Sofia touching herself on the bench and Severin beating Rob. As the song grows wilder in this second section, the on-screen action also escalates. Sofia masturbates more and more frantically, and Severin strikes Rob more violently — everyone is trying to make a connection, trying desperately to feel something. The dialogue between Severin and Rob bleeds over into Sofia's fantasy, and Sofia's expression indicates that she, like James, is distracted by her inner thoughts about her primary relationship. While James's epiphany seems to be that his true place is with Jamie, Sofia's seems to be that she can no longer be happy with Rob. The scenes end with James looking off into the distance after he pushes Caleb away, Severin screaming for Rob to look at her, and Sofia screaming at the sputtering street light. The sequence ends with a citywide blackout, and the song fades out before any character is able to climax; neither the song nor the characters find resolution.

'Winter Love' could be said to evoke the experience of the female orgasm; while the male orgasm ends with the release of semen, providing a definite end point (Tantric practices aside), the female orgasm has commonly been described in terms of 'waves', a series of ever-expanding ripples that could go on indefinitely. Susan McClary writes that "female erotic pleasure" can be conceived of musically as "pleasure that is not concerned with being somewhere else, indeed, pleasure that need not even be thought of as tied specifically to sexual encounter, but pleasure that permits confident, free, and open interchange with others" (McClary, 1991: 124) and that "combines shared and sustained pleasure, rather than the desire for explosive closure" (*ibid.*: 130). By contrast, most western art music, conceived of as 'masculine', drives towards a cadence, or climax, just as the male orgasm does. The song 'Winter Love' does build to a climax but then keeps going, just as a multi-orgasmic female theoretically could. Rather than celebrating this capability, however, the second 'Winter Love' scene shows that this type of orgasmic response ends only in frustration, as none of the characters actually climaxes and the song eventually just fades out. The montage ends with Sofia screaming, not from pleasure but from frustration. The message seems to be that in order to be truly satisfied, she must learn to "come like a man", and have one powerful, goal-directed orgasm.

'In The End', the song over the film's final sequence, provides that dramatic climax to the plot, both musically and sexually. The scene begins with Scott Matthew dreamily plucking his guitar at the Shortbus as Justin Bond and others move through the communal space lighting candles in response to the blackout. We are reminded again of the authenticity of the diegetic music: Matthew plays haltingly, pausing between shortened phrases. Other musicians join in off screen as we see shots of the characters from the previous scene (the second 'Winter Love' occurrence) individually or in pairs making their way to the Shortbus. The ensemble builds to include a string quartet, led by the incongruous-looking Bitch in dreadlocks playing a violin, then stops and restarts as the scene cuts back to the stage, emphasizing the diegeticity of the performers, who must play acoustically during the blackout. After another brief pause, Justin Bond begins to sing. The lyrics of 'In The End' speak to the loneliness of all the characters and their search for meaning: "We all bear the scars/Yes, we all feign a laugh/We all sigh in the dark/Get cut off before we start". The culminating line of the chorus is "We all get it in the end", which functions as a quadruple entendre for being penetrated, coming to a self-realization, and reaching death (both the 'little' and the 'big').

As Justin Bond sings, the reunited Jamies begin to kiss; Sofia alternates between kissing Nick and Leah on either side of her; and Ceth impulsively kisses Caleb. After Bond sings the last line, the music begins to fade out, but then the strains of a brass band are heard, as the Hungry March Band enters. Everyone interrupts what they are doing to watch the band; Sofia immediately returns to kissing the couple, evidently not as distracted by this music as she had been by Rob's (here, unlike in the earlier scene, the music is both diegetic and participatory). The shots intercut between Sofia, Nick and Leah; Bond singing through a megaphone to be heard over the band; and Ceth and Caleb watching the Jamies. Bond calls for "everybody" to sing, a double cue that leads to everyone not only joining in the chorus, but also resuming or initiating their sexual activities. Rob begins kissing a woman next to him, and Bond licks the mayor Tobias's face. Only Severin is alone, though as she stated earlier, she prefers it that way. Everyone is participating, either musically or sexually, or both; the musical union of brass band and rowdy group chorus underscores the merging of the flesh. After this final scene, when Sofia finally reaches orgasm, the second section of 'Winter Love' returns, sounding even wilder and producing a musical climax to go with the sexual one. In the end, the music signifies both sexual climax and the coupling of the 'little death' with the big death, as well as the realization that getting *off* requires a certain amount of self-awareness, or getting *it*. Sofia had stated earlier, to Rob, that she (using the pseudonym of Cheryl) "has to claim it [her orgasm] for herself", but the reality for Sofia is that she needs the communal experience, at least for the first time, in order to reach climax. She finds release in an almost casual communal experience, in front of a group of people cheering her on. As she reaches orgasm, lights go on all over the city, ending the blackout and stressing the notion of sex as an interconnected experience. Jid's scenario of "shooting out creative energy into the world, and … merging with other people's energy" has proven true for Sofia's experience. Her one powerful, goal-directed orgasm has furnished light for the entire city.

Just as the energy produced from Sofia's orgasm has been extended to include the whole of New York City, by the end of the film, the image of the Shortbus as a "salon for the gifted and challenged" has been expanded to include the viewing audience, which may feel a sense of community with the characters at the salon. John Cameron Mitchell has used the experiences of a group of characters to bring a positive view of sexuality into a public forum. In contrast to the experience of porn, in which the viewer is expected to be alone (even in a movie theatre) as s/he watches the images on screen, when watching *Shortbus* the viewers are meant to feel included, part of the carnival atmosphere, through their voyeurism-as-participation.[11] Rather than feeling that "time had stopped and I was completely alone" (which rings truer for 'real' porn than for the *Shortbus* experience), the viewer may come away with the feeling that a wider array of lifestyles exists of which s/he was unaware, and that each is as valid as the next. We are all welcome to get on the Shortbus, and to get off on it too.

Acknowledgements

Thanks to Christine Kraemer, Mark Pittman, Richard Letts, Bruce Johnson, Mark Evans and two anonymous reviewers for their comments and critiques.

Notes

1. Interview with John Cameron Mitchell, online at http://www.shortbusthemovie.com/thefilm.php (accessed 30 January 2008).
2. Unattributed, '*Shortbus*: porn, art, or a bit of both?', 4 October 2006, online at http://www.msnbc.msn.com/id/15129045/ (accessed 12 June 2008).
3. Interview with John Cameron Mitchell (see note 1).
4. There exists, of course, the possibility that the music is mimed, but it is treated as a live performance for the purposes of the narrative.
5. See http://www.bitchmusic.com/bbio.htm (accessed 3 June 2008).
6. Interview with John Cameron Mitchell (see note 1).
7. Written by Louis Jordan and Billy Austin in 1944, 'Is You Is?' has been recorded by a number of artists, and was used in a famous 1946 Tom and Jerry cartoon called 'Solid Serenade'. See http://www.louisjordan.com/ and http://www.tomandjerryonline.com/musiclistings.cfm (both accessed 4 May 2010). Anita O'Day released the song on her album *Once Upon A Summertime* (Glendale Records, 1963). See http://www.last.fm/music/Anita+O%27Day (accessed 4 May 2010).
8. A Shabbas goy is a Gentile who performs tasks forbidden for observant Jews on the Sabbath, such as turning on the lights or the oven.
9. The 'Lee' of Lee and Leblanc is Sook-Yin Lee, who plays Sofia in the film.
10. Lyrics from http://www.scottmatthewmusic.com/ (accessed 2 July 2008).
11. I encountered several groups of 'alternative' people locally who arranged to view the film together and even held discussion groups afterwards; the same would undoubtedly not be true for a traditional 'skin flick'.

References

Dargis, M. (2006), 'Naughty and Nice in a Carnal Carnival', *New York Times*, 4 October; online at http://movies.nytimes.com/2006/10/04/movies/04shor.html?ref=movies (accessed 4 May 2010).

Gerosa, M., and Thompson, A. (1990), 'How the X Got Axed', *Entertainment Weekly*, 12 October; online at http://www.ew.com/ew/article/0,,318334,00.html (accessed 4 May 2010).

Maus, F. (1993), 'Masculine Discourse in Music Theory', *Perspectives of New Music*, 31(2), 264–93.

McClary, S. (1991), 'Getting Down off the Beanstalk: The Presence of a Woman's Voice in Janika Vandervelde's *Genesis II*', in *Feminine Endings: Music, Gender, and Sexuality*, Minneapolis: University of Minnesota Press, pp. 112–31.

O'Hehir, A. (2006), 'Beyond the multiplex: Cannes', *Salon*, 22 May; online at http://www.salon.com/ent/movies/feature/2006/05/22/btm/index.html (accessed 4 May 2010).

Ridley, J. (2006), 'The harder they come: the subversive mainstream friendliness of John Cameron Mitchell's sex-positive cheer', *Village Voice*, 26 September; online at http://www.villagevoice.com/film/0640,ridley,74639,20.html (accessed 4 May 2010).

Tamaki, M. (2006), '*Shortbus* at Toronto International Film Festival: Behind the scenes/ Getting off by getting on', *Xtra!*, 31 August: online at http://www.xtra.ca/public/viewstory.aspx?AFF_TYPE=3&STORY_ID=2022&PUB_TEMPLATE_ID=2 (accessed 4 May 2010).

Verge, S. (2006), 'Keeping it real: Sook-Yin Lee bares all in John Cameron Mitchell's controversial new *Shortbus*', *Toronto Life:* online at http://www.torontolife.com/insiders-guide-film-festival/features/sook-yin-lee/ (accessed 4 May 2010).

Zacharek, S. (2006), 'Shortbus', *Salon*, 4 October; online at http://www.salon.com/ent/movies/review/2006/10/04/shortbus/index.html?source=search&aim=/ent/movies/review (accessed 4 May 2010).

13 In Extremis
The Roots, Soundscapes and Significations of Twenty-first-century Zombie Porn

Ralph G. Marsh

Introduction

Between them, sexuality and violence are the major reasons for restricted ratings of films, DVDs and television programmes. Due to (rather than *despite*) this, combinations of the two have recurred in independent cinema and non-theatrical videos and DVDs. This cross-over had its heyday in the 1970s, when directors such as Joe Davian and Mario Bava churned out low-budget exploitation films that combined explicit (and often coercive) sex and (sexualized) violence. The furor about so-called 'snuff' movies, which allegedly included actual shots of women being murdered for the camera,[1] represented a 'logical' extension of this vector (even if the film at the centre of the scandal, Michael and Roberta Finlay's *Snuff* [1976] was later revealed to be pure fiction).[2] In similar taboo-breaking fashion, a number of (fiction) films have represented necrophilia in various ways. The most notorious examples are Jörg Buttgereit's features *NEKRomantik* (1987) and *NEKRomantik II* (1991), which include several explicit sequences of sexual activities with corpses. The compendium of Charles Bukowski stories adapted in *Crazy Love* (Dominique Deruddere, 1987) also features an episode with a morgue attendant and a young female corpse. This is – as you would expect in an art movie – 'tastefully' done (and mostly suggested rather than depicted). Into this dark, disturbing mix a new element has arisen: zombie porn.

Zombie porn is an emergent proto-genre that combines graphic representations of sexuality and scenes of horrific dismemberment and cannibalism. Zombies occupy a peculiar position with regard to mortality. They are un-dead, i.e., neither dead nor alive. In this regard they resemble vampires but are not blessed with the physical completeness and (often) magnetic sexual allure of their Transylvanian relatives. Indeed, they usually appear as lurching, drooling, semi-animated, gore-splattered, cannibalistic psychopaths. Unlike the dark, brooding counts and buxom temptresses represented in Hammer vampire films, zombies make for less obvious pin-up material. Zombie porn hits a very precise niche, addressing an extreme transgressive fantasy that is designed to amuse and appall (in equal measure). In doing this it revels in the visceral potential of the audio-visual medium, foregrounding explicit images in conjunction with dramatic sonic effects and musical stings, scores and textures. This chapter addresses the latter elements and, in particular, how they deploy the sonic conventions of porn and horror cinema in combination with hard rock styles such as death metal to create singularly intense sonic impressions. Linked to this, the chapter also details the close connections between rock culture and the creative personnel involved in the proto-genre and the processes of interaction that have produced the films.

Zombie history

The contemporary cinematic zombie derives from earlier zombies represented in Caribbean-themed movies associated with voodoo rituals and beliefs. The first example of these was Victor Halperin's *White Zombie* (1932), which was set in Haiti and starred Béla Lugosi (with a soundtrack including material by Cuban-American bandleader Xavier Cugat). Jacques Tourneur's RKO thriller, *I Walked with a Zombie* (1943) revisited similar themes with considerable visual panache, a subtle creepiness and an eerie orchestral score by Roy Webb (together with diegetic songs from Trinidadian calypsonian Sir Lancelot). Historically, the key pivot between the early to mid-twentieth-century Caribbean-themed zombie films[3] and the later explosion of the genre was John Gilling's 1966 Hammer horror feature *Plague of the Zombies*. Set in Victorian England, the plot involves a dastardly local squire who uses voodoo magic he has acquired in Haiti to revive corpses to labour in his tin mine. But whatever the antecedents, the definitive product development of the modern zombie occurred in George Romero's *Night of the Living Dead* (1968). Romero's film was a low-budget, black-and-white feature that depicted corpses returning from the dead to attack and eat living humans. While slow, clumsy and predictable in their plans of attack, the sheer numbers of 'living dead' make them a formidable, pitiless and terrifying foe. The director's 1978 follow-up, *Dawn of the Dead* upped the ante, being made in colour and featuring music from fellow horror director Dario Argento and his regular collaborators, the progressive rock band Goblin. Further sequels followed, including *Day of the Dead* (1985), *Land of the Dead* (2005) and *Diary of the Dead* (2008), and the director's remake of his earlier *Dawn of the Dead* (2004). But while Romero's own work remains among the strongest contributions to the field, other directors have imitated, extended and/or parodied the rampaging zombie formula, including the notable series of *Resident Evil* films (2002, 2004, 2007) spawned by the initial computer game, launched in 1996. To date, in the region of 80-plus zombie-siege feature films have been released, a significant proportion of which feature rock music and, in particular, hard rock, in their soundtracks. Indeed, two – *Hard Rock Zombies* (Krishna Shah, 1985) and *Death Metal Zombies* (Todd Mason Cook, 1995) – develop this connection into major plot elements. The former film concerns a rock band booked to perform a gig in a remote, violent inbred town called Grand Guignol (!), where they are murdered by locals, only to be raised from the dead when a local girl plays back one of their tracks that is based on an ancient resurrection chant. The 1995 film involves a fan of the death metal band Living Corpse, who acquires a recording of a song entitled 'Zombified' that transforms the living into zombies when they hear it, and features tracks by ensembles such as Anal Cunt, Brutality and Dead World.

These films reflect a more general association between heavy metal, and in particular death metal, and horror/pagan/satanist themes, such as those featured prominently in many bands' lyrics, album cover artwork and videos. This association dates back to the late 1960s, when bands such as Black Sabbath and Black Widow combined demonic themes with hard-rock arrangements, creating a template that death metal bands such as Death and Morbid Angel adapted into a faster, more furious and lyrically explicit style. While more stylistically syncretic than core death metal ensembles, the British band Cradle of Filth, formed in 1991, developed a reputation for controversial themes and images on its early releases, embracing horror fiction in albums based around popular works, such as *Dusk ... And Her Embrace* (1996), inspired by the work of Sheridan Le Fanu, and *Cruelty And The Beast* (1998), based on the life of (and mythology accruing to) the Hungarian countess Elizabeth Báthory.[4] In 2001 the band collaborated in the production of a feature film by their regular video director Alex Chandon entitled *Cradle of Fear*. This developed a number of the band's lyrical themes and involved graphic images of death, dismemberment, demonic foetuses and murderous zombies.

Sexuality and zombie movies

The association of zombies with sexuality, or, rather, with sexual activities per se, was first broached by the Italian exploitation film-maker Joe D'Amato[5] in *Le Notti erotiche dei morti viventi* (1980) (released in English-language versions as *Erotic/Sexy Nights of the Living Dead*).[6] Accompanied by a prominent and atmospheric synthesizer rock score attributed to Pluto Kennedy (a pseudonym used by Italian composer Marcello Giombini[7] for his work on exploitation features), the film is bookended by mental-hospital scenes, posing its narrative as a flashback. The film's scenario involves an amorous American entrepreneur, Wilson (played by Mark Shanon), who secures the lease to a resort site and hires a boat-owner to take him and his girlfriend to its location, the supposedly uninhabited Cat Island. Upon arrival, the trio encounter a mysterious old man and Luna, a nubile young female (played by Laura Gemser) who turns out to be a ghost able to shift between human and cat form. After numerous sex scenes in port, en voyage to Cat Island and on shore, the horror element occurs in the latter part of the narrative when the undead emerge at night to menace the trio. Wilson falls victim to the zombies after he encounters Luna one evening. Pretending to acquiesce to his erotic intent, she fellates him only to bite off his penis at the shaft, allowing her zombie associates to follow up and gorge on his (other) flesh. Transformed into a zombie himself, he then attempts to menace his girlfriend and the captain before they escape their zombie pursuers, to awaken at dawn on a beach, permanently unhinged by their experiences. Three subsequent exploitation features also partially presaged the 2000s zombie-porn cycle discussed below by including sexualized female undead. In *Night of the Living Babes* (Jon Valentine, 1987), the two male protagonists visit a bordello expecting conventional action only to find it staffed by zombie hookers; in *Zombie Nympho Coeds* (Tommy Dammit, 1993) a number of girls are drugged, killed and (semi-)revived to participate in carnal activities; and Hugh Gallagher's *Gore Whore* (1994) features a murderous prostitute who turns out to have been chemically resurrected from the dead.[8]

The arrival of sexually rapacious female zombies in the early 2000s was substantially precipitated by developments in what has come to be termed 'alt.porn' – a new visual styling/aesthetic of photo, DVD and performance porn that used models and actors whose Goth/punk tattoos, hairdos, piercings, (occasional) costumes and general demeanour were diametrically opposite to the purring siliconed kittens who star in mainstream porn. The performers' subcultural associations were underlined by the prominence of 'alternative' music genres: punk, Goth, industrial (and also, on occasion, techno and rave) in videos and live performances.[9] This porn style was specifically targeted at a youth market and first attracted substantial attention through the images featured on (and general design of) the website GothicSluts.com, established in 1999, which featured pale (and often pseudo-vampiric) models and BDSM fetish clothing and accessories. SuicideGirls.com, launched in 2001, succeeded in gaining a more extensive profile by including a wider range of model types and styles (including punk, retro 1950s and various hybrids thereof) and developing a group of female models, blogs and online networks that its operators and many members claimed rendered it more of an alternative online community and sexual style movement than a pay-for-porn web service.[10] Since its inception the operation has also diversified into radio (SG 103.1 FM in Los Angeles); live burlesque tours, starting in 2004; and feature-length videos (including a video record of their first live sets entitled *The First Tour DVD*). Their stage shows and DVDs featured extensive use of rock music and the *First Tour* DVD also featured a video clip for Probot's 2004 single 'Shake Your Blood', which includes over fifty SuicideGirl models as extras. Along with SuicideGirls.com, BurningAngel.com, initiated in 2002, promoted a similar aesthetic (as typified by its founder and lead performer Joanna Angel[11]) and, significantly for this analysis, extended this into film production.

Zombie-porn productions

Repenetrator (2004)

One of BurningAngel.com's first video productions was an 8-minute-long sequence originally intended as a Halloween treat for site habitués. The film featured Angel, in role as the revived 'corpse girl', and her professional partner, Tommy Pistol, as the mad scientist; it was written and co-directed by Doug Sakmann (who had just completed the rock/horror feature *Punk Rock Holocaust* [2004]). The model for the film was Stuart Gordon's famously gory *Re-Animator* (1985), a splatter-ridden feature in which a crazed scientist revives corpses. Gordon's film, in turn, was a loose interpretation of H. P. Lovecraft's short story 'Herbert West; Reanimator'. Lovecraft's story, originally published in 1922, provided a notable precursor to later cinematic zombie fiction through its representation of the revived dead as violently psychopathic. Along with Gordon's use of gore, the film's notorious scene in which a woman receives cunnilingus from the mad scientist's severed (but still functioning) head[12] is the other element of the film most obviously cuing *Repenetrator*'s re-interpretation.

The film's plot is relatively simple. A mad scientist injects a hefty amount of green serum into a female corpse's vagina in order to reanimate her and imbue her with an intense craving for sex. The process is successful and the two couple enthusiastically before she intensifies things by goring his neck, slashing and disembowelling him and gnawing on his entrails. Then, obviously disappointed at his sudden passivity and demise, she hits on the idea of reanimating *him*.

Somewhat surprisingly, for a minimally budgeted, one-set production, the soundtrack is varied, apt and, on occasion, humorous. The film opens with laboratory noises and stereotypical Gothic organ lines, then switches to a surprising slow vibraphone melody plus bubbling noises that (in combination) evoke Arthur Lyman's (very different) tiki lounge ex-/er-oticism. The moment of the woman's revival is (like that of the revived female corpse in James Whales's *Bride of Frankenstein* [1935]) signalled by her eyes suddenly opening. Unlike Franz Waxman's brief (and pioneering) 'stinger' used to jolt the audience in Whales's film, the moment is synched to the beginning of a stilted digital dance rhythm ('Head Waltz', by Hick, Nick and Jew of the Dead). This playfully alludes to the very different kind of 'dance' that the couple is about to enact. After several halting attempts to speak, the revived corpse finally voices what she craves most – the scientist's cock – and, as the scene switches to an overhead shot of them fucking, a grungy guitar riff comes in and becomes more intense, like their exhortations, as he squirts more serum over her. After a scene cut and a moment's silence, he goes down on her and the riffing starts up again. Blood squirts noisily from her vagina as a high synthesizer melody develops. After another cut and sound pause, a riff leads to a full-on rock passage as he penetrates her again, with the fast-paced rhythm of the Secretion's aptly named 'Fucking Zombie' synched (more or less) to the couple's fucking rhythm. After another cut and sound pause, sizzling electronic tones and a slow keyboard melody predominate as she first bites into his neck, then rips his entrails out. Grounding things, the surgery couch creaks audibly as she continues to straddle him as he expires, his demise being sonically mirrored by a disintegrating rock rhythm and screaming vocals. As the narrative ends and the credits roll, the soundtrack plays suitably soothing classical music, providing a moment of respite in conventional horror-film fashion.

The film proved controversial and popular in equal measure, as Angel has recalled:

> We put it on Burning Angel, and our billing company wrote us a few days later and said "You gotta take that down," because it was too bloody and violent. It sucked – everybody liked it so much. I said, "Will you just let me

> *keep it up for Halloween," and they said "Okay, all right," and I kept it up for a week for Halloween. I thought that would be it, but then, nobody left me alone – for six months I got an email every day asking where Repenetrator was. I thought maybe we should shoot five more scenes and put together a whole DVD, but people couldn't wait – they wanted it! So we put it on DVD even though it's one scene ... And it won most outrageous sex scene at last year's AVN awards.*[13] (Homicide, 2007)

The continuing popularity of the video led to its re-release in 2006 with an alternative director's cut and a 'making of' documentary,[14] suggesting the viability of zombie/horror porn as a niche product.[15]

Grub Girl (2005)

The second in the contemporary zombie-porn film cycle comprised the screen adaptation of horror-fiction author Ed Lee's *Grub Girl* narrative. Lee first introduced his zombie hooker character in a short story published in 1988 and it gained a minor cult following after it was adapted into graphic narrative form by Simon Morse for publication in *Verotika* magazine.[16] The key figure involved in the adaptation of Lee's story into further media forms was Glenn Danzig, the singer, songwriter and multi-instrumentalist who came to fame with the band that bore his surname in the late 1980s. Indeed, the film version of *Grub Girl* substantially represents an interpretation of Lee's original property through the lens of Danzig's particular preoccupations and sensibilities. Danzig's band mixed hard rock and punk influences on albums such as their eponymous 1988 debut, *Lucifuge* (1990) and *How The Gods Kill* (1992). The lyrics of many of the band's songs proved controversial as a result of their explicit references to rape (e.g., 'Power Of Darkness'), extreme violence against women (e.g., 'Sacrifice'), (mutual) sexual satisfaction supposed enacted by the latter (e.g., '7th House') and associated psychic/supernatural transcendence (e.g., 'Blackacidevil'). Danzig's first involvement with *Grub Girl* entailed his acquisition of the story for adaptation into comic format for his magazine company Verotik, which he had established in the early 1990s as an outgrowth of his teenage interest in horror comics. After the success of its graphic adaptation, Danzig commissioned Lee to develop a screenplay for the film; this was originally pitched to Hustler Video before Danzig settled on a collaboration with Craven Moorehead, a friend who had directed over ninety hardcore porn productions, including series such as the (self-explanatory) *Deep Throat This* numbers 1–18. In an interview prior to the film's release on DVD, NorthStar's marketing director Michael Atkins identified the rock/horror/porn connection as an attractive and potentially lucrative one:

> *Craven has been a shooter for us for quite some time and has always delivered a great product, while Glenn Danzig has sold millions of records worldwide and is a major rock legend and influence ... It is a perfect match ... With all the success of the Rap and Hip Hop porn that has come to the market we wanted to bring something to the metal and rock fans ... This*

> *collaboration between a legend like Glenn Danzig and the directing and shooting expertise of Craven is like throwing gas onto an already blazing fire.*
> (Necro, 2004)

Capitalizing on Moorehead's specific expertise, the cast includes experienced porn performers, such as Britney Skye in the title role, and the film comprises extended sex scenes, introduced and linked by brief narrative/explanatory sequences.

The film opens with a credit sequence accompanied by an unresolved piano motif and added digital strings, creating a sense of unease. After a brief montage of action images, the film provides an explanatory introduction, where the hooker heroine relates how she was killed by nuclear pollution emanating from an experimental military aircraft. The scene then cuts to a morgue where two attendants admire, grope at and then engage in lengthy rough sex with the corpse. After numerous penetrations, one attendant withdraws and ejaculates over her groin. Suddenly reviving, she opines that she has just experienced "the worst fuck of my life", pushes him away and pulls his colleague over and into her, exhorting and abusing him until he climaxes, then stabs her hand into his chest, killing him (and licking her fingers afterwards). A second direct-to-camera sequence follows in which she explains that she returned to work after her revival with the added advantage that "grub" (i.e., zombie) hookers are unable to contract diseases. The film then moves to another extended rough sex sequence after she is picked up and taken to a couple's room. Before commencing her interaction with them she explains a second 'advantage' – that they can be as rough as they want since she can't feel pain. The couple respond enthusiastically to this information and perform similar rough sex to the morgue scene (with the additional deployment of a strap-on dildo and vibrators). The third scene features her fellating her pimp in an alley. Eventually losing patience with his abuse, she bites his cock off and gores his entrails. These three extended sex scenes are accompanied by a predictable series of exhortations, non-verbal utterances and slapping and squelching noises mixed over extended versions of industrial rock tracks. The latter are provided by the emerging Los Angeles-based ensemble Skumlove (which released its debut album *Songs Of Lust And Corrosion* in 2008). While the extended mixes are primarily instrumental/textural, elements of the lyrics – where discernible – are lyrically congruent with the narrative themes, most pointedly (and, it transpires, ironically) in the third sequence where the song and lyrical hook, as if expressing the pimp's opinion of himself, states, "I am your God".

After having dispatched her pimp, the heroine declares her intention to open her own brothel. The final section comprises an extended interaction between two other grub girl hookers and a female client at her establishment, underscored by an extended mix of Danzig's track *Unspeakable* (originally released on their 1999 album *6:66 Satan's Child*). While musically similar to Skumlove's material used in the previous scenes, the track's more intelligible lyrics address the very temptations of engaging in the unspeakable that the brothel client is participating in. The film closes with a final direct-to-camera sequence where the lead grub girl reaffirms her zombie hooking activities and declaims, direct to the audience, "Don't act like you never thought of it before ... Why else would you be watching this crummy movie?"

In the combination of its specific elements with minimal narrative the film adaptation of *Grub Girl* can be seen to draw on alt.porn aesthetics and to use Lee's zombie theme as an enabling device. The film's music principally supports the film's general grunge/alt. aesthetic and, through the intelligible aspects of the song's lyrics, provides an appropriate thematic colour. Surprisingly, despite her death from military pollution, her necrophilic abuse at the hands of morgue attendants and mistreatment by her pimp and clients, Skye's character is not shown to be motivated by vengeance against the living nor, indeed, against men per se, but is shown as negotiating the everyday nature of her transformed existence as a professional sex-industry worker (albeit one 'with a difference').

Porn of the Dead (2006)

Like *Grub Girl*, the production team of *Porn of the Dead* also had close associations with the rock sector. The film was directed by punk rock musician, porn-film performer and producer, Rob Rotten.[17] Rotten began appearing in porn films in 2002 and directed his first film, *Fuck the System*, in 2005. This took alt.porn's rock stylings to a logical extension, featuring music by bands such as Deicide, Decapitated and Gorerotted together with a scene that features Rotten being fellated in a bar by a female punk during a performance by the Californian punk band Smut Peddlers.

Porn of the Dead, like *Grub Girl*, is based around a number of extended sex scenes. Unlike its predecessor, the narrative of the film unfolds in a non linear fashion and without the benefit of direct-to-camera links. Indeed, the identification of a credible narrative structure is difficult. One interpretation would be that the film's central section constitutes the narrative's starting point and provides the rationale for the existence of a rapacious female zombie (performed by different actresses) who features in three of the film's four other scenes.[18] With admirable self-reflexivity, the central scene begins with a quasi-verité sequence of a porn film crew shooting a nighttime sequence of a couple interacting in a forest clearing, accompanied by loud ambient sound and crew dialogue. The shoot is interrupted by the arrival of three zombies, who gore and dispatch the crew and male actor and engage the actress in a gangbang that she rapidly warms to and actively participates in. The sequence finishes with the zombies ejaculating over the actress, who appears otherwise unharmed by the encounter (making it unclear whether the activity has turned her into a zombie). By contrast, the film's opening sequence provides a subtle atmospheric introduction to the subsequent mayhem. The film opens with a woman walking awkwardly away from a car, accompanied by an unsettling left-hand piano motif and prominent ambient sounds, including buzzing flies. A male wearing a mouth-mask takes her back to the car and then to a darkened house with a pit set in the floor. After pushing her into it, he returns wearing a full anti-contamination suit, only to find her missing. She then looms above him, throws herself on him and rips at his clothes before engaging him in frenzied sex. After he reaches orgasm she bites his penis off. The film's final scene, showing a zombie being molested by an asylum attendant, ends in similar fashion, confirming the action as this proto-genre's equivalent of mainstream porn's ejaculatory 'money shot'.

As in *Grub Girl*, the film's extended sex scenes are accompanied by metal music. But unlike Moorehead's film, which features extended mixes as relatively smooth underscores for the noises and vocalizations of its sex scenes, Rotten's film includes its selection of material (by death metal bands Decapitated, Blood Red Throne, Gorerotted, Exmortem, Impaled and Deicide) in sound montages that accompany sex scenes, with track sequences fading in and out of the mix, rising and falling in prominence and/or pausing with little narrative logic – adding to the film's amorphous textual sprawl.

Zombie Strippers (2008)

While the three films discussed above do not present themselves as overtly political, *Zombie Strippers* offers itself for interpretation in a similar manner to that accorded to Romero's pioneering zombie features. As critics such as Elliot Stein have identified, *Night of the Living Dead* (1968) can be seen as a subversive reflection on its sociohistorical moment and the American values informing the decade:

> George Romero's remarkably assured debut, made on a shoestring, about a group of people barricaded inside a farmhouse while an army of flesh-eating zombies roams the countryside, deflates all genre clichés. It traded the expressionistic sets of the traditional fright flick for a neorealistic style – Romero's use of natural locations and grainy black and white gave his gorefest the look and feel of a doc. And this was not Transylvania, but Pennsylvania – this was Middle America at war, and the zombie carnage seemed a grotesque echo of the conflict then raging in Vietnam. (Stein, 2001)

Similarly, the rise of the zombie-porn proto-genre in the terminal stage of Bush-era America suggests a similar context (if not direct inspiration for) the films. The suppression of details of troop deaths, the murky shadow world of 'extraordinary rendition' of terror suspects, the abuses at Abu Ghraib and the continuing scandal of the Guantanamo Bay prison camp provide considerable fuel for phantoms in the early twenty-first-century USA. This background is overtly signalled in Jay Lee's *Zombie Strippers*, set in a near-future America (2012) where President George W. Bush has been re-elected for a fourth term (along with vice-presidential running mate Arnold Schwarzenegger) at a time when the USA is embroiled in conflicts across the Middle East, France, Canada and Alaska. Faced with a severe shortage of troops to sustain its military ventures, the government has authorized a programme to reanimate the dead to serve as soldiers. Early indications suggest that this is less than entirely successful. While female zombies maintain some degree of mental control and, indeed, gain enhanced physical abilities, male zombies rapidly regress to an entirely bestial state.

After an opening that includes an introductory news broadcast and sequences showing the zombie contagion escaping its restricted military zone, the majority of *Zombie Strippers'* action takes place in an illicit venue, a strip club that continues to operate in defiance of President Bush's ban on public nudity. The film's two narrative threads combine when a zombie enters the club; he attacks and passes the contagion on to the club's star performer, Kat (Jenna Jameson). After reviving in zombified form Kat bemuses the club's owner Ian Essko (Robert Englund) by returning to the stage, with blood still caked on her throat and chest, and performing an intensely aggressive number that causes a frenzy amongst the initially stunned crowd of patrons. Impressed by Kat's zombie energy and demeanour, Lillith (Roxy Saint) volunteers to be infected by her and also revives as a hyper-assertive, highly energized sexual predator. Unable to compete with their zombified colleagues' routines, many others offer themselves up for conversion. Inflamed by their on-stage performances, the dancers routinely drag male patrons backstage, arouse and then gore them to death, producing an increasing stock of deranged male zombies that Ian has to keep locked in a cellar. The denouement arrives when the zombie patrons and dancers turn on the small band of living staff shortly before a rescue squad arrives to dispatch the undead.

Though micro-budgeted (in Hollywood terms), *Zombie Strippers* emerged from a more mainstream position than the previously discussed trio of productions and achieved a (limited) cinema release in North America due, in no small part, to the casting of veteran horror actor (and *Nightmare on Elm Street* star) Englund and renowned porn actress/internet star Jameson in lead roles. Writer/director/cinematographer Jay Lee began directing feature films in the early 2000s after working on independent film and television productions in the 1990s. After a series of short arthouse-style films Lee moved into commercial genre production with his critically praised 2006 horror feature *The Slaughter* (2006). Somewhat unusually for a lowbrow production starring a porn actress, Lee has identified the French/Romanian dramatist Eugène Ionesco's 1959 play *Rhinoceros* as the model for *Zombie Strippers*. In Ionesco's drama the citizens of a small French town gradually turn into rhinoceroses, and it has been widely interpreted as an absurdist representation of the transformation of a civil society into a totalitarian one, echoing the rise of Fascism and French collaboration with the Nazis during World War II. In interviews accompanying the release of *Zombie Strippers*, Lee recounted how the initial idea behind the film derived from a throwaway comment he made during the production of *The Slaughter*:

> Once upon a time we were making socially relevant indie films that no one seemed keen on buying. So we made 'The Slaughter'. Though it had our own personal message, it was a shamelessly marketable horror movie (or more so a parody of one, which was part of the message). I started joking that at least the film wasn't something like 'Zombie Strippers'. This got a laugh every time I said it. So it makes me think, why not do zombie strippers, the title writes itself, it gets a reaction, and something as ridiculous as zombie

> strippers was about as ridiculous as French people turning into rhinos – and it just clicked. I could bring our socially relevant films together with shameless marketing and hopefully produce a successful, moneymaking, entertaining film with a message. (Meh, 2008)

Inspired by Ionesco's model, Lee's engagement with horror was informed by his perception that the genre operates as

> a minefield of metaphor and allegory, there is often so much more than meets the eye in horror films, such as the deep exploration of the fragility of the human psyche, the evils inherent in our society and in ourselves, and so on. This is some deeply profound and tragically human ground to tread. (ibid.)

While Lee's film may have been informed by cultural reflections and inspired by a specific mid-twentieth-century drama text, it also has a direct connection to the alt.porn/independent rock nexus described above through the casting of Los Angeles-based alternative rock performer Roxy Saint as the Goth-girl stripper Lillith and through the film's extensive use of rock music.

Saint began to attract attention in 2003 through live performances with her band the Blackouts and she established a reputation as a flamboyant and sexually explicit performer whose demeanour and visual style evoked the template laid down by the Suicide Girls and BurningAngel.com. Unusually for an unsigned artist, her first commercial product was a self-funded DVD entitled *The Underground Personality Tapes* (2004). It featured videos shot by a variety of directors which expanded her songs' lyrical themes and her visual performance style into vivid scenarios, many of which drew on horror, porn and/or science-fiction themes and imagery. The opening track, 'Rebel', serves as a signature to Saint's performance persona, with its opening lines declaring, "I'm danger, beware/ I'll be your worst nightmare". Other video tracks address sexual desire, such as 'Fuck Song' (directed by Saint), in which she performs sex-industry roles (hooker, stage performer) and sings and dances in skimpy attire; and 'Firecracker' (directed by Eric Zimmerman). The title of the latter serves as a metaphor for her more general sexual volatility, as she is shown picking up men in the street, cavorting with a trio of other semi-dressed women, being wrapped in cling film by one, and appearing in a bath, tinting its waters red with her menstrual blood.

Zombie Strippers features two main types of music: an introductory pastiche-1950s title sequence and atmospheric digital-orchestral and rock/textural sequences provided by Billy White Acre[19] and pre-recorded hard rock songs selected by Jay and his partner Angela Lee.[20] As part of his brief to White Acre, Lee supplied the composer with reference folders of what he referred to as "old school" and "new school" zombie-film music. The latter included a lengthy extract from the score to British zombie-comedy *Shaun of the Dead* (Simon Pegg and Edgar Wright, 2004). Lee described this reference as a "halfway stage" to what he was after in his film. This highlights the elaborate intertextuality and layered tradition in the *Zombie Strippers'* score, since the score for the British film also consciously reworked elements of classic horror and offset these with rock and dance tracks. Co-director Edgar Wright has described the inspiration of the score for *Shaun of the Dead* as follows:

> *Certainly with the score the idea was we wanted to do a 21st Century update of John Carpenter and Goblin. So the score is definitely influenced by* Assault on Precinct 13, The Thing, Suspiria *and* Dawn of the Dead. *There was a use of Goblin about half way through [that] came about because … it's a fantasy sequence, I thought in their heads* Dawn of the Dead *music is probably playing, we used that music as temps and then we thought "fuck it" we should just try and clear it. We also used the library music from* Dawn *at the very beginning of the film and at the very end because a friend of mine had just released … the unofficial score of* Dawn of the Dead[21] *so we cleared some of (the) tracks from that which is brilliant.* (Brown, 2004)

Expanding on this approach, Lee briefed White Acre that the music he was after should be "louder, cooler, dirtier and noisier" than the *Shaun of the Dead* score (personal communication with the author, July 2008).

The pre-recorded rock songs are mainly used for the on-stage sequences that comprise a significant portion of the narrative. The film introduces the audience to each of the featured strippers by showing their (pre-zombified) performance styles to a series of rock tracks, then contrasts these to their post-zombified ones. It then combines various zombified dancers on stage who interact in dance and, finally, physical combat between Kat and her professional rival Jeannie (Shamron More). While far from interchangeable, the styles of the tracks are similar, comprising intense, mid- to fast-tempo rock arrangements and strained, aggressive vocals. Saint and her band contribute two tracks and she sings on a third, entitled 'Smother You', written and produced by White Acre. 'Smother You' serves as the film's de facto theme tune, appearing once as a diegetic track and again over the end-credits. The track marks a significant transition point in the film. The first club sequences introduce the strippers backstage and dancing individually. Their dances are accompanied by loud rock tracks, produced to sound as if they emanate from the venue's sound system. After her zombification Kat returns to the stage to perform to 'Smother You' – beginning jerkily and uncoordinated before switching into a markedly more intense and energetic routine than the women's previously represented ones. Kat's vigorous performance complements Saint's intense and abrasive delivery of the song's dark lyrics and the jagged, distorted sound and fast pace of its accompaniment. Inspired by Kat's dance, Lillith also elects to become a zombie and returns to the stage to deliver a demonically sexual (not to mention acrobatic) routine to Saint's own (ironically entitled) 'Don't Kill The Star'.

The film's most remarkable sonic sequences accompany the intense visceral action of its final section. This comprises two intercut sequences, the final face-off between Kat and her (now-zombified) rival Jeannie and the zombies' escape from the basement and assault on the club's human staff. The Kat versus Jeannie sequence begins with taunts, before moving to the most sonically sublime moment of the film. As they face each other, the vestiges of humanity peel away and raw primal energy emerges as the two exchange deep, inhuman howls that shock the patrons into a chilled silence. In elegant allusion to the Absurdist inspiration of the film's drama, sound designer/foley artist Andrew Knox mixed rhinoceros roars and other animal sounds to emphasize the essential animal combat between the two.[22] Fired by this exchange, the rival strippers then engage in a dance duel, vying for audience approval. This gives way to actual combat between the two as they strike, dismember and slash at each other (and, in Kat's case, fires balls from her vagina at her adversary), with Jeannie gaining the upper hand before their fight is brought to an abrupt close by the arrival of a military squad who terminate them. Meanwhile, off stage the staff are engaged in a hopeless rearguard action that involves them blasting away at zombies before they succumb. The sound mix for these sequences, provided by Glen Schricker, and particularly for the on-stage combat, is a dense and complex wall of sound, comprising digital orchestral rumbles, riffs and jarring chords mixed with an array of roars, crunches, swooshes, clangs and explosions that anchors the audience in the action even as its gymnastics and visual effects shift into (small 'a') absurdity. As the action reaches its peak, with Kat slashed to ribbons and with the staff overwhelmed, the arrival of the military quietens the anarchy enacted in the club by eradicating (all but one of) the undead and imposing calm upon the 'scorched earth' of the club's terrain.

This combination of hard-edged rock music, abrasive digital orchestrations, primal howls and the sound of physical disintegration represents the most intense sonic distillation of the themes of the zombie-porn cycle addressed in this chapter. Unlike the stereotypically bland soundtracks of mainstream porn cinema, *Zombie Strippers* conveys a sonic intensity cued by the confrontational traditions of death metal and the in-your-face aggression of punk. In many ways, Kat and Jeannie's showdown and the physical dismemberment that eventuates represent the essential (stripped-down) expression of *thanatos* and *eros* that underscores both the whole tradition of sex and violence in western cinema and the specific impulses that underpinned the inauguration of the zombie-porn cycle.

Conclusion

The four zombie-porn films analysed in this chapter draw on both heavy rock genres and contemporary film-scoring traditions in a variety of ways. Somewhat surprisingly, for a minimally budgeted short that was produced as a Halloween treat for porn-site habitués, *Repenetrator* has the most varied use of musical styles, combining sonically dense and abrasive hard rock tracks with pseudo-classical and vibraphone passages. *Grub Girl* and *Porn of the Dead* feature heavy metal tracks that are less synchronized to particular action sequences and which primarily function to provide external musical backdrops to sustained scenes of violent sexual interaction. *Zombie Strippers* has the most accomplished and coherent soundtrack, both in its diegetic uses of music (predominantly for the strippers' routines) and score and its complementary sound design and overall mix. Despite their soundtrack differences, all four films draw on rock music's energy and, more particularly, the aura of rebellion, transgression and excess that heavy- and punk-rock bands, their promoters, fans and journalists have attempted to sustain as a core element of their appeal.

In this manner, there is a significant convergence, as the transgressive content of zombie-porn films is as complex, contradictory and flawed as rock's own occasional claims to counter-hegemonic radicalism. Yet, like certain rock acts, texts and/or moments, zombie porn – at very least – provides dark and complex meditations on violence and hetero(sexuality) that can be interpreted as wilfully deviant responses to state-sanctioned militarism and moral majority-ism. Indeed, Republican presidential candidate Bob Dole explicitly acknowledged this in 1996 when he condemned death metal band Cannibal Corpse in a campaign speech that climaxed with the declaration that "Those who cultivate moral confusion for profit should understand this: we will name their names and shame them as fanatics out of step with America."[23]

There is, of course, a wide range of perspectives on how productive and/or progressive such social taboo-breaking is. This has been exemplified by the wide variety of responses to alt.porn. One snapshot of these was provided by a spirited interaction in the New York press in 2005. Following an article in the *New York Times* profiling the production of *Burning.Angel.com: The Movie* that lauded its stars for their "empowered" sexualities (Lanham, 2005), social commentator Rochelle Gurstein provided a powerful riposte. Gurstein, the author of *The Repeal of Reticence* (1996), a conservative and cautionary history of the loosening of censorship and obscenity laws in the United States, lambasted alt.porn's claims to radicalism and Joanna Angel's invocation of punk-rock as a (legitimating) reference point. Taking a very different tack, she linked alt.porn production practices and sensibilities to the notorious abuse of Iraqi prisoners by US service personnel such as Lynndie England and her boyfriend Charles Graner,[24] arguing that

> England's sadism, along with the fact that she and Graner not only made but circulated pornographic videos of themselves, speak[s] to the coercive and brutalizing nature of the pornographic imagination so prevalent in our world today. (Gurstein, 2005)

There is obviously some pertinence to this linkage. But there is also substantial slippage. The associations between England's and Graner's behaviour, the military culture of violence it was nourished within and the development of alt.porn are complex and open to debate.[25]

It would be disingenuous to argue that there is any clearly articulated (let alone programmatic) ideological underpinning to zombie porn's distillation of elements of pornography, horror and rock culture. That, after all, isn't the way that popular culture operates. Authors produce texts that enter into social spaces in which they are interpreted by a range of users and promoters. In this context, the dark, dynamic texts of zombie porn invite engagement through their excess and facilitate this through the elements of familiarity of their individual components. Whether identified as prime examples of what Dole referred to as "moral confusion for profit" (*op. cit.*), as extreme manifestations of what Gurstein (2005) calls the "coercive and brutalizing nature of the pornographic imagination", or as more radically transgressive texts from a social underground, the films are unquestionably confrontational. They avoid easy reduction and provide representations of contemporary culture *in extremis*.

Acknowledgements

Thanks to members of the *Zombie Strippers'* production team for their research assistance, to Philip Hayward and anonymous referees for advice and guidance on previous drafts and to Cradle of Filth for providing a research soundtrack.

Notes

1. An activity that had been foreshadowed in British director Michael Powell's controversial *Peeping Tom* (1960). The existence of snuff movies was also a central plot element of Paul Schrader's feature *Hardcore* (1979) and Joel Schumacher's similarly themed *8mm* (1999).
2. As is Sean Tretta's *The Great American Snuff Film* (2003), which (inviting comparison to the *Blair Witch Project*) purports to document (and include actual footage shot by) a real-life serial killer named William Grone. For reasons that can only be speculated upon, there has been a recent crop of productions on the topic, including *Amateur Porn Star Killer* (Shane Ryan, 2007), *Home Made* (Jason Impey, 2008) and *Slaughtered* (Anthony Doublin, 2008).
3. Which also included such oddities as *King of the Zombies* (Jean Yarbrough, 1941) and *Zombies on Broadway* (Gordon Dines and Gordon Douglas, 1945).
4. The album included a guest appearance by veteran Hammer actress Ingrid Pitt, as narrator, reprising her title role from the 1971 feature *Countess Dracula* (Peter Sasdy).
5. Joe D'Amato was one of several pseudonyms used by Aristide Massaccesi.
6. The film was released in two versions, one with the more sexually explicit material removed. The version discussed here is the R-rated one.
7. He is best known for his modern Christian music written in the 1950s and 1960s, such as *La Messa dei giovani* for rock ensemble and vocals, which was premiered in Rome in the Oratorio di San Filippo Neri in 1966.
8. Foreshadowing the wider development of horror-porn styles in the 2000s, the 1998 compendium film *Terrors from the Clit* (Robert Black), compèred by Dukey Flyswatter (aka Michael Sonye), the front man of mid-1980s schlock-horror metal

band Haunted Garage, features an episode of male zombie rape alongside sexual scenes with vampires and Frankensteinian monsters.
9. There's also something of a pre-history to this association of new wave and porn in the person of British avant-garde/new wave musician and Throbbing Gristle member Cosi Fanni Tutti (Christine Newby) and her parallel careers as a stripper and soft- and hardcore porn performer in the 1970s and 1980s. For an illuminating interview on her attitudes towards her sex-industry work, see 'Cosey Fanni Tutti – time to tell', in *Compulsion: Alternative Culture*, online at http://www.compulsiononline.com/falbum2.html (accessed June 2008).
10. Courtney Love, for instance, has been an active member, frequently posting quirky reflections on fame and sexuality.
11. See Lanham (2005) for background on the performer and her operation.
12. This sequence was cut from the cinema-release version and some subsequent video and DVD releases.
13. *Adult Video News* Awards, an annual US industry event.
14. Subsequent BurningAngel titles included Angel's (self-directed) features *BurningAngel.com: The Movie* and *Joanna's Angels* (both 2005). Directors such as Eon McKai developed further engagements with the alt.porn aesthetic in films such as *Art School Sluts* (2004), the trilogy *Kill Girl Kill 1-3* (2005) (marketed with the tagline 'Boys kill with violence ... Girls kill with sex') and *Neu Wave Hookers* (2005). The latter (which also stars Joanna Angel in a leading role) revisits Gregory Dark's 1985 feature *New Wave Hookers* via a complex plot that involves a group of young women who become fixated with the film and set out to investigate its history and background (accompanied by the music of acts such as Gold Chains, Electrocute and Dirty Sanchez).
15. The film has been subsequently reissued together with Sakmann and Angel's later collaboration, *The XXXorcist* (2006) (a porn revisioning of William Friedkin's *The Exorcist* [1973]) on a single DVD entitled *The Sick & Twisted Horror of Joanna Angel* (2008).
16. Initially in issue no.8 and subsequently repackaged in various formats.
17. See Taormino (2006) for background on Rotten.
18. The remaining scene features a 'normal' human female masturbating and subsequently dreaming of frenzied sex with a shadowy male (who might possibly be a zombie). While accompanied by the same style of music and audio as the remainder of the film, its relation to the zombie theme and implied narrative of the rest of the film is unclear.
19. Composer of scores for previous films such as Jay Lee's *Noon Blue Apples* (2002) and the SF comedy *Tammy and the T Rex* (Stewart Raffill, 1994).
20. By Saint (three tracks), the Dirt Bombs (two), Yeva (two), Kozy (one), Vistalance (one) and three tracks attributed to Andre Morawek, Sebastian Grund, Tom-Eric Morawek, Nick Wachsmuth and Sebastian Rioche.
21. Various artists, *Dawn Of The Dead – Unreleased Soundtrack Music* (2004).
22. Thanks to Andrew Knox for his discussion of the sound design and production.
23. A section of this speech is archived online at http://www.tombofthemutilated.net/Bob-Dole-Cannibal-Corpse.html (accessed 19 June 2009).

24. England attracted international media attention when she was shown gleefully posing in photos (taken by Graner) next to naked and humiliated Iraqi inmates. Subsequently sentenced for mistreatment of prisoners, she has entered popular cultural mythology. Austrian metal band Pungent Stench, for instance, featured a composition entitled 'Lynndie (She-Wolf Of Abu Ghraib)' on their 2004 album *Ampeauty*. The title is significant, comparing England to Ilse Koch, the notoriously sadistic wife of a Nazi concentration camp commander (who was herself the inspiration for Don Edmond's gruesome 1975 sexploitation feature *Isla, She Wolf of the SS*.). In a more mainstream context, TV shows such as *The Simpsons* and *South Park* have also alluded to England's activities and her infamous photo poses, further entrenching her in the popular imaginary.
25. Gurstein's article is artfully written. Despite its title's suggestion of a direct connection between a 'taste-free', sexualized society and barbaric, violent excess ('On the Triumph of the Pornographic Imagination' — note those first three words, invoking Leni Riefenstahl), the article avoids engaging with the extent to which the actions of a few scapegoated service personnel reflect and were engendered by the state-sanctioned sadism endemic in US prisons in Iraq. It's the couple's unfortunate visual representation of their abuses that becomes the focus of the issue.

References

Brown, D. M. (2004), '*Shaun of the Dead* — interview with director Edgar Wright', *Digital Retribution*; online at http://www.digital-retribution.com/features/0003.php (accessed June 2008).

Gurstein, G. (1998), *The Repeal of Reticence: A History of America's Cultural and Legal Struggles over Free Speech, Obscenity, Sexual Liberation, and Modern Art*, New York: Hill and Wang.

Gurstein, G. (2005), 'On the Triumph of the Pornographic Imagination "Wearing Nothing But Attitude"', *New Republic*, 18 May; online at http://www.artsandopinion.com/2008_v7_n1/gurstein-3.htm (accessed June 2008).

Homicide, J. (2007), 'Joanna Angel interview', *Eroszine*; online at www.eros-ny.com/articles/2007-02-06/joanna_angel0206/ (accessed June 2008).

Lanham, R. (2005), 'Wearing Nothing But Attitude', *New York Times*, 1 May; online at http://www.robertlanham.com/burningangel.html (accessed June 2008).

Meh (2008), '*Zombie Strippers* director interview', *HorrorMovies.ca*; online at http://www.horror-movies.ca/horror_11203.html (accessed June 2008).

Necro, D. (2004), 'Craven Moorehead directs Verotik's Grub Girl', *Crypt Magazine*; online at http://www.cryptmagazine.com/175675.html (accessed June 2008).

Stein, I. (2003), 'The Dead Zones', *Village Voice*, 7 January; archived online at http://www.villagevoice.com/2003-01-07/film/the-dead-zones/ (accessed June 2008).

Taormino, T. (2006), 'Sex, Drugs, and Punk Rock Music: Rob "Don't Call Me Alt" Rotten Talks about His Unique Kind of Porn', *Village Voice*, 10 October; archived online at http://www.villagevoice.com/people/0641,taormino,74720,24.html (accessed June 2008).

Index

Note: Film/DVD titles are in italics; album titles are italic, with 'album' in parentheses; song titles are in quotation marks; book titles are italic; musical works are either in italics or quotation marks, with composer's name in parentheses.

A Rebours (Huysmans) 61
Abducted by the Daleks/Daloids 135
Abe, Sada 91–101
Abrams, J. 174
Abu Ghraib 225, 233
acousmêtre 6
Acre, Billy White, *see* White Acre, Billy
Adamson, Al 116
affect 2, 67, 76
African music 58
Age of Innocence, The 64
Ai no borei ('Empire of Passion') 100–1
Ai no korida (*In the Realm of the Senses*) 1, 4, 7, 89–101
Aihara, Kyoko 100
Algar, James 20
Alice in Wonderland (Lewis Carroll) 5, 70, 71, 74, 76, 84, 116
Alien 102
Alien Probe 129
Alien Probe II 129
Alpha Blue 117–19, 120
Also sprach Zarathustra (Richard Strauss) 46, 112, 113
Altman, Rick 2, 9, 194, 199
Amateur Porn Star Killer 231
Amazing Stories (magazine) 103, 104
Amelie 86
American National Parent/Teacher Association 147
Ampeauty (album) 233
Anal Cunt 219
... *And God Created Woman*, *see* Et Dieu créa la femme
Andersen, Gotha 32
Anderson, Paul Thomas 153, 158
Anderson, Paul W. S. 137
Andrews, David 66, 72, 85, 122, 126, 127, 171
Angel, Joanna 220, 221, 230, 232
Animal Collective 205, 207, 210, 211
Antonioni, Michelangelo 83
Apatow, Judd 137
Arab music 24
Argento, Dario 218
Armstrong, Neil 121
Armstrong, S. 39, 46, 49
Armstrong, Samuel 20
Arnaldi, Stefano 63
Arsan, Emmanuelle, *see* Marayat Rollet-Andriane
Art School Sluts 232
arthouse films 6, 80, 84, 226
Asian cinema 89, 90

Asimov, Isaac 130
Assault on Precinct 13 228
Astaire, Fred 131
Astley, Edwin 104
'Astronomy Domine' 81, 82
Atkins, Michael 222
Augoyard, J.-F. 10
Aury, Dominique (aka Pauline Reage) 86
Austin, Billy 215
Austin Powers movies 46
Australian Classification Board 170
Avon Science Fiction Reader (magazine) 104
Avon Theater, New York 78

'Baby Did A Bad Bad Thing' 181–2
Bacchus, John 120, 128, 137
Bach, Johann Sebastian 62
Bachelet, Pierre 68, 71, 72, 74
Bacon, Francis 54
Bailey, Fenton 122, 136
Baker, Jack 143, 150
Baker, Rick 114
Ballard, Hank, and the Midnighters 164
Band, Charles 126
Bangs, Lester 141
banjo 47
Barbano, Nicolas 35, 36
Barbarella 5, 107–11, 113, 115, 119, 120, 122, 127, 134, 135, 136
Barbato, Randy 122, 136
Barbieri, Gato 54, 55, 57
Bardot, Brigitte 68, 107–8
Barker, Raphael 204
Baron, Red 79
Barr, M. 145
Barrington, Kristara 146, 151
Barron, Bebe 109
Barron, Louis 109
Barthes, Roland 90, 100, 169
bass (instrument) 26, 27, 41, 48, 63, 71, 75, 134, 208
Bataille, Georges 83, 87
Báthory, Elizabeth 219
Batman (TV series) 41
Batman Forever 137
Bauer, Chris 164
Bava, Mario 107, 217
Baxter, Les 106, 107, 121
Bazelon, Irwin 191, 195
Beamish, Lindsay 204
Beatles, the 21

'Beautiful' 205, 210
Behind the Green Door 85, 113–14, 117
Beneath the Valley of the Ultravixens 42
Benveniste, Michael 122, 127
Bergson, Henri 153
Bergstrom, J. 154, 155
Berkeley, Busby 143
Bernds, Edward 121
Bernstein, Charles 111–12
Bernstein, Elmer 104, 121
Bertolucci, Bernardo 4, 54–65
Besieged 57, 62
'Best Of My Love' 161
bestiality 20, 21, 22, 36
Better Luck (album) 144
Beyond the Valley of the Dolls 46, 50, 51
Big Chill, The 171
Billen, Andrew 36
Bimbo Cheerleaders from Outer Space 126
Bitch (poet/actor) 206, 209, 210
biwa 96
Black, Robert 231
Black Rebel Motorcycle Club 192
Black Sabbath 138, 219
Black Throat 150
Black Widow 219
'Blackacidevil' 222
Blacklode 126
Blackouts, the 227
Blade Runner 102, 145
Blair Witch Project, The 137, 231
Blondie 141, 155
Blood Red Throne 225
'Blue Danube, The' 31, 132
Blue Lines (album) 131
'Blue Sofa' 144, 151, 152
bluegrass music 47
blues 131, 151
'Blues In' 169
Body Double 8
'Bolero' (Ravel) 133
Bond, James 5, 14, 86, 106
Bond, Justin 205, 207, 209, 211, 231
Bone, John T. 126
Boogie Nights 154, 158–73
'Boogie Shoes' 167
Bordellet 12, 15, 16, 17, 29–33
Bordello, *see Bordellet*
Bormann, Martin 44, 45
Bornoff, Nicholas 100
Borodin, Alexander 31, 121
Bowles, Paul 60
'Boys Of Melody' 205
Bradby, Barbara 155
'Brand New Key' 162
Brando, Marlon 54
Brannan, Jay 207, 210
Brasher, John 115
brass instruments 41, 42, 44, 46, 47, 48, 55, 58, 109, 110, 131, 133, 161, 214

Brasso, Tinto 120
Brecht, Bertolt 118
Bride of Frankenstein 114, 221
Brigman, W. E. 170
British Sound 123
Brooks, Anthony, *see* Raymond Phelan
Brooks, Mel 132, 133
Brooks, Richard 159
Brophy, P. 67, 83
Brown, Clifford 167
Brusendorff, Ove 15, 16
brutality 219
Buchanan, Larry 121
Buckalew, Bethel (aka Seymour Touchus) 106
Buhler, J. 175
Bukowski, Charles 217
burlesque films/music 5, 40, 105, 106, 120, 121
BurningAngel.com: The Movie 231, 232
Bush, George W. 225, 226
Butkus, Clarice 4
Buttgereit, Jörg 217
Byrd, Thomas 10
Byrne, David 60

Cabaret 117, 118, 123
Café Flesh 117–19, 125
Califia, Pat 87
Camison, Matt 71, 72
Campanile, Pasquale Festa 120
Campion, Jane 171
Candy Goes to Hollywood 154
Cannibal Corpse 230
Canterbury, Stewart 129
'Careful With That Axe, Eugene' (aka 'Murderistic Women' and 'Come In Number 51, Your Time Is Up') 81, 82, 83
Carell, Andy 137
Carey, Lynn 49
Carlisle, Una Mae 208
Carlos, Walter (aka Mister K.) 72
Carlton Cinema, Copenhagen 15
Carmassi, Denny 119
Carpenter, John 228
Carrie Nations, the 48–9
Carroll, Lewis 116
Carson, Shanti 206
Casablanca 3
Castleman, William Allen 114
Cat Ballou 108
Cat on a Hot Tin Roof 159
Cat-Women of the Moon 104
Catholic League of Decency 122
Caton-Jones, Michael 137
celesta 121
censorship 13, 17, 69, 99, 107, 113, 115, 127, 159, 170
Centre de recherche sur l'espace sonore et l'environnement urbain (Cresson) 3
'Champagne Galop' (Lumbye) 23, 36
Chandon, Alex 219

236 Index

Chant d'amour, Un 36
Charlie's Angels 137
Chastagner, C. 147, 149
Chen, Joan 61
Cheung, Tequila 80
Chevalier, Maurice 32, 36, 37
Chibnal, S. 121
Chinese Mask, The 15, 16, 17, 19–20, 33, 34
Chinese music 19, 20, 60, 61
Chinn, Bob 113
Chion, Michel 2, 9, 67, 72, 73, 174, 199
Chopper 171
Christine, Henri 37
Cinderella (children's story) 86, 116
Cinderella 2000 116
Claim, The 64
Clarida, Bob 6, 9, 10
Clary, Corinne 86
Clash, the 155
classical music 18, 21, 47, 60, 79, 89, 112, 205, 221
Clean Breast: The Life and Loves of Russ Meyer, A (autobiography) 39
Cleland, John 29
Clifford, M. 78, 79, 82, 87
Clifton, Kevin 51
'Climb Every Mountain' 138
Clockwork Orange, A 10, 72
Cloonan, Martin 8, 10
Clover, C. 148
Clown Porn 51
'C'mon C'mon' 192
Cobb, Jodi 100
Coe, Frank 106
Coltrane, John 63
'Come In Number 51, Your Time Is Up', *see* 'Careful With That Axe, Eugene'
'Come With The Gentle People' 49
comedy films 8, 29, 32, 33, 42–4, 132
Commodores, the 167
Conformist, The 58, 62
Conviene far bene l'amore 120
Cook, J. R. 138
Cook, Todd Mason 218
Corbett, John 3, 7
Cornelius, Henry 123
Costello, Elvis 119
Countess Dracula 231
country and western music 89
Cox, Alex 154, 174–5
Coyle, Rebecca 113
Cradle of Filth 219, 231
Crazy Love 217
Crewe, Bob 110, 122
Crowded House 119
Cruelty And The Beast (album) 219
Cruise, Tom 174, 177, 178
Cruzados, the 154
Cugat, Xavier 218
Cumming, Alan 183

cunnilingus 79, 82, 90, 96, 118, 128, 150, 208, 221
Cuny, Alain 68
Curtiz, Michael 73
Cyborgasm 4

daiko drum 96
Dalby, Liza 100
D'Amato, Joe (aka Aristide Massaccesi) 219, 231
Damiano, Gerard 85, 87, 114, 117, 136
Dammit, Tommy 220
D'Andrea, Franco 55
Dandy Warhols, the 192
Danforth, Jim 114
Daniels, Stormy 132, 137, 138
Danzig, Glenn 222, 223
Dargis, Manohla 204
Dark, Gregory 140, 142, 144, 154, 232
Dark Brothers, the 140, 142, 150, 153
Dark Victory 56
Davian, Joe 66, 67, 78–85, 217
Davis, Bette 56
Davis, Julienne 181
Dawn of the Dead 218, 228
Dawn Of The Dead – Unreleased Soundtrack Music (album) 232
Dawson, Paul 204
Day of the Dead 218
Day the Earth Caught Fire, The 102
de Berg, Jean 70
de Lauretis, Teresa 194
de Mandiargues, André Pieyre 69–70
de Palma, Brian 8
de Sade, Marquis 81, 84
Dead World 219
Death 219
Death Metal Zombies 218
'Debbie' 195
DeBoy, PJ 204
Decapitated 224, 225
Deep Throat 114, 117, 136
Deep Throat This series 222
Deicide 224, 225
Del Naja, Robert ('3D') 131-3, 134, 137
Del Rio, Vanessa 79, 82, 83, 84, 87
Delerue, Georges 58, 62
'Den grimme dreng' ('The Naughty Boy') 12
Denis, Kay 116
Denny, Martin 105
Deruddere, Dominique 217
Dery, M. 145
Desperate Housewives (TV series) 73
Det erotiske museum, *see* Museum Erotica, Copenhagen
Det tossede paradis ('Goat in Paradise') 13, 36
Deutsch, S. 41
Devil Girl from Mars 104, 110
Devil in Miss Jones, The 114, 117
Diary of the Dead 218

Index 237

diegetic music/sound 2, 6, 32, 47, 58, 59, 68, 73, 76, 79, 81, 92, 93–5, 96, 98, 99, 109, 110, 127, 128, 148, 160, 161, 164, 167, 168, 169, 175, 181, 183, 184, 192–3, 200, 205, 206, 207, 209, 210, 213, 214, 218, 228, 230
Dillon, Dan 115
Dines, Gordon 231
Dirt Bombs, the 232
Dirty Sanchez 232
Disco volante, Il 120
Disney, Walt 20
Doane, Mary Anne 194, 195, 201
Doctor Who (TV series) 120, 135, 138
Dole, Bob 230, 231
Domination Blue 78, 82
Dominik, Andrew 171
'Don't Kill The Star' 228
Doublin, Anthony 231
Douglas, Gordon 231
Dr. Dopo Jam 36
Dr Goldfoot and the Bikini Machine 106
Dr Goldfoot and the Girl Bombs 106–7
Dr. Strangelove 10
Drew, Kenny 25, 26, 27, 28
Dribben, N. 49–50
drums, *see* percussion
Dukey Flyswatter (aka Michael Sonye) 231
Dumont, Sky 181
Duran Duran 108, 154
Durbin, K. 170
Dusk ... And Her Embrace (album) 219
Dworkin, Andrea 70, 86
Dyer, Richard 142
Dyrehausbakken, Copenhagen 32

Eastern music 18, 48, 142
Ebb, Fred 123
Ebert, Roger 43–4, 46, 52
Edmond, Don 233
Egan, Walter 163
Ege, Ole 9, 12–37
8mm 231
Einstein, Albert 108
Elbow 192
'Electrify Me' 144, 151
Electrocute 232
Elliot, B. Ron 103
ELO 153
Emmanuelle 68, 70, 85
Emotions, the 161
England, Lynndie 230, 233
Englund, Robert 226
Ensemble Nipponia 95
Eros Cinema, New York 78
Erotic Adventures of Zorro, The 114
Erotic House of Wax, The 127
Erotic/Sexy Nights of the Living Dead, *see Le Notti erotiche dei morti viventi*
Erotic Time Machine II, The 127

Erotic Witch Project film series 120, 128, 137
erotica (films) 1, 2, 5, 6, 7, 8, 12, 26, 29, 33, 34, 35, 38, 49, 67, 68, 69, 70, 114, 121
Erotica 2000 16
Erotiske drømme (Ole Ege) 16
Escort (magazine) 16
Esquivel, Juan Garcia 164
Esturaku ('Pleasures of the Flesh') 100
Et Dieu créa la femme 107–8
Eurythmics 108, 154
Evans, Mark 4, 10, 35, 36, 171, 214
Event Horizon 137
Exmortem 225
Exorcist, The 232
extra-diegetic music/sound, *see* non-diegetic music/sound
Eyes Wide Shut 2, 174–89

Fairuz (singer) 23, 36
Falsetto, Mario 174
Fanny Hill, *see Memoirs of a Woman of Pleasure*
Fantasia 20
Fantastic Stories (magazine) 103
Fantasy Reader (magazine) 104
Farmer, Philip José 103, 116
Faster, Pussycat! Kill! Kill! 41, 42, 48, 51
Fatal Attraction 111
Federal Office of Film and Literature Classification (Australia) 170
fellatio 48, 50, 75, 82, 90, 93, 94, 96, 118, 128, 130, 146, 150, 207, 219, 223, 224
Fellini, Federico 39
Femalien 127
Femalien 2 128
Ferraro, Ralph 114, 115, 123
fetish/fetishism 38, 49, 60, 67, 81, 86, 104, 107, 117, 134–6, 141, 220
Fetishes of Monique 78, 79–81, 85
Feuer, Jane 34
Field, Todd 183
Fields, Dorothy 208
film noir 63, 102, 113, 154, 166
'Find It' 49, 50
Fingered 154
Fini, Leonar 85–6
Finlay, Michael 217
Finlay, Roberta 217
Fire Maidens from Outer Space 121
'Firecracker' 227
First Tour DVD, The 220
Fischer, C. 42
Fitzgerald, Jon 122
Flash Gordon films 114
Fleming, Peter, *see* Ole Ege
Flesh Gordon 113–15, 119, 120, 127, 135
'Flesh Gordon Is Dead' 115
Flesh Gordon Meets the Cosmic Cheerleaders 115
folk music 21, 36, 94, 205
Fonda, Henry 108
Fonda, Jane 68, 108–11

238 Index

For Your Eyes Only 86
Forbidden Planet 109
Ford, Anitra 111
Ford, John 108
Forest, Jean-Claude 107, 108
Fort Apache 108
40-Year-Old Virgin, The 137
Fosse, Bob 117, 123
Foundation trilogy 130
Fox, Charles 110, 122
Fox, Scotty 136
Franz Ferdinand 192
Freeman, Robert 114
Freud, Lucien 54
Freud, Sigmund 153
Friedkin, William 232
Friedman, David 103
Frith, Simon 147, 149, 193, 195
From Dusk Till Dawn 154
From Here to Eternity 160
Frontiere, Dominic 135
Froom, Mitchell 119, 123
Fuck the System 224
'Fucking Zombie' 221
Fuji, Tatsuya 100
Full Moon (production company) 126
Fung, Richard 150, 155
funk music 47, 48, 112, 116, 133, 145
'Funky Shit' 137
Furlong, John 41, 43

Gaarde, Ingerlise/Inger-Lise 32
Gabor, Zsa Zsa 121
Gaillard, Slim 121
Gainsbourg, Serge 68, 85
Gale, Mike 109
Gallagher, Hugh 220
Galliano, L. 101
Gardens, Max 106
Garner, Errol 28
Garofalo, R. 140, 149, 151
Gavin, Erica 41
Gemser, Laure 219
Gendron, Bernard 141, 151, 155
Genet, Jean 36
Gerosa, M. 203
Gilling, John 218
Gillis, Jamie 141
'Gimme That Old Time Religion' 45
Giombini, Marcello (aka Pluto Kennedy) 219
'Girls On Film' 154
Gishiki ('Ceremonies') 100
Giuffre, Liz 155
Go, Jade 60
Goblin 218, 228
Godard, Jean-Luc 57, 123
Godzilla 135
Golden, Arthur 100
Gold Chains 232
Goldfrapp, Alison 196, 197
Goldfrapp (band) 196
Goodbye Emmanuelle 85
Goodbye to Berlin (Isherwood) 123
Goodman, Miles 116
'Goody Goody' 167
Gorbman, Claudia 2, 9, 175, 178, 184–5
Gordon, Dexter 12, 22, 23, 25, 26, 27, 28
Gordon, Stuart 220–1
Gore Whore 220
Gorerotted 224, 225
Gorfinkel, E. 36
Gori, Lalo 107
Goulding, Edmund 56
Graduate, The 6
Graham, Heather 162
Graner, Charles 230, 233
Graveyard Tramps, see Invasion of the Bee Girls
Great American Snuff Film, The 231
Green, Al 155
Greer, Germaine 36
'Grey Clouds', *see* 'Nuages gris'
Griffith, Patrick M. 137
Grodal, T. 174
Grone, William 231
Grub Girl 222–4, 225, 229
Grund, Sebastian 232
Guantanamo Bay 225
Guest, Val 102
guitar 36, 64, 74, 75, 76, 82, 83, 109, 110, 112, 116, 127, 131, 132, 142, 145, 197, 207, 211, 213, 221
Gurstein, Rochelle 230, 231, 233

Halaby, John R. F. 137
Hall, Terri 87
Halperin, Victor 218
Hamano, Sachi 91
Hammer films 112, 217, 218, 231
Hammerstein, Oscar 138
Han, Maggie 62
Hannan, Michael 122
Hard Gore 81
Hard Rock Zombies 218
Hardcore 231
Hardman, Adam 207
Harlan, J. 188
Harman, Robert 115
harmonica 58
harp 145
Harrison, H. 121
Harron, Mary 158
Harry, Deborah 141
Hart, Daniel 105
Hasan, M. 74, 76, 86
Haunted Garage 232
Hawks, Howard 45
Hayes, Isaac 112
Hayward, Philip 9, 10, 35, 51, 102, 104, 110, 111, 121, 231
Hayward, Susan 68

'Head Waltz' 221
'Heart Of Glass' 155
Hebdige, D. 141, 149
Hedwig and the Angry Inch 206
Hefti, Neil 41
Heifetz, R. 101
Heins, M. 170
Heiseiban Abe Sada: Anta ga Hoshi'i ('Sada Abe in the Heisei Era: I Want You') 91
Hell House 87
Henderson, E. 40
Hendrix, Jimi 10
'Herbert West; Reanimator' (H. P. Lovecraft) 221
Herrmann, Bernard 104
Hersh, Stuart 105
Hick, Nick and Jew of the Dead 221
Hicklin standard 170
Hilmer, Jan 206
Hilton, Arthur 104, 121
hip-hop 2, 89, 222
Hirose, Ryohei 101
Histoire d'O (Pauline Reage) 68; see also *The Story of O*
Hitchcock, Alfred 5, 160
Hoang, N. T. 150, 155
Hoffman, Philip Seymour 165
Hoffman, Samuel 121
hogaku, see Japanese music
Hole 64
Holiday, Billie 64
Hollywood Blue 114
Home Made 231
Hori, H. 91
Horner, Mike 132
Horowitz, Richard 59, 60
'Horse Tears' 196
Hosokawa, S. 138
Hot Chocolate 165
House of de Sade 67, 78, 81–4, 85
How The Gods Kill (album) 222
How to Make a Doll 107
Howard, Richard 100
Howlett, Liam 131–3, 134, 137
Hugo Award 103
Hullick, James 55, 58, 64
Hungry March Band, the 205, 213
'Hunter Gets Captured By The Game, The' 137
Hustler (magazine) 152
Huysmans, Joris-Karl 61
hyggefilm 29

I Am a Camera 123
'I Can't Give You Anything But Love, Baby' 205, 208, 212
'I Only Have Eyes For You' 181
'I Surrender, Dear' 165, 166
I Walked with a Zombie 218
Ichiyanagi, Toshio 101
'If You Fall' 205
Ifukube, Akira 135

Image, The (Jean de Berg) 70, 86
Image, The (film) 85
Immortal Mr. Teas, The 38, 39, 44, 51
Impaled 225
Impey, Jason 231
'In Flight Data' 131
'In The End' 205, 206, 207, 213
'In The Long Run' 49
In the Realm of the Senses, see *Ai no korida*
'Incense And Peppermints' 46
Innocents of Paris 36
Inoue, T. S. 154
Inside Deep Throat 122, 136
'Interstellar Overdrive' 135
'Intro' 161, 162
Invasion of the Bee Girls (aka *Graveyard Tramps*) 111–13, 119, 120
Ionesco, Eugène 226, 227
'Is You Is Or Is You Ain't My Baby?' 205, 206, 215
Isaak, Chris 181–2
Isherwood, Christopher 123
Ishida, Kichizo 91–100
Ishii, Maki 101
Ishii, Teruo 91
Ishiro Honda 135
Isla, She Wolf of the SS 233
'It's A Good Day' 166
'It's Not Safe' 205, 209

Jackal 137
Jackson, Reverend Jesse 147
Jaeckin, Just 2, 66, 67, 68–78, 84, 85, 86
Jaffrey, S. 121
Jameson, Jenna 226
Japanese cinema 89–90
Japanese music 93, 95, 99
Japrisot, Sébastien 70, 71
Jaws 45, 188
jazz 5, 18, 21, 35, 36, 44, 47, 48, 54, 56, 57, 58, 64, 89, 105, 106, 110, 120, 121, 129, 165, 167, 176, 180, 181, 195, 205, 207, 208
'Jazz Suite no. 2 for Jazz Orchestra' (Shostakovich) 176–80
Jazzhus Montmartre, Copenhagen 25
Jefferson Airplane 142
Jein, Greg 114
Jeremy, Ron 126
'Jesse's Girl' 168
Jitsuroku Abe Sada ('A Woman Called Sada Abe') 91
Joanna's Angels 232
Joensen, Bodil 15, 17, 20–2, 35, 36
Johnny Wadd 113
Johnson, Bruce 4, 8, 10, 35, 159–60, 214
Johnson, William 100
Jones, Wayne Scott 128
Jordan, Louis 215
'Jordu' 167
Joyce, James 42

240 Index

Juva, Anu 35
Juva, Johannes 35

kabuki theatre 96
Kael, Pauline 61
Kander, John 123
Kantor, Igo 41, 44
Kaplan, E. Ann 142, 154
Kapsalis, Terri 3, 7
Kasdan, Lawrence 171
Kassabian, Anahid 161
kazoo 116
KC and the Sunshine Band 166
Kelman, Robert 117
Kendrick, Walter 4
Kennedy, Pluto, see Marcello Giombini
Kern, Richard 154
Kerr, Deborah 160
Kessel, Barney 121
keyboard instruments 31, 32, 36, 44, 45, 48, 54, 57, 58, 63, 68, 72, 74, 75, 82, 83, 106, 110, 112, 115, 117, 118, 121, 127, 129, 131, 132, 133, 134, 145, 163, 164, 175, 186, 192, 195, 196, 197, 205, 207, 208, 221, 223, 224
Kid, Gary D. 80
Kidman, Nicole 174, 177
Kiki and Herb 205
Kill Girl Kill films 232
King, Joy 138
King Of Cool, The (album) 123
King of the Zombies 231
Kinkle, R. D. 37
Kinsey Report 103
Kirsten, S. 121
Kiss Me Quick 106, 119
Klein, Joshua 123
Knox, Andrew 229, 232
Kobayashi, Tadashi 100
Koch, Ed 209
Koch, Ilse 233
Koestler, Arthur 153
Kohlbrenner, John 137
Kohler, P. 137
'Kolla Kolla' 205
koto 96, 97, 99
Kotz, Liz 197
Kovi 133
Kozy 232
Kraemer, Christine 214
Kristel, Sylvia 68
Krzywinska, Tanya 1, 11, 159, 170
Kubrick, Stanley 2, 46, 72, 112, 113, 132, 174, 175, 177, 178, 180, 188
Kumonosu-Jo (*Throne of Blood*) 90
Kurosawa, Akira 90

'La Bamba' 155
Laderman, Carol 191
Laing, D. 141, 150

Lancaster, Burt 160
Lancelot, Sir (calypso performer) 218
Land of the Dead 218
'Land, the Sea and the Sky, The' 23
Landis, B. 78, 79, 82, 87
Landis, John 38, 78, 79, 82
Lane, Desiree 146
Lang, Nick 130
'Language' 205, 210
Lanham, R. 232
Larriva, Tito 154
Last Emperor, The 54, 60–2, 64
Last Tango in Paris 4, 54–9, 60, 62, 63
Latin American music 36, 41
Lavender, Asa 42
Lawrence, D. H. 58
Le Fanu, Sheridan 219
Leaky Brain, see Brian Rogers
Leather, Richard 129
Léaud, Jean-Pierre 57
Leblanc, L. 141, 150
Lee, Angela 227
Lee, C. 155
Lee, Debbie 79
Lee, Ed 222
Lee, Jay 226, 227, 228, 232
Lee, Peggy 166, 167
Lee, Sook-Yin 204, 215
Lee and Leblanc 210, 215
Legrand, Michel 58
Lehman, Peter 143, 152–3, 198, 199, 201
Lelong, Jean-Pierre 72, 86
Lennox, Annie 154
Let Me Tell Ya 'Bout White Chicks 150
Letts, Richard 214
Levey, William 115
Levy, W. 36
Lewis, Herschell Gordon 107
Leydon, R. 109, 121
Life (magazine) 109
Ligeti, György 184, 185, 188
Link, Stan 10
Liquid Sky 154, 155
Liszt, Franz 186, 188
'Little Bird' 205
Little Buddha 64
Little Prince, see Daniela Sea
'Livin' Thing' 153
Lofficier, J.-M. 107
Lolida 2000 127
'Look On Up At Bottom' 49
Lords, Traci 154
Lorna 42
Losfeld, Eric 107
Lost in Space (TV series) 120
lounge music 41, 44, 46, 47
Love, Courtney 232
Lovecraft, H. P. 221
Lovell, Jacqueline 127
Lucas, George 102, 130

'Lucifer Sam' 138
Lucifuge (album) 222
Lugosi, Béla 218
Lui (magazine) 68
Lumbye, H. C. 22–3, 36
Lunch, Lydia 141, 149, 154
Lust in Space 128
Lyman, Arthur 105, 221
Lyne, Adrian 111
'Lynndie (She-Wolf Of Abu Ghraib)' 233

Macbeth 90
McCarthy, T. 39
McClary, Susan 213
MacDonald, David 104
McG 137
McHugh, Jimmy 208
McHugh, K. 73
McKai, Eon 155, 231
McRobbie, Angela 147, 149
'Machine Gun' 167
Mad Doctors 107
Madonna 201
Maetzig, Kurt 110
'Magnet And Steel' 163, 167
Major, Jack 126
Malkovich, John 59
Malm, W. 97
'Mama Told Me Not To Come' 165
Mandell, Alan 209
march music 18, 41, 44, 79, 131, 142
March of the Penguins 86
Marietta (model/actor) 106
Mark of Zorro, The 114
Mars Needs Women 121
Marshall, Grant 137
Martin, N. 43
Marvelettes, the 137
'Masked Ball, The' (Jocelyn Pook) 188
Massaccesi, Aristide, *see* Joe D'Amato
Massive Attack 131
Masters, Rick 129
Mastsuda, Eiko 100
masturbation 79, 83, 119, 144, 145, 146, 148, 151, 196, 197, 201, 203, 208, 212, 232
Matrix, The 137
Matsudaira, Yoritsune 101
Matsumura, Teizo 101
Matthew, Scott 205, 209, 210
Matton, Charles 120
Maus, Fred 206
Mayer, William 105
Meese Commission 78, 87
Meh (pseudonym) 227
Meiji restoration, the 90, 95
Meiji, Taisho, Showa; Ryoki onna Hanzaishi ('History of Women's Grotesque Crimes') 91
Melanie 162
Melford, George 23
Melvins, the 142

Memoirs of a Woman of Pleasure (Cleland) 29
Messa dei giovani, La (Marcello Giombini) 231
metadiegetic music/sound 175, 184, 186, 188
metal (music) 5, 6, 219, 222, 225, 229, 231–2
'Metal Postcard' 137
Metzger, Radley 71, 85, 122
Mexican music 155
Meyer, Nicholas 111
Meyer, Russ 5, 38–53, 122
Microcosmos 86
Miki, Minori 95
Milczaca Gwiazda (*Der schweigende Stern*) 110
Mildred Pierce 73
military music, *see* march music
Miller, O. O., *see* Doris Wishman
Millerman, John 129–30, 137
Miller-Young, Mireille 2, 9
Milton, Berth 129, 137
'Mindfields' 137
Minogue, Kylie 108
Minor, Mike 114
Mirotznik, J. 123
Mister K., *see* Walter Carlos
Mitchell Brothers, 85, 114, 117
Mitchell, John Cameron 203–4, 214, 215
Mitchell, Sharon 79
Mizuno, Shuko 101
mockumentaries 49
Mol, Gretchen 162
Mole People, The 135
Mona – the Virgin Nymph 114
Mondo Topless 42
money shot 7, 125, 147, 166, 174, 188, 225
Monkees, the 49
Montel, Michèle 72
Monty Python (comedy team) 51
'Moon Doll' 105
Moorehead, Craven 222, 223, 225
Morawek, Andre 232
Morawek, Tom-Eric 232
Morbid Angel 219
More, Shamron 228
Morgan, Jonathan 132
Moroccan music 59
Morricone, Enio 54
Morris, Gary 51
Morse, Simon 222
Mosellie, B. 123
Mothers of Invention, the 36, 122
Motion Picture Association of America 170
Mr Norris Changes Trains (Isherwood) 123
'Mucha Muchacha' 164
'Mudmen' 81
Mulvey, Laura 194
'Muderistic Women', *see* 'Careful With That Axe, Eugene'
Muren, Dennis 114
Museum Erotica, Copenhagen 12, 16, 18, 35
Museum Erotica: An Erotic Musical 18, 36

242 Index

Museum of Modern Art, New York 38
Music Out Of The Moon (album) 105
'Musica Ricercata' (Ligeti) 184, 185, 187
musicals (films) 3, 17, 18, 34, 36, 45, 67, 142, 159
My Darling Clementine 108
My Fair Lady 13
'My Favourite Things' 63
Myers, Mike 46
Myrick, Daniel 137

Nation, Carrie A. 49
National Catholic Office for Motion Pictures (USA) 107
National Film Theatre, London 38
Natsu no imoto ('Dear Summer Sister') 100
Nebula Award 130
necrophilia, *see* zombie porn
NEKRomantik 217
NEKRomantik II 217
Nelson, T. 174
Neu Wave Hookers 155, 232
Neumeyer, D. 175
Neville, Richard 36
New Wave cinema 57
New Wave Hookers 5, 140–57, 232
new wave music 5, 140–2, 145–9, 155, 231
Newby, Christine (aka Cosi Fanni Tutti) 232
Newman, Randy 164
Newsweek (magazine) 107
Newton, Thandie 62
ney 59
Niblo, Fred 114
Nielsen, K. Axel 13
Nietzsche, Friedrich 113
Night of Submission 78, 82
Night of the Living Babes 220
Night of the Living Dead 218, 225
Night Ranger 168
Nightmare on Elm Street 226
9 Songs 9, 35, 190–202
No Protection (album) 131
nohkan 96
non-diegetic music/sound 2, 6, 31, 47, 48, 72, 92, 95–9, 109, 160, 161, 163, 167, 168, 169, 175, 180, 182, 188, 191, 193, 195, 196, 207, 208, 209, 210, 211
Noon Blue Apples 232
North, Peter 155
Norton, Bret 100
Notorious Bettie Page, The 158–73
Notti erotiche dei morti viventi, Le (*Erotic/Sexy Nights of the Living Dead*) 219
Nouvel Adam (magazine) 68
'Nuages gris' (Liszt) 186–7
Nude on the Moon 104–5, 119, 120
Nyman, Michael 64, 195–6, 197

Obayashi, Nohubiko 91
O'Brien, Kieran 191, 200

O'Brien, L. 142
Octopussy 86
O'Day, Anita 207, 215
O'Hehir, A. 204
Oliver, M. 51
Once Upon A Summertime (album) 215
Opening of Misty Beethoven, The 3, 43, 85
opera/operetta 18, 21
orgies 31, 79, 82, 83, 84, 93, 94, 126, 183, 185, 186, 187
Osco, Bill 116
O'Shea, Milo 109
Oshima, Nagisa 1, 89–101
Outer Limits, The (TV series) 135

Packman, Jeff 191
Palmer, Gail 154
Paramenter, Melissa 196
Parents' Music Resource Center (PMRC) 147
Paris, Henry 43
Parker, Charlie 121
Parks, Gordon 112
Partner 54
Pastoral Symphony (Beethoven) 21–2
Paulhan, Jean 70, 73, 77, 85, 86
Peary, D. 41
Pedersen, Niels-Henning Ørsted 25
Peeping Tom 231
Pegg, Simon 227
Penley, Constance 66, 71, 72, 85, 87, 140, 143, 152
Pepper, Art 169
percussion 5, 25, 27, 44, 48, 49, 54, 59, 61, 62, 71, 74, 75, 76, 82, 83, 84, 109, 110, 112, 118, 119, 127, 128, 131, 134, 195, 200, 207, 211
Peterson, Oscar 28
Petkovich, A. 142, 144
Pfeiffer, Chelsea 134–5, 136
Phair, Liz 64
Phelan, Raymond (aka Anthony Brooks) 104
Phillips, Stu 49
phrygian mode 98
Piano, The 171
Pink Floyd 81, 82, 84, 135, 138
pinku eiga (pink film) 90; *see also* pornography
pipa 61
Piper From The Gates Of Dawn (album) 82
Pistol, Tommy 220
Pitt, Ingrid 231
Pittman, Mark 214
Plague of the Zombies 218
Planet of the Dead, see 211 First Spaceship on Venus
Planet Stories (magazine) 104
Plasmatics, the 150
Playboy (magazine) 50, 107, 109
Playboy Book of Science Fiction, The 121
Pleasure Dome: The Genesis Chamber 129
Plugz, the 144, 151, 152, 154, 155

Pollack, Sydney 177
Pommer, Kristian 36
Pook, Jocelyn 188
Poole, Gaye 4, 159–60
Pop-arp (album) 72
Porn of the Dead 224–5, 229
Porn Wars 133, 135, 136
pornography 1, 2, 4, 5, 7, 8, 12–37, 38, 40, 43, 66, 67, 68, 71, 74, 78, 79, 80, 81, 87, 90, 111, 114, 115, 117, 119, 123, 125–33, 140–57, 158–72, 190, 191, 198, 200, 203, 218, 220–33
Pornography 12, 15, 16, 17, 21, 22–9, 33, 36
'Pow R. Toch H' 138
Powell, Michael 231
'Power Of Darkness' 222
Powrie, P. 171
Presley, Elvis 108
Press, J. 149
Primal Scream 192
Prince Igor (Borodin) 121
Private Media Group (PMG) 129–30, 134
Prix de Deux Magots 69
Probot 220
Prodigy 131
Pungent Stench 233
punk rock 49, 50, 140–2, 144, 145, 149, 151, 155, 156, 220, 221, 222, 224, 229, 230
Punk Rock Holocaust 220
'Put Yourself In My Place' 108

Quaglio, Laurent 72, 86
Queen of Outer Space 121
Quitmeyer, David 51

Raffill, Stewart 232
ragtime 48
Raincoats, the 149, 155
Ranvaud, D. 57
rap 6, 151, 222
Rapaport, Pola 77, 87
Ravel, Maurice 133
Read, Dolly 49, 50
Reagan, Ronald 87
Reage, Pauline (pen-name of Dominique Aury) 68, 69, 70, 73, 77, 85, 86
Re-Animator 220–1
'Rebel' 227
Reddington, H. 141, 149, 155
reggae 131, 141–2, 146, 147, 151, 155
Reilley, John C. 163
Reiner, Rob 52
Relics (album) 82
Renegades 129
Repenetrator 220–2, 229
Repo Man 154
Reservoir Dogs 171
Resident Evil films 218
Revel, Harry 121
Revenge and Punishment 78, 79, 80–1, 85

Reynolds, S. 149
Reyolds, Burt 161
Rhinoceros (Ionesco) 226
Rialto Cinema, New York 78
Richards, Sybil 127–8, 137
Richardson, Marie 183
Richie, Donald 90
Ridgely, Robert 165
Ridley, J. 204
Riefenstahl, Leni 233
Right Side of My Brain, The 154
Riisfeldt-Clausen, Kim 12, 36
Rioche, Sebastian 232
Rivas, Ray 209
Roach, Jay 38, 46
Roach, Max 167
rock music 36, 48, 49, 76, 89, 110, 120, 127, 129, 131, 135, 142, 147–8, 149, 151, 201, 218, 219, 221, 222, 223, 224, 227, 228, 229, 230, 231
Rocket Girls 129
Rocky Horror Picture Show 76
Rodgers, Richard 138
Rodriguez, Robert 108, 154
Roemheld, Heinz 138
Rogers, Brian (aka Leaky Brain) 132, 137
Rollet-Andriane, Marayat (aka Emmanuelle Arsan) 68, 70
Rolling Stones, the 201
Romero, George 218, 225
Romney, Jonathan 174
Ross, J. 43
Rotten, Rob 224, 232
Roy, Herve 68
Rubin, Gayle 87
Ryan, Shane 231

'Sacrifice' 222
SADA 91
sadomasochism 24, 66–78, 134–5, 155, 207, 212
Saint, Roxy 226, 227, 228
Saint, Sylvia 130
Sakamoto Ryuichi 59, 60, 61
Sakmann, Doug 220, 231
Salter, Hans 138
Samson, JD 210
Sánchez, Eduardo 137
Sanders, Denis 111, 122
Sandrelli, Stefania 62, 64
Santana 15, 28, 35
Sarno, Joe 71
SAS (Scandinavian Airlines) 28
Sasdy, Peter 231
Satisfiers of Alpha Blue, The, see Alpha Blue
'Saucerful Of Secrets, A' 81
Saucerful Of Secrets, A (album) 82
Sawtell, Paul 41
saxophone 5, 20, 41, 47, 54, 55, 58, 63, 151, 180, 208

244 Index

'Say You'll Be There' 49
Sayadian, Stephen (aka Rinse Dream) 117, 118, 123
Schaefer, Eric 38, 40, 50
Schneble, Sylvia 111
Schneider, Maria 54
Schnitzler, Arthur 180
Schrader, Paul 231
Schricker, Glen 229
Schubert, Franz 10
Schumacher, Joel 137, 231
Schwartz, Adolph 39
Schwarzenegger, Arnold 225
schweigende Stern, Der (*Milczaca Gwiazda*) 110
Science Fiction Writers of America 130
sci-fi films 5, 102–24, 125–39, 144, 154, 227
Scorsese, Martin 64
Scott, C. 46, 48
Scott, Ridley 102
Screech, Timon 100
Sea, Daniela (aka Little Prince) 206
Secretion 221
Sergeant York 45
'Set The Controls For The Heart Of The Sun' 81, 82
Sevastakis, M. 51
'7th House' 222
Sex in the City (TV series) 73
sex muzak 5, 129
Sex Trek film series 12, 136
Sex World Girls 126
'Sexy Ways' 164
Seymour, Frances Ford 108
Shaft 112
Shah, Krishna 218
'Shake Your Blood' 220
Shakespeare, William 90
shakuhachi 96, 97, 98, 99
shamisen 93, 94, 95, 96, 98
Shanon, Mark 219
Shaun of the Dead 227, 228
Shaw, Artie 165
Shaw, Vinessa 183
'She Wants My ... Love' 151
'She's A Lady' 74, 76
Shefter, Bert 41
Sheik, The 23
Sheltering Sky, The 54, 59–60, 64
Shimizo, Osamu 101
Shitsurakuen ('Lost Paradise'; novel) 91
Shortbus 203–16
Shostakovich, Dmitri 175–80, 182, 184, 185, 188
Shumway, David 160–1, 171
Sick & Twisted Horror of Joanna Angel, The 232
Sickels, R. C. 170, 171
Sikov, E. 56
silence 4, 9, 56, 57, 58, 60, 73, 166–9
Silent Star, The, see 211 First Spaceship on Venus
Silverman, Kaja 2, 9, 67, 70, 198, 199
Silverstein, Eliot 108
Simone, Nina 64
Simpsons, The (TV series) 233
singing/vocalization (voice as bearer of extra-lexical messages) 20, 42, 49, 54, 55, 58, 59, 60, 62, 67, 71, 72, 73, 74, 75, 76, 77, 79, 80, 81, 82, 83, 84, 92, 93, 94, 96, 105, 109, 110, 112, 115, 116, 118, 119, 127, 128, 133, 134, 135, 145, 147, 151, 152, 158, 162, 163, 165, 166, 167, 168, 181–2, 187, 190, 192, 194, 195, 196, 197, 199, 200, 201, 207, 210, 211, 213, 214, 221, 223, 227, 228, 229, 231
Siouxsie Sioux 141
Siouxsie and the Banshees 137, 141
'Sister Christian' 168
6:66 Satan's Child (album) 223
Sjöberg, T. 130
Skaros, Nick 135, 136, 138
Skumlove 223
Skye, Britney 223
Slaughter, The 226
Slaughtered 231
Slits, the 149, 155
Sloopys, the 107
'Smack My Bitch Up' 137
Smith, Jeff 123, 146, 152, 153, 154
Smith, Patti 50
Smith, William 112
'Smother You' 228
Smut Peddlers 224
Snow White 86
Snuff 217
Sobieski, Leelee 183
Sockets, the 154
'Soda Shop' 205, 210
Soila, Tytti 13, 29, 36
Solid Serenade 215
Songs Of Lust And Corrosion (album) 223
sonic anaphones 5, 10
sonic phenomenology 3–4, 7
Sontag, Susan 70
Sony, Michael, *see* Dukey Flyswatter
Sound of Music, The 13
South Park (TV series) 233
Space Balls 132
Space Nuts 132, 133, 134, 136, 137, 138
Space Thing 103
SpaceGirls! 134–5
Spaceship Venus Does Not Reply, see 211 First Spaceship on Venus
'Spanking' 36
Spears, Britney 142
Sperb, J. 174
Spermula 120
Spice Girls, the 49
Spie vengono dal semifreddo, see Dr Goldfoot and the Girl Bombs
Spielberg, Steven 45, 188
Spoto, Chris 51

Springfield, Rick 168
Sprinkle, Annie 79
stag films 40, 125, 143
Stahl, Jerry 118
Staiger, Janet 194
'Star-spangled Banner, The' 205, 211
Star Trek TV series 122, 124, 129, 134
Star Trek: The Wrath of Khan 122
Star Trek VI: The Undiscovered Country 122
Star Wars films 102, 129, 130, 132, 133, 165
Star Whores 128
Stealing Beauty 56, 64
Stein, Elliot 225
Stein, Herman 138
Steiner, Max 56
Stephens, C. 170
Stevens, Chuck 108, 122
Stevens, Roger 120
Stewart, Alexandra 72, 73, 74
Stewart, Dave 108
Stickles, Peter 206
Stilley, Margot 191, 199
Stone, Evan 132
Storey, M. 121
Story of Joanna 85, 87
Story of O, The 2, 5, 67, 69–78, 80, 83, 84, 85, 86, 87
Strange Relations (P. J. Farmer) 103
Strasberg, Lee 108
Strauss, Johann, II 23, 31, 32, 132
Strauss, Richard 46, 112, 113
Strawberry Alarm Clock 46
stringed instruments (western) 19, 20, 31, 32, 55, 58, 59, 60, 61, 62, 63, 64, 74, 75, 76, 109, 112, 133, 138, 155, 211, 213, 223
Stuttgart Ballet Company 87
Sublime 142
Sugarman, Sparky 116, 133
Summerday, A (*A Summer's Day*; *A Summer Day*) 9, 12, 14–15, 17, 20–2, 35, 36
Sunday in New York 108
Super Furry Animals 192
'Superpredators' 137
Supervixens 41, 44, 45, 46, 47, 48
Supremes, the 106
'Surgery' 205, 209
Surrender Cinema 126, 127
Suspiria 228
'Sweet Talkin' Candy Man' 49
Switched-on Bach (album) 86
symphonic music, *see* classical music

Tagg, Philip 2, 6, 9, 10
Tajiri, Shinkichi 14, 15, 20, 21, 36
'Take Me To The River' 155
Takemitsu, Toru 100
Talking Heads 155
Tamaki, M. 204
Tamkin, David 138
Tamla Motown 106, 137

Tammy and the T Rex 232
Tanaka, Noboru 91
Tango Lesson, The 86
Taormino, T. 232
Tarantino, Quentin 38, 51, 171
Tasker, William 44
Taurog, Norman 106
Taylor, Elizabeth 159
Taylor, Lili 164
Taylor, Vanessa 127
Teague, Jack 79
Tease: The Beat Of Burlesque (album) 121
techno music 131, 205, 211, 220
Teenage Jesus and the Jerks 149
Tengo, Yo La 209
Terrors from the Clit 231
Tevis, Peter 122
Tewksbury, Peter 108
theremin 116, 121, 134
Thestrup, Knud 13
Thewlis, David 62
Thing, The 228
'This House' 205
This Is Spinal Tap 52
'This Piece Of Poetry Is Meant To Do Harm' 205
Thomas, Kevin 39
Thompson, A. 203
Thompson, Nathanial 86
Three Colours: Blue 86
Three Colours: Red 86
Three Dog Night 164
thrillers 5, 58, 111
Throbbing Gristle 232
Throne of Blood, see *Kumonosu-Jo*
'The Tide Is High' 155
Tillman, Charles 45
Tiomkin, Dmitri 104
'Titan' 131
Tivoli Gardens, Copenhagen 23, 28, 34
To Catch a Thief 160
Tokyo senso sengo hiwa: Eiga de isho o nokoshite shinda otoko no monogatari ('The Battle of Tokyo') 100
Tom and Jerry (cartoon characters) 215
Torgue, H. 10
Toth, Cy 121
Touchus, Seymour, *see* Bethel Buckalew
Tourneur, Jacques 218
Traumnovelle (Schnitzler) 180
Tretta, Sean 231
Tricky 137
trip-hop music 131
Triplets of Belleville, The 86
Truffaut, François 57
Tutti, Cosi Fanni, *see* Christine Newby
2001: A Space Odyssey 10, 46, 112, 132
211 First Spaceship on Venus (*The Silent Star, Planet of the Dead* and *Spaceship Venus Does Not Reply*) 122
Tyler, Liv 64

Tzara, Tristan 86

Ultravixens 42, 44, 45
Ulysses (Joyce) 42
Underground Personality Tapes, The 227
Ungari, E. 57
'Unspeakable' 223
'Upside Down' 205, 209
Uranus Experiment, The 129–30, 131–3, 134, 135, 136
Uranus Experiment 2, The 132

V-Magazine 107
Vadim, Roger 107, 108, 111, 127
Valentine, Jon 220
'Valentine' 31–2
Valentino, Rudolph 23
Van Druten, John 123
Van Leeuwen, T. 171
Venus Cinema, New York 78
Verge, S. 204
Vermue, Reg 209
Verotika (magazine) 22
vibraphone 221
vibra-slap 44, 51
Villadsen, Ebbe 12, 13
violence 5, 50, 66–78, 153
Virgins of Sherwood Forest 127
Virtual Encounters 127
Virtual Encounters 2 127
Vistalance 232
Vixen 38–9, 41, 44, 48
Vlad, Alessio 63
vocoder 71, 72
Vogel, Virgil 135
Vogue (magazine) 68
voice, *see* singing
Von Bondies, the 192
Vowles, Andrew 137

Wachowski Brothers 137
Wachsmuth, Nick 232
Wagner, Richard 31
Wahlberg, Mark 162
Walker, A. 174
Wallace, Richard 36
Waller, Fats 208
'Waltz no. 2' (Shostakovich) 175–80, 182, 188
War of the Worlds 102
'War Pigs' 138
Warhol, Andy 5
Wasson, Craig 9
Waters, John 38
Waters, Roger 83
Waxman, Franz 114, 221
Webster, Ben 25
Wells, H. G. 102
Wemba, Papa 62

West, Mae 122
Westerns 5, 44, 108
Westworld 145
Wet Dream Film Festival 14, 20, 21, 28, 35, 36
Whales, James 221
Wham Bam Thank You Spaceman 115–16, 119
'When I Fall In Love' 181
White, David 116
White Acre, Billy 227, 228
'White Rabbit' 142
White Zombie 218
Wilcox, Fred 109
Williams, David 82
Williams, John 188
Williams, Linda 1, 2–3, 4, 5, 6, 7, 9, 10, 18, 34, 38, 45, 50, 51, 66, 67, 76, 77, 79, 80, 81, 83, 111, 117, 122, 125, 128, 131, 136, 142, 143, 144, 146, 149, 150, 158–9, 160, 170, 171, 196, 199
Williams, Longjohn 134
Williams, Wendy O 141, 149, 154
Wilson, Stuart 199–200, 201
Winger, Debra 59
Winkel, Margarita 100
'Winter Love' 205, 206, 207, 211, 212, 213, 214
Winterbottom, Michael 64, 190, 199, 200
Wishman, Doris (aka O. O. Miller) 104
'Wizard's Sleeve' 205, 209
Wood, Ollie 127
Woods, P. 38, 40, 43
woodwinds 36, 47, 58, 109, 165
Wright, Edgar 227, 228
Wright, Robb 144

XXX Files, The (TV series) 120
XXXorcist, The 232
xylophone 109
Xzibit (aka Alvin Nathaniel Joiner IV) 142

Yarbrough, Jean 231
Yeva 232
'You Sexy Thing' 165
Young, Ralph 105

Zabriskie Point 83
Zacharek, S. 204
Zappa, Frank 36, 122
Ziehm, Howard 114, 115, 122, 123, 127
Zimmer, Hans 131
Zimmerman, Eric 227
Zinnemann, Fred 160
Zombie Nympho Coeds 220
zombie porn 5, 217–33
Zombie Strippers 225–9, 230
Zombies on Broadway 231
Zorba the Greek 13
Zuromskis, Catherine 159, 160, 169–70